The Union Challenge
to Management Control

The Union Challenge to Management Control

By NEIL W. CHAMBERLAIN

ARCHON BOOKS, 1967

Library of Congress Catalog Card Number: 67–19507
Printed in the United States of America

C O N T E N T S

INTRODUCTION

This is the first of a series of books to be issued under the auspices of the Labor and Management Center at Yale University. The objective of the Center is the promotion of the public interest and welfare through the improvement of the diagnosis of rather than the writing of prescriptions for problems in the field of relations among management, unions, and workers. We seek to do this by means of studies of:

The determinants of the actions of workers, management, and union leaders.

The interests, objectives, traditions, techniques, structures, and survival requirements of unions and private enterprise.

The basic human, economic, and social factors to which the parties to industrial and labor relations must adapt themselves.

The techniques and rules of their relationship.

The conditions of their peaceful interaction and the reduction of conflict.

The impact of individual interests and practices of management and unions on the efficiency and survival requirements of the other, and on the public interest and welfare.

Whatever the subject of a particular investigation, it is designed to contribute to the development of principles of human behavior, useful in understanding why men behave as they do, the motives which set in motion, and the circumstances which mold the character of policy, decisions, and practice.

One policy of the Labor and Management Center should have clear statement. Our research directors and authors have ultimate freedom in the presentation of their findings. They have the advantage of consultation with and criticism from other members of the staff. But we believe that greatest progress will come from permitting a wide latitude of individual freedom and the genuine acceptance of individual responsibility. Members of the staff have been chosen on the basis of their scientific ability and integrity. They are in accord with the basic assumptions which our Policy Committee, composed of three representatives each from management, organized labor, and the university, has determined shall underlie the work of the Center. These assumptions are as follows:

It is desirable to preserve and perfect democracy, free unions, free management, and free enterprise.

These institutions will survive or fall together.

There is a large area of common interest among these institutions but the conflicts among them are real.

It is desirable to reduce the conflicts, which if unresolved endanger the survival of all of them.

Freedom of inquiry and expression by men who meet these qualifications is a basic policy of the Labor and Management Center.

The present work is focused on a problem of great importance to all parties including the public. Collective bargaining and unions are present facts of American industrial life. If private enterprise is to survive in the presence of these facts, an effective integration of unions with the management of private enterprise must be found. This book does not prescribe the form such integration must take. That form must be hammered out by the parties immediately involved in view of all the specific factors with which only they can be familiar. Dr. Chamberlain has contributed a careful and penetrating analysis of the present progress toward such integration and has evaluated the steps taken in the light of the underlying survival requirements of management and unions.

E. WIGHT BAKKE
Director

P R E F A C E

Like all research in the field of union-management relations, this study is subject to charges both of partiality and impartiality, and for the same reason: those who see good in the convictions of one side only will scarcely approve an investigation which recognizes merit, where it is thought to exist, in the opposition's beliefs. Yet insofar as it is possible to do so, this analysis aims at an objective approach to the important issue of the impact of the union on managerial authority in the large corporation.

Both management and labor are now going through a difficult process of adjustment. One cannot be familiar with their persuasions, aspirations, and fears without acquiring a sympathy for both which sometimes makes judgment difficult. Except for a few paid mouthpieces on both sides, the proponents of one party can be no more charged with selfish interest than the advocates of the other. Selfish interest is involved in both cases, but along with it go genuine concern for institutions and social faiths, attachment to ideals, a sense of justice. These, it must be repeated, are found in both protagonists. If the position of either is presented here inadequately it is not for want of trying or for want of sympathy, but for lack of understanding. If the logic is faulty, it is not because the heart has directed it.

The factual material contained in these pages is dated as of October 1946. In a field where the day-to-day relationships of unions and management change the structure of data on which analysis rests, it has been impossible to revise assertions of fact down to the date of publication. The renegotiation of collective bargaining agreements has already modified the accuracy of some of the statements contained in this study. New legislation may soon contribute to the temporary quality of other statements which are presently correct. Nevertheless, the conclusions which have been reached do not depend for their validity upon any one of a number of facts, but upon the conditions and situations which collectively they reveal.

An important amount of information has been obtained in interviews with company and union officials, and a lesser amount in correspondence. With few exceptions, such material has been supplied on the condition that the anonymity of the source shall be preserved. It has therefore been necessary, in numerous instances, to quote such men or cite their opinions without identifying them, except perhaps in a most general way. Likewise in some cases there was a reluctance to link particular arbitration decisions in grievance proceedings with the company or union con-

ix

cerned. This reluctance has been met, in the four appendices relating to specific industries, by avoiding documentation. No less care has been taken in the use of such materials for analytical purposes, however, than if the most thorough documentation had been made.

This study was made possible through a research grant from the Social Science Research Council, whose generosity is acknowledged with deepest thanks. To all those officials of both companies and unions who have given of their time to discuss the problems raised herein is owed a debt of gratitude. No words can adequately convey my appreciation of the aid given by Professor E. Wight Bakke, Director of the Yale University Labor and Management Center, with whom was discussed the preliminary outline and who has examined critically the complete manuscript, suggesting numerous improvements.

Acknowledgment is made of permission to quote from the following sources: *The Dynamics of Industrial Democracy*, by Clinton S. Golden and Harold J. Ruttenberg, and *The New Outlook in Business*, edited by Bronson Batchelor, both published by Harper & Brothers; *The Modern Corporation and Private Property*, by A. A. Berle and Gardiner C. Means, published by The Macmillan Company; *American Labor Dynamics*, edited by J. B. S. Hardman and published by Harcourt, Brace and Company; and from articles in the *Harvard Law Review*, the *Chicago Law Review*, *Public Opinion Quarterly*, and *Fortune*.

NEIL W. CHAMBERLAIN

September 1947

PREFACE TO THE 1967 EDITION*

One recent day at a small cement plant near Palo Alto, Calif., the boss strode up to one member of a two-man crane-operating crew. The boss asked if he'd step down off the giant machine now and then, walk a few paces to the side, and punch a button that would start or stop the conveyor belt being used to haul sand and gravel into the plant. The oiler complied.

A couple of days later, this matter came to the attention of a business agent for the International Union of Operating Engineers in San Francisco. The union speedily dispatched a representative to the scene. He instructed the oiler that henceforth he wasn't to set foot off the crane while on duty. Next morning an additional man appeared on the job to run the conveyor belt.

Incidents such as this—in which unions, rather than management, decide where workers are to work, and what they're to do—are provoking a management counterattack that's far broader than generally realized. While the battles over "featherbedding" in the steel industry, the railroad industry, and on the East coast docks have been grabbing the headlines, the fight also is being waged in a variety of other businesses, large and small across the country.[1]

The interpretation of management rights has become important as an arbitrable matter and the management rights issue remains prominent. In the immediate postwar days, when management rights clauses were being introduced in contracts, many observers believed these clauses to be window dressing. It seemed that acknowledged rights of management were being formally put into words, and this formalization had no value except possibly for public relations purposes.

Now it is being realized that perhaps there is greater substance in these clauses than was thought and that they do have a bearing on the interpretation of other clauses in the contract. Consequently, we may need to take a new look at what they mean. Indeed, there seems to be a feeling across the nation that rights which had once been conceded to the union are again under scrutiny, that privileges which unions thought had been won in the postwar decade are being re-examined and subjected to hard bargaining. Assignment of work and subcontracting are just two of these controversial areas, areas which in their larger setting are generally referred to as disputes over managerial prerogatives and the unions' attempted invasion thereof.

What is involved here is a power struggle, a conflict of relationships which has gone on over the decades, perhaps over the centuries. This phenomenon should be viewed in historical and philosophical perspective.

From this perspective what we are interested in are the points of similarity

*This material first appeared in somewhat different form in *Industrial and Labor Relations Review*, Vol. 16, No. 2, January, 1963.

[1]James R. MacDonald, "Work Rules Battles," *The Wall Street Journal*, Nov. 4, 1959, p. 1, col. 1.

between the situation today and situations in the past. We are also interested in the ways in which today's situation may be distinguished from those involving the same kind of dispute, the same kind of argument over prerogative power relationships in previous years.

THE ISSUE OF PREROGATIVES

At the outset, it may be suggested that the issue of management prerogatives, of authority prerogatives, is as old as the master-servant relationship. Wherever there is an authority which presumes to direct a subordinate and to determine paths of conduct and routines of behavior, there will inevitably be protest from those to whom the assignment is made. The subordinates will question the basis for the authority and the reasonableness of its exercise. So let us not assume that this is an issue which somehow has suddenly been precipitated into our midst. It is one which has been experienced in human relationships in a variety of forms over hundreds and thousands of years.

This issue studs the history of the union-management relationship. Every bit of progress the unions have made, every achievement they have won, has been realized in the face of charges that they were invading the prerogatives of others, that they were assuming authority which should be the proper preserve of some other group, generally a managerial one. Unions have become somewhat inured to this charge of invasion of others' prerogatives.

They were so charged when they sought to reduce the twelve-hour, indeed even the sixteen-hour, workday. They were so charged when they first attempted to have some say on so elementary a matter as wages. When they first attempted to bargain on these matters they were met by the counteroffensive that such matters were really in the hands of those who represented the workings of a systematic order, perhaps even in the hands of God. One need but remember some of the quotations which are part of the lore of labor relations from those who presumed that they were spokesmen of higher order, vessels of an authority which was greater than their own, and whose righteous position was being challenged by renegade, upstart, rebellious groups who really had no ground for such a challenge.

A typical illustration of this can be found in an editorial which appeared a little more than a hundred years ago, in the *Journal of Commerce* published in New York City.

On an occasion when the printers' union was attempting to negotiate on such matters as restriction of number of apprentices, the employment of women as compositors, child labor, and female labor (viewed as a threat to the position of the old established compositors), the editorial attacked the union in this fashion.

Who but a miserable craven-hearted man would permit himself to be subjected to such rules, extending even to the number of apprentices he may employ, and the manner in which they shall be bound to him; to the kind of work which shall be performed in his own office, at particular hours of the day, and to the sex of the persons employed, however separated into different apartments or buildings. For ourselves we never employed a female as compositor, and have no great opinion of apprentices; but sooner than be restricted on these points, or any other, by a self-constituted tribunal outside of the office, we would go back to the employment of our boyhood and dig potatoes, pull flax, and do everything else that a plain honest farmer may properly do on his own territory. It is marvelous to us how any employer having a soul of a man within him can submit to such degradation.[2]

This is characteristic of the heights (or the depths) of feeling which can be stirred by such challenges to one's authority. It is interesting to note how this reference to the position of the plain honest farmer who controls his own destiny has always seemed to be an escape hatch for managements beset in this fashion. About a hundred years after the appearance of this editorial, Charles E. Wilson, when president of General Motors, was faced with a demand from his union for a union security clause. He replied: "I would not have a closed shop. I am never going to sign one. When it gets around to that, it will make a farmer out of me." This thought of a return to the soil as a means of escaping the depredations of unions seems to have persisted over the years and has perhaps been a comforting reassurance to management that if the unions become too persistent, there is always a way out.

In certain respects the issues we are examining have continuities with the past and ties to history of which we can remind ourselves. But there are also elements of difference. One peculiarity of the present labor-management relationship is that, so far as I know, for the first time in history our society has given, not only legal sanction, but a measure of encouragement to those whose very function is to challenge a vested authority.

We realize that the very role of unions is to act as a challenge to management. Nonetheless, our society has since 1935 given legal protection to those seeking to attack the wielders of established authority in the business setting. This has been forcefully brought home to many managements in the form of NLRB decisions dealing with the duty to bargain over a large variety of issues.

We may recall the Circuit Court decision which upheld the National Labor Relations Board in its ruling with respect to the Phoenix Mutual Life Insurance Company.[3] In that case, a group of insurance salesmen had decided that the frequent turnover of the cashier in the office was a handicap to them. They banded together in order to support the appointment of a new cashier after the latest one had left the company, preparing a petition in which they urged the appointment of the person who was then acting as assistant cashier. This came to the attention of the office manager before the petition was formally presented, and the two ringleaders were fired.

[2]George A. Stevens, *New York Typographical Union No. 6*, Annual Report of the Bureau of Labor Statistics, New York State Department of Labor, 1911, Part 1, pp. 240–241.
[3]Phoenix Mutual Life Insurance Co., 73 NLRB 1463 (1947).

This was an informal kind of action. No union was involved. But because it was considered concerted activity, a charge was filed with the National Labor Relations Board. The Board supported the two discharged men and ordered their reinstatement. A majority of the Circuit Court upheld the Board and said that the salesmen's interest in the appointment of the cashier was reasonably related to the conditions of their employment. This evoked a very strong dissent from one judge who said that the choice of a cashier was purely a management affair and that: "To put it bluntly, their grievance was directed at a matter which was none of their business or concern."[4] He then went on to say that he supposed, under the construction given by the majority, the employees would have been protected if they had concerted regarding the naming of the company president, or directors of the company, or the general counsel of the company, or other officials who were important to the conditions of their employment. This is an interesting example of a case in which an arm of the government is protecting a group of employees who are contesting a managerial right or are at least seeking to influence a managerial prerogative of appointing company staff.

The issue has come up in numerous other ways. The appropriateness of stock options as a subject of mandatory bargaining has been upheld. The cases in which the Board has held a subject nonbargainable are rare.

CONFLICT IN VALUES

Now to examine the underlying value conflict that permeates this kind of relationship. Sometimes we feel that this attempted union invasion of management rights represents an aggressive, a novel, an intruding, a radical kind of approach—that it puts the unions in the position of urging radical institutional reforms. To some degree one might defend that argument.

It could be said, using a sociologist's phrase, that this is an unintended consequence of purposive action. In fact, the union's actions have been motivated by a conservative point of view. The underlying rationale is one, usually, of trying to preserve a relationship rather than trying to establish a new one. The latter is sometimes present, but the former is much more prevalent.

This reminds us of the functions performed in this sort of controversy by management and union, and the conflict of values represented in their functional roles. The conflict which is engendered by disputes over managerial prerogatives is not simply one of a right or a wrong in a particular situation, but is a conflict of values which is virtually inherent in the parts which are played by the two parties.

We must remember that management in the performance of its function is necessarily an instigator of change and a responder to change. Management is operating in an economic environment within which change is the rule. The

[4]NLRB v. Phoenix Life Insurance Co., (C.A. 7th, 1948), 22 LRRM 2089 at 2095.

pressures of economic competition force it to be responsive to changes that are occurring around it. For management, change is the law of life. Unions, on the other hand, frequently are cast in the roles of forestallers of change. They are seeking to preserve positions involving security for their members.

In its role, management, almost of necessity, seeks to achieve certain well-focused objectives. It may be seeking to pass a competitor in total sales. It may be trying to bring a new product to the market before a rival does so. It may be trying to open up new territory, establish a new plant, or effect a merger with another company. These can be fairly major objectives, but they are almost always quite concrete in their execution.

On the other hand, unions are usually engaged in a drive for what may be termed satisfactory states of existence for their members—a morale-building relationship with supervisory foremen, the respect of others for good performance, a physical or a material situation which is comparable to that of their fellow workers or their neighbors. These are not the pinpointed, well-focused objectives which management has before it.

And yet both organizations must try to achieve these different objectives through the same medium—the business, the firm, the corporation. Management's goals frequently involve a restructuring of the organization of the company. The union goals, on the other hand, very often require adherence to the status quo.

Even the vocabulary of the two organizations differs in ways that strikingly point up the values conflict. For example, management will regard efficiency as being a good word, a good objective, something which is conducive to the health of the organization. To the union, efficiency usually connotes some attempted means of chiseling the workers out of something which they have earned for themselves. Security becomes, in the union vocabulary, the desirable counterpart. But this very word, in reverse, usually chills management. It is not the kind of a word to which management can respond.

Or take the word "ability." Again, to management this connotes a positive, affirmative quality, the kind of a criterion which should be used in the management of an organization. But to the union the term, ability, may represent the way in which management seeks to weasel some short-term employee into a position which is really due to the long-term employee. Seniority becomes, in their vocabulary, the preferable kind of attribute.

Or take the term "incentives." Again, for management this connotes something good, a driving force of which they are a necessary integral part; whereas, on the union side, incentives are usually tied up with rate busting, and undue pressures on the workers to achieve, or to produce. The responses are similar in connection with the term "scientific management," and the illustrations could be multiplied.

Out of this background, and compounded by unremitting competitive pressure facing it in the performance of its duties, management views unions as a force which interferes with its legitimate objectives. The union looms as an intruder which tends to frustrate the attainment of what management considers socially desirable ends.

In the light of this inescapable and continuous conflict between the parties, it is well to take brief note of the defense positions which each has prepared and the kind of rationale which each has mustered in defense of its attitudes.

MANAGEMENT AND UNION POSITIONS

The issues have seldom been more sharply posed than in a discussion which took place some few years ago before the National Academy of Arbitrators between James Phelps of Bethlehem Steel and Arthur Goldberg, then of the Steelworkers' Union. Phelps rested his position almost exclusively on the doctrine of residual rights. The following quotation indicates the reliance which he placed on this argument.

The job of management is to manage. The operation of the enterprise at its maximum efficiency [one of the vocabulary words which is peculiar to management] is management's responsibility and obligation. If a management believes that, in order to discharge its obligations, it must retain in full measure the so-called prerogative of management, it has the right to refuse to agree in collective bargaining to restrict those rights. If the management should agree to limit its exclusive functions or even to delegate certain of its duties to a union, it can enter into an agreement that will clearly define how far it has agreed to go.

To the extent the parties have not seen fit to limit management's sphere of action, management's rights are unimpaired by the contract.[5]

This is the doctrine of residual managerial rights which can only be given away by specific contract entered into in collective bargaining. Opposed to this is a philosophy which comes from a different set of values and which rests its argument primarily on the concept of consent of the worker, the basis for challenge of authority over history immemorial.

Arthur Goldberg said:

A backlog of rights and practices and precedents does develop as the collective bargaining relationship continues, based not on pre-union history but based on the period of the collective bargaining relationship.

. . . the practices which grow up during decades of a collective bargaining relationship cannot be swept aside . . . [they] inevitably represent the set of circumstances which formed the backdrop of the negotiation of the current agreement. . . . To the extent that present conditions and methods for change are not revised, they are accepted. Therefore, each party has the right to assume that changes in wages, hours, or working conditions not provided for by contract can be made only by mutual agreement or by following practices for making changes

[5]James C. Phelps, "Management's Reserved Rights: An Industry View," *Management Rights and the Arbitration Process*, Proceedings of the Ninth Annual Meeting, National Academy of Arbitrators (Washington, D.C.: Bureau of National Affairs, 1956), p. 117. The phrase in brackets is, of course, mine, not Phelps's.

which have existed during the collective bargaining relationship or [and this is a phrase which has always puzzled me] by virtue of management's exercise of an exclusive right (such as the introduction of new products, new machines, new material, new methods of manufacture, etc.). [The rationale for the inclusion of these specific items was never very apparent.] To suggest that management can make changes at will unless the contract specifically bars it is unfair and can lead to placing so many bars in the contract as to make successful negotiation increasingly difficult and operations less and less flexible, with detailed consideration of the facts and merits of each case replaced by precise rules and regulations.[6]

Both of these positions represent indefensible extremes. On the one hand, Mr. Phelps would seem to relegate the union to the role of a simple supplier, a supplier of services akin to the supplier of materials and having no more stake in the continuing operation of the company. But, of course, collective bargaining itself imposes continuing obligations, including obligations of consultation. The element of mutuality applies to the relationship, and it is not simply a matter of legal contract that is involved.

On the other hand, Mr. Goldberg seems to limit management initiative, with a few exceptions that have been given no rationale, to situations in which the union has given its concurrence, which is not, in my lexicon, initiative at all but a method of converting the individual firm into a kind of legislative forum. This, it seems to me, is an indefensible attack upon that necessary functional aspect of management, the right of initiation. Somewhere there must be a middle ground between these two positions.

One of the problems confronting us is how to establish that middle ground. What kind of resolution can we bring to a conflict which is necessary, inescapable, and continuing? The conflict is one which cannot be easily or permanently resolved. But perhaps something can be done to lessen the conflict, to smooth the relationship between the parties, to reduce the areas of tension and to build up areas in which the parties can effect an adequate working relationship.

Some mitigation of this inescapable conflict has come over the years. We have made progress, in part by improved understanding on both sides, management and union. Whether this can be ascribed to the development of the human relations philosophy which has had such wide circulation, one does not know, but it probably has had something to do with it. But certainly both sides have become much more enlightened in their dealings with each other. There is growing appreciation of the idea that both the simple demands of a democratic relationship—namely, consent of those over whom authority is wielded—and the realistic pragmatic necessity of getting something done require this accommodation. It is only good management to seek to secure consent of the governed who could otherwise make it impossible for management to achieve the very objective which it has set for itself. This, it seems

---

[6]Arthur J. Goldberg, "Management's Reserved Rights: A Labor View," *ibid.*, pp. 125–126. Again, the bracketed comment is mine and not Goldberg's.

to me, represents a forward advance, and I do think there has been an increasing degree of enlightenment and understanding of the human relationships involved in the process.

One of the really great instruments for resolution of the difficulties which have been pointed out here is the grievance procedure. Where the parties are willing to experiment with an increasing use of this device (not more frequent use, but a wider scope for its operations, a more flexible approach to it) and where there is a willingness to experiment with ways in which grievance procedure can be used, we may have one device which can, in the future to a greater extent even than in the past, be made an instrument for resolving on an ad hoc basis the kinds of disputes we encounter as we move along.

It should be added that in this process the terminal role of arbitration will continue to be a necessary one, even though the role of the grievance procedure may spread beyond the simple adjudication of terms of an agreement. The grievance procedure can operate at its most effective level when there is recognition on the part of all the parties to the process that what is necessary to observe is both the logic of the rule and the logic of the situation. These two are not always the same.

There is a need for somehow effecting an adequate compromise between the common rule, which applies in all situations, and the extraordinary solution which may represent deviation, a deviation which does not destroy the rule but only keeps the rule flexible enough to preserve it. This sort of experimentation involves developing a philosophy of the grievance procedure along lines which I think still lie largely ahead of us.

There is room for a more extended and deeper delving into the functioning of the grievance procedure in the union-management relationship than has been done. We need to explore, perhaps in a clinical fashion, some of the differences between grievance procedures which are on their face quite similar; the differences that exist between, for instance, the UAW-Ford relationship when Harry Shulman was umpire and that at GM when Ralph Seward was umpire. An intensive examination of the differences in these two relationships, what each was able to effect, and the difficulties that each encountered might help us in seeing more clearly in the future the ways in which this extremely important device, this invention which is one of our truly great social innovations, can be made even more fruitful in the future.

I have suggested that there are elements of similarity with the past in the conflict over managerial prerogatives as the union seeks to exercise them, and that there are also elements of dissimilarity. One of the important dissimilarities is that of giving legal sanction to the invasion by one group of the authority of another. I should like, finally, to focus on another dimension of this. It concerns the interrelated roles of productivity and efficiency in our economic processes and brings in several avenues of discussion and controversies ranging over a very wide economic area. Galbraith's concept of the "affluent society" is pertinent here, as is the long-standing dispute between the railroads and the Railroad Brotherhoods over featherbedding. It is the question of the relative importance of efficiency and productivity in our economic life.

EFFICIENCY AND PRODUCTIVITY

In recent years there has been a tendency to take the position that we are sufficiently wealthy in this country to allow us to be unconcerned about waste as it accumulates. Daniel Bell has put this into the thesis that one of the fruits of increasing productivity is the ability to be wasteful.

There is a measure of truth in this proposition. It is true that we can be less concerned about the need of exacting every last measure of human effort because of the increasing efficiency of our productive machine. But I am somewhat fearful that the doctrine of the "affluent society" has reached the point where it is sapping some of our needed interest in efficiency and productivity.

This, for two reasons. On the domestic scene we are reaching a position where there will be an increasing confluence of views from all shades of political opinion—over the next five, ten, fifteen years, it is difficult to say just when—that the affluence about which we speak is in the private sector, but that in the public sector we are really facing a pretty shabby and run-down society. Our housing situation, our transportation situation, our educational establishment, our recreational facility are but portions of our public plant which in many respects is operating at a very low level. It is not getting any better but is, in fact, deteriorating.

I would expect as the years move by we will find, not that we feel we are living in such an affluent society, but that we must recognize and give up an increasing measure of private wealth to enable us to put back in working shape and improve our public plant. This will mean that we are going to need the fruits of a productive and efficient economy, so we cannot afford to be wasteful in this respect.

Second, moving from the domestic to the international scene, there is similarly no doubt in my mind that as the years go by we will have imposed on us as a society inescapable responsibilities to help improve the economic lot of underdeveloped countries abroad. In the same way that we now take it for granted that citizens of New York, by a progressive income tax, are helping to improve the lot, let us say, of residents of Oklahoma, or of Montana, or of other less wealthy states, the same kind of a demand will be imposed on us for overseas assistance, and we will in time learn to accept this. But it is also going to impose strains on our productive efficiency and we will find that we do not have quite the degree of affluence we once thought if we are to turn out this mountain of wealth which is going to satisfy our private wants, our public needs, and the international demands upon us. We will find that we have to produce and produce effectively to meet all these requirements. This may also mean that, to the extent our national objectives of increasing the productivity of other countries abroad is successful, we are rearing more effective competitors for our own economy. What we are trying to do seems almost quixotic—attempting to create a more rigorous competition for ourselves. Yet, over the long haul, this is surely the only way to accomplish our aims.

If change is the law of life in industry, and if one of the functions of unions is to try to insure that change does not do damage to the morale and material security positions of its members, then it becomes increasingly incumbent upon all of us to find more effective means of resolving the conflict. The means developed to eliminate wasteful practices from the industrial scene must be such that they do not damage those who are a necessary and integral part of that scene.

I do not think we can go on indefinitely assuming that the union position must be always accepted when it claims that practices which have been developed in the past should be left untouched in the present. There may well be instances where the extraction of a greater measure of productive efficiency will require an increasing acceleration of innovation, new processes, and new methods in the industrial scene. But this only underscores the necessity of our turning a much more critical eye to the question of how we can make such changes come about without exacting a price from those on whom the burden will rest. In this process we must try to establish ways, procedures, and new devices by which we can meet the legitimate demands, the necessary functional position, of the union when it seeks to conserve the security and the position of its membership.

The Union Challenge
to Management Control

C H A P T E R 1

The Problem

The date is January 17, 1940. Around a long table in a Cleveland hotel room and in chairs facing the table sit a group of men engaged in an important collective-bargaining conference. It is not an industry-wide negotiation, but out of the conference will come an agreement which will set the pattern for agreements throughout the industry, for the two largest companies in that industry are jointly bargaining with the national officials of the union representing a large number of the employes of that industry. Their determinations will provide a "contract leadership" for the numerous smaller companies producing similar products. Representing the two companies are twenty-three men. Appearing for the union are forty-four.

After the usual preliminaries, the director of labor relations for one corporation leads off:

"I expect it is not necessary to be in any way formal about this and stand up while you talk about this matter. So long as you can all hear, we would just as soon sit down. . . .

"This agreement that you have given to us is rather unique in its make-up, and while it does not say closed shop in so many words, it is perfectly obvious to us that that is what it means. . . .

"In addition to that, there are at least ten paragraphs in this proposal that to the men on this side of the table mean a wide exploration into the realm of collective management. I know of no organization that has adventured into the field of collective management as you men have indicated here. Even the strongest organizations in the country recognize the rights of the management to run their business without first consulting the organization, and these ten paragraphs, at least, diverge widely from that field, and even make it an impossibility—if I may use such a word at this time—to even consider such a paragraph. . . .

"In the sum total of these proposals, gentlemen, we just cannot believe that you know what it means yourselves. We cannot believe that you even know that your proposal means, in effect, $5 million a year at least, and that is not the end, because you have proposed—committee discussions

1

here on something—and the Lord only knows what, so far as we are concerned—in any event, we suppose that it all means additional cost, so that to say that these companies are angry about this is not true. There isn't anybody on this side that is angry about it—we are amazed; amazed to the point of humiliation, I might say, to find that after trying for five or six years to get closer together, that instead of getting closer together, we find ourselves farther apart than at any time in the history of collective bargaining between these two companies and your organization."

The speaker turns to the executive vice president of the second company. "Now, Mr. Vice President, if you can elaborate on that a little bit, I wish you would."

The executive vice president takes up the story. He mentions a few figures bearing upon the proposal. He considers the implications of some of the union's requests. And then he concludes:

"With all my personal relations with a great many of the boys in this room, I had had a feeling, after putting in a lot of time on it myself and getting close to you boys and getting together on the troubles, I had thought we were perhaps as close in our cooperative thinking in the last six months as we ever were. Well, now you take all that and throw it out in the air. I am not mad about it—I don't know that I am disgusted; I am just bewildered. What are we going to do with it? I can't believe that you boys know what you are asking."[1]

What were the subjects of the union's proposal which prompted this concern by company officials for the preservation of managerial authority and evoked the damning epithet "collective management" with which to brand the proposal? Seniority provisions; automatic supply to the union of service records and employment lists; promotion schedules; matters of hiring and firing; employment of idle men on repairs rather than the contracting out of such repairs; an incentive system; equal distribution of orders among each company's plants; production speeds. In the companies' view, on these matters management must have the final determination. In the union's view, they were subjects for joint agreement.

The determination of the appropriate subjects for collective bargaining, and the definition of the spheres of company policy-formation which are of sole concern to management is one of the burning problems of industrial relations. In the words of a leading newspaper, "The question how far employes should have a voice in dictating to management is at present one of the hottest issues before the country."[2] It is an analysis of that problem to which this study is addressed.

[1] Quoted excerpts are taken from verbatim minutes of these negotiations.
[2] Editorial in the *Washington Post*, January 10, 1946.

The language in which the problem is customarily presented by management groups is in terms of "the invasion by the unions of managerial functions," and "the encroachment by labor on managerial prerogatives." There is no question where managements stand on the issue. They are convinced that the unions are seeking such inroads, that the attempt holds grave dangers for our social economy, and that it must be halted. They are not certain how the union effort is to be stopped, or even whether it can be stopped.

Let us briefly consider the prevalent management position, as presented by company spokesmen:

... union representatives are demanding and succeeding inch by inch in obtaining the demand that they exercise judgment before management can act. ... If the management representatives must talk to the union representatives before they can act or make a decision, then management has lost [its] management function. The function is then being discharged by the party with whom management must consult before acting, and the party whose approval must be obtained. That is the drive that is being made. ...[3]

Heretofore such encroachment upon management has been exercised only by such regulatory bodies as the Interstate Commerce and Public Service Commissions when dealing with public utilities. To yield to such a demand would mean the end of free enterprise with efficient management. ...[4]

The issue is not confined to whether the unions shall have a voice in matters which may be described as borderline, such as use of the seniority principle in governing promotions, where the basis of the worker's interest is perhaps more evident. Management is convinced that it faces a fight along a wide front to preserve its discretionary freedom in more basic matters. "The *unions* now attempt to make management's decisions on prices, on profits, on production schedules, on depreciation reserves, and on many other phases of industrial operation."[5] This challenge management would meet by recognizing certain reciprocal rights of the parties to the bargaining process. As expressed by H. E. Lewis, Chairman and President of the Jones & Laughlin Steel Corporation, "The right of labor to organize and bargain *and* the right of management to manage are in-

[3] Testimony of George Romney, General Manager, Automobile Manufacturers Association, in *Investigation of the National Defense Program*, Hearings before a Special Committee Investigating the National Defense Program, United States Senate, 79th Congress 1st Session, Part 28 (1945), condensed from pp. 13127 and 13135.

[4] Statement of Walter Gordon Merritt, counsel for General Motors, before the Truman Fact-Finding Board, *New York Times*, December 29, 1945.

[5] Statement of Ernest T. Weir, Chairman, National Steel Corporation, on a radio program sponsored by American Iron and Steel Institute, January 7, 1946, published by the Institute in pamphlet form. Italics in the original. H. W. Prentis Jr., former president of the National Association of Manufacturers, declared before the National Labor-Management Conference that in the last two or three years there had been "a definite tendency to extend the process of collective bargaining into fields that clearly trespass upon management functions." *New York Times*, November 7, 1945.

herent in the system of free enterprise that has made this country the leading industrial nation of the world."[6]

There is a conflict here which the management formula does not resolve, however. The issue of managerial prerogatives has arisen precisely because the "inherent" right of unions to organize and bargain has run counter to the "inherent" right of management to manage. If businessmen believe that the problem can be resolved to their satisfaction by recognizing *both* rights, is it because of an unconscious harboring of the mental reservation that management rights are prior and controlling, before which the union right to bargain must give way when conflict arises? If so, this is hardly a solution which the labor interests can be expected to accept.

What of the union position on this important issue? It is not easy to define if one is guided by the statements of labor officials. Some have disclaimed any attempt to penetrate management functions, recognizing, in unequivocal statements that would receive the endorsement of any business leader, a field of management which must remain inviolate to union penetration.

The union has abandoned its rightful function—that of protecting the worker—when it participates in management's function.[7]

The automobile worker does not seek to usurp management's function.[8]

Collective bargaining in industry does not imply that wage-earners shall assume control of industry, or responsibility for financial management. It proposes that the employes shall have the right to organize and deal with the employer through selected representatives as to wages and working conditions.[9]

The presidents of both the American Federation of Labor and the Congress of Industrial Organizations have signed their names to a "New Charter for Labor and Management," to which the United States Chamber of Commerce is likewise party, containing among other policy statements the following: "The inherent right and responsibility of management to direct the operations of an enterprise shall be recognized and preserved."[10] A similar charter drawn up in the City of Toledo, approved by members

---

[6] From a radio broadcast of January 14, 1946, sponsored by the American Iron and Steel Institute and published by it in pamphlet form. Italics supplied. Wayne L. Morse has similarly expressed this thought in "The Scope of Arbitration in Labor Disputes," *Papers Presented at Fourth Stanford Industrial Relations Conference,* Stanford University, 1941, p. 115: "There are certain rights which are not arbitrable, such as the inherent rights of management and the inherent right of labor to organize and function as a union."

[7] *U. E. Guide to Wage Payment Plans, Time Study and Job Evaluation,* United Electrical, Radio and Machine Workers, 1943, p. 98.

[8] From the preamble to the Constitution of the United Automobile Workers (CIO). Other union constitutions contain similar pronouncements.

[9] Samuel Gompers, "Collective Bargaining," *American Federationist,* vol. 27 (March 1920), p. 259.

[10] *New York Times,* March 29, 1945.

of the AFL and CIO as well as by industrial leaders and public representatives, contains among its governing principles a like provision.

Such pronouncements as these might lead one to the conclusion that the difference of opinion between management and labor as to the areas of management discretion is not a deep-seated one, insusceptible to settlement by discussion and agreement. The recognition by both parties of the existence of managerial functions not subject to union participation would seem to offer the necessary common basis of approach essential to such an agreement. This is not the case, however.

Not only have some union officials refused to concede the existence of privileged fields of managerial competence; there has been no willingness on the part of even those labor leaders recognizing managerial prerogatives to attempt a definition of precisely what managerial prerogatives they are recognizing.

It is my opinion we are going to succeed, meanly or greatly, in the field of industrial relations, only in so far as we can widen the area of collective bargaining to include not only questions of wages but many other questions relating to management's conduct.[11]

Within each level of organization, the union must be conceded the right to bargain respecting all functions of management, including determination of the production policy, the sales policy, the price policy and the financial policy.[12]

We are always trying to encroach on the managerial prerogatives. . . . We don't know what those prerogatives are. They change from year to year. . . .[13]

More significant even than such pronouncements are the practices of union representatives in bargaining conferences. At one time or another, in one industry or another, there is scarcely a function of management which has been impervious to union penetration.

Between the point where business managers retain the unchallenged exercise of a particular function and the point where the union succeeds in subjecting that function to joint policy determination is usually an intermediate stage, in which the union employs its privilege of critically examining managerial methods and determinations. It is this stage which seems to characterize the relationships of management and labor to a large extent at the present time. Financial and price policies of businesses are being brought more and more under the analytical survey of union officials and their research assistants. The productive efficiency of the managers is being accorded close scrutiny. Insofar as there is union dissatisfaction

---

[11] M. H. Hedges, Director of Research, International Brotherhood of Electrical Workers, "Time and Motion Study Under Collective Bargaining," *Advanced Management*, vol. V (1940), p. 90.

[12] From an interview with a national CIO official, who was expressing not present norms. but future goals.

[13] Matthew Smith, Secretary, Mechanics Educational Society of America, in *Investigation of the National Defense Program,* Part 28, p. 13249.

with management's discharge of its functions, it may be expected that labor officials and representatives will seek to secure a voice in the determination of business standards and policies, that they may be brought in line with its objectives, whatever the latter may be. Moreover, there is every reason to conclude that at least in certain instances participation in general policy formation is itself a union objective, sought not only for the concrete results expected from it but also because this participation is conceived as an important element of "industrial democracy."

It is difficult to reach any conclusion but that union officials, regardless of public statements, have generally adopted a flexible and evolutionary approach to the question, with the consequence that into any statements acknowledging and accepting the existence of managerial prerogatives must be read the addendum "as of this moment." The functions of management left untouched by the most recently concluded collective-bargaining agreement are the managerial prerogatives which labor will not seek to invade—"as of this moment," that is, for the life of the contract, or until new circumstances, a change in economic or social conditions, the accumulation of greater strength, the pressure of a drive to power, the need for new goals, or any other of a number of incentives may prompt a fresh assault upon some "right" which management had theretofore possessed unquestioned. The memories of union officials need not be long to recall days when the *joint* determination of wages and hours and working conditions, hiring and firing provisions, seniority rights and union security clauses was challenged by the managers as an invasion of their *sole* right to manage. There is no reason to expect that the unions will accept managements' determination of their spheres of discretion today any more than they respected such ex parte determinations in the past. We find here, then, the same sort of mental reservation that we found in the managers. When the "rights" of management conflict with the "right" of the union to bargain there are few union officials who would not act upon the premise that the "right" of the union is paramount.

The issue, thus sharply drawn, hung over the National Industrial Conference called by President Wilson following World War I, and was implicit in the question of employe representation over which the conference finally broke down.[14] Twenty-six years later the National Labor-Management Conference called by President Truman following World War II split on this problem even more sharply. Separate reports were submitted by the labor and management members of the Committee on Manage-

[14] The story is related in "National Industrial Conference, Washington, D. C.," *Monthly Labor Review*, vol. 9 (1919), pp. 1342–1351, especially 1348. Canadian experience provided a parallel, as noted by Leifur Magnusson, "First Canadian Industrial Conference," *Monthly Labor Review*, vol. 9 (1919), pp. 1353–1364, especially 1355.

ment's Right to Manage. The difference in viewpoint was marked. Said the management members:

> Labor members of the Committee on Management's Right to Manage have been unwilling to agree on any listing of specific management functions. Management members of the committee conclude, therefore, that the labor members are convinced that the field of collective bargaining will, in all probability, continue to expand into the field of management.
>
> The only possible end of such a philosophy would be joint management of enterprise. To this the management members naturally cannot agree. Management has functions that must not and cannot be compromised in the public interest. If labor disputes are to be minimized by "the genuine acceptance by organized labor of the functions and responsibilities of management to direct the operation of an enterprise," labor must agree that certain specific functions and responsibilities of management are not subject to collective bargaining.

The union members of the committee reported, in part:

> It would be extremely unwise to build a fence around the rights and responsibilities of management on the one hand and the unions on the other. The experience of many years shows that with the growth of mutual understanding the responsibilities of one of the parties today may well become the joint responsibility of both parties tomorrow.
>
> We cannot have one sharply delimited area designated as management prerogatives and another equally sharply defined area of union prerogatives without either side constantly attempting to invade the forbidden territory, thus creating much unnecessary strife.[15]

What lies at the roots of this conflict? What is the nature of this issue which has arrayed the autonomous organizations of business against the autonomous organizations of workers? It is in part legal, in part economic, in part technical or technological, in part political, in part ethical. To understand the problem and to form intelligent judgments it is therefore necessary that we separate these aspects of the problem, insofar as that is feasible, and analyze them in their respective details.

The problem has its legal elements. The rights and duties of owners, managers, workers, and unions are caught up in the controversy. So too are their privileges, which impose no duties on others and which may be more difficult of defense. Where does the managerial "prerogative" fit into the complex of legal relationships? Where enters the "right" of unions to bargain? The law of social relationships has sprung both from the legislatures and from the courts, both from the federal government and from the state governments, both from the authorities of one period and from those of succeeding periods. Has this diversity of sources created confusion as to where "rights" "inhere," and why?

---

[15] *The President's National Labor-Management Conference*, November 5–30, Summary and Committee Reports, U. S. Department of Labor, Division of Labor Standards, Bulletin No. 77. Quoted extracts are from pp. 56–57 and 61.

The problem has its important economic aspects. Industrial authority implies power to determine the lines of production and the distribution of income. It is this latter phase which has received primary emphasis in most discussions of the question. The conflict is conceived in terms of the workers' fight for "more," and in line with the materialistic foundations of our social thinking the "more" is construed as more pay, more prosperity, more goods, more real income. There is a large measure of truth in this assumption, but it is not the whole story. How much of the problem it encompasses and how much it leaves untouched is important to determine, even though quantitative measures are not available.

The problem has its technological considerations. A smoothly operating, well-integrated industrial system is essential to a strong society. What is the nature of the managerial authority required by such an industrial system? With the growth of our society, in area and population and wealth and material complexity, there has been an accompanying specialization of economic activity by business units, demanding intricate business arrangements—some planned and others not—enmeshing the seemingly infinite parts of our industrial society into a working unity. What is the necessary function of management, and what are the desirable roles of managements and unions, in achieving this industrial order?

The problem has its political implications. We are groping our way towards the definition of the place of autonomous organizations in our political scheme. We are seeking the elaboration of a constitutional theory of the government of organized groups within our society. Where fit the revolutionary aspects of freedom of association within our political framework? How may we achieve unity while encouraging diverse groupings of interests, balance without playing off power against power; how relate the functional groups in the broader polity?

The problem is highly charged with an ethical content. Judgments are required as to the moral validity of legal relationships, the justification for economic powers and distributive shares, the degree of weight to be accorded technological efficiency, the philosophical foundations for political arrangements. Here indeed lies the final basis for decision. We should be missing the heart of the problem if we failed to realize that legal and economic arguments, technological and political considerations must give way before widely held moral convictions. What is the ethical basis of the workers' struggle for increasing participation in business decisions? On what standards of justice and rightness does management rest its defensive tactics? Such questions should not produce wry smiles from those recalling union terrorism and intimidation, and management use of *agents provocateurs*, bribery, and tear gas. Such condemned activity reveals the deep roots of ethical persuasions. (We may remember that men killed men in the name of Christianity.)

We have thus set ourselves a task of no little magnitude in undertaking to examine unionism's attack on the citadel of managerial prerogatives. It is therefore perhaps desirable at the outset to agree to confine the scope of our study within limits.

For our purposes, we shall survey the broad problem of the impact of collective bargaining on managerial functions only in the large corporation. An exact measure of size is not especially important; we may, if we wish, define large corporations as those possessing assets of approximately fifty million dollars. This delimitation of the scope of the investigation may be defended on several grounds.

There is no longer any argument as to the overwhelming importance of the large corporations in American economic life. There is no need to marshall here an array of facts which has become familiar reading —the proportion of corporate wealth, of business wealth, or of national wealth controlled by the 200 largest corporations, the size of the employe populations of these giant businesses, and the ramifying effects of their corporate decisions. This material is readily available for those who wish to review it.[16] Since it is at best difficult, if indeed not impossible, to arrive at significant generalizations based on all forms of American business, disregarding the type and scale of organization, we shall confine our attention to that form of business which is recognized as of dominating importance in our economy.[17]

One evidence of the dominance of the large corporation is especially pertinent to the present investigation. It is not infrequently the case that the agreement signed by the union with the leading company or companies in an industry will set a pattern for the entire industry. Agreements with the smaller producers will follow the terms of the leading contract in most important particulars, with some deviations arising as a result of local conditions. This principle applies in the steel, coal, and flat-

[16] It may be found, for example, in A. A. Berle and Gardiner C. Means, *The Modern Corporation and Private Property* (1932), especially chap. 3; Twentieth Century Fund, *Big Business, Its Growth and Its Place* (1937); National Resources Planning Board, *The Structure of the American Economy*, Part 1, especially chap. 7 and appendices 7 through 11; Temporary National Economic Committee Monograph No. 27, *The Structure of Industry* (1941); R. A. Gordon, *Business Leadership in the Large Corporation* (1945), chap. 2; Gardiner C. Means, "The Growth in the Relative Importance of the Large Corporation in American Economic Life," *American Economic Review*, vol. 21 (1931), pp. 10–42.

[17] Support for this procedure may be found in William O. Douglas, former chairman of the Securities and Exchange Commission and one well versed in the characteristics of American business enterprise. Douglas has spoken of the desirability of "particularization of types of problems and of types of controls needed" along lines of business size. "Directors Who Do Not Direct," *Harvard Law Review*, vol. 47 (1934), p. 1306.

glass industries, for example, and only to a somewhat lesser extent in other industries which recognize a dominant company (or association) influence. The significance of this practice was seized upon by the federal administration during the reconversion period following World War II, when wage increases were permitted where a "pattern" had been established; a "pattern" customarily resulted from agreement between a national union and a dominant corporation or group of corporations. It is therefore reasonable to expect that insofar as unions are able to secure from the large corporation contract rights impinging upon formerly recognized managerial functions, contract leadership will result in extending such rights over a much wider area.

The problem to which we are thus addressing ourselves is that of the impact of collective bargaining on managerial authority and functions, with its legal, economic, technological, and political implications. We shall attempt to assess the motivating forces behind the unions' persistent drive to achieve a voice in the councils of management, and behind management's stubborn reluctance to concede the justice or wisdom of that endeavor. We shall consider possible resolutions of the conflict. And we have defined the area in which we shall study this broad problem as one including only the large corporations in American industry. As the first stage in this investigation let us undertake to analyze the nature of one of the two principals in the bargaining process—management.

C H A P T E R **2**

Management in Theory and Practice

THE LEGAL POSITION OF MANAGEMENT

The legal status of corporate management forms an important part of the vast body of corporation law. The jural complexities surrounding the nature of the corporation continue to confuse even lawyers and courts and we must tread our way here carefully. For our limited purposes, we are interested only in how managerial authority is derived and what it constitutes.

In the same manner that a union may be considered as simply the aggregate of its members, no more and no less, the corporation has been held in law to *be* the stockholders. As is true of so many phases of corporate law, this theory has not gone unchallenged. Yet it does enjoy such important support that it is at least correct to say that strong probability exists that cases will still be decided by courts of law on the presumption that the United States Steel Corporation or the General Motors Corporation are merely associations of several hundred thousand people whose common interest is that they all possess shares of stocks in those corporations. "The idea that the corporation is an entity distinct from the corporators who compose it has been aptly characterized as 'a nebulous fiction of thought.' . . . When all has been said, it remains that a corporation is not in reality a person or a thing distinct from its constituent parts, and the constituent parts are the stockholders, as much so in essence and in reality as the several partners are the constituent parts of the partnership."[1]

The association of individuals combining to do business together receives its corporate character from the statutes under which it comes into being. These corporation laws and the certificate of incorporation or charter which the newly formed organization receives upon meeting

[1] *Cincinnati Volksblatt Co.* v. *Hoffmeister,* 62 Ohio St. 189, 200; 56 N.E. 1033, 1935 (1900). This view has been strongly upheld by two eminent students of the law, Wesley Newcomb Hohfeld and Max Radin, as for example, in the former's "Nature of Stockholders' Individual Liability for Corporation Debts," *Columbia Law Review,* vol. 9 (1909), p. 310; and Radin's "The Endless Problem of Corporate Personality," *Columbia Law Review,* vol. 32 (1932), pp. 665–666.

11

the requirements of the law define the legal powers of the corporation. In the absence of any statutory or charter provision to the contrary, these powers are vested in the stockholders, as themselves the management of the business.[2] As a matter of practice, however, almost invariably provision is made either by statute or charter for the direction of the company by a specially selected board of management, commonly known as the board of directors, designed to act on behalf of the body of incorporators. ". . . The corporation is altogether a distinct body from the directors, possessing all the general powers and attributes of an aggregate corporation, and entitled to direct and superintend the management of its own property, and the government of the institution, and to enact bylaws for this purpose. So far as the act delegates authority to the directors, the latter possess it and may exercise it, not as constituting the corporation itself, but as its express statute agents, to act in the ordinary business of the institution. The directors are created a board, and not a corporate body."[3]

As a framework for the exercise of the powers so conferred upon the board of directors to act on behalf of the corporation, the bylaws drafted and accepted by the stockholders join the statutory corporation law and the charter or certificate of incorporation as the articles governing the conduct of the business in its broad outlines. It is customary for the bylaws to specify the powers which the stockholders grant to the board of directors to act on their behalf, but it is important to note that these are limited powers only insofar as the statutory law and and the charter have not themselves conferred additional powers upon the board. In practice, the limitations are not great, for it has been quite customary for the bylaws (if, indeed, not the statutes) to confer broad grants of power upon the board. It is by no means unknown for the board to be provided with authority to amend or enact the bylaws themselves.[4] We shall consider at a later point, but for the sake of emphasis mention here also, a fact which becomes cardinal in discussing the nature of managerial authority in dealing with labor unions: limitations upon the board's powers have not been, primarily, with respect to the type of actions which it may take but, rather, with respect to the purpose and intent of the actions taken under the almost limitless powers granted to the board.

So sweeping is the legal authority of the board of directors in the

[2] Thomas Conyngton and R. J. Bennett, *Corporation Procedure* (edition revised by Hugh R. Conyngton, 1927), p. 129. *Union Pacific Railway Company* v. *Chicago Railway Company*, 163 U.S. 564, 596 is illustrative.

[3] *Bank of U.S.* v. *Dandridge*, 12 Wheat. 64.

[4] This power is exampled in *Realty Acceptance Corporation* v. *Montgomery*, 51 F. (2nd) 636, and is further discussed by William J. Grange, *Corporation Law for Officers and Directors* (1935), pp. 69–70.

management of the company that it has sometimes been said that the stockholders possess the power to elect the directors, but having elected them are virtually powerless to take further action with respect to the conduct of the business which they own.[5] They are "helpless as against their board of directors,"[6] so long as the board operates within the extremely broad spheres of authority allotted to it and in the interests of the stockholders. "The corporation is the owner of the property, but the directors in the performance of their duty possess it, and act in every way as if they owned it."[7]

We are here not concerned with the theory of the separation of ownership and control which has become associated with the names of Berle and Means and which involves the institutional processes by which managements may perpetuate themselves in office irrespective of the wishes of the stockholders, and the possible divergences which may arise thereby between the interests of those who manage and those whose property is managed. We are here concerned only with such separation of ownership and management which is provided for in law; we are interested only in the legal nature of the managerial authority in the corporation. This authority, we discover, is profound. Indeed, so singular, so undivided, is the power of management in the corporation that it has been held to exist independently of the stockholders themselves. "But in corporate bodies the powers of the board of directors are, in a very important sense, original and undelegated. The stockholders do not confer, nor do they revoke those powers. They are derivative only in the sense of being received from the State in the act of incorporation. The directors convened as a board are the primary possessors of all the powers which the charter confers. . . ."[8]

It is not material in this connection whether one considers that the authority of the board derives from the laws of the state or is conferred by the stockholders, or obtains in part from both sources. It was long settled in the common law that the powers of the board extended to all subjects connected with the management of the company, and unless specific restrictions were imposed such powers were virtually supreme. The delegation of authority to the board in statutory law was thus no more than legislative recognition of a legal relationship already existing before the courts. To the extent that state law does not confer managerial powers upon a board, in the absence of any specific limitations on the board's authority such powers will still be inferred from the common law.

---

[5] Earl A. Saliers, *The Handbook of Corporate Management and Procedure* (1929), p. 275.
[6] Conyngton and Bennett, *Corporation Procedure*, p. 129.
[7] *Manice* v. *Powell*, 201 N.Y. 194, 201. *Manson* v. *Curtis*, 223 N.Y. 313, and *Blancard* v. *Blancard & Co.*, 96 N.J. Eq. 264, also illustrate this principle.
[8] *Hoyt* v. *Thompson's Executor*, 19 N.Y. 207.

Statute law merely reinforces common law in vesting in the board of directors almost exclusive powers of management.[9]

If the grant of managerial authority to the board of directors is so unconfined as to spheres of competence, there is nevertheless an important limitation upon the board's discretion in the exercise of its authority. All decisions made and actions taken by the management must be in the interests of the stockholders whom it represents. There has been no end of discussion as to whether this obligation places the directors in the relation of agents, trustees, or fiduciaries to the stockholders for whom they act. As regards our investigation, this discussion is not relevant except insofar as it establishes that, whatever the nature of the relationship of the directors as management to the stockholders as owners, the managerial authority is to be exercised solely on behalf of the stockholders, within the general legal framework of the political jurisdictions within which the corporation operates.

The obligation of corporate management to the owners is not subject to any fixed set of rules.[10] "As a result, though attempts have been made at various times in trust instruments to confer absolute powers on the trustee and to exempt him from any and all liabilities in connection with the use of such powers, the law has almost invariably declined to honor the exemption from liability and has imposed its own standards on the trustee. All that the trust instrument can do is to say what the trustee's *powers are;* where and when he is permitted to use them depends upon a set of standards which the courts will impose independently of the agreement, contract, or constitutive documents."[11] However broad or precise the grant of powers in statute, charter, or bylaws, the directors as the management of a corporation are subject to this limitation on the

---

[9] It is legally incompetent only in such spheres as may be specifically set forth in the statutes, charter, or bylaws. In practice, these limitations run only to such acts as increasing the capital stock, leasing the corporate property, or winding up the corporate business, in the absence of stockholder approval.

[10] This point is developed by Rudolph E. Uhlman in "Legal Status of Corporate Directors," *Boston University Law Review,* vol. 19 (1939), p. 16. Codes of conduct have been elaborated, but application of their principles has been by no means uniform. Conyngton and Bennett have thus enunciated five general requirements for the conduct of directors (*Corporation Procedure,* pp. 210–211):

    1. Use of the same care and diligence in the conduct of corporate affairs which any prudent businessman would exercise in conducting his own business. (This becomes, to a degree, a question of prevailing business practice.)
    2. Scrupulous good faith in all matters relating to the corporation.
    3. Lack of self-interest as a motivation for actions or decisions.
    4. No business relations as a third party with the corporation for personal advantage.
    5. No profit-seeking at the expense of the stockholders.

[11] A. A. Berle, "Corporations and the Public Investor," *American Economic Review,* vol. 20 (1930), p. 67. Italics in the original. It is hardly necessary to point out that the "set of standards" by which directorial action is judged changes with geography, time, and personal viewpoint.

use of those powers, that they shall be exercised only for the best interests of the stockholders as a body, on behalf of the stockholders as a corporation.

"The ordinary trust relation of the directors to the corporation and stockholders is not a matter of statutory law, or of technical law. It springs from the fact that the directors have the control and guidance of the corporate business affairs and property, and hence of the property interests of the stockholders. Equity, at least, recognizes the truth that the stockholders are the proprietors of the corporate interests and are ultimately the only beneficiaries thereof. Those interests are, in virtue of the law, intrusted, through the corporation, to the directors, and from that condition arises the trusteeship of the directors with the concomitant fiduciary obligations."[12]

We may conclude, then, that regardless of whether the authority of corporate management is derived by direct delegation of the stockholders or by legislative fiat, the legal basis of that authority rests ultimately upon an accompanying obligation to serve the interests of the corporators. Without the acceptance of that obligation there is no legal foundation for management's assumption of authority. The powers of management are conferred as the result of a legal relationship with the stockholders. If management is considered as agent for the stockholders, its authority is limited to actions on behalf of the principals. If management is considered as trustee, its authority is confined to actions in the interest of the *cestui que trust*, that is to say, of the stockholders again.

The legal relationship established between management and owners involves more than the conferring of powers. With the powers of management goes the liability of the stockholders, as a corporation, to the fulfillment of such obligations as may be assumed on their behalf. With this liability of the stockholders is associated their right to a managerial performance designed for their advantage; with management's power is bound up a duty to act only for the preferment of the interests of the body of shareholders. Other legal elements than these powers and liabilities, rights and duties, are bound up in the management-stockholder relationship, but for our purposes these are the essential ones. The rights and duties limit the powers to be exercised and the correlative liabilities which may be imposed upon the corporation as a property-owning aggregate or association.

Thus far we have been considering managerial authority in relation to its source, but this has been only preliminary to determining its relations with third parties. The power conferred on management by virtue of its legal relationship with the stockholders enables it to exercise, as respects

---

[12] *Kavanaugh* v. *Kavanaugh Knitting Mills*, 226 N.Y. 185, 123 N.E. 148.

its legal relations with other parties, all the rights, privileges, powers, and immunities associated with ownership, except as these have been reserved from its field of competence by statute, charter, or bylaw. It has, for example, the right to forbid the entrance of others on corporate property except in accordance with terms mutually agreed; the privilege of employing corporate capital along lines deemed most advantageous in its own judgment, the power to contract with others respecting the sale of corporate products or the hire of labor with corporate funds; immunity from interference with the enjoyment of corporate rights or claims except through the operation of due process of law. This complex of rights, privileges, powers, and immunities is probably what businessmen have most frequently in mind when they speak of the prerogatives of management, though such intent is not always clear. Again, however, it is important to observe that, before the law, management is entitled to this legal authority not by virtue of anything inhering in its management function,[13] but solely by reason of its relationship with the owners of the corporation. Authority comes into its possession when management is chosen to that office, but legal sanction for that authority continues only so long as management fulfills its obligation to act solely on behalf of those who have designated it as management.

Unless we understand this legal framework, it will be impossible for us to understand an important part of management's case with respect to "union encroachment on managerial rights." Because of its single responsibility to the stockholders, a responsibility imposed by law, management resists granting to a party whose interests do not coincide with those of the owners a "right" to share in managerial determinations. In management's view, to accede to such a demand by the union would be to violate the obligations inherent in its own legal relationship with the owners. Other elements are involved in the managers' position, it is true, but it is impossible to deny that this legal ground is a dominating consideration.

The refusal of some managements to submit disputes of interests to arbitration stems from the same view, and it is in such instances that business representatives have been most articulate in stating their position.

The very act of accepting authority constitutes an agreement to exercise it in accordance with the aims and interests of the person from whom it is obtained, and the use of the authority in a contrary manner is a violation of the terms of its acceptance. . . .

It is essential, then, that authority be delegated only to those who will act exclusively in the interests of their superior. For example, the Army would not think of appointing

[13] This is still with respect to third parties. It is of course true that certain rights are inherent in the managerial function relative to the stockholders, such as, for example, the right to inspect the corporate books, records, and property.

an officer who is also an officer in the Army of another nation, since his loyalty would be seriously in question.

This same principle applies in business. The Management, in its delegation of authority, is bound to make certain to the best of its ability that the authority will be used in accordance with the interests of the business. This precludes it from delegating authority to anyone whose interests may be in conflict with those of the owners of the business.

These are the principles that are involved in so many of the labor controversies of the moment. As a part of its basic responsibility, a Management must make every effort to maintain its labor relations on a basis of harmony that will further the best interests of the business as a whole. In all labor controversies which threaten to disrupt the orderly conduct of the business, it should make every reasonable effort to settle the differences. As a matter of principle, it should always be willing to submit debatable questions of fact to qualified impartial fact-finding agencies.

But in any case in which compromise would mean serious injury to the true long-term interests of the institution and the purposes for which it was created, no Management can be excused if it voluntarily submits the issues to any form of arbitration which involves an irrevocable agreement to abide by the decisions of another party or agency.

Suppose, for example, that the Management of a company in a given industry, employing a specialized kind of highly skilled workman, was presented with a demand for a reduction in hours which would so reduce the supply of skilled labor that before sufficient additional workers can be obtained and trained the business as an institution would be irreparably injured. The Management, of course, should attempt to compromise at some point which would not produce this serious result. It would attempt to establish to the satisfaction of the men that the request is unreasonable. It should seek by all possible forms of mediation and conciliation to effect a settlement of this nature. But should all of these attempts fail, the submission of the matter to the unlimited, binding arbitration of an outside party would be dereliction and the investors would be fully warranted in discharging the Management forthwith.[14]

In similar vein, the General Motors Corporation, through Mr. H. W. Anderson, vice president in charge of personnel, refused the request of the United Automobile Workers to arbitrate issues in dispute in the 1945–1946 negotiations. Anderson replied to the union:

Actually your proposal means that an arbitration board would assume the responsibilities of management; that it would assume responsibility for determining what is a sound financial and economic policy for General Motors; that the presently constituted management would relinquish functions which have been assigned to it by the owners of the business—the stockholders; that the duly elected officers of General Motors would surrender their functions and responsibilities to outsiders including a representative of the union. . . .

Such functions of management cannot be delegated to anyone not responsible for the continuing success of the business. They will not be surrendered to the union. . . .[15]

The management argument might be briefly summarized as follows: If

---

[14] Stephen M. DuBrul, director, labor economics section, General Motors Corporation, in an address, *Authority and Responsibility in Industrial Management,* presented to the Institute of Public Affairs, University of Virginia, July 14, 1934, mimeo., pp. 7–9. Italics in the original.

[15] *New York Times,* November 24, 1945.

the stockholders are to have their interests faithfully served, the fullest possible discretion must be preserved to their elected representatives. Thus in fighting for managerial freedom, management is only fulfilling its trustee function of attempting to secure the advantage of the stockholders. Insofar as management has consented to any dilution of its authority not required by law, it has presumably done so only because it believes that course of action to be in the best interests of the owners —perhaps by improving the morale of the workers, stimulating greater cooperation by the union, or by forestalling or settling a strike.

It is important to note, however, that although management *may* construe its legal duties to require resistance to union penetration of its authority, the legal power to grant unions a voice in managerial determinations exists. As we have noted, managements of corporations are virtually unlimited in the permissible scope of decisions and actions. The principal limitation upon their legal capacity to act lies in the intent and the prudence of their judgment. If upon serious consideration of the issues managers are led to believe that it is in the interests of the stockholders to grant the union a more significant role in policy formulations, there is no reason to believe that any court of law would raise a barrier. The legal requirements of managerial responsibility do not therefore preclude managements from sharing their authority. It is quite true, however, that they cannot equally share their responsibility. The consequences of any business policy must be shouldered by the management alone. The statement that management can delegate but cannot share responsibility is to be considered, then, not as raising an insurmountable impediment to a union's sharing the managerial authority, but simply as a reminder of management's legal status as the sole agency which the law will hold accountable for the protection of the stockholders.

We have been discussing here the status of the corporation and its management in the eyes of the law. In recent years there has been a growing belief that this legal basis of corporate action is inadequate. Spokesmen have not been lacking to proclaim that more than the interests of the stockholders is involved. "That lawyers have commonly assumed that the managers must conduct the institution with single-minded devotion to stockholder profit is true; but the assumption is based upon a particular view of the nature of the institution which we call a business corporation, which concept is in turn based upon a particular view of the nature of business as a purely private enterprise. If we recognize that the attitude of law and public opinion toward business is changing, we may then properly modify our ideas as to the nature of such a business institution and hence as to the considerations which may properly influence the conduct of those who direct its activities."[16]

This view that the responsibilities of corporate management run to other parties in interest than the stockholders has been enunciated by an increasing number of businessmen. Representative of this group, Owen D. Young has said:

> If you will pardon me for being personal, it makes a great difference in my attitude toward my job as an executive officer of the General Electric Company whether I am a trustee of the institution or an attorney for the investor. If I am a trustee, who are the beneficiaries of the trust? To whom do I owe my obligations?
>
> My conception of it is this: That there are three groups of people who have an interest in that institution. One is the group of fifty-odd thousand people who have put their capital in the company, namely, its stockholders. Another is a group of well toward one hundred thousand people who are putting their labor and their lives into the business of the company. The third group is of customers and the general public. . . .
>
> I think what is right in business is influenced very largely by the growing sense of trusteeship which I have described. One no longer feels the obligation to take from labor for the benefit of capital, nor to take from the public for the benefit of both, but rather to administer wisely and fairly in the interest of all.[17]

We shall have occasion to examine later similar statements by other business leaders. The assumption of broader social responsibilities than is implied in an agency or fiduciary relationship to the group of stockholders has become commonplace in the public pronouncements of our business managers. It is no impugnation of their good intent, however, to say that we must not expect such assertions to determine conduct on critical, specific issues. The fact remains that irrespective of personal wish on the part of few or many of the managers, the law binds them to a course of business conduct in the sole interest of the corporate owners. It is the single standard by which the law will evaluate their conduct.[18]

The validity in practice of this legal theory of managerial responsibil-

---

[16] E. M. Dodd, "For Whom Are Corporate Managers Trustees?" *Harvard Law Review*, vol. 45 (1932), p. 1163.

[17] Quoted in Dodd, *Harvard Law Review*, vol. 45, pp. 1154–1155.

[18] This is the basis for the reply to Dodd by A. A. Berle in "For Whom Corporate Managers *Are* Trustees," *Harvard Law Review*, vol. 45 (1932), p. 1365.

There is a question whether the National Labor Relations Act has introduced a change in this respect. Insofar as the Act imposes upon managements a legal duty to bargain collectively with unions of the employes' choosing, it appears to be specific recognition of a legal claim to an interest in the affairs of the corporation by a party other than the stockholders. True, the legal obligations of the management to the owners who choose them may require that it strike the bargain most favorable to their interests, denying union claims whenever possible, negotiating so effectively that it concedes to the union only the bare minimum necessary to prevent or settle a strike, or to win its cooperation. Moreover, the Act requires no agreement. Nevertheless, the National Labor Relations Board's construction of the duty to bargain as embracing the obligation to submit counterproposals to union demands contains elements of a legal claim to a continuing interest in the corporation. This is perhaps a change in corporate law and philosophy of the first magnitude, which we shall want to examine at greater length elsewhere.

ity is not here in question. Whether managements represent the free choice of the stockholders or are self-selected is not material at this point. Whether their actions are in fact guided by the purpose of serving the stockholders or whether other motives play their part is not now in issue. If the legal theory is only fiction, there is reason to re-examine it for purposes of bolstering or modifying it, enforcing or replacing it. But so long as the laws of managerial responsibility remain unchanged, we cannot ignore them. We have been concerned at this stage of our investigation only with description of the law and not with reform.

THE FUNCTIONAL DEFINITION OF MANAGEMENT

The legal status of management is determined by its connection with the corporate owners. Its legal authority derives from a relationship of trust or agency with the stockholders. This is one important aspect of management's position in the corporation, and one significant method of defining management. The status and authority of management are derivative from other sources than the law, however; there are other aspects of management's position in the corporation which are equally important, and other ways of defining management. From preoccupation with the legal basis for management, let us now turn to an examination of its functional role.

"Whether capital be supplied by individuals or by the State, whether labour be by hand oι by machine, whether the workers assume a wide control over industry or are subjected to the most autocratic power, the function of management remains constant."[19]

This assertion that the management function remains constant under all forms of industrial organization raises a number of challenging questions.

What is it that characterizes management; that is to say, what is the "management factor"? What *makes* management management? What powers or characteristics or qualities does management require in order *to be* management?

When business groups declare that it "should be an obligation on the part of unions to recognize, and not encroach upon, the functions and responsibilities of management,"[20] are they concerned with management functions which might be considered "inherent," or are they speaking

---

[19] Oliver Sheldon, *The Philosophy of Management* (1924), p. 48; like expressions may also be found on pp. 281–282 and 284. Robert M. C. Littler, one of the most ardent advocates of managerial freedom, has similarly remarked in "Managers Must Manage," *Harvard Business Review*, vol. 24 (1946), p. 376.

[20] Statement of management members of the Committee on Management's Right to Manage, in *The President's National Labor-Management Conference*, p. 57.

of management functions as they have developed historically in the American capitalistic system?

Professor Holden and his Stanford University research associates have broken down "top management" into three zones with specialized functions. The first of these zones they have called "the trusteeship function" which includes among its responsibilities the representation, safeguarding, and furthering of the stockholders' interests.[21] As we have already seen, this is a legal duty of management as trustee or agent for the corporate owners. Is it, however, a function of management as management, or is it a function of management as trustee; can the two functions be separated? *Is* there a management function regardless of the ownership or control setting?

In attempting to answer these questions we shall be troubled at the outset by the abundance and variety of the definitions of management. Of recent years the managers have been subjecting themselves and their operations to an increasingly critical self-examination, seeking to determine the essence of their reason for being. Management societies, associations, and conferences have paraded programs of analysts dissecting managerial life into its cellular parts. Out of the wealth of this discussion has emerged no sharp conclusion as to the fundamental nature of management, the irreducible minimum without which management ceases to be management. This is not surprising, for the very richness of the manager's occupational life makes it difficult for him to seize upon any factor or factors as being more fundamental than any other.

Let us plunge into the problem by indicating some of the definitional difficulties. Professor Balderston and his associates have listed fourteen of the many synonyms for "managing" which have been used at one time or another: to direct, guide, control, govern, regulate, administer, conduct, "boss," discipline, make obedient, supervise, superintend, cope with, carry on.[22] Others might be added: to initiate, correlate, coordinate, take charge, oversee, execute. Each of these tends to emphasize some aspect of "management" and implies, by that emphasis, varying interpretations of what is fundamental in the function of a manager. Which emphasis is correct? Or should all of these aspects be accorded equal weight?

Let us set about answering these questions which we have raised.

Within the corporation, as within any organization, we may note three distinct phases of doing business. We may call these direction, administration, and execution. In addition, there is perhaps a fourth, less distinct but nonetheless important, which we may designate as compliance. We

21 Paul E. Holden, Lounsbury S. Fish, and Hubert L. Smith, *Top-Management Organization and Control* (1941), p. 15.
22 C. Canby Balderston, Victor S. Karabasz, and Robert P. Brecht, *Management of an Enterprise* (1937), p. 3.

shall examine all of these functions in turn. First in any organization must come the definition of objectives, the determination of what is to be done. This is the function which we have called *direction*. It is associated only with the highest and ultimate level of authority in the corporation. Thus, when the foreman tells his crew what is to be done, he is not exercising the directive function. The function which he is exercising we shall examine in a moment. Direction ordinarily is concerned only with deciding the broad goals of the business, but the scope of its objectives is not the determinant of the directive function. In the final analysis, that determinant is whether there is a higher authority within the management organization which may overrule the objective set forth. If there is such a higher authority, direction is not being exercised.

Typically in the large American corporation, the function of direction is found in the board of directors, or in some combination of the board of directors and the top officials, or in the top officials solely. The exact location is dependent upon whether in fact the board controls management, whether final authority is shared between them, or whether top-management controls the board. Wherever decisions may be made without fear of their being set aside, there lies direction.

We have said that direction ordinarily concerns itself only with broad goals. It may thus determine the line of products which shall be produced by the corporation, the methods of raising capital funds, the capital structure of the business, its relations with the public or with its employes, or other matters of similar importance. It may, however, concern itself with much smaller details, as for example whether a new office of vice president shall be created or whether paid holidays shall be granted to the working force. The essential character of direction is thus its ultimate authority, the finality of its decisions. Attempts to define direction by the broadness of its decisions, the importance of its goals, the basic nature of its determinations lead only to confusion. It is invariably possible to point to decisions made by officials lower in the corporate hierarchy which are broader than some reached by the directive officers, goals which are more important and determinations which may be considered more "basic" than those established by the directive authorities.

It is clear from what has been said above that direction is not concerned solely with the development of policy. Considerable confusion has developed around the very meaning of the word "policy," but we may consider it as a standard governing present and future actions and decisions within a defined area of operations, a meaning which finds some agreement among management specialists.[23] The directive authorities will indeed enunciate policies in this sense, but they need not stop with

[23] As, for example, Holden, Fish, and Smith, *Top-Management Organization and Control,* p. 79.

such an exercise of their function. Any decision as to *what is to be done* which emanates from them must be considered as direction.

Moreover, *levels* of policy are determinable only by the degree of authority attached to them. Any efforts to define "basic," "general," or "department" policy except by reference to the source of authority are doomed to confusion. The content of the policy itself does not offer a basis for classification. The Stanford survey of top-management organization points up the difficulty in this respect. It suggests that basic policies are those which establish the long-range objectives and chart the destinies of the company, while general policies are those which are of short-range or everyday operating significance. It offers as an example of basic policy, found during the course of the survey, that "Compensation for all employees shall be at or above prevailing rates"; as an example of general policy, "Until further notice the company will meet all competitive prices."[24] It is evident, however, that these two policy statements, judged on content, are of the same order, declaring that the company will meet both the wage rates and the prices of its competitors. One may be as long-range or as short-range as the other—only time will tell. They may logically be called basic or general only on the ground that one has emanated from a higher authority than the other.

If direction establishes what is to be done, *administration* determines how to do it. Several important characteristics of administration must be noted. First, it operates within a framework of discretion. Given the statement of what is to be done, administration is faced with a choice of alternatives as to how the objectives may be accomplished. The degree of discretion is limited only by the preciseness of the directive.

Second, administration, like direction, may or may not be concerned with policy formulation. Administrative decisions may establish continuing standards of action by which directives may be met. They may likewise effectuate directives by examining each set of circumstances as a basis for a unique decision. The field of pricing provides a good example of these differing approaches. A directive that the price of each product must permit a profit may be carried out by establishing a price policy providing continuing standards for determining a price, or it may be effectuated by considering all the facts of the case afresh whenever a price is fixed. Both methods are administrative.

Third, in the corporation the directive may only be implied. In the price example given above, the administrative authorities may have been given no explicit directive that the sales prices of their products must afford a profit, but at least in certain situations the directive may be fairly inferred from the nature of corporate activity. In business, direction is fre-

24 Holden, Fish, and Smith, *Top-Management Organization and Control*, pp. 80–81.

quently much less explicit than in government. There is no constitutional limitation upon delegation of authority except in a few stated spheres, such as the choice of the chief executive or the declaration of dividends. In practice, corporate administrations are granted broad discretion, extending even to the authority to accomplish objectives which must be assumed if they are not stated.

Fourth, administration may always be overruled by direction. It does not constitute a source of final authority. If the directive authorities are dissatisfied with the administrative method of accomplishing their objectives, they may secure a change by making the directive more explicit. If administrative authorities take action on the basis of what they believe to be an implied directive, the directing officials may take exception to the inference by ordering abandonment of the practice found objectionable.

If direction determines what is to be done and administration establishes how it is to be done, *execution* is responsible for seeing that it is done. Because the area of decision-making captures the spotlight of public attention, involving as it does the accommodation of conflicting interests and the actual determinations which affect men's lives, it has overshadowed that aspect of managerial responsibility which merely sees that decisions, once made, are carried out. To quarrel with this attitude would be difficult, for unquestionably it is the decision which is of primary importance. At the same time, the significance of the executive function should not be lost sight of, for unless a decision is carried out it may as well not have been made, and unless it is carried out as was intended it is in fact not the same decision.

The essential feature of execution is therefore effective compliance with the statement of objective and the method of attaining it—in the corporation the executive possesses no power of veto. This calls for widely varying degrees of responsibility and capability. Certain executive performances may be entrusted only to the chief executive, others to a foreman. It is important to observe, however, that execution is distinguished from direction and administration by an almost complete absence of discretion. The area of free choice is narrowly restricted, since the objective and the method have previously been determined. It is not for that reason an unimportant responsibility, however. A high order of intelligence may be required to execute a mission by the method prescribed.

Lastly, there is that fourth aspect of business operation, less well defined than those which we have been discussing, which may be called compliance. It is essential that some means be provided for determining whether executive management has actually complied with administrative determinations, and whether administrative management has carried out directives. Some method of checking on performance is required, even though this requirement has frequently been neglected in the practice of many business corporations.[25] Where undertaken, it has generally been considered a matter for investigation and action by those primarily interested; that is to say, those who make the decisions and policies are responsible for reviewing the actions and decisions made in accordance with them. A notable exception to this practice is the employment of an auditing staff responsible for a check upon performance in matters relating to monetary responsibility, and occasionally upon compliance in the fields of price quotations, credit and discount actions, and purchases as well.

The operation of a business, then, calls for the three functions of direction, administration, and execution. Compliance may lay claim to constituting a fourth. These functions are not always easily distinguishable. One reason is that typically in the American corporation they have been performed, to an important degree, by the same persons. With such central coincidence of these functions, it has not been easy, nor has it seemed especially necessary, for the Pooh-Bahs of industry to identify an action as directive, administrative, or executive in nature, or as involving compliance.

The confusion between direction and administration has been pointed up by the discussion of "inside" and "outside" directors. In some instances the entire board of directors consists of men who are at the same time administrative officials within the corporation. "Those who do not agree that the directorate has been eliminated realistically in such cases must admit the anomaly of a management reporting to, supervised by, and responsible to itself."[26] Yet even if the directorate as a body has been "eliminated realistically" in such cases, the directive function has not. A corporation could not function without direction, an ultimate source of authority providing final determination of what is to be done. Similar confusion obtains in those instances where the administrative officials, through corporate machinery, are in a position themselves to choose the directors.[27] Though a nominal distinction between the directive and administrative authorities may have been retained, it does not conform to the fact of where final authority actually resides. If administrative officials make decisions which are not subject to reversal by a higher authority, or which are reached without regard to any nominally superior body, they are in fact exercising the directive function.

Because direction and administration have become so intermingled in

---

[25] The Stanford survey found that none of the 31 large corporations studied had hit upon any inclusive scheme by which policy interpretation or compliance could be checked. *Top-Management Organization and Control*, p. 82.

[26] George E. Bates, "The Board of Directors," *Harvard Business Review*, vol. 19 (1940), p. 79.

[27] Gordon, *Business Leadership in the Large Corporation*, p. 109, provides a brief discussion of this practice.

the American corporation, there have been some who have dropped direction from the picture altogether, and have spoken only of administration as the authority responsible for determining objectives and establishing a framework within which executive management operates.[28] Such a construction may be appreciated for its effort to bring theory into line with the fact of the confused mingling of the two functions, but it is indefensible in logic and undesirable as a statement of corporate organization. Logically, there must always be something to administer; that something is supplied by direction. Desirably, there should be a more precise identification of final authority within the corporation; reduced to simplest terms, the functions of the directors, about which so much has been said, should be clarified. Shall the board of directors be considered simply as another set of administrators, or as an advisory body without powers, or as a figurehead? Who, in the face of such defection, should exercise that directive function which is and must be an integral feature of corporate conduct? Or should the directive authority of the board be rejuvenated? As we shall see in a later chapter, these questions are by no means impertinent to a study of union-management relations.

In the same way that direction and administration have become intertwined, so too have administration and execution. In some instances the two functions may be performed concurrently and by the same people. To revert to our pricing illustration, if administration establishes no formula by which executive authority may compute prices, and the pricing process proceeds on the basis of a unique determination using the relevant facts (as, for example, in the setting of the price of a new-model automobile), the price may be determined by the same officials who decide what weight shall be accorded the various factors entering into the pricing problem—a combination of the administrative and executive functions, simultaneous determination of how the price is to be set and the actual setting of the price in accordance with the determined procedure. Economists have long been accustomed to speaking of prices so arrived at as administered prices, thus emphasising the planned manner of their determination.

We have been speaking of the functions of direction, administration, and execution in the corporation, but as yet we have not identified any of these with management. As a matter of fact, except in a popular sense there is no common agreement as to what the *managerial* function is. Some experts have identified it with the executive function, thus distin-

---

[28] H. S. Person, in "Research and Planning as Functions of Administration and Management," *Public Administration Review*, vol. 1 (1940), pp. 65–67, is one who thus telescopes the functions of direction and administration with an explicit recognition of what he is doing.

guishing management from administration.[29] It is doubtful, however, if such a distinction would be accepted by the managers themselves, by the public, or even by other experts.[30] There is, moreover, little to be gained by it. It seems more useful to accept the more general if less specialist view that management embraces all those functions which we have enumerated. At the same time, it is essential that the nature of the functions be kept distinct and separate. For purposes of reference, we may—when emphasizing one aspect of management—speak of directive management, administrative management, and executive management.

The importance of these distinctions for our study should now be apparent. When business groups raise a protest against "union encroachment on managerial prerogatives," are they concerned with all their functions equally, or with one or two in particular? Are they distinguishing as to the nature of the "encroachment" at all? It is probable that different problems are involved here that may require differing treatment.

A NOTE ON COORDINATION AS A MANAGEMENT FUNCTION

There are undoubtedly some who would add a coordinating, organizing, or integrating function to the functions of direction, administration, and execution on which emphasis was placed in the foregoing analysis. It cannot be questioned that the ability to coordinate all the decision-making and action-taking phases of the business enterprise is a *sine qua non* in the large corporation. One writer has called it the "very heart of the leadership function."[31]

Coordination has not been given the status of a function of management in this study since it does not appear to be a separable function. It is involved in the formation of policies and the making of decisions. It enters into the operations designed to effectuate them. It is *not* pursued independently of directive, administrative, and executive management.

There would seem to be no more reason for establishing coordination as a separate function in business than there would be for naming it as such in government. Coordination *operates* in the legislative (directive), administrative, executive, and judicial (compliance) functions. It has no separate existence. It is, of course, possible to maintain that legislative or administrative action involves more than decision, that it includes

---

[29] This point of view is adopted by Sheldon, *The Philosophy of Management*, p. 32; Person, *Public Administration Review*, vol. i, p. 67; Ordway Tead, *Democratic Administration* (1945), p. 67.

[30] Holden, Fish, and Smith, for example, include in top-*management* the directors as well as general and divisional officials.

[31] Gordon, *Business Leadership in the Large Corporation*, p. 56.

coordination as well. Nevertheless, coordination would form only one element of the lawmaking process, one requirement for successful administration. It would discharge no final responsibility. Policy and decision-making along with effectuation would still remain as the ends to be served.

We may recognize that in the large corporation complexities of organization may so underscore the necessity for coordination that staff agencies are established to formulate policies *on* coordination, and officials are appointed to execute those policies. If this occurs, then "coordination" merely becomes one of the areas of management, similar to "personnel," "budget," or "credit." As in those areas, the corporation's purpose would be served through the functions of direction, administration, and execution, in this case in the field of coordination.

This note is not intended to minimize the importance, indeed the essentiality, of coordination in business. It is added only because, since it is of such significance, some question might be raised as to why it was not accorded the dignity of being listed as a function of management in its own right.

THE STRUCTURE OF MANAGEMENT

Viewing the corporation as a whole, there is only one source of directive authority, though that authority may be shared, as for example between directors and top officials, or may be divided jurisdictionally, as among committees of the board of directors. Administration and execution, however, are scattered throughout the corporation, in its various levels. They are found in the general management level, in the divisional, the departmental, the general foreman, and the foreman levels. The relationships of administration in these various stages may be illustrated by tracing the development of a policy through the first few brackets of management, though this is not intended as an implication that only policy decisions follow this course. (As we have seen, any decision determining how an objective is to be achieved may flow through the administrative network.) As an example, directive management may enunciate the rule that each product shall bear its own cost of production. General administrative management, on the basis of this standard, may further specify that whenever the annual volume of a product falls below an economic manufacturing lot size, the product shall be considered for elimination. Divisional administrative management may then carry the matter another stage by establishing that when orders are accepted in lots of less than one hundred, no promise shall be made as to date of delivery, delivery being dependent on accumulation of other orders in sufficient quantities to permit profitable production of a single lot. In this example divisional management exercised discretion in determining *how* to effectuate the policy handed down from general management. It had, however, no discretion as to *whether* that policy should be effectuated. General management, in turn, established in its discretion a policy designed to assist in carrying out the directive handed to it. It might have adopted a different policy but it could not avoid the compulsion of effectuating the given directive.

This example suggests that although there is only one source of direction in the corporation viewed as a whole, viewed from any one level of management the decisions handed down from the level above, regardless of its position in the managerial hierarchy, must be considered as *in the nature* of a directive. For such decisions establish *what is to be done.* Thus in the case above, the administrative decision of general management when passed to divisional management assumed the form and force of a directive from the former to the latter. So far as divisional management was concerned, the policy handed to it was a final statement the authority of which was not subject to question. There remained for it only the administrative question of how it was to be accomplished and the executive problem of seeing that it was accomplished. Once the administrative question was settled to its satisfaction, it could relieve itself of the problem of execution by passing the matter on to the next lower level, where the process may be repeated, until at some level final action is taken. This is not a process of buck-passing. It is a process of getting things done by narrowing a problem to dimensions where its effectuation can be safely entrusted to those in the next lower level of management. To narrow a problem beyond this stage is what businessmen mean when they say that someone concerns himself too much with administrative details.

Considering the corporation as a whole, then, there is only one *source* of direction, vested in the top level of management. Considering each individual level of management in its organizational context, however, direction lies in the level immediately above it, to which it is responsible. This method of operation has been called by Person the "frame-within-frame" technique.[32] If we consider the various levels of the organization as "frames," *within any given frame* the functions of the officials are administrative and executive relative to the frame above them, but directive relative to the frame below them. It must be clearly remembered, however, that this is true only when adopting the viewpoint of officials within an organizational frame. It cannot be too often repeated that in the corporation as a whole there is logically only one source of final or directive

---

[32] Person, *Public Administration Review*, vol. i, p. 67.

authority, even though that authority is shared among a number of people or divided among them on jurisdictional lines.

Reference to Figure 1, which illustrates in a simplified form the frame-within-frame organization, will perhaps assist in understanding it. We may recall that the traditional managerial pyramid is based on the numbers of men exercising authority at various levels of operations. It thus

THE
"FRAME —WITHIN— FRAME"
ORGANIZATION of LARGE CORPORATIONS

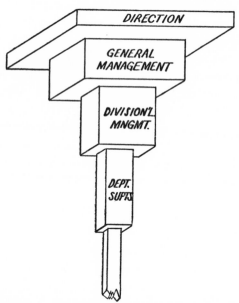

FIGURE 1. The broad surface area indicates the decision-making (directive or administrative) function of management at each level. The depth of each layer of management indicates the executive or decision-effectuating function. In each frame of the corporate structure, the decision-making and decision-effectuating functions operate *within* the boundaries supplied by the frame above.

shows a broad base of lesser supervisors or foremen, supporting a smaller group of general supervisors, who in turn are surmounted by a still smaller group of department heads, and so on until at the apex of the organizational structure is found a small board of directors or even the single authority of the president. This traditional pyramid we have reversed, since we are not here concerned with the numbers of men at each layer of the managerial hierarchy. Our interest lies in the functioning of management.

As a result, Figure 1, which is designed to show the structure of corporate authority, is necessarily an inverted pyramid. As one proceeds up the management ladder, the area of discretion increases, and the broadest area of authority is to be found at the top of the management framework. Moreover, the three-dimensional character of the pyramid must be indicated if the frame-*within*-frame plan is to be visualized and if the multiple role of management is to be emphasized.

The broad surface area of each frame may be considered to represent the decision-making area of management within that frame. For the top frame, where resides the ultimate and final authority within the organization, this is the managerial function which we have called direction, the determination of what is to be done. For all subsequent frames this becomes the administrative function of determining how it is to be done, when the corporation is viewed as a working whole. From the viewpoint of management at any particular level, however, the decision-making function of those managers in the frame above assumes the *nature* of direction, of final authority. This is indicated in the diagram by showing that the decision-making function within any frame must operate within the outlines prescribed by the frame above.

The depth of each frame may be viewed as the executive function. It too operates within the area of decision of the frame above. It is evident from the diagram that the decision-making functions (direction or administration) are at their maximum at the top of the organizational hierarchy, becoming less and less important in successive frames. It is likewise clear that the reverse is true of the executive function. Nevertheless, there are some executive actions required even at the top managerial level, in those cases where the directors execute their own decisions,[33] and there are some administrative decisions required in the lowest frame of the corporate structure, such as the problem which a foreman faces in deciding how to accommodate an urgent order without delaying the scheduled completion of jobs already on hand.

In practice many decisions and policies originate in frames several stages removed from the directive level, and are forwarded up through the organization for approval. Some of these may be administrative or-

[33] Equally important, when the corporation is viewed not in isolation but in its social context, geared into the legislative and institutional framework of the economy, it becomes at once apparent that what may be construed as the exercise of the directive function *within* the corporation, in some instances is in reality the exercise of an administrative or executive function, involving the fulfillment or effectuation of a directive which has originated *outside* the corporation. Thus, for example, the choice of a chief executive is not a matter of discretion with the board of directors, since it is compelled by state incorporation laws, charter, or bylaws to provide such an office; the choice of a chief executive may more appropriately be viewed as an executive action taken in accord with a directive emanating from a higher authority than any within the corporation itself. The registration of securities or the choice of an accounting firm may be similarly viewed.

ders on which higher approval is sought because *how* is considered almost as important as *what*. Others are decisions made without benefit of previous direction, or on the basis of an implied or assumed directive. In these latter cases the decision is forwarded for the approval which will *make* it a directive. This procedure is no different from that which is found in government circles, where the administration prepares a proposed measure for the consideration of the legislature, without whose approval the measure would remain only a wish or a verbal exercise.

An important decision or a broad policy may therefore be formulated at any level in the corporation. It must, however, travel up through the organizational structure, frame by frame, until it reaches the level of those delegated sufficient authority to make it effective.

COMMITTEE ACTION WITHIN THE CORPORATION

In the typical large corporation, directive and administrative decisions are seldom the product of one man. Collective action characterizes these managerial functions. Within any frame direction and administration are customarily the work of a committee consisting of a number of the managers within that frame, to whom are not infrequently added certain managers from the frame immediately below.

Regardless of the degree of activity of the board of directors in the conduct of the business, the fact remains that *if* the board is active it operates as a board or through committees. In the eyes of the law, certain powers of the board may not even be exercised except through the board as a whole. In other matters committees may be selected, ranging in size from three to nine members, empowered either to take final action or to investigate and report to the entire board. Among such committees are to be found executive, finance, auditing, investment, pension, and various special committees. While it is obviously true that powerful individuals may dominate a board, or indeed an entire company, it is equally true that board action in the establishment of basic business policies is generally a collective effort, in practice as well as in theory.

The line of division between direction and general management is not hard and fast, as we have had occasion to note previously. One important reason for the vagueness of the distinction lies in the overlapping of personnel, in some companies carried to the point where there is an identical composition of these two management frames. In these cases where the left hand approves what the right hand has initiated there may be difficulty in establishing in what sense the directive frame controls general management. Bearing this in mind as a possible limitation on the accuracy of the previous diagrammatic presentation, we may, however, go on to examine the manner in which general management, operating *within* the frame which represents directive action, reaches decisions on its own level.

Here the possibilities for the chief executive to "run the show" on the basis of his personal leadership are great, particularly if he is a strong-willed, forceful individual who seeks quick results and immediate action. It is significant, however, that even in those corporations whose organizational structure is such as to make the president the chief source of general management policy, there is a prevailing tendency for the president, despite his concentrated authority, to consult with subordinate officers on all major decisions. Indeed, such collaboration is so close as to "approximate council action."[34]

In almost two-thirds of the companies surveyed by the Stanford group, formal procedures were found for securing committee action on the broad administrative problems of business operation. These companies were observed to fall into one of two major categories. In one, the executive council was composed primarily of members of divisional management, the frame just below general management. In the other category, executive council members were full-time representatives of the general management frame itself.

Those companies which draw their general executive council from among the divisional managers were generally found to have councils composed of from five to seventeen members, with an average of eight. They hold meetings at regularly stated intervals, council duties being only part-time obligations. Their principal interest and responsibility lie in their divisional job, as head of a department, a plant, a region, or perhaps a subsidiary. Their capacity to act as general management, through the executive council, is a power delegated by the chief executive. It will be noted that as general management they are participating in the formation of policies and the making of decisions to which as divisional management they must subsequently conform. This may contribute to a fuzziness of the boundaries between the respective frames, as was true between the directive and general management frame, though this is not an inevitable result. For here there is no suggestion of the council's controlling the president and his immediate executive assistants. The latter benefit from the council's advice, they may even accept its decisions in preference to their own tentative opinions, but decisions resulting from action of the executive council are promulgated with the force of authority attached to the general management frame; the divisional managers have

[34] Holden, Fish, and Smith, *Top-Management Organization and Control*, pp. 21–22. Pages 22–27 present an elaboration of the functioning of general management on the lines set forth here.

no authority residing in their own positions which enable them to modify or discard general administrative orders to which they may object, even though they may have originally participated in their formulation.

Those companies employing permanent full-time executive councils normally place on such a body from three to nine top-ranking executives, including the president and a number of vice presidents selected for their wide range of training and experience. Sometimes this group meets at no stated intervals, though it does meet frequently, in some cases daily, as the situation demands. Its members are ordinarily saddled with no other responsibilities than this over-all supervision of the company's affairs. However, they often are specialists in some phase of the business, and in council sessions are looked to by the others for expert opinion in such matters. Because of this specialization, divisional managers may contact a member of the council for advice on problems within his field of special competence. Divisional members are responsible to the council as a body, however, and not to any one member. "In almost no case would a divisional executive expect to receive a 'yes' or 'no' decision from an individual council member; such decisions emanate only from the council as a whole. In this connection, it is noteworthy that even the president usually takes action through the council rather than as an individual."[35]

The committees which we have just been considering are known as general management committees. They are responsible for the over-all guidance of the corporation. In addition, there are functional committees which operate within a narrower sphere, concerned with decisions on a particular aspect of the company's business—personnel, price policy, manufacturing, distribution, and the like. These committees may have on them some of the same personnel as is found on the executive council but include as well members of divisional management with special interest in these fields. It is in these committees, operating in the general management frame, that broad policies are developed within specific categories of operating problems.

It is in the formulation of such specialized policies that staff agencies, too, play their part. These agencies are established to assist management, operating in a service capacity. They may advise, they may survey the results of policy to determine its effectiveness, they may assist in the execution of administrative decisions, they may coordinate the activities of those responsible for execution. They themselves seldom have the authority to make decisions binding upon any frame of management; their authority is confined to the operation of their own agency. Nevertheless, they may and do play a vital role in assisting management in its directive or administrative function.

[35] Holden, Fish, and Smith, *Top-Management Organization and Control*, p. 25.

Below the general managerial frame this same pattern of committee organization is apparent. Within the divisions of the company, executive committees will be found, forming policies and making decisions applicable to the division as a whole. Functional committees will concern themselves with the development of divisional policies respecting the relevant areas of management. Staff agencies will provide assistance. In the lower managerial frames, the collaborative or collective aspects of management become less and less formalized, depending for their operation upon informal consultations and cliques. Indeed, in the frame of foremanagement "boss" action may all but obliterate the committee method. Even here, however, there is a distinct tendency for the foreman to act only after sounding out the assistant foreman and other key men within his group. With the advent of the shop steward, directly representing the men, the need for such collaborative action has, if anything, increased.

Decision-making in the large corporation, then, is commonly a group function. Consultation and collaboration may occur through formal mechanisms, such as established councils, or through informal discussion and agreement. This occurs in all frames of management. One recent study concludes that "the prevalence of group, instead of individual, action is a striking characteristic" of the large corporation, and finds further that the degree of such group activity is correlated positively with the size of the business.[36] The importance of decisions in the large corporation is such that there is a strong incentive to spread the responsibility for them. This is not to deny the existence of personal responsibility nor the dominating influence of the forceful individual possessing extensive authority. The question whether some individuals possess the authority to make decisions and formulate policy on their own initiative is not involved; rather we are concerned with the practice.

This prevalence of group activity in the large corporation necessitates the development of centers of coordination. These centers of coordination are of two types: those occurring at the point of contact between two organizational frames, where the lower frame may be seeking approval or the frame above may be seeking advice; and those occurring within a frame to determine common action or policy, frequently as a preliminary to interframe coordination. The importance of group decision-making and the diffusion of responsibility have made the smooth functioning of such centers of coordination an imperative for the large corporation. Their formalization as standing committees or continuous councils stems in part from the necessity of isolating and identifying at least the primary centers so that authority and responsibility for their performance may be delegated. Such delegation is frequently but not always to a single in-

[36] Gordon, *Business Leadership in the Large Corporation*, pp. 99, 105.

dividual, such as the president, an operating vice president, or a division manager, but a clear distinction must be made in these cases between the *personal* responsibility for effective coordination and the *group* nature of decisions resulting from it.

IMPACT OF THE UNION

We have to this point been concerned with what might be termed the "pure" theory and practice of management in the large corporation. Considerations attending the entrance of a union into corporate operations have been intentionally excluded. Questions which the advent of the union raises have been left unanswered. It now becomes necessary to examine the impact which the union makes upon the theory and practice of direction, administration, execution, compliance, the frame-within-frame structure, and committee action.

First, we may note that if unions share in the policy- or decision-making process at the highest managerial level, they are sharing in the directive function. This result is commonly achieved in the collective-bargaining process, where union and top company officials jointly agree upon policies which are to govern the business in certain areas of operation. However, if the bargaining conference occurs and the agreement is reached in a business frame below the directive frame, the choice of the policies in question is determined in some measure by higher policy or at least is subject to review by higher authority. Here the union is sharing the administrative, not the directive, function. Assume, for example, that directive policy provides that all layoffs and rehiring shall be based on seniority. Exercising its discretion as to how this directive shall be carried out, general administrative management may declare that the seniority principle to be followed shall be determined by agreement between company and union officials in the respective plants of the company. *Relative to the plant managements,* this administrative decision constitutes a directive. If by joint agreement with the union at a particular plant it is determined that plant-wide seniority shall govern, this again is an administrative order, which responsible officials must execute whenever workers are laid off or rehired.

If the unions seek to participate in the decision-making function in the corporation, they must recognize that *except for the top frame* this is a function of an administrative management which is powerless to act outside of the standard established by the higher policy which controls its actions and decisions. In the above example, if union members at a given plant of the company should object because they were laid off when members with less seniority were retained at another plant, they must recognize that their quarrel is not with *plant administrative policy* (since that policy is controlled by general administrative policy with respect to the condition that seniority should operate only within the confines of a plant). Nor is their quarrel with *directive policy*, since that policy simply establishes the seniority principle but leaves its working out to management down the line. The union might, however, seek a reformulation of *general administrative policy*, since management at that level is left free to determine the type of seniority to be adopted. It is controlled in the exercise of its discretion only by the directive that seniority *shall* govern layoffs and rehiring. It is therefore possible for the general administrative management to determine that company-wide rather than plant seniority shall prevail, and it is within the general management frame that union pressure should be brought if a change is desired.

This analysis suggests several corollary arguments:

1. If company officials wish to localize disturbances and friction within the industrial organization, it would seem desirable for them to make more explicit the company organization plan and the frames within which have originated those business policies and decisions of interest to the union. A union dissatisfied with a particular policy or decision might then be directed to those officials responsible for it and authorized to amend it so long as they conform to the standard laid down by any higher controlling authority.

2. A company official to whom is delegated administrative authority should be encouraged to accept his full responsibility. He should be discouraged from any attempts to "pass the buck" back to higher officials whose decisions have permitted the latitude of discretion within which he may act. If friction is to be localized by directing the union to its source, equivocation by company officials who refuse to accept responsibility must be minimized. This again calls for careful statements of areas of discretion allowed to officials within each successive business frame, so that responsibility may be isolated and identified.

3. When union members or officials become dissatisfied with a decision or with the operation of any given policy, they should first ascertain that the company officials with whom they customarily negotiate have the authority to modify it. If the local union is bargaining with plant officials, and the decision or policy complained of is one which is controlled by general management, it would be clearly useless—or at best wasteful of energies—for the local union to bring pressure on the plant management to amend a decision which it never made and concerning a matter over which it has no control. It therefore seems incumbent on top union officers to train their members and subordinate officials to clear disputes over business decisions and policies with those union officials who *are* in a bar-

gaining relationship with the company executives responsible for the decisions complained of.

This is simply a recognition that in the large corporations unions too have their frames-within-frames, represented by national officials, divisional or departmental officials, regional directors, and local officials, with their various subordinate breakdowns. Officials in each of these frames are in bargaining contact with management in a corresponding company frame. For union pressure to be brought to secure a change in company policy, efficiency and economy of effort and concern for minimizing the degree of disruption to the industrial organization would seem to impose this requirement: Responsibility within the union for securing a desired change should be shifted up or down the union organizational hierarchy to that union frame whose officials are in a bargaining relationship with those in the company frame responsible for the policy.

4. In the same way that corporations should make more explicit the source of various decisions and policies and the authority of various officials, unions should accomplish a similar clarification of responsibility for policy and a like delineation of degree of authority for the benefit of company officials who may seek to discuss changes.

5. In the above discussion we have been speaking of company policies and union policies. That each of these organizations has its respective policies should need no elaboration nor argument. But that in the operation of the business there can be only one policy or decision on a given subject in a given area is equally evident. One method of determining business policies and making business decisions to which both company and union officials must conform is supplied by the collective-bargaining process. As we have seen, collective bargaining resulting in agreement is a method of directive and administrative management. Decisions of the bargaining table must therefore, as an organizational principle, be accorded as full compliance by each of the parties as though enunciated by their own leaders singly. The joint conference and agreement become a unitary and responsible source of authority within an enterprise. It is equally deserving of recognition, however, that the bargaining process is the union's only organizational method of participating in the directive and administrative functions. As a result, those areas of business operation which are untouched by the existing agreement must be accepted as lying outside the union's purview, and in those areas it cannot organizationally participate in direction and administration as long as the agreement remains unchanged. It may, of course, seek to extend its directive and administrative competence in such untouched areas in future negotiations.

What considerations are raised when we move from the fields of directive and administrative management to that of executive management? Where does the union fit into the managerial function of seeing that decisions are translated into completed actions?

Direction and administration theoretically can and in practice often are shared functions, since they involve the exercise of discretion. Consultation and compromise are possible in the directive determination of what is to be done and the administrative decision of how to do it. This occurs in practice both within the management family itself and in its collective-bargaining relationship with the union. In the executive function of accomplishing what has thus been decided, however, there is small opportunity for the play of discretion. Discussion and compromise are inappropriate at this stage, as the only basis for disagreement lies in whether the executive action in fact complies with the directive and administrative decisions. Any other disagreement constitutes a dispute not with executive management but with direction or administration.

This distinction is sometimes difficult to perceive when the functions of administration and execution are performed by the same individual. Let us assume a typical shop situation. The general foreman calls in the shop foreman and says to him, "Joe, we have a rush order here for 500 valves of such and such specification to be ready for shipment by Thursday night. I want you to get 'em done without delaying any of your other jobs. I don't care how—just get 'em done."

The general foreman has handed Joe a difficult problem. Joe's shop is already loaded with jobs. How accommodate the urgent order? This is an administrative problem with which Joe is now wrestling—the question of *how*. In solving it he may consult with his assistant or call together his leaders. At this stage discussion, compromise, and agreement are possible. Once the decision has been reached, however, the administrative function has ended. Now remains the executive task of doing, of translating the decision into accomplishment. Discussion and compromise at this stage are not possible—their place, if at all, was in the phase of administrative planning.

"I don't think we even ought to try to get things done by Thursday night," complains one worker. "It's pushing us too hard." His complaint is with the general foreman's administrative decision (which from where Joe the foreman sits constitutes a directive). Joe can do nothing about this complaint.

"I don't think we ought to do it this way," another worker criticizes. "If we did it my way we'd get it done easier." His complaint is with Joe's administrative decision, which it is within Joe's discretion to modify. The criticism, however, comes late if the job is already in process.

"You're not handling this the way you told us you were going to," remarks one of the leaders. "You're letting one job get in the way of another." His complaint is with Joe's executive management. He is not criticizing Joe's discretionary decision but his failure to adhere to it. Joe can correct his executive shortcoming without modifying his administrative determination. Any other criticism would, however, be directed against Joe—or the general foreman—as an administrator.

The functional requirements of business organization thus demonstrate that executive management—divorced from any administrative aspects—cannot be a shared function. With discretion at a minimum, with compliance all that is needed, joint execution would be out of place. *Either* the union steward *or* the foreman, for example, may have full authority in executing decisions, or they may divide the area within which each exercises authority, so long as each conforms to administrative orders. In the event of such division of the job, both will be executive managers within their respective areas, and for this purpose the steward will cease to be a union official, becoming instead a part of management, officially delegated responsibility for this function. While we have been speaking here of executive management in the shop, these statements are equally applicable in all frames of the business.

Unions sometimes now are recognized by company officials for the performance of executive functions. When the union or closed shop is accepted as business policy for the enterprise, the union officials are delegated certain managerial responsibilities for the execution of that policy: they apply the standard and make final determinations as to whether a worker shall be permitted to continue working; they certify to the appropriate officials in the company hierarchy *of which for this purpose they are a part* the names of those men who are to be discharged for nonmembership. In cases of the closed shop they participate in determining which men shall be hired, in line with the policy laid down in the agreement. In some instances, as in the printing trades, certain union bylaws are accepted as part of the collective-bargaining agreement, thereby becoming business policies of the enterprise. In the execution of such policies union officials exercise a managerial function. During World War II, when problems of discipline and absenteeism became pressing, in a few companies union officials were all but added to the company payroll and were actually given company desks as "personnel officers." Their formal and informal contacts with the employes were utilized for the more effective execution of administrative decisions in the field of manpower mobilization and scheduling, which, while jointly reached, ran counter to union policy—well inculcated in its membership—of the preceding years of peace and depression.

In recent years company representatives have been expressing increased concern that unionization of foremen poses a potential threat to effective executive action. The question is raised as to whether administrative decisions to which employes object will be given full compliance if this class of executive management owes responsibility to the same union which represents the production workers it superintends, or even to an independent union which, however, maintains sympathetic relations with the rank-and-file organization. Additional concern is voiced that in some instances the executive position in the shop is undermined by a diversion of authority to an official or unofficial union leader within the group, often the shop steward. In these instances an order emanating from the foreman, valid under the directive or administrative terms of the collective agreement, may be challenged by a union official—modified and occasionally even countermanded. If the loyalty of the workers runs primarily to their own leaders rather than to the foreman, as executive authority, they will follow the dictates of the former. Thus the industrial relations director of one large rubber corporation says, "We recognize that in some of our shops the union committeeman exercises greater authority than the foreman." And an automobile executive, speaking of this problem, goes so far as to maintain that "If any manager in this industry tells you he has control of his plant he is a damn liar." In frank moments some union officials will admit the existence, though not the prevalence, of this situation.

Without passing on the desirability of the unionization of foremen or possible moral justification for a challenge of a supervisor's orders in a given situation, we must nevertheless recognize the *organizational* necessity of full executive compliance with directive and administrative decisions. If there is dissatisfaction with those decisions, they themselves should constitute the target of attack by the dissatisfied. Any attempt to subvert them by the subtler process of inducing executive noncompliance would raise dangers to the whole business structure.

So much for the union's role in direction, administration, and execution, and the necessities of fitting its exercise of those functions into the frame-within-frame structure of the organization. There remains the matter of compliance. We have previously noted that in practice those who formulate policy and make decisions are responsible for reviewing the actions taken in accordance with them. The union is therefore interested in securing compliance with those decisions and policies which it helped to formulate through joint conference and joint agreement. For this purpose the grievance procedure is employed, and *for this purpose* it is intended not to permit the union to exercise a control over administrative decisions or to share executive authority but to check on managerial compliance with policies and decisions which have already been jointly reached.

In the first step of the grievance procedure, the union attempts to demonstrate to management that policies have not been complied with, and that certain decisions or actions should therefore be modified, revoked, or remedied to conform with policy. If there is no settlement at this stage, the case progresses up through successive joint conferences until it finally reaches those officials who themselves were the authors of the policy or decision in question. Even here there is sometimes a difference of opinion, depending upon the sincerity with which the case is approached and the degree to which there was a meeting of the minds when the policy was established. If no concurrence is obtained at this level, in an increasing number of corporations the case is referred to an "impartial umpire."

To a large extent the question of compliance with policies and decisions is a judicial question. The impartial umpire is intended to supply this judicial function, and by a weighing of facts and by his unbiased judgment conclude whether there has been managerial compliance with directive and administrative orders. This judicial function is of course confined to questions of compliance with matters jointly determined, but to the extent that unions succeed in widening their scope of influence in corporate affairs the impartial umpire will become an increasingly important agency within the corporation. It must be stressed, however, that the grievance procedure culminating in the impartial umpire is, *as a compliance system,* no mechanism designed to permit the union to participate in direction, administration, or execution. It is a means of testing managerial conformance to decisions and policies which have been determined jointly by union and company officials, who together comprise the directive or administrative management within the area of the agreement.

Since in most companies the grievance procedure is seldom used solely as a check on compliance but is often made to serve additionally as a medium for bargaining (that is to say, for changing the terms of directive or administrative orders), a confusion of purposes and functions may result. It may be conceded that no great harm is done if the grievance machinery is used for bargaining purposes providing two conditions are present: that the participants have sufficient delegated authority to modify the administrative decision complained of; and that there is agreement as to the desirability of the change, so that the rule as amended may be accepted as an administrative guide for future executive action. The danger arises, however, that where compliance machinery is used for negotiation, the *administrative* decision (compliance with which is in question) will be modified from case to case, to suit the convenience of one of the disputants, thus eliminating all prospect of establishing a standard by which future compliance may be judged.

Lastly, we may recall that decision-making in the large corporation is a group process. Now collective bargaining likewise is a group process. The question therefore asserts itself as to why there is managerial opposition to group decision-making through collective bargaining when group action is the norm in corporate practice.

The answers, which are several, will be explored more fully later. A few of the considerations more pertinent to the functional analysis may be touched on now. First and foremost, the group process in the corporation revolves around centers of coordination which are established to guarantee that decisions are reached. Within each such collaborative group or at each such center of coordination resides full authority to discharge that function. The authority may be and frequently is vested in a single individual, to whom the group constitutes an advisory council. In those cases where authority and responsibility are delegated to an entire group, such as the board of directors, a simple majority vote will ordinarily suffice to determine policy. This placement of authority insures that a decision is reached when a problem is faced. Failure to reach a decision would mean an abdication of responsibility which could be met only by a reassignment of authority. For the business to operate there must be answers to problems faced; an organizational procedure assuring such decisions—involving delegation of adequate authority and responsibility —cannot therefore be avoided. Except for corporations in a pathological condition there is always an organizational process available by which decisions may be readily forthcoming, and there is always a source of sufficient authority which may be drawn upon to resolve differences of opinion within a group. This is not true of the bargaining relationship. Here differences of opinion over matters of interest within the group, between the corporate managers and the union managers, are not subject to speedy resolution by an authority which both recognize. There is available no organizational procedure for insuring that the necessary decisions are reached. The terms "deadlock" and "impasse" have no place in describing corporate centers of coordination. They recur frequently in describing the bargaining relationship. Management is therefore reluctant to substitute the group process of collective bargaining for its own group processes because it involves the possibility that business operations will be brought to a dead stop by deadlock within the group.

Second, the harmony which characterizes group corporate processes is not carried over to group bargaining processes; that is, the admission of union representatives to managerial collaboration destroys the solidarity of the group. Between the union managers and the corporate managers there do not exist the same general objectives, the same loyalties, the same legal responsibilities, the same codes, the same philosophy. Instead, the group becomes bifurcated, with two competing sets of objectives, loyalties, responsibilities, codes, and philosophies. Cohesion and integration are destroyed. In addition to lack of common authority, there is lack of a common basis for agreement. Each of the two groups lives within its distinct structure of living.

Third, because of the lack of common authority and of a common basis for agreement, the established pattern of frame-within-frame organization essential to the operation of a large corporation is weakened if not broken down. Corporate management operates within a framework of delegated discretion which it cannot transcend; in every frame the boundaries of its discretion are outlined by the frame above. This is also true of the union. However, neither corporate management nor the union is always willing to recognize such a delimitation of discretion on the part of the other. If within the divisional frame, for example, the union presses for a decision to which corporate management, within its discretionary framework, is powerless to agree, resolution of the deadlock is necessarily thrown into a higher frame where both parties to the group possess sufficient authority for compromise. The union, however, may consider such referral only as stalling, and press for immediate action. At the least, such action may hinder the effective functioning of both the frame in which the question is raised and that to which it must be referred, in the case of the former by preventing the exercise of such discretion as has been delegated, in the case of the latter by contesting authority after it has been exercised within its appropriate discretionary framework. Substitution of group bargaining processes for group corporate processes therefore may constitute a threat to the very organizational structure of the business.

These considerations constitute a serious challenge to the unions. If the unions are to be integrated within the business, answers to these objections must be found. On the other hand, an equally serious challenge is offered corporate management. For if the unions remain as an important part of our institutionalized society, existing corporate practices, developed when no union was involved, must necessarily be changed to accommodate the presence of unions in the business process. Assuming that unions are here to stay, management too must therefore prepare itself for change.

We may now summarize briefly some of the more important of our findings:

The union becomes part of directive management when it signs a collective-bargaining agreement determining what is to be done within certain areas of corporate activity. It becomes part of administrative management when it concludes subsidiary agreements determining how these decisions are to be accomplished. It becomes executive management when it is delegated (and accepts) the responsibility and authority for translating such decisions into action.

The union has one other function which may, perhaps, be considered managerial—that of seeking operating compliance with the policies of the agreement. Company officials likewise are interested in adherence to the agreement. Grievance procedures have therefore been established, frequently culminating in the judicial office of impartial chairman, to test compliance.

This analysis has nothing to say as to what the area of agreement should be. It seeks only to clarify the managerial functions which the union exercises within the corporation and the method of their exercise.

We may now also return to the question which was previously raised: What is it that characterizes management, what is it that makes management management? It is the organizational authority to determine policies and make decisions and to execute them, within the legal framework of the society of its origin. This function is indeed one which exists regardless of the nature of that legal framework, independently of the ownership and control setting. The latter will determine the objectives and the method of the exercise of managerial authority, but the basic function of management persists in any society, by whomever exercised. The intervention of unions in the American industrial scene thus affects the procedures to be adopted in the management of the business enterprise. It affects the objectives of management. The *function* of management, however, remains unchanged.

THE AREAS OF MANAGEMENT

As a further aid in understanding the operations of management in the large corporation, and of analyzing the problems introduced by the participation of unions in the functions of management, we may delineate the important areas of business enterprise within a single company. In addition to defining management by its legal status and functional role, we are in effect thus defining management by the nature of the operational problems which it faces.

For our purposes we may distinguish principally two types of approach. The first defines the areas of management without regard to relation or category. This method has the advantage of permitting precise and complete coverage. Some areas are difficult to fit into specific categories or classes, but with simple itemization there is no necessity of forcing them into an operational group with which they have only slight affinity, or of assuming them covered by an operation to which they have a surface family resemblance. Thus no managerial field is slighted of considera· tion; as many fields may be listed as have any claim to separate distinction.

The second approach is to consider the areas of management by categories, groups, or classes of related activities. This method has the advantage of indicating more clearly where a particular area of management fits into the operation of the business. It gives pattern and design. It places emphasis by highlighting the major phases of business operation, but at the same time permits detail by clustering around them the subordinate activities necessary to their realization. If precision is sacrificed, comprehension is gained.

It is this second approach which we shall adopt in this study. There is another reason than that given above for this choice. We shall shortly be concerned with the degree of penetration by labor unions of the areas of managerial responsibility, and with the problems that follow from such penetration. It seems probable that once a union has successfully asserted its voice within one of the broad categories of management authority, it is a somewhat simpler matter for it to spread its penetration within that category, among the several managerial areas comprising it. For example, if the union succeeds in participating in the formulation of policy relating to production techniques, it would probably be easier for it to extend its influence to the types of machinery and equipment which shall be used (a matter of expanding its penetration within the same category) than it would be to secure a voice in the determination of the financial procedures to be adopted to raise new capital (requiring initial penetration within a totally different category). This is the principle of the "entering wedge." If applicable to the subject of our investigation, it indicates that the fact of the union's penetrating one of an itemized list of areas of management is more significant than appears on its face; for it provides a beachhead from which further penetration may be carried to *related* activities.

In this study we shall make use of six categories: finance, personnel, procurement, production, distribution, and coordinate or cabinet activities. Under these broad categories the principal areas of management may be grouped as follows:

I. *Finance—control over money*
    1. Raising of necessary capital; the capital structure
    2. Dividends
    3. Reserves
    4. Amortization and depreciation
    5. Accounting procedures

6. Insurance
7. Budgeting

II. *Personnel—control over men*
  1. Type of personnel
  2. Size of force
  3. Hiring, dismissal, allocation, and discipline of work force
  4. Wages and hours
  5. Employe advancement policies (vacations, pensions, etc.)
  6. Promotions
  7. Health, safety, and social conditions

III. *Procurement—control over materials*
  1. Purchase of raw materials
  2. Organization of suppliers and subcontractors

IV. *Production*
  1. Design and engineering
  2. Types of machinery and equipment
  3. Job content
  4. Methods of operation
  5. Rates of operation
  6. Standards of quality
  7. Maintenance

V. *Distribution*
  1. Quantities of production
  2. Sales policies
  3. Distributing organization
  4. Marketing
  5. Advertising
  6. Inventories
  7. Credit policies

VI. *Coordinate or cabinet activities*
  1. Line of products
  2. Company organization
  3. Selection of key personnel
  4. Research and development
  5. Extension or contraction of capacity
  6. Location of plants
  7. Prices of products
  8. Collective bargaining
  9. Trade and industry relations
  10. Public relations

This last category of coordinate or cabinet activities consists of those areas so intimately affecting many or all of the other five groupings that they can be successfully managed only by general integrated action. They are activities which could not adequately be administered by any one of the other five functional organizations even on standards set forth in basic policies.

No special claims are made for the above classifications. It is more than likely that some would place one of the specific areas under another category, or perhaps prefer a different set of groupings altogether. However, the given breakdown has sufficient logical consistency and ease of manipulation to make it useful in our later investigation. It is adopted not with any thought of its superiority to other presentations, but because it is better suited to our purposes.

The People of Management

MANAGEMENT AS A PARTICULAR GROUP OF PEOPLE

At the National Labor-Management Conference held in Washington in the fall of 1945, management representatives voiced troubled concern over union efforts to "encroach" on the functions of management. They drew up a list of "management prerogatives" which they maintained should not be invaded by the unions. They were, however, unsuccessful in obtaining agreement by the labor representatives to this or any other compilation of "exclusive rights of management."

This move on the part of management has a significance deeper than appears on the face of it. It carried the definite implication that management was a function which could be exercised only by a constituted group or class of people. Others not so constituted were to be barred from sharing it. They sought to secure union compliance with the jurisdictional areas which they had delimited for their sole exercise of the management function. *This effort on the part of the managers to obtain recognition from the unions is as significant a social struggle as the earlier effort of unions to obtain recognition from the managers.*

We have already observed that management may be defined and understood on the basis of its legal relationships, of its organizational function, and of the types of problems which it is called upon to face. The question may now be raised whether there follows from these three definitions of management a fourth—an identification of management as a particular group or class of people. In essence, what we are now seeking to discover is whether there is such consistency between the variant definitions that we may say that management by one description is the same as management by another.

Earlier in our investigation we examined the legal basis for managerial authority. We discovered that management in the corporation must, under the law, be considered as the representative of the owners of the corporation, to whom it owes the duty of a trustee or agent. This trustee and agency relationship carries with it the legal rights, privileges, powers, and immunities of property ownership, to be exercised on behalf of the stockholders as owners. In this sense, the managers of a corporation are a group of persons whose basis for authority is a defined legal relationship to the owners. No person or group of persons not possessing this legal foundation for authority has any claim to managerial status. This obviously excludes the unions.

From this viewpoint management representatives, in seeking to define the areas of their sole competence, are simply attempting to get the unions to agree to the legal requirements of the situation. If the authority of management derives only from a legal relationship with the owners and if its validity is dependent upon the performance of a legal duty to exercise that authority solely on behalf of the owners, how *can* management consent to any watering down of its competence? To do so would be to violate its trust. To violate its trust would be to destroy the basis of its authority.

Management thus conceives that its loyalty must run to the stockholders, as the corporation. Any recognized loyalties to its employes, customers, or the public stem from the conviction that justice and fair play to these groups will inure to the benefit of the owners. They must, therefore, be modified loyalties, valid only insofar as they do not establish loyalties equal or paramount to its fealty to the owners. A broader and wiser recognition of how consideration for participating groups other than the stockholders will result to the advantage of the stockholders, at least in the long run, has been the chief characteristic of what has been called "enlightened management." But no degree of enlightenment will permit managers conscious of their legal obligations to sacrifice to the interests of other groups their loyalty to the corporate owners.

This legal consideration provides the ground for defining management as a class of people designated under the law to conduct the affairs of the corporation. It is not a social class but a legal class.

As a matter of practice, this position is becoming more and more untenable. Broad areas of management are now subject to joint policy determination by the appointed managers and union officials. It is necessary to examine only casually a collective-bargaining agreement to perceive the important limitations which have been placed upon management's freedom to conduct the business on behalf of the owners. In these areas the union shares the management function. Collective bargaining, as we have seen, is a method of directive and administrative management. Yet the union officials thus participating in the management of the corporation recognize no legal obligation to the owners. They owe no primary loyalty to the stockholders. On the contrary, their union office imposes upon them a first loyalty to a different group of people, the employes of the corporation. If the unions are thus exercising a managerial role, can we define management as a class of people whose claim to authority rests upon its legal relationship with the owners?

Strict realism requires the admission that there is a group of people whose claim to managerial authority in the corporation rests upon a legal representation of the owners but that this group does not constitute the whole of the business management class. The definition is not an all-inclusive one. Moreover, as we shall see later, the claim of what we may call "legal management" to an authority which has its foundation in the law is accompanied by no adequate legal means of defending that authority from dilution. The definition of management merely as a class whose position is established by law appears only partially accurate for our day and age.

If the law provides no acceptable basis for defining management as a class from which the unions are excluded, this does not mean that the legal managers will necessarily abandon their efforts to secure union recognition of their sole competency, at least in certain areas of business operation. On the basis of a kind of functional approach they likewise assert the necessity of limiting "management" to the constituted group of people which they comprise. "Protection of management rights is not a matter of defending technical legal rights alone: it is simply and fundamentally a matter of *protecting the freedom and authority that management must have if it is to discharge its responsibility of managing the business.*"[1]

This is a view the meaning of which is difficult to grasp. If, as is the case, it is intended to justify a bar to further union participation in management functions, then proponents of this view owe its further explanation. First, they must explain the grounds—*other than legal*—on which "freedom and authority" should be restricted to a *particular* group of people, the presently constituted managers. Second, either they must admit that the whole institution of collective bargaining is undesirable since it limits the "freedom and authority" of the constituted managers, or, alternatively, they must explain why collective bargaining may safely be permitted in some areas of business operation but in no others.

As we have seen, collective bargaining is in fact a *method* of management. It might be contended, it is true, that it is an inferior type of management. Compromises will necessarily be called for. Judgment will be affected by displays of bargaining power. Discretion may be vested in those who are not familiar with the facts on which decisions should be based, or who are incapable of using information to arrive at inescapable conclusions, or whose very ability has been tested only by their popu-

---

[1] Lee H. Hill and Charles R. Hook, Jr., *Management at the Bargaining Table* (1945), p. 58. Italics are in the original.

larity with a mass following. To dignify with the name of management the making of business decisions under such circumstances may be considered an abuse of language.

It seems probable that some consideration such as this must prompt the view that managers must be those constituted with undivided freedom and authority to conduct operations. At root it is an efficiency or engineering concept of management, which excludes more than one set of hands in the guidance of the business machine. Introduce the union and you have, at best, a back-seat driver; at worst, sand in the gears or even a complete breakdown.

This may be one concept of management, but it is by no means the only possible one. Efficiency in the engineering sense is a necessary element of business, but it is not the only element, and many people, including a number of managers, have raised the question as to whether it should even be considered the dominant one. Numerous restrictions on management's freedom and authority to run the business have been imposed—some by society, some by business competition, some by business association, some by the unions. There is no reason to believe that further restrictions will not be imposed in the future. Is the managerial function thereby frustrated? Do managers therefore cease to exist?

Freedom and authority to operate the business there must be, of course, but such freedom and authority may operate within a framework of limitations and may in some aspects also be shared. Freedom and authority are not necessarily attributes which must be "protected" by one group from enjoyment by another. "To accept the idea that the president of any industrial concern because of his position is competent alone to decide every question affecting the enterprise as a whole, or the employer-employee relationship in particular, is going counter to all human experience. Such an attitude is opposed to the now generally recognized theory of management by functions as contrasted with management through title, position, ownership, or salary."[2]

The conclusion seems inescapable that management cannot now be defined as a particular class or group on the basis either of legal status or efficiency concepts. Management in fact is composed of all those who participate directly in the formulation of decisions as to what is to be done and how to do it, and who are responsible for the execution of those decisions. The personnel who compose management can best be defined on the basis of their function.

It is true that even in the not-so-distant past the divergence was imperceptible between those who exercised the function of management and those who held the legal authority for that exercise. Within recent years

[2] Morris L. Cooke and Philip Murray, *Organized Labor and Production* (1940), p. 85.

that identification has been losing its validity, however. Those who have been delegated managerial authority under corporate laws no longer represent the whole of the management group. Increasingly, as the legal managers will themselves testify, corporate authority has been passing to the hands of union officials, who in collective-bargaining conferences discuss many of the same problem areas with legal management; together they seek agreement on business actions to be taken.

We discovered earlier that management was a function which exists independently of a particular ownership and control setting, though the latter may determine its objectives and methods. We have reverted to that principle in answering our question of whether management consists of a particular group of people. The rights of ownership still play the predominant part in our corporations today, at least nominally. The authority of those whom we are accustomed to designate as managers flows from a responsibility to ownership. But at their side now sit men wielding a remarkably similar though not an equal authority, derived from other sources than the owners and with responsibility to others than the owners. These leaders of the unions are exercising, too, a managerial function, though independently of the ownership setting.

From this conclusion follow certain important corollaries:

1. Management cannot be considered as a class distinct from union officials. Union representatives become *part of* directive or administrative management through the collective-bargaining process and the resulting agreement. They become *part of* executive management whenever they are charged with the responsibility and delegated the authority to carry out any policy set forth in the collective agreement.

2. Management can be considered only as a *functional* class, in the same way in which one might speak of newspaper reporters, college professors, or doctors as functional classes. People become management by the role they play in the business corporation, by what they do, just as people become reporters, professors, and doctors by performing the functions of those professions. Some people become full-time managers just as some people become full-time reporters; others are part-time managers—or professors or doctors. Union officials are usually part-time managers, just as are corporate directors.

3. The authority of management in the legal sense is vested only in certain members of the managerial profession. These are subject, in addition to their managerial duties, to the duty of trustee for the stockholders.

4. Union officials who exercise managerial functions are not similarly bound by trusteeship obligations to stockholders. They have a political but not a legal responsibility to the employes who have elected them.

5. Within those business areas where union managers and corporate

managers exercise concurrent or joint responsibility, the divergent allegiances and loyalties provide grounds for conflict. This conflict among the "managers" may increase as unions penetrate additional areas of business operation.

6. Conflict among the "managers" can be confined to matters of direction and administration. Once the agreement sets forth the decisions and policies jointly established, the basis for conflict is at an end for the life of the agreement. This is true, however, only if an adequate compliance procedure has been established as a check upon executive and administrative management and is respected by both corporate managers and the union.

7. Part of the existing conflict among the "managers" arises from the fact that corporate managers have not yet become accustomed to accepting union officials as comanagers in those areas of business operation in which the union has been accorded a voice. Part of the conflict also arises from the fact that union officials have not become accustomed to thinking of themselves as co-managers in those areas. The function of manager requires certain privileges and certain obligations. Corporate managers have been reluctant to grant those privileges to the union managers, though they cannot prevent the union officials from managing. Union managers have been slow to accept the obligations of their corporate positions.

8. When we speak of management in the sense of a group on the other side of the bargaining table from the union, we must be aware that this is only a loose usage of the term, an historical persistence. But too long a persistence in considering management as something necessarily distinct from the unions, as a constituted class rather than a group of people exercising the same function, will make a solution to the problem of how to resolve the conflict of opposing interests doubly difficult to achieve. Even now our difficulties in grappling with the problem of the union's participation in corporate affairs have been augmented by our confusion of management as a function with management as a special class of people.

There is an unfortunate lack of suitable terminology in this field of industrial relations. We shall ourselves continue to use the old historical terms in our investigation, for want of something better. We are interested in the very problem of who are the managers and how their authority is to be exercised. But we are starting from present positions, and so commonly is the conflict considered as between the union on the one hand and management, in the sense of the legally constituted management, on the other hand, that we shall continue to use those terms for the sake of clarity. But we must do so with the recognition that so to speak is no longer to speak accurately. For already the managerial group includes within it others than those who have achieved their positions through common corporate procedures.

CORPORATE MANAGEMENT DEFINED BY ITS STRUCTURE OF LIVING

Although it is apparent that that group of citizens we have customarily labeled management is not the only group of individuals concerned with the functions by which and problem areas within which direction, administration, and execution of industrial operations are carried on, nevertheless they have much in common. In a sense they form a *social* group whose "structure of living"[3] is different from that of other participants in the operations of enterprises. Their goals, routine behavior, personal and social resources, their codes, philosophy, symbols, and ritual bear the stamp of the world of management. The functions they perform are an important part of this structure of living even though some of these functions are shared in varying degrees with persons outside of "management" as usually defined. But the structure of living has other elements which make of them a psychological group, conscious of their unity of interest in distinction from other groups. This awareness of being alike and the desire to protect the system of business operations and structure in which the alikeness is experienced are important factors in determining the reactions of management to the developing participation of unions in those operations.

By no means can we, even implicitly, assume that some common mold or matrix has formed the managers. At the same time we should be overlooking an important phase of our investigation if we failed to try to understand in what manner their position as the legal guardians of the corporate owners and the legal enterprisers of the business world has contributed to a structure of living distinguishing them from others in society. We must choose our terms with care to state and achieve our purpose. By "distinguishing" them from others in society we do not mean to isolate them from the social setting. Quite the contrary, it should be our intent to discover characteristics of their *interactions with* society.

We may start with the initial hypothesis, then, that management's actions and reactions in society are a reflection of its total structure of living. We may define structure of living to include the goals and objectives which management is pursuing, the environmental obstacles to achieving its goals and the techniques it has developed to overcome them, the op-

[3] An elaboration of this concept with specific reference to its applicability in union-management relations is contained in E. Wight Bakke's *Principles of Adaptive Human Behavior*, Reprint No. 4 of the Yale University Labor and Management Center (1947).

portunities and aids to achieving its objectives present in its social setting and the methods of exploiting those opportunities which it has developed, the reenforcements and supports which it has built up around its methods and practices such as codes, rights, status, and philosophy. That there are similarities present in the structure of living of the legal managers as a group is recognized whenever we speak of "business as a way of life."

It should be clear that we are not here concerned with managers as a functional class. Union officials who exercise the managerial function have a structure of living all their own. Similarly, those in the groups commonly referred to as middle management and supervisory management are differentiated in many respects from the top managerial groups in the corporation, and we should not render our analysis vague and fuzzy by attempting to describe them in the same terms. We are here concerned only with those legal managers who are responsible for the success of the business, who are thus entrusted with guiding its destinies, charting its course, and controlling its evolutions.

The pertinence of this approach to our study is apparent. To *understand* the managers and their ways of living and thinking is to assist in understanding their attitude to the unions and the efforts of the unions to share in their function. We shall here be able to hit only the highlights, but even this should be of importance to us. We shall consider only two elements in the structure, goals and philosophy, which help to make of managers a self-conscious group.

What are the motivations compelling a man to seek the position, with its attendant burdens and responsibilities, of managing a corporation? In the literature of management, and in discussions with management both incident to and independent of this investigation, three primary compulsions which define the goals of the managers have stood out: recognition, self-expression, and personal security, mixed in varying proportions.[4] An observation is immediately in order. It might equally be held that these three objectives characterize not only the managers but all individuals in society. The difference between the goals of the managers and the goals

---

[4] These terms are of course not generally employed by the men to whom they apply. The Yale University Labor and Management Center, which has been conducting extended studies of this aspect of the human relations problem in industry, believes it has identified six goals. These are: (1) respect of fellows; (2) creature sufficiency; (3) increasing control over one's own affairs; (4) understanding; (5) capacity performance, and (6) integrity or wholeness. Further explanation of these terms will be found on page 247. For purposes of the present analysis these six goals have been reduced to the three here discussed. Respect of fellows is treated as recognition. Creature sufficiency, control over one's own affairs, and understanding are joined together as security. Capacity performance and integrity are condensed into self-expression. While this treatment sacrifices certain desirable detail, it lends emphasis to the points pertinent to the present study. At the same time, the resulting stress on certain goals involves no inconsistencies with the more elaborate structure.

of other individuals lies in the placement of emphasis among these simultaneous objectives and the degree of compulsion which they exert upon the individual; it lies also in the choice of means to achieve these goals.

The rise and growth of the large corporation in America, its power and influence in our economic and social life, are material evidence of the results of these three compulsions upon those of our society whom we call the managers. We need not concern ourselves now with why the results in America differ so strikingly, both in degree and form, from those achieved by similarly compelled individuals in other countries and times. At the same time, the present existence of our industrial giants provides immediate incentive to those who seek the achievement of their goals through the business medium to struggle upward to the controlling positions in those corporations where recognition is greatest, self-expression is possible on the grand scale, and personal security is enhanced.

Is there any doubt as to the recognition which comes with a top managerial job in the large corporation? Within the corporation there is of course the deference paid to authority. Within the business community there is the mutual respect of the fraternity of the successful. But more, in no other country has the opinion of the successful businessman been so respected by the churches, followed by the small businessmen, supported by the press, accorded deference by the politicians, and even accepted by many of the workers—witness the difficulties of the unions in breaking down opposition to organization among employes where managements have sought to discredit the union. To introduce a man as a vice president of U.S. Steel, the president of General Motors, the secretary of Westinghouse, the treasurer of Standard Oil of New Jersey is to stamp him with success, prestige, and authority. He has indeed achieved recognition by his fellowmen. Why recognized? Partly perhaps for an ability which is implicit in his attainments. Perhaps for personality traits which his office has developed in him—capacity for logic, decision, cooperation, action. Even more, however, for the power of his position. Even the critic frequently turns sycophant in the presence of the great.

Is there any question as to the possibilities for self-expression inherent in the managerial role? To bring together men and materials, to organize them for a purpose, to improve upon that organization, to integrate it with the community are creative projects. When the organization is numbered in thousands or hundreds of thousands of employes, when the materials are assembled from depots throughout the world, when the organization required is the government of an industrial state the creative element assumes majestic proportions. The freedom from restrictions except those contained in the framework of society has permitted this self-expression with few inhibitions. At the top of the managerial hierarchy, power has been close to absolute. Self-expression has labored under little restraint. Well might two labor leaders say, "The managers of industry naturally enjoy a means of self-expression in their daily work, because it is essentially creative and gives their personalities dignity and their lives a meaning. For them, in the main, their jobs are a pleasure. When they brag about working fifty, sixty, or seventy hours a week, management officials are to be neither honored nor pitied, but envied."[5]

Can there be any skepticism as to the personal security that comes with high managerial office? This is a security which stems not solely from the size of salary—the creature sufficiency—though that may be important. It is equally if not mainly the security that comes from controlling rather than being controlled. Business decisions direct lives; they determine what shall be done, how it shall be done, and who shall do it. It is "safer" to apply policy than to have it applied to one's self. The technology of production is altered, the method of distribution is changed, an experimental department is wiped out, a plant is shut down, a business slump forces curtailment, the requirements of a job are modified—these are the decisions which emanate *from* top management with catastrophic impact upon those affected. The closer to the apex of the managerial pyramid, the fewer there are to make decisions applicable to one's self, the fewer there are to criticize performance. Power may be sought not only for the opportunity to achieve by controlling others, but to achieve by freeing one's self from control by others.

We have been speaking here of the compulsions motivating the managers. But what of that motivation which has received such single emphasis in so much of the popular—and even professional—discussion of the day, the profit motive? Does it too not play its part, constituting a goal the pursuit of which releases springs of energy and determines managerial behavior? Though the answer must be negative and though we must admit that in the large corporations profit as such is not the goal of most of the managers who conduct their business, this is far from denying the importance of profit in our economy.

The large corporation provides the example par excellence of the separation of ownership and control. This separation is not entirely complete. Those who control still retain some ownership in the corporation, but it is the rule rather than the exception when the ownership investment constitutes only an insignificant sum, both proportionally and absolutely.[6] At best, then, the ownership role of the managers provides only a degree of personal security. Recognition, self-expression, and the largest measure

[5] Clinton S. Golden and Harold J. Ruttenberg, *The Dynamics of Industrial Democracy* (1942), p. 239.

[6] Gordon, *Business Leadership in the Large Corporation*, chap. 2, with summary on p. 45, provides concise evidence for this statement.

of personal security come out of the managerial rather than the owner-ship function. Profit may control the owners' decisions; it is only one factor to be weighed by the managers. Profit may be sought to the exclusion of all else by those who will benefit from it; the salaried manager directly benefits from it only a little and is unwilling to make of it a polar star. His satisfaction comes more in the doing than in the reaping.

Yet if profit cannot be viewed as the manager's personal motive, it is important in our system as an indicator of the measure of his success. In the words of one manager, "profit becomes numbers on a score board."[7] It measures the extent of his recognition, satisfies himself as to how capably he has created, and influences the security of his position. Profit is not sought as an end in itself but as the yardstick of achievement. A winning ball club cannot "pocket" the runs which made it champion, nor can a manager "pocket" the profits which show him to be a business success. Both runs and profits are simply scores which add up to a demonstration of performance. The profit "motive" is simply one of the rules of business which must be respected by the managers if they are to achieve their personal goals of recognition, an opportunity for self-expression and personal security. There is, indeed, some indication that profits are no longer being accepted as the final measure of success in the way they once were;[8] nevertheless, nothing else so concrete has as yet taken their place.

We may say, then, that the personal goals sought by the legal corporate managers are recognition, self-expression, and security to be attained through the corporation as medium and measured by its profit-position under their guidance.

Because of the possibilities for goal-realization which high managerial office presents, we may at this point reasonably inquire as to the supports and influences which assist men in climbing to such a favorable position. The American tradition suggests that every boy has a chance to become president of the United States or at least president of a corporation. The advantages inhering in the manager's position would lead one to expect that many would make the effort. The characteristics of those who have succeeded in attaining a top-managerial rank may throw some light upon possible requirements for such a position—not with respect to personal abilities, which are difficult to assess as between those who succeeded and those who did not, but with respect to environmental factors, which are more easily determinable. We may ask ourselves, for example, what are the occupational backgrounds of these men, their social backgrounds,

---

[7] Beardsley Ruml, *Tomorrow's Business* (1945), p. 106.
[8] This fact has been briefly mentioned in Chapter 2, page 19, and is further developed in Chapter 9.

their educational training? Are there influences here which contribute a common element to their structure of living?

A comprehensive study of the characteristics of some 8,749 American business leaders was undertaken by Professors F. W. Taussig and C. S. Joslyn in the period 1928–1932. One of the significant conclusions of that study was that the typical American business leader was neither the son of a farmer nor the son of a wage earner, but a businessman's son. Of the group surveyed only 12 per cent came from farming families, approximately 10 per cent had fathers who were manual laborers, while 56.7 per cent were sons of business owners or executives.[9] Moreover, indications were found that the proportion of businessmen's sons who become business leaders was on the increase.

At the time this study was made, the laboring class—both skilled and unskilled—composed approximately 45 per cent of the population, yet contributed only 10 per cent of the business leaders. The professional and business classes combined accounted for only about 10 per cent of the population, yet contributed 70 per cent of the business leaders. These figures may be taken to indicate not only occupational backgrounds of our businessmen, but to a large extent the nature of their social backgrounds as well, insofar as the social environment reflects family income and occupational differences. It is worth noting, too, that about 40 per cent of those business leaders who were the subjects of this investigation had profited from their social environment by the receipt of help or by the assistance of influential connections at the time of embarking upon their careers.[10]

As regards degree of schooling, the evidence showed that of the 8,749 business leaders in the sample, about 25 per cent had no more than a grammar school education; 28 per cent had a high school training or its equivalent; and approximately 45 per cent had received college training, with 32 per cent receiving degrees. Of importance for our purposes, it was found that the proportion of college graduates among the business executives increased with the size of the firm. Thus 43 per cent of the executives of large-scale businesses were college graduates.[11] This observation is further borne out by a more recent investigation which found that of the presidents of 100 of America's largest corporations, 54 had been to "a college of some sort."[12]

It is most difficult to assess the above statistical information. On the one hand, it may be taken to indicate that a large proportion of our business leaders are drawn from the favored classes, that their family, social,

[9] Taussig and Joslyn, *American Business Leaders* (1932), p. 234.
[10] Taussig and Joslyn, *American Business Leaders*, pp. 241 and 247.
[11] Taussig and Joslyn, *American Business Leaders*, pp. 247–248 and 250.
[12] "The 30,000 Managers," *Fortune*, vol. 21 (February, 1940), p. 61.

and occupational backgrounds provide early familiarity with the world of industry, influential connections, and advanced education permitting them to skip lightly over many rungs of the career ladder. On the other hand, it may be asserted that these in themselves count for little if there is not innate ability to support them once on their own, and that the above figures merely indicate a concentration of ability in certain classes.[13] It is the old controversy of environment versus heredity, which cannot be answered by stressing one to the exclusion of the other.

The results of the study of Taussig and Joslyn may be thrown into a different light by pointing out that although over two-thirds of the sample of business leaders came from favored families, some 60 per cent of the total sample had *not* benefited from influential connections or financial assistance and 55 per cent had never entered a college classroom. Advantages of family, if significant, must therefore have operated in subtler ways in an important number of instances.

The inconclusiveness of these results is further shown by the *Fortune* survey of 1940, which found that of the presidents of 100 of our giant corporations, "thirty-two at the very least can be called self-made men in the fullest sense of the word. Twelve of the sixty men in the industrial group quite as clearly inherited their jobs."[14]

There is thus no conclusive testimony that opportunity to rise to top-management ranks is limited to those possessing favorable environmental factors of social and occupational background or educational training. There is, however, a rather high correlation between managerial status and a business or professional family background. The significance of this correlation is difficult to determine, but it would indeed be superficial to dismiss the possibility that the advantages of such a family background are of little or no assistance in the upward climb to positions of business responsibility, whether or not those advantages operate through the medium of influence, of supply of capital, or provision of education.[15] One

---

[13] This is the opinion of Taussig and Joslyn, who conclude that their study "strongly suggests, if it does not prove, that inequality of earnings between the several occupational classes has its origins in a fundamental inequality of native endowments, rather than in an inequality of opportunities." *American Business Leaders*, p. 268.

[14] *Fortune*, February, 1940, p. 61. The other 56 presumably began with advantages that favored them, but achieved their positions only through demonstration of personal merit.

[15] Taussig and Joslyn seem all too optimistic in their discussion of the relative opportunities of the American boy born of poor parents. Perhaps one element of decisive importance is the possible lack of direction given to such a boy, particularly if the experience or education of the parents is limited, as is likely to be the case. The channeling of incentive, initiative, and ability is of central importance in succeeding in business as in other fields of endeavor.

It may be well to emphasize at this point that Taussig and Joslyn are speaking of management in the traditional sense, that is, of those whom we have referred to here as legal or corporate managers. If managers in the functional sense are included, it would obviously no longer be true that such a small percentage comes from working-class background, since union officials conducting collective-bargaining negotiations would also have to be included.

conclusion to be derived from this high correlation may, however, be stated with greater assurance. It is almost certain that a large proportion of our managers have come from families in which a business philosophy was recognized and accepted. This leads us to another element in the structure of living which welds managers together as a self-conscious social group.

It is extremely doubtful that most businessmen would be able to elaborate their philosophy, much less classify it according to the philosophical school or schools embraced by it. Nevertheless, the necessity for making decisions which daily faces the manager requires him to adopt some philosophical approach if incoherence in business practice is to be avoided. It is not a matter of choosing which philosophical system is most adapted to his needs—the process is not such a conscious one. The very act of making business decisions, however, contributes to the development of a way of business life which may be called a philosophy. To the extent that many of the decisions facing managements, in whatever companies, are decisions of the same order, operating within the same economic and social setting and, indeed, operating on each other, we may expect certain similarities of approach among them. One professional philosopher believes that typically the businessman employs a "combination philosophy" of realism, idealism, and pragmatism, with special emphasis on realism.[16] The technical nomenclature need not bother us, as the discussion will make evident what these terms imply.

Realism is rationalism, a concern with "real" things and not with products of the mind. In business it is represented by a concern for facts on which to rest decisions, by the drive for systematization and standardization. It is the basis for the frequently encountered statement that if the facts are carefully and fully assembled, the business decision will flow out of them. Accounting, auditing, and budgeting procedures are manifestations of it. The development of hiring standards and the use of time-motion studies are evidences of it. The atomization of the production process into numerous stages which may be readily mastered—the whole field of specialization of labor on the basis of engineering studies—are part and parcel of it. The cold calculation of advertising appeal, the survey of potential markets, and the media best suited to reach those markets are based on it. Sales techniques—analyzing the customer and giving him what he wants or making him want what is offered—are primed with it. The organization of research along systematic lines, decisions as to plant locations, the determination of pricing policies are all business realism in action. This concern with things as they are and not as they should be

---

[16] Rupert C. Lodge, *The Philosophy of Business* (1945).

is a strong element in business philosophy. The value of change must be demonstrated by facts. Experience, not theory, is the guide.

Idealism embodies the speculation of the mind, the vision of the dreamer, as opposed to the hard world of reality. It is thus contrasted with realism. If realism so dominates the businessman's philosophy, one would expect little room for idealism, and such is the case. But there is at least a touch of idealism in the businessman's world—and even in his office. It concerns primarily his vision of what the corporation might become, his dream of what the "ideal" corporation would be like. As such it is a star that beckons even if it can never be attained. The map of the world on his office walls or the terrestrial globe on his desk may be concrete evidences of this inner urging for the spread of his corporation's influence, as likewise may be the architect's drawings for the corporate headquarters of the future. These distant goals exert the pull of the future and constitute a perpetual challenge. Idealism is probably most important to the man at the top of the managerial structure. For him there is no higher critic prodding him to greater efforts. The incentive must come from within, and it is his idealism which inspires it. There is thus some room in business for the dreamer. At the same time, the realist element of business philosophy will never let the manager escape from the hard fact that it is only mastery over things, the physical harnessing of physical forces—manpower and materials and capital—which will permit the climb upward and onward toward the ideal. The ideal leads but it cannot control. There is always the hard world of reality with which to cope— today.

Pragmatism emphasizes growth, change, choice, and consequence. For the pragmatist "facts" do not lead to a single conclusion, but to a number of alternatives, the best among which is to be determined by its results. Moreover, the results by which actions are to be judged must be in terms of their effects upon people. It is a philosophy of opportunism and improvisation. "Things" do not remain the same; there is constant change in the world, and the individual must adapt himself to it. But pragmatism calls for more than mere adaptation. By stressing choice among alternatives it emphasizes the freedom of the will; by emphasizing change it lays open the possibilities of progress, of movement toward goals realizable in the "here and now," rather than in the idealist's "perhaps sometime." The business manager's pragmatism finds its outlet in his search for technological improvements and the pioneering of new products, in contrast to mere exploitation of existing lines. It is evident in the improvisation that comes in the early stages of mobilizing the economy for full war production, when safety-pin factories turn to making gas masks, washing-machine assemblies produce turrets, and automobile plants change over to tanks. It shows, though somewhat randomly and sometimes misguidedly, in concern for employes' welfare and the company's role in the community.

Of these three, then—realism, idealism, and pragmatism—is the managers' philosophy composed. As among managers, the emphasis upon them may be distributed differently, but it is safe to assume that by far the dominant element is realism. The fact compels. What is, must be faced. The organization of vast numbers of workers, the provision of great quantities of materials from a multitude of sources, the development of machinery and production techniques, and the coordination of all three as to time, place, and method require a rigid adherence to system and standard, to the "hard facts" of economic and industrial life.

In part, the codes of business conduct so frequently elaborated by trade associations stem from the realistic necessity of being able to predict another's behavior, of being able to count upon a business world in which certain standards are observed, becoming part of the facts with which the manager must deal. In part, the doctrine of final authority, of "freedom to manage the business," arises from the realistic desire to make decisions on the basis of facts as the top managerial authority sees them, undiluted by compromises to secure the following of associates or subordinates: it is, as we have seen, an efficiency concept, with efficiency rooted in realism.

This is the business philosophy which is part of the social setting in which many—between one-half and two-thirds—of our managers mature from adolescence. It is part of their ways of thinking before they enter business. It is not only true that business itself conditions the minds of the managers: business has conditioned, through family influence, the minds of a large proportion of our managers before they come in direct contact with it. If true, this conclusion is vitally important. It establishes a certain continuity of business behavior founded on a continuity of business philosophy handed down from father to son. It renders business less susceptible to change by limiting the number of those entering business and ultimately reaching managerial status who do not already have some rather fixed philosophical beliefs of the nature of business activity. This should not, however, be overstressed, for influences other than family will act upon the rising manager, and those influences may reflect social changes. But insofar as family influence is important, the growth of future managers in the families of present managers preserves, as we have said, a certain continuity of business philosophy.

The goals of the legal managers are recognition, self-expression, and personal security. The philosophy guiding management is predominantly realism, tinged with idealism and a form of pragmatism. The goals and the philosophy of management *are bound up in the corporation.* Their objectives are found and their philosophy expressed *in the corporation.* To a very important degree, for the managers, personal achievement is corporate achievement; personal philosophy becomes corporate philosophy.

This is significant for our study. It provides one clue to managerial opposition to sharing its authority with the unions. Union penetration of the managerial function constitutes a threat to the goals of the legal managers and a challenge to their philosophy. To share the managerial function would be to share—that is, dilute—recognition;[17] it would limit the freedom of self-expression;[18] it would weaken personal security.[19] To share the managerial function with the *unions* would be, as many managers believe, to remove business decisions from a factual foundation and rest them upon social considerations, political predilections, or even mental vagaries.[20]

Managerial opposition to the sharing of their authority with the unions is rooted in part, therefore, in a defense of personal objectives and personal philosophy. This must be said in no condemnation. Such motives inevitably play their roles in every movement seeking change as well as in every resistance to change. They could not do otherwise, since they

[17] Thus note this statement of one company official: "It is not so much that they [the union leaders] win loyalty for the union—but they do it by . . . wanting credit for everything, even when it is management's own idea." Such sharing of recognition is not only in the eyes of employes, however. Particularly if unions should extend their interest to broader spheres of corporate policy would the legal managers be forced to share with them public recognition for corporate achievements.

[18] The following comment of a corporate manager is pertinent in this respect: "Restriction on management freedom is a big issue. This isn't breast-beating. We've got heavy responsibilities for making quick, accurate, and effective decisions. Sometimes there are considerations that we can't divulge or that wouldn't be understood if we did. We're held responsible for the success of them but the Union isn't. It takes complicated maneuvering to run a business and all of the parts have to be kept working together. You have to have a good deal of free play in the rope for that. Sometimes there's a particular restriction but on the whole it's the overall sense of being closed in on and the anticipation of more of the same that gets you. It's the cumulative effect of one area of freedom after another being reduced and the promise of still more that gives us real concern. But you make adjustments and go on to every particular one. It's not impossible. But you wonder how long it can go on and leave you able to meet your responsibilities." This and the quotation in note 17 are from E. Wight Bakke, *Mutual Survival: The Goal of Unions and Management* (1946), pp. 34 and 29.

[19] Through union attacks on the size of salaries of corporate officials, its ability to subject managerial efficiency to critical inspection, and limitations on the freedom *from* control of the top managers.

[20] Thus, the assistant production manager of one large corporation writes: "Factual support is secured for all arguments presented to the union negotiators. Company records and statistics, government publications, and other sources are freely used to substantiate and justify stands made by the management. However such factual evidence has not been very successful in convincing union representatives of the justice of management's position on any point." For other expressions on the lack of attention accorded factual data in collective bargaining, see N. W. Chamberlain, *Collective Bargaining Procedures* (1944), chap. 6, "Use of Economic Data."

arise out of the very structure of living of those who participate in the conflict.

INFLUENCES ON MANAGERIAL DECISIONS

The issue of union participation in managerial determinations is sometimes raised in terms suggesting that "outside" influence is a problem confined to relations with organized workers. It is scarcely necessary to do more than state that this is not actually the case. The large corporation has frequently been analogized to an industrial government; as in the case of governments, the corporation is subject to the pressures and influences of a variety of groups. It is important to realize that such pressures spring from organized collectivities including competing or collaborating corporations and trade associations as well as labor unions. In bringing their pressures and influence to bear, they frequently indulge in a process which can be recognized only as collective bargaining, in one form or another.

Collective bargaining has commonly been considered as a device peculiar to workers seeking to overcome the economic inequality facing the individual worker in reaching terms with his employer. So conceived, its more general significance is overlooked, for such a view sees collective bargaining as a device compensating economic inferiors for their individual weakness. If, however, collective bargaining is understood not as a compensation for individual weakness but as an expansion of individual strength, its larger import becomes apparent. It would be fatuous to assert, for example, that the investment house of Dillon, Read and Company, in the determination of the terms of a security issue which it may handle, resorts to collaboration with other investment houses[21]—collectively bargaining, that is to say—as a compensatory measure. To recognize, however, that by collective action this firm may expand still further

[21] *Investment Banking*, Hearings before the Senate Temporary National Economic Committee, part 24 (1939), pp. 12652–12653, records the memorandum of a conversation between members of the First Boston Corporation and Dillon, Read and Company, relating to a proposed issue of Shell Union Oil Co.: ". . . He is sure that the company will be shocked at the proposal he has in mind making and that their first impulse will be to try to go somewhere else. You will recall that the syndicate in the last issue was a pretty comprehensive one and he thinks that the only possible place that they might go to is Kuhn Loeb, and there are probably reasons why they would not go even to them. He is anxious, however, to have his group present a solid front to the company and, in effect, to agree that if the Shell Union does not trade with the Dillon Read—Hayden Stone—Lee Higginson group, the members of this group will not join any other bankers who may attempt to form a group to figure on the business. In view of the well-known trading proclivities of the Shell people, I have agreed in principle to Mr. Mathey's suggestion on the theory that if our large and strong group cannot get the business on terms that we feel attractive, we will be better off to be out of the business." Even the traditional boycott as a support to bargaining power is present in this example.

its bargaining power is to recognize the general applicability throughout the economy of the collective-bargaining concept.[22]

Not all pressures and influences upon managerial decisions result from bargaining power expressed through collective bargaining, however. Others may spring from the advantages of a strategic position. In this study we will do no more than suggest some of the areas in which the bargaining power and strategic positions of various groups interested in the conduct of a corporation may determine in some degree the decisions of corporate management.

As has already been intimated above, financial groups such as commercial and investment bankers and insurance companies may influence and even form management policies and decisions. For the most part the interests of these groups have centered in the financial affairs of a corporation, as might be expected,[23] but at times it has been difficult to dissociate financial considerations from decisions of another nature. Thus, part of the price of financing may be appointment of the bankers' representatives to directorships in the corporation, in which capacity they in fact become part of management and eligible to share in nonfinancial as well as financial decisions. Speaking before the Bond Club of New York in 1937, William O. Douglas, then Commissioner of the Securities and Exchange Commission, pointed out that not only in cases of such appointments is this result possible, moreover.

All of the hazards and dangers to investors arising by reason of the fact that bankers are represented on the boards of issuers may continue though such relationship is abolished. Such hazards and dangers are inherent in control. That control may result not only from having a representative on the board but also from having a voting trusteeship or a strategic investment position (usually though not necessarily in stock); or it may result from subtle ties of friendship, from long periods of association, from favors rendered, from zones of influence in financial circles, or from an inertia which has never been challenged.

When I speak of control I do not speak legalistically. . . . I mean not only working control but also domination and controlling influence over policies however obtained or preserved. You know better than I do how subtle that control is. You also know better than I how valuable it is or can be. Certainly when that control is in the form of directorships, voting trusteeships, or a strategic investment position, the bankers who have it can commonly claim that company as their own. It amounts to a "no trespassing" sign on a financial empire.[24]

[22] Similarly, collective bargaining in labor relations, though it does compensate the worker for his individual economic weakness, may more realistically be viewed as expanding his bargaining power. Certainly the employer who complains of being pressed to the wall as a result of union demands could describe collective bargaining as a compensatory device only in terms of overcompensation.

[23] Gordon discusses "The Influence and Leadership Activities of Financial Groups" in chap. 9 of *Business Leadership in the Large Corporation.*

[24] Address as released by S.E.C., mimeo., pp. 2–3. Reproduced in substantially the same form in *Democracy and Finance,* collected statements of Justice Douglas (1940), pp. 32–33.

To some extent this condition has been remedied by the "arm's-length bargaining" and competitive bidding rules of the Securities and Exchange Commission,[25] but it has not been eliminated.

Union officials in certain industries have been particularly sensitive to what they identify as "banker domination" of the companies with which they bargain. Thus the Railway Labor Executives' Association has charged: "Railroad operations are no longer actually directed by the highly competent and responsible railroad officials who know how the railroads should be run. Railroad policy now for a number of years has been controlled by bankers and financiers whose one purpose has been to take from the railroad industry all that the industry could give at the moment . . ."[26] Similarly, A. F. Whitney, President of the Brotherhood of Railroad Trainmen, in private correspondence has asserted: "Railroad labor has always had the problem of overcoming the pressure exerted upon management representatives by railroad bankers. Management representatives have many times indicated that they were not free to give a decision on the basis of their own convictions. Management representatives generally take the position that they 'have a job to do.' " And in the anthracite coal industry, a representative of the United Mine Workers unofficially asserted that "the operatators' negotiating committee was always hog-tied to the domination of the banking interests and was never free to execute a wage agreement in accordance with their working knowledge of the anthracite industry."

The degree and nature of financial influence on corporate decisions are not matters of concern here, nor is any moral judgment implied respecting such influence. It is of immediate interest only that banking groups, and other institutional suppliers of capital,[27] do affect, in some measure, the course of corporate conduct.

Corporate affairs may likewise be made the concern of other businesses having no financial relationships. Competitors, customers, and suppliers, for example, if strategically situated, may be able to exert strong influences in bargaining with a corporation.[28] The decisions affected may concern price, sales policy, quality and lines of merchandise, and even labor relations. The impact of chain-store and mail-order merchandisers on the

[25] These rules and their genesis are set out in the Commission's *Tenth Annual Report* (1944), pp. 105–107.

[26] *The Wages of Railroad Labor—1938*, p. 26. This charge has been taken up more recently by the chairman of the boards of the Chesapeake and Ohio Railroad and the Alleghany Corporation, who charges that "for three generations Morgan and Kuhn, Loeb have dictated the policies of the American railroads . . ." *New York Times*, March 1, 1946.

[27] Robert A. Gordon, in his recent study, *Business Leadership in the Large Corporation*, p. 216, finds that "The influence of insurance companies has increased."

[28] Gordon in *Business Leadership in the Large Corporation*, pp. 246–255, discusses these influences.

policies of the principal tire manufacturers is too well known to be re-counted.[29] It has been charged that in negotiations with the unions the automobile body and parts manufacturers are guided to a large extent by what they "infer" to be the wishes of the automobile makers.[30] A United Mine Workers' official privately writes that "Even in the days of the four-state competitive field—West Virginia, Illinois, Pennsylvania and Indiana—which served as the base wage-making territory, representatives of railroads, utilities, and other large consumers of coal, as well as the steel industry, intervened in a sort of 'third-house' lobby in wage conferences between bituminous coal operators and the coal miners."[31] This situation has not changed, he charges.

In many industries some of these business influences have become formalized through trade associations. The degree to which such associations affect corporate decisions is difficult to assess, but that some measure of influence exists is possible to establish. It ranges from the formulation of policies for the violation of which a member may be fined or expelled to the mere provision of a leadership which it is inexpedient to ignore.

Other forms of intervention in managerial decisions may be presented, but these are sufficient to establish the point of present interest—namely, that collective bargaining with unions is not the only means by which management shares its authority. By bargaining with other collectivities, and by responding to the influences of strategically situated "outside" groups of financial houses, suppliers, customers, competitors, and trade associations, it is likewise sharing authority. The procedures may be less formal, the results less openly arrived at, the relationships more traditional. Nevertheless, it is clear that the unions are breaking no new paths in seeking to participate in the determination of corporate policy. Since this is so, the question arises why there has been more widespread managerial opposition to granting the unions a voice in business decisions than there has been to the intervention of other pressure groups.

There is no single, clear-cut answer to this question. First we must

[29] The story is well told in Walton Hamilton and Associates, *Price and Price Policies* (1938), pp. 98–116.

[30] William McPherson, *Labor Relations in the Automobile Industry* (1940), p. 40. It has likewise been charged by union men in the flat glass industry that while some of the major producers in that industry have accepted the union shop in principle and practice, they have refused to commit it to the written agreement for fear of offending the automobile companies, who are important customers.

[31] "Going back to 1922," says this official, "the railroads, the Morgan interests, and all the big consumers, as well as the steel companies, insisted that the operators force a wage reduction in the bituminous coal industry. Some railroads, some manufacturers, and steel companies bluntly told coal operators that unless they deflated the mine workers' wage scale, which was holding up wages in steel and other industries, that they would give their business to non-union areas, regardless of transportation costs. This interference caused the Western Pennsylvania operators to decline to meet in the wage negotiations of 1922, with a resultant five-month stoppage in both the bituminous and anthracite industries."

recognize that there *has* been resistance to the penetrations of management authority by other pressure groups besides the unions. Companies have not willingly succumbed to the insistences of banking groups or the demands of important customers. Trade associations sometimes face the possibility of disintegration or secession as the result of the refusal of members to accept as binding the decisions of the group. At the same time, there does not appear in these instances the same continuing managerial opposition as is expressed towards the unions. Such interventions by pressure groups as are frequent in the large corporation are more often than not accepted once they are established. In some instances, as we have noted, a place for their representatives is made on the board of directors of the corporation.

To some extent this attitude is based on a feeling of dependency and necessity. A place was made for bankers in the counsels of industry because they held the key to needed capital. Gentlemen's agreements among banking houses often eliminated the possibility of a competition among themselves that might have destroyed their bargaining power and strategic positions. Established relations with a given banking firm were also valued by management itself because they permitted calls for assistance in times of financial distress that in the absence of such long-standing associations would have gone unheeded. Similarly, the suggestions and even dictates of important suppliers and customers have been accepted because without suppliers and customers there could be no business. Because trade associations are voluntary, membership itself constitutes proof that the advantages of collaboration with competitors outweigh the disadvantages of extracorporate influence. In the case of unions there is seldom, however, the same feeling of dependency and necessity. Companies would continue to operate even with the demise of the union. The power of individual unions has been subject to wax and wane throughout American history, and there is always the fortuitous possibility that tomorrow may see another wane. This is particularly true when union fortunes are so vitally linked with the national political complexion, which too is subject to change. The increasing power of a particular union at the moment, then, *may* be accepted by management not as indication of its necessity or the company's dependence upon it, but as a spur to increased resistance, that the union's power may be dissipated if not broken in some future-to-be-hoped-for. Since the passing of the crusading fervor of the early New Deal administration, seldom has a session of Congress passed without the introduction of some measure designed to achieve this purpose.

As another consideration, except for the unions there has never been any single problem of outside intervention common to all managers at any one time, upon which common antagonism could be centered. The threat of banker control was not presented to all corporations simultaneously. It had already been established in some companies when others faced the problem. Some have escaped it altogether. The bargaining power and strategic positions of suppliers and customers are far from the same in all industries. In some these groups are dominated rather than dominating. Trade associations often rely for their strength upon the large corporation, which may control the group in its own interests. In any event, their growth, powers, and purposes vary between industries and regions, presenting few common problems. Particularly in recent years, this has not been true of the unions, however. Their rise in an industry has sometimes been the signal for a general attack by all employers in that industry and even outside it. The unions constitute the one pressure force operating upon the corporation which has been faced with concerted opposition from the managers. They most nearly, of all group interests, represent a problem of intervention common to all managements at one time, permitting a common antagonism.

Another basis for greater opposition to the unions than to other "outside" forces has been the openness of their challenge and its operation without the legal framework. Managers have shown greater willingness to accommodate pressure groups which have acquired their power in behind-the-scenes moves bringing less loss of prestige and often resulting in a merger of forces rather than surrender. Moreover, the power game is played within an accepted legal framework. Except for the piratical methods of a few operators who have flouted the law, power within a corporation has been acquired through pressures legally exercised. Bargaining power and strategic position play through established corporate procedures and business methods—the acquisition of stock, the supply or withholding of capital, materials, or markets. Physical force and contests of human endurance seldom enter the picture. In the case of the labor unions, however, their influence in corporate affairs can be acquired only by outright challenge to the constituted interests, with bargaining power resting upon the strike weapon and the picket line, often with violence attending. Their position is secured outside of recognized corporate and business procedures and to a large extent outside of the framework of law.[32]

Basically, however, the answer to the question of why management has more willingly accepted outside intervention other than that from unions lies in the fact that, except primarily for the unions, outside intervenors

[32] An interesting analysis of this aspect of the union-management relation is offered by Marvin Barloon in "Violence and Collective Bargaining, " *Harper's Magazine* (May, 1940), p. 625.

have shared with management the same social and economic beliefs, the same goals, the same philosophy, the same legal responsibilities. In short, management and such outside pressure groups have a common structure of living. Business is part and parcel of this structure of living. Banking houses, suppliers, customers, and competitors are all themselves business corporations faced with the same kinds of problems as the businesses with which they deal, and meeting them in the same manner. Trade associations are merely such corporations in collaboration. Sharing authority with such groups might mean a loss of personal power (though in some instances it means an actual expansion of power, an enlargement of the area within which authority is exercised). It involves no violation of the system of authority itself, however, or of the business framework. It constitutes no threat to the social position of the managers. It is, in fact, part of "the game." To win at the game may therefore be accepted merely as evidence of ability, commanding respect and providing an example for emulation, so long as one observes the codes and rules. The significant fact is that managers have been more willing to accept outside intervention when brought by those who are themselves "in business." To sum it briefly, they understand each other.

To this structure of living of the managers the unions, however, pose a threat. They seem to endanger the organizational framework and the system of authority throughout the corporation. Their philosophy has idealistic values foreign to the predominantly realistic outlook of businessmen. They challenge the accepted codes and rules. They substitute for the legal responsibilities of the managers political responsibilities of their own. Their program is revolutionary insofar as it seeks not merely a shifting of authority within the existing system but modification of the system itself. How common it is to hear the managerial condemnation that the methods and objectives of the unions "won't work" in a competitive business society.

It is this challenge to the way of life of the managers that provides them with their sterner attitude to the intervention of unions than to the intervention of other business groups. There is not the same basis for mutual accommodation. "So many of their [the unions'] appeals, activities, and attitudes are colored by value to the *movement*. Businessmen are used to dealing with other businessmen on a business basis and are puzzled by this point of view of the union. . . ." Seeking a *modus vivendi* with the unions is not so much part of "the game" as it is a struggle for survival. "It is not so much the aggravation of hearing violent and untrue things said about management—that is bad enough. But it is the basic assumption which is clear, namely that collective bargaining is a battle and the ordinary rules of peaceful, reasonable procedure, and mutual respect don't hold."

The unions were not first, then, nor are they alone, in seeking to share authority within the corporation. Aside from the state itself, however, they are alone in arousing an "employer solidarity in never giving in on anything which jeopardizes the institution of their company and of management."[33]

---

[33] The above three quotations are from interviews with management officials by E. Wight Bakke, in *Mutual Survival—The Goal of Unions and Management*, pp. 33, 34 and 40.

Degree of Union Penetration
of Managerial Areas

What is the nature of the union drive to share managerial authority with the legal managers? To this point we have been concerned only with the fact that labor *is* penetrating into areas of managerial responsibility. We shall now make a limited attempt to measure that penetration by seeking to establish the number of areas where unions now share, in some manner, the decision-making power, and by attempting to estimate the importance of their share in those areas.

This undertaking is a difficult one. In some degree the measure of the union's influence may be taken from the collective agreements now in existence. This procedure would not reveal, however, union power which may be derived from other sources than the agreement, or the manner in which the agreement provisions may be interpreted to permit exercises of influence not readily apparent from a casual reading. Analysis, then, must rely on practice as well as on the contractual word.

Furthermore, in discussing the impact of the union within the corporation it is necessary to distinguish between official union actions or policies, the actions or policies of organized groups within the union which may not have official sanction but are nonetheless important, and the actions of individual union members who may attempt, through union membership, to exert a personal "managerial" influence. These three aspects of the problem are all significant, but of a descending order of significance. Again, it is essential to distinguish between actions or attitudes which may appear in isolated instances, and those which have the status of continuing policy.

Our analysis will necessarily have to be limited. It will be confined to six major industries: automobiles, steel, rubber, electrical equipment, meat packing, and public utilities. All of these industries with the exception of public utilities are dominated by a very small number of large corporations. In public utilities the situation is somewhat different. The telephone industry is virtually identical with one huge corporation possessing a number of large subsidiaries. The telegraph industry is likewise dominated by a single corporation. In the field of gas, light, and power,

74

large corporations are prevalent but the number of them is likewise large, only a few of which have here been considered.

The results of the investigations into these six industries have been summarized in this chapter, to give an admittedly rough measure of the extent and intensity of the union's participation in management functions in corporations of the size with which we are concerned. This brief recapitulation is based upon a much more detailed analysis, industry by industry, than is feasible to present in the text of the study.[1]

FINANCE.

None of the unions in the six industries has sought a voice in methods of raising capital or the capital structure of the companies. In varying degree, all have shown an interest in the size of dividends to stockholders but have asked for no direct share in this determination. All have likewise been concerned with the accounting procedures of the business, though primarily for purposes of estimating a company's financial ability to stand wage increases rather than for establishing an area of joint interest. To a lesser extent there has been a similar interest in the size and employment of reserves.

It is probably possible to establish a negative and a positive interest of the unions in this category of finance. The negative interest lies in demonstrating that a company's wage-paying ability need not be accepted as confined within the bounds of the financial showing of a company as unilaterally determined. This position has been well stated by the president of a union in another industry, railroads, who has said: "Our criticism of these [financial] policies does not mean that we propose to oust the management and conduct the policies for ourselves. It only means that our criticism is a defense mechanism against the claims of the railroads that the employes are 'racketeers,' or that the employes are selfish or are making unreasonable demands, or that the railroads cannot afford to give the employes fair wages and working conditions."[2] Such a purpose may be accepted as of general incidence among unions. Behind it lies no intent of seeking to share in managerial decisions relating to finance. It may and sometimes does, however, imply a union disregard or nonacceptance of managerial decisions on which money issues of the bargaining table are based.

The affirmative interest of the unions in the financial affairs of the corporations with which they bargain must be stated somewhat more tenu-

---

[1] Those who are interested in examining the summarized findings of specific industries will find in the appendices reports covering the automobile, steel, meat packing, and public utility industries. Space limitations have necessitated omission of the findings for the rubber and electrical equipment industries.

[2] From private correspondence, December 8, 1941.

ously. First, it is probably true that although profits are legally the property of the owners of the business, they are actually regarded by the union as a proper subject for bargaining, so that it becomes difficult to distinguish between what might be considered as bargaining for wage increases and what might equally be considered as bargaining for profit-participation. Recognition of this economic philosophy injects greater significance into the comment of the executive vice president of one large corporation, made at a bargaining conference where union representatives pointed to the favorable profit position of the company as ground for wage increases:

> . . . And then I just wondered whether you boys—and I don't mean to imply that you didn't go at this seriously, but I wonder if you have any conception of the vast amount of money that you have cut up and as to this new spread—that's one thing. If, on the other hand, you just have a misconception that this is some golden cheese that we are going to cut up now and whack it up, no matter what the amount is, I don't see that we are going to get anywhere at all. If that is the conception, we have a very bewildering situation. We might expect our customers to say, "Whenever you are making a profit, you must immediately reduce the price, and whenever we are making a profit you immediately ask us to increase the cost of labor. When you get those two things together, there is no profit.

Secondly, bargaining over *profits*, if intelligible, naturally leads to a concern about such managerial areas as methods of raising capital, the size of dividends, amounts set aside for reserves and the purposes for which set aside, provisions for depreciation and amortization, and other accounting policies. For decisions in these areas will determine the profits available for bargaining. Thus it is that one leading union official has joined in the statement that under a profit-sharing scheme, "The workers must see the monthly statement of profits and have a voice in deciding on unusual expenditures which will tend to reduce profits temporarily in the expectation of increasing them at a later period."[3] Thus it is that one independent union in the utility field made the demand in negotiations that dividends to corporate stockholders be limited, by collective-bargaining agreement, to six per cent. If all negotiations for wage increases above some basic or minimum figure are understood as a form of profit-sharing, then union interest in the mechanics of profit determination becomes more than a defense mechanism.

It would not be accurate to say that unions now actively espouse this view. Nevertheless, it is current. The ability-to-pay argument which loomed so importantly in 1945–1946 wage negotiations is shot through with this thesis. The general defensive attitude on the part of managements respecting authority in this category in all the industries analyzed,

[3] Cooke and Murray, *Organized Labor and Production*, p. 121.

with the exception of rubber, is evidence that they anticipate a struggle to retain that authority.

It is reasonable to conclude that the unions have not actively sought the right of joint determination of financial matters except in isolated cases, that they are not now preparing any planned or concerted attempt at penetrating this category, but that the logic of their position is drawing them in that direction.

PERSONNEL.

Union incursions into areas of management have been at their deepest and broadest within this category.

With respect to the *type of personnel* to be employed, unions in the automobile, steel, rubber, electrical equipment, and meat-packing industries have promoted, with some degree of success, a policy of nondiscrimination on the basis of race, color, creed, or sex. Jointly with management, they have participated in the formulation of apprenticeship programs designed to foster professional competence. In the public utility field, unions have in some instances joined in writing the qualifications required of applicants for given types of employment.

The impact of collective bargaining has been felt on decisions as to the *size of the work force*. As regards the total number of employes on the payroll, the unions have exercised influence by obtaining agreements to share work before force reductions are instituted, thus maintaining the attachment of a larger number of workers to their jobs while total man-hours of employment decline. Particularly in public utilities, and to a much more limited extent in steel, there has been recognition of the principle that employes whose jobs are eliminated by technological changes should be reabsorbed into other jobs. Expansion of this principle is sought with a view to making mandatory such an arrangement, requiring the carrying of displaced employes until jobs open for them through normal turnover. Some effect on manpower available may result from agreed-upon limitations of the number of apprentices. A relation between the number of workers on a given operation and the work load has also been established in some companies in all of the industries reviewed.

Union plans for a guaranteed annual wage are being pressed in automobiles, steel, and meat packing. These plans as now formulated constitute a guaranteed income to a guaranteed number of workers. This latter condition would establish a minimum size of the work force for the life of the contract or for a period specified in the contract. Within this period this minimum work force would be in the nature of a fixed charge on the company.

Control over *hiring* practices is shared by the union in various ways.

In filling a vacancy, management may be obligated to give preference to specified types of workers under given conditions, such as to men previously laid off, existing employes who prefer the vacant job to their own, former employes who have lost their seniority standing, experienced workers or union members whether or not previously employed by the company. Rehiring following layoffs is commonly in the inverse order in which the work force was reduced. In a few instances in the public utility field there is provision for a closed shop, under which employes are supplied by the union upon request by the company.

Unions likewise participate in the determination of procedures governing *layoffs*. In all cases they have sought to make seniority the governing factor in determining which workers shall be dismissed, with varying success within and between industries. Straight seniority is probably applied most rigidly in the rubber industry, by agreement, but by practice it has become the major factor controlling layoffs in all industries analyzed. In some instances where ability is still given consideration, as in automobiles and steel, the union has successfully insisted that management must be able to prove the existence of greater ability, by objective measurement, before retaining junior employes while dismissing men with longer service records.

The principle of work-sharing down to a specified minimum number of hours before reducing the work force has become contractually established in many companies in all six industries. In some instances the union is accorded the right to review dismissal schedules. Advance notice to employes selected for layoff, of varying length, is commonly prescribed. Reductions in force due to mechanization have been hedged, particularly in public utilities, by various provisions calling for reabsorption of those displaced, or retraining to fit them for the new skills required or for other suitable employment, or lengthy advance notice, or severance pay. In other industries such displaced workers are handled under provisions for reassignment of employes.

Questions of the *allocation* of workers are subject to joint decision in important particulars. The goal of all the unions is agreement that transfers to better jobs shall be based on greater seniority while transfers to less desirable jobs shall be based on lesser seniority. This goal has been largely obtained in rubber and to a considerable extent in automobiles. It is practiced to some degree, even when not appearing in contract clauses, in the other four industries.

An employe's consent to be transferred must be obtained in the meatpacking industry, and under certain conditions in automobiles, rubber, and public utilities. The packinghouse workers have also secured the right to seek transfers on their own initiative, with an effective system, based upon seniority, to make that right a real one.

The area of *disciplinary control* over employes has been subject to an intensive penetration by the unions. In some companies they have participated in the formulation of the rules of conduct for breach of which agreed penalties may be imposed. In all cases an employe charged with an offense is entitled to representation by his union in a grievance procedure culminating in arbitration. Where permanent offices of arbitration have been established, filled by an official who is continued from case to case and whose services may be readily invoked, a body of doctrine or precedents governing the disposition of such cases is being established. This is true in automobiles, steel, and meat packing, in particular. Among such rules or principles are found the following: employes must have prior knowledge of the causes for which disciplinary penalties may be imposed; there must be reasonably certain knowledge of the penalties attached to the offense; employes must have knowledge of the offense with which they are charged; there must be adequate evidence to support the charge; any disciplinary penalty imposed on employes must conform to the charges. Managerial action found to have violated one or more of these principles is generally rescinded by an arbiter or umpire, if the case comes to a hearing before him. In such event, the employe is commonly made whole for any loss sustained as a result of the discipline imposed.

In the steel industry, agreement has been reached on a procedure preliminary to suspension or discharge, under which a temporary suspension of no more than five days is imposed, during which time a hearing is held to determine what final action shall be taken. Management's decision, again, is subject to grievance proceedings.

The complaint is encountered in virtually all major companies of the six industries here discussed that the union has been responsible for an even greater loss of managerial disciplinary power than contract provisions or their application would indicate. It is charged that unofficial group action in the shop has succeeded in intimidating many foremen, leading them to believe that to impose discipline will only result in loss of production through a protest work stoppage, or in a contest of power in which their authority may suffer more than it would by permitting laxities in the shop, or possibly in an over-ruling by higher management or the umpire which may likewise constitute erosion of their authority. In the automobile and rubber industries management admits that in certain shops the union steward exercises greater power than the foreman. It is not necessary to rely upon such unofficial inroads to demonstrate the impact of the union in this area, however. By the contractual means already discussed they have succeeded in sharing a very great measure of authority in the disciplinary control of employes.

Wages represent one of the oldest fields of collective bargaining, and it is to be expected that the influence of unions here has been an important one. The union's impact on general wage increases needs only mention. In addition, in all six industries a system of job classifications has been instituted, which the union participates in establishing either through initial negotiation or by challenging management's classifications via the grievance procedure. To each job classification a wage or wage bracket is attached, generally by managerial determination but again subject to amendment in the grievance procedure. The automobile, rubber, and packinghouse workers are seeking a more direct participation in the setting of such wage rates. By policy or practice it is usually agreed that once an individual rate has been set it may not be altered except as a result of changes in methods of production, equipment, or materials. Any general wage increases negotiated are added to the basic rate structure.

In most industries there are provisions, often numerous, for special cases, providing for such contingencies as the wage to be paid a worker temporarily assigned to another job than his own, or the provisional rate to be paid pending the setting of the permanent rate, or the rate to be paid when production must proceed under handicaps. Certain general conditions are likewise established, as for example the payment of equal wages for equal work, of differentials in favor of night workers, of overtime or penalty rates under given circumstances, of minimum "call-in" time when employes report for duty without previous advice that work is not available.

In the steel and meat-packing industries, there is a minimum daily guarantee equal to the basic hourly rate for the job times the number of hours worked, designed to protect the earnings of piece workers. In meat packing there is likewise a minimum weekly guarantee which becomes operative when an employe starts his second day of work, assuring him a minimum number of hours of work or equivalent pay for that week.

The automobile, steel, and packinghouse workers are now pressing for a guaranteed annual wage, and in a few utilities such a plan has already been instituted. The elimination of geographical differentials also stands high on the program of most of the unions here considered.

Hours, like wages, constituted one of the areas of management first penetrated by the unions. One result has been a joint specification of the hours and days which make up the normal work week. Hours or days worked outside of those so specified are paid for at penalty rates. Changes in shift hours may often be made only after advance notice to or discussion with the union. The principle of equalization of hours of work has gained a strong hold in all six industries, applying to part-timing in the event of decreased production and the spread of overtime hours on increased production. Contractual definition of hours of work has been attempted in all cases, and includes such expenditures of time as for reporting or calling in, for rest periods, for traveling, for preparing tools or receiving instructions, sometimes for changing clothes and handling grievances. In rubber, meat packing, and public utilities, unions are seeking greater control over the scheduling of overtime.

In the area of *employe advancement policies,* unions in all six industries have been successful in securing collective agreements establishing paid vacations, and have joined in writing the conditions for eligibility and the method of computing vacation payments. Payment for holidays not worked is common only in public utilities, but in all cases the union has had a voice in setting forth the holidays on which work may not be required except by payment of penalty rates. With only a few exceptions, most of them concentrated in public utilities, social security plans have remained under the control of management. In all industries, however, unions are making demands for joint administration of retirement funds, dismissal payments, sick leave, and group insurance systems.

All unions in the six industries discussed have sought to establish the principle that selection of employes for *promotion* shall be based on seniority. They have succeeded in obtaining recognition of the seniority factor in varying degree. In automobiles, steel, electrical equipment, and some public utilities seniority controls only where merit and ability are equal. In rubber, meat packing, and other public utilities seniority governs if the employe is capable of learning the job within a reasonable "breaking in" period. Arbitration decisions in the automobile and steel industries have laid down the rule that where management bases promotion on ability rather than seniority it must be able to offer objective proof of the greater ability of the employe selected. A single decision in the meat-packing industry has reversed this rule, requiring the union to demonstrate that management's decision as to lack of ability on the part of a senior employe failing to be promoted was not made in good faith before remedial action will be ordered.

Provision for the *health and safety* of employes while on the job still rests largely with management. In all industries unions have often obtained agreement that management "shall continue to make proper provisions" for health and safety. Since such clauses are subject to arbitral determination as to what constitutes "proper provision," they are more than innocuous expressions. In some cases there has also been agreement on some specific phase of the health and safety program, such as the furnishing of protective clothing or safety equipment.

PROCUREMENT.

The unions have shown little interest in this category. Their only effort has been directed against the hiring of outside contractors where the effect would be to reduce employment opportunities for their own members. Agreements to prevent such a result have been reached in the automobile, rubber, and public-utilities fields. The Steelworkers have so far unsuccessfully sought to secure the acceptance of this principle.

PRODUCTION.

With respect to *machinery and equipment,* none of the unions here discussed has any official policy of opposition to technological improvements. They uniformly insist, however, that such changes in technology shall not operate as threats to job or wage security. In isolated instances, organized groups without official sanction may seek to forestall the use of new machinery by refusing to work it or demanding wage rates too high to make installation profitable. The impact of the union in this area, therefore, operates officially and even unofficially primarily through decisions in other fields, such as wages and layoff policies. Its influence is felt not in decisions as to whether new technological processes shall be installed or old ones modified, but in decisions governing the circumstances of installation or modification.

The system of job classifications has in some ways eliminated questions as to *job content* and in other respects has raised new questions. As long as duties required fall within the description of the classification covering the worker, there has been only infrequent and spasmodic resistance by employes, individually or in groups, to work assignments which they may not normally perform. There has been increasing opposition, however, to the performance of duties outside the employe's regular classification unless he is paid the higher of the two rates involved, on temporary work, or is reclassified to a higher position, where the assignment is permanent. Such objections have usually been sustained in arbitration at the terminal step of the grievance procedure.

In all industries unions have succeeded in affecting the job content of foremen and first-line supervisors by agreements forbidding their engaging in production operations except in specified situations.

Rates of operation have been affected by the union primarily in two ways: through official protests of production standards and unofficial attempts to limit production. In all industries management retains the right to set work standards or production quotas, which, however, are generally subject to union challenge through the grievance procedure as being excessive or as failing to satisfy the requirement, established in a number of companies, that earnings shall not suffer as a result of changes of standards. The effect of such a challenge may be a retiming of the operation. In some instances an arbiter has resorted to an independent engineering firm to obtain an impartial expert report.

Management is deeply concerned over its inability to secure what it considers a fair day's work from its employes. In the steel industry a positive program to obtain joint agreement on what constitutes a fair day's work on any operation is being undertaken. In the automobile, rubber, and meat-packing industries the unions offer as an answer to management's problem a proposal for joint initial determination of the rates of operation, claiming that workers will live up to standards which their representatives have participated in setting.

DISTRIBUTION.

In the automobile, steel, and meat-packing industries union leaders have expressed deep interest in regularizing the flow of products to the market, eliminating seasonal peaks where practical. They have likewise shown concern with the total volume of marketable products of their industries in terms of sustaining regular employment of attached workers. There has been little attempt to convert such an interest into a positive program presented to management for adoption, however.

In one important way have unions affected the quantities and flow of output. Strike action inevitably results in at least a temporary falling off of distribution of the product—from producer to wholesaler if not to retailer and the public. In some instances a permanent decrease may occur, as in those instances when coal users have converted their heating and power plants to oil burners because of prolonged and repeated stoppages in the supply of coal, or when a potential buyer of a General Motors automobile, in the event of protracted shutdown of its plants, turns to one of the other producers for his purchase.

COORDINATE ACTIVITIES.

The foreman has become a focal point in issues revolving around the *organizational structure* of the company. Managements are seeking to find the answer to at least three questions in which he is vitally concerned. One has been raised as a result of the unionization of foremen. In some industries, such as meat packing and power and light, this membership drive has been undertaken by the same union that represents the production and maintenance workers. In other industries, such as automobiles, steel, and rubber, an independent union has sought to enroll the supervisory employes. This distinction has not seemed especially significant to some managers, who believe that a strong community of interest will be established between any foreman's union and the production union. The result, they fear, will be a shifting of the foreman's loyalty from the company to his union and its program, including collaboration with the organization of rank-and-file workers. Under these circumstances, they believe, discipline will not be adequately enforced in the shop, the collective agreement will be read by him in favor of the employes, and his function as management representative in the first stage of the grievance procedure will become meaningless.

A second problem which management sees in this area is not premised on the spread of unionism among supervisory employes. Even in the absence of foremen's unions, company officials believe that the production unions have become so powerful that they may successfully contest a foreman's authority in the shop. If he exercises the power of his position, he may confront a walkout or threat of walkout, noncooperation, or slowdown. The result in some cases has been outright intimidation of supervisors and the usurpation of authority by shop stewards. Warnings of discipline are only met with threats of strike. Management officials have tended to regard this situation as a breakdown of the organizational structure.

A third problem relates not to the responsibility or authority of supervisory employes, but to their integration into the promotional sequence. In some companies workers promoted out of the bargaining unit lose their accumulated seniority and if demoted or laid off therefore lose its customary protection. Where promotion to the rank of foreman may thus mean promotion into insecurity, management has sometimes had difficulties in finding suitable candidates for supervisory roles. The status of foreman has thus lost some of its luster.

These three considerations have made "the foreman question" important. Since first-line supervisors are the meeting place of management and men, responsible for effective execution of managerial directive or administrative orders in important areas, the manner in which are solved the problems raised by the union impact on the foreman will have a profound effect upon the organizational structure of the large corporation.

Aside from the strategic importance of their relation with the foreman, the unions have left their mark upon corporate structure in another significant way. They have been instrumental in securing the establishment of the office of impartial chairman, board of arbitration, or umpire, empowered to decide all disputes relating to the interpretation or application of the collective agreement. The founding of this branch of management whose sole function is to test executive compliance with administrative decisions, or administrative compliance with directive determinations, constitutes an innovation in management methods. In such industries as automobiles and steel and meat packing, the provision of a permanent office of arbitration has made possible the resolution of difficulties which might otherwise have erupted as work stoppages or lockout. It becomes less feasible for either management or union to take an unmovable stand upon their interpretation of what the agreement means, as this new branch of management has been designated for that interpretive purpose, empowered to override decisions of management or positions of the union.

While the unions referred to in these pages, or their leaders, have been occasionally interested in such areas of management as *line of products* (as in automobiles), *location of plants* (as in rubber), and *research and development* (as in meat packing), there have been no planned programs to share authority in these areas. The unions have made proposals but have not supported them with bargaining strength. They have withdrawn when rebuffed by management. At the same time there is no indication that such reception has resulted in their losing interest in these fields, or in renouncing future action when deemed desirable for the protection or advancement of their members.

The United Automobile Workers has been the most aggressive of the unions in these industries in attempting to share in the determination of *pricing policy*. At the same time there is reason for believing that a more sustained interest has been shown by some unions in the public utility field, whose pressure is brought not upon management directly but upon the governmental agency or commission charged with the setting of rates.

Determination of the procedures of *collective bargaining* has almost of necessity been a joint affair. Little attention has been paid to the process of arriving at agreement on the contract terms, the only requirements customarily being notification by one party to the other of an intent to raise issues, and joint meeting, both within a specified number of days before the expiration of an existing contract. The grievance procedure, designed to resolve disputes as to the interpretation and application of the agreement, has been more detailed. It permits the worker or the union as his representative to protest managerial actions considered violative of the contract in a series of steps, beginning with the foreman and ending with the arbitrator. As Professor Shulman of Yale University, fulfilling the latter function in The Ford Motor Company, declared in a decision:

In any industrial plant, whatever may be the form of the political or economic organization in which it exists, problems are bound to arise as to the method of making promotions, the assignment of tasks to individuals, the choice of shifts, the maintenance of discipline, the rates of production and remuneration, and the various other matters which are handled through the grievance procedure. . . . Such disputes are not necessarily evils. They are the normal characteristics of human society which both arise from, and create the occasion for, the exercise of human intelligence. And the grievance procedure is the orderly, effective and democratic way of adjusting disputes within the framework of the collective labor agreement. It is the substitute of civilized collective bargaining for jungle warfare.

The definition of this grievance process, including the highly important office of arbitrator, has itself been a collective-bargaining matter. The union has participated in establishing the industrial government of which it is a part.

It is appropriate to note at this juncture, though briefly, one of the most significant ways in which unions have shared authority with the legal management. Little has been revealed in the industry analyses which indicates that the unions seek to influence management's *choice of key officials*. There have, indeed, been occasional instances when pressure groups of the shop, sometimes with the sanction of lesser union officials, have sought to exercise a veto power over the appointment of minor supervisory officials—a foreman who has incurred the enmity of the shop force, even a department superintendent indisposed to "cooperation" with the union. The infrequency of such occurrences testifies to their relative unimportance, however.

Of really first-line significance, on the other hand, is a more direct method by which unions influence the choice of key officials. If the line of analysis adopted in this study is accepted, then union officials must themselves be considered as an important branch of management, defined in functional terms. We are not now talking of the desirability of their exercising the managerial function, but of the fact of their exercising it. We are not discussing their competence but only their role. We are not speaking of the legal criteria as to who constitute management, but of functional standards by which the managers may be identified. The fact that union officials do share with legal management authority in some of the key areas of business operation is itself indication that they constitute an element of the managerial hierarchy, unless we choose to ignore the plain results of their actions. It is of course true, as has already been stressed, that their responsibility runs to their membership rather than to the owners of the business. This distinction, however, is only to state the heart of the labor-management problem. It does not destroy the fact that union officials now participate in determining the nature of business operations, sharing in the making of directive and administrative decisions, and in compelling executive compliance with those decisions. Legal corporate management has nothing to say as to the choice of the union leaders selected for this purpose. Indeed, they are barred by law from influencing the actions of the rank and file of workers in their choice of leadership. We may thus say that while unions, by and large, have not shared in legal management's choice of key officials, they have shared in the process of electing key officials whose actions are part and parcel of the operations of the enterprise. In this area of management, legal management and the unions act unilaterally; the result of their unilateral action, however, is a form of joint management in the areas where authority is shared. In a sense, recognition of this fact provides a summation of the discussion of this chapter.

It is evident that the unions' penetration of the managerial function has been deepest and widest within the category of personnel practices. There is not an area of that group of business decisions in which they have not shared some control: type of personnel, size of force, hiring, layoffs, allocation, discipline, wages and hours, employe advancement policies, promotions, and health and safety. And there are numerous areas in this category where the authority which they share runs deep: discipline, wages and hours in particular, but likewise layoffs, rehiring, allocation, and promotion, where they have secured acceptance of the seniority principle.

Next to personnel, the category of production has been most affected by the union program. In particular, labor participation in business decisions has been felt within the areas of job content and rates of operation. The increasing interest in the effects of technological changes is more and more focusing union attention on types of machinery and equipment and methods of production. A union-management cooperation program such as that sponsored by the Steelworkers emphasizes these same areas from the viewpoint of efficiency, so that greater gains may be shared by workers, management, and owners. It may prove to be a safe guess that the next category of managerial authority in which the unions will seek to deepen and widen their participation will be this category of production.

It is not especially significant that in some instances agreements touching one of the areas of management may only embody prior managerial practice. For by the very process of subjecting to joint agreement matters which had previously been solely determined by legal management, the fact of union interest is established. A change of decision or practice then becomes possible only through further joint agreement. The spread of union power within the corporation proceeds by a sharing of authority which in innumerable cases originally takes only the form of a contractual acceptance of existing company practices.

A conscious effort has been made in this chapter not to build up a "case" showing union participation in an area of management where none exists or where the union role is tenuous. Similarly, union "interest" in an area of management where it has not actually sought a voice has been mentioned only where that interest has appeared significant. The importance of union participation in managerial functions is demonstrable without a stretching of facts or use of the imagination.

Above all it must be stressed that no value judgment is intended by the present examination. We have sought for the present only to determine the extent of union penetration and interest, not its rationale nor its merits. Some may find in such a factual presentation grounds for wonder that the union has not sought a voice in certain areas where its interests and the welfare of its members are evidently involved. Others may find cause for concern at the dilution of the authority of legal corporate management. These matters we shall examine later. They are not at issue now.

In a previous chapter we have examined the directive, administrative, and executive functions as they are found in corporate practice. In the present chapter we have inquired into the extent to which unions have sought a voice in those processes. The problems engendered by the apparent inconsistencies between, on the one hand, corporate decision-making and decision-effectuation procedures as we have become accustomed to think of them, and the shared authority of collective bargaining, on the other hand, require more careful statement and analysis.

Before turning to those problems, however, it will be helpful to consider more fully the nature of unions, which constitute the challengers of present management practice. What are the purposes and the compulsions behind their drive to secure an expanding role in managerial decisions? By what techniques have they implemented their purposes? What is the role of the union personnel—membership and leaders? What resources and facilities are available to them, that enable them to perform the managerial functions they have acquired and which they seek? These are the questions to which we shall next direct our attention.

The Union in Management

THE PURPOSES OF UNION PENETRATION

"We have no plan. Unions work from particulars to generals. We are empiricists without knowing it. It is simply a matter of meeting problems as they arise."

In these words a union official summarizes his views as to what leads a union to seek an expanding role in the management of a business. A handful of management people agree with his diagnosis. The union, they say, is moved by expediency. Its demands are governed by what it conceives to be its needs of the moment. There is no broader plan or purpose.

There is an element of truth in this view, but it is inadequate as an explanation of motivation. It is important to understand the factors which lead a union to appraise a situation as requiring its corrective action. On what basis does it assess its needs of the moment? What is the nature of the particular problems from which it works to general solutions? In what situations does it feel the compulsions to challenge the remaining structure of managerial "prerogatives" rather than seek satisfaction through the areas of joint interest already established? What goals does it strive to reach by a spread of its power within the corporation?

Virtual unanimity of opinion exists among the union leaders that any managerial decisions or authority threatening the security of the workers must be regulated. They interpret security in a broad sense as anything affecting the material well-being of the membership.

This position of the union officials merits emphasis. The stress laid upon it in all types of unions in all industries stamps it as constituting their primary rationale. It involves more than wages. We will do well to consider their own words, as given in the following quotations, each from a different union leader.[1]

---

[1] In the chapters which follow we shall call rather extensively upon both union and management representatives for their expressions of opinion. Unless otherwise indicated, such opinions have been given in personal interviews or private correspondence in connection with this investigation. Again unless otherwise noted, such opinions were expressed in confidence and the personal source cannot be identified.

A drive for security lies behind the union's interest in management matters. It brings along with it a democratization of industry, true, but this is not an independent drive. Any leader who speaks of democracy in industry as a drive is indulging in intellectualization which the worker thinks little of in such terms, though he may think of it in terms of his having greater protection, greater voice in the decisions that affect him—*not for the sake of participating but for what participation can do for him.* The end result of the drive for security *may* be a form of socialism, but if so it will be reached on its own merits and not as the objective of a program. As such it can be discussed on its own merits. Is there anything so radically wrong with worker participation in management that it must be avoided because it challenges a prevailing system?

The union doesn't want to run the business. It doesn't want to take over management. At the same time, while we don't attempt to usurp management's prerogatives, we do attempt to mitigate them so that their exercise cannot endanger the security and well-being of the workers.

The union doesn't want the responsibility of management but sometimes it has to assume it because a management doesn't do its job. As a general proposition, the union won't seek to move in on a management "right" unless management has lost that "right" by default. Some abuse of its power will necessitate the union's doing something just to protect the workers. It's simply taking up a grievance on a larger scale. The union's outlook is one of correcting abuses of authority, and it will generally wait until after the abuse, then moving in reluctantly, rather than take a preventive step of moving in to forestall the misuse of managerial power.

The worker has a bigger stake in certain management policies than anyone else— stockholder, consumer, or management. Take the problem of seasonal fluctuations in production. Management says this is a matter of scheduling, and therefore its sole prerogative. But to the worker it is his livelihood. Who has more of an interest than the worker in the decisions reached in scheduling production if seasonal layoffs are involved? The same is true of many other issues where the management has denied the union an interest.

If the unions are *planning* a drive to secure a greater voice in management, I haven't heard of it. Of course, it may work out that our program will lead into socialism, as they worry about, but it won't be because we planned it that way. The basic motivation is security. As long as management's decisions don't adversely affect the security of the workers or their union, we are glad to let the management run the business—we don't want any part of that responsibility. But when management's decisions affect the workers' security, the union will be right in there fighting.

This quest for security can be broken down into several components. To paint in only the most important issues involved in a complex subject, let us consider only three of the factors making up the security which workers are seeking through their unions and which unions are seeking through a greater sharing of managerial authority. First, let us examine the wage issue.

The union starts with the premise that economic security demands steady employment providing an adequate income. Its conception of what is adequate is subject to upward adjustment. Security is not defined as subsistence. It involves progressive improvement of the workers' economic status.

Moreover, union leaders, particularly of the younger school, have advanced in economic sophistication. They are aware that the wages of the workers are in a real sense limited by a company's financial competency. "The profits a company makes should be of the greatest interest to every employe. The workers must understand the company's finances if their demands for increased wages are to be supported by facts and figures that prove the company's 'ability to pay.' "[2] At least in important wage conferences, it is the older, one might almost say obsolete, type of union negotiator who must argue, as one did in a 1940 conference with a small company in the fur and leather industry: "Maybe you have lost there, but I am certainly taking the position that it is not because of the high-priced labor. It may be poor salesmen or poor management or something, if they are losing that much, because it is not on account of your labor cost, it doesn't seem to me." Union leaders increasingly are not satisfied with a *belief* that it must be "poor management or something" which makes for a poor profit showing. They want to *know*.

To satisfy this demand for knowledge unions have established and expanded research agencies of their own. They have become more facile in the use of information gathered by governmental and private agencies. But more has been needed. They have sought to require managements to justify, by informative analysis, their inability to sustain or increase wages. Listen to a union official speaking at the 1938 wage conference of the American Flint Glass Workers Union and the National Association of Manufacturers of Pressed and Blown Glassware:

Another matter that we wish to bring to the attention of the manufacturers at this time is that of management and management's responsibility for lack of business and lack of employment in some factories. If we submit to wage reductions, before doing so, we are going to insist upon knowing more about the affairs of management, profits, and the background of some companies.

The Flint Glass Industry is a small industry and we appreciate that we cannot take out of the industry more than it can afford to pay, so we have very largely a mutual proposition, and as such, the representatives of the workers should know more about the business and the manner in which it is being taken care of insofar as some of the companies are concerned.

And later in the same conference ensued the following colloquy:

Union official: We asked for facts and the manufacturers asked for facts. Some manufacturers gave us facts and others did not. What were your earnings, payroll or profits for the first six months?

[2] United Electrical, Radio and Machine Workers Handbook, *How Corporations Conceal Profits,* p. 8.

Company official: We just about broke even. I don't think it is your business as to what our profits are. I believe you are all wrong.

Union official: We are not wrong; the industry is small and we feel we should know something about your profits. We know you can't take more out of the industry than there is in it. You ask that wages be reduced and we want to know why.

Your company has done very well in the years you have been in business. We are not willing to accept idle statements as a basis for legislation on wages. We insist on knowing about your business before we reduce wages and thereby enrich the employers. . .[3]

At times business officials have encouraged this union interest in the total picture of corporate operations. Thus in the 1946 negotiations the president of the General Electric Company advised the unions to take into account, in formulating their demands, such factors as "material costs, labor costs, manufacturing facilities, price controls, supply and demand, selling costs, and the one inevitable and inexorable fact that we first have to produce and sell our goods before we can collect our price from the customer."[4] At the same time, such management people hesitate to proceed to the conclusion many union leaders are now reaching, that if these factors so vitally affect the wage potential they may at times become bargainable issues in themselves.

The unions' increased knowledge of corporate operations and their recognition of the impact of managerial decisions in many areas upon the company's wage-paying ability have thus inspired some unions to seek economic security in the broad sense by seeking a voice in vital corporate decisions. The 1941 collective agreement in the ladies' garment industry in New York City, a field of little businesses, embodied this new approach by giving the union a collaborative role in improving the efficiency of the industry—even to the extent of testing the efficiency of its employers. The motive was a desire to recoup wage losses suffered during the depression. Said the initiating union official, "A demand for increased wages of 14 per cent, backed up by a strike threat, might have done it. But there was a strong possibility that the result would have been a further loss of business and therefore no gain in the total pay roll."[5] Similarly, among those large industrial unions which now are pressing for a guaranteed annual wage there is the attitude that if a company finds itself unable to make good on its guarantee to the covered employes, the union will discuss possible retrenchment, but only after it has been accorded an opportunity to appraise the necessity of such action by a thorough examination of managerial policies and practices.

[3] American Flint Glass Workers Union, *Conference Circular* No. 286, Toledo, August 30, 1938, pp. 5282 and 5317.

[4] *New York Times*, January 20, 1946.

[5] Julius Hochman, "Dressmakers' Union Promotes Industry Planning," *Labor Information Bulletin* (U. S. Department of Labor), May, 1941, p. 2.

In the light of the above considerations, there is more content than meets the eye in the statement of the president of one powerful railroad brotherhood that "It is only when management policies have a material effect upon the welfare of the workers we represent that we propose to have a voice." The significance of this statement lies in the fact that the management policies referred to may arise in any of the areas of business, whether or not traditionally reserved to management discretion. This is not a tortured construction of the attitude of a number of strong unions, as many a management official can testify. It is explicitly set forth in the written statement submitted by a representative of a large and strategic union: "The union does not envision any desire to share the managerial role as business agent. This means that the union is not concerned with the strictly 'business procedures,' such as budgeting, raising the necessary capital, capital structure, dividends, reserves, types of machinery and equipment, advertising or credit policies, etc. It should be noted, however, that should *any* policies of the company adversely affect the wages and working conditions of its membership, the union would have to challenge management's unilateral authority over the problem."

The union's quest for security for its members may thus lead it to challenge managerial authority on matters affecting the company's wage-paying ability. The same quest may likewise lead it to challenge managerial authority on other fronts. With the wage issue as the first constituent of economic security, let us now examine the second component with which we shall here deal. We may label this a drive for the rationalization of personnel policies.

The economic security of an employe is bound up not only in the wage level of his company but also in management's personnel actions—in its selection of employes for layoff, rehiring, and promotion, in the assignment of employes to jobs, in their transfer, in the disciplining of employes. If decisions of this order are the result of subjective evaluations or capriciousness, there is no security. If such decisions are, however, governed by stated rules which are enforceable by the employe or his representative, there is a relatively larger measure of security. It is this rationalization of personnel policies which the unions have sought in increasing measure—witness the intensity and extent of their penetration of the areas of management in the personnel category, as discussed in the previous chapter.

It is difficult to overstate the importance attached by the workers to union controls of this nature. The feeling of independence, the relief from insecurity attendant upon the rationalization of personnel policies can be appreciated only when contrasted with the feeling of subservience and the despised need for bootlicking of previous days. Nowhere is this truer than in the large corporation. It is exampled in the report by an independent source of the situation existing in U. S. Steel in 1936, prior to the impact of the United Steelworkers.

Although U. S. Steel established central employment offices in 1919, control of jobs, the rotation of work, was left in the hands of foremen. In stable periods this power is relatively unimportant. In a depression-ridden steel town, where getting a day's work has been as prized as finding a nugget, it increased in importance a thousandfold. . . . The power to assign work in such a situation means the difference between living or being destitute to the man who receives it, and the reminiscences of steelworkers are filled with stories of money lent to foremen after a better-than-usual pay, and never repaid or expected, of minor officials who have small business interests that men patronize in the hope of getting more work.[6]

To eliminate such favoritism and willfulness, the unions have sought and obtained a sharing of authority in the areas of concern. The seniority principle is its answer to situations such as that described above. To charges that seniority gives no heed to a man's ability or even his need, a union man will reply that at least it is objective. He knows where he stands. There is a rule, and a union to enforce it on his behalf. Likewise in cases of discipline, there are principles on which he can rely, before an impartial judge if he so desires, to secure an even application of industrial justice. As much as any wage, this means security.

A third element of the worker's search for security involves an attempt to enlarge the area of control over his own affairs. So long as the decisions which affect his opportunities for continued gainful employment and satisfaction within the company remain in the hands of officials who are not responsible to him, he believes there is no real security. He may successfully pressure for higher wages. He may achieve a satisfactory rationalization of personnel policies. But if the vital decisions as to the scale and schedule of production, the introduction of labor-saving devices which may sever him from a chance to use his skill, the closing or relocation of plants remain outside his effective influence, there is no real security for him. He experiences a cold reaction to such statements from management representatives as: "It is axiomatic, of course, that the ultimate success of any given employee comes only through the success of the company."[7] He wants to know what the chances are for his success *within* the company: will new machinery reduce him from a skilled operative to a member of the custodial force? He wants to know what are his chances for continued attachment *to* the company: what means "the success of the

[6] From "The U. S. Steel Corporation: III," *Fortune*, May, 1936, p. 141.
[7] *The Open Door*, a message from [President] I. L. Perry to the employes of Carnegie-Illinois Steel Corporation [undated], p. 6.

company" to him if in transferring its operations from New Bedford to Charlotte he is severed from the payroll?

This rationale of the union's drive is implicit in a union official's reminder to members of the American Management Association that cost reduction, method improvements, cost-saving equipment, and technological change are inseparably associated in the mind of the worker with mass unemployment, wage reduction, thousands of employes placed on unemployment rolls, and working himself out of a job.[8] These are actions which may guarantee the success of the company. They contain no similar guarantee to the individual worker.

Without any form of control over the men whose decisions spell out his future, the worker feels at the mercy of the benevolence—or the lack of it—of the managers of the business. "Boards of Directors sitting in the financial centers of the nation pass economic legislation, based exclusively on their profit and loss statements. In one decision they wipe out a complete mill and ruin an entire town, and they do it apparently without any thought of responsibility for the social consequences of their decision."[9] If the necessity for such decisions is tied to the capitalistic system and the inescapable imperatives of business competition, it is small wonder that private enterprise has sometimes been the butt of the worker's attack. Bosses without control, whether in business or government, are synonymous with autocracy. His is not an attack on authority, but on uncontrolled authority. The intervention of his union in the decisions of management is one method by which he seeks to secure some measure of control over his own affairs.

The security which we have been discussing this far as motivating a union's desire to gain a more important voice in corporate operations is security within the firm. It is related to the wage-paying ability of a particular firm, to the personnel policies of that same firm, and to the responsibility of authority within the firm. Under the impact of the Great Depression and the postwar reconversion period, unions have begun to turn their eyes outward from the company. They have come to appreciate that security cannot always be guaranteed even by the most favorably disposed management. There are factors operating throughout the economy to which the individual company must adjust itself. In the same manner in which some unions have felt the necessity of sharing the managerial function because of its significance to the workers' security, so too have some unions felt that these general economic conditions must be controlled in the interest of their members. This presents a problem of

[8] *New York Times*, October 30, 1945.
[9] Philip Murray, *Technological Unemployment* (Steelworkers Handbook, undated), p. 13.

greater magnitude. It points to the maintenance of a full employment economy as the essential without which economic security cannot be guaranteed in the firm. The goal has been succinctly stated by the report of the American Federation of Labor Committee on Post-War Planning:

> We want a regime of economic freedom, but our enterprise system must demonstrate that it can function so as to husband and utilize, not to waste and dissipate our natural resources. We want free enterprise, but our productive system must be committed to the progressive raising of the national income and the maintenance of full employment. Such a system is necessarily opposed to all tendencies toward monopolistic restriction. We want free enterprise, but we also want an economy which will provide ample support for the health, educational, recreational and similar public services so essential to the welfare of the working people in our industrial society. Finally, we want a program of economic enterprise which will not be repressive but will support the free exercise of civil and political liberties.[10]

To attain this goal, both the AFL and the CIO have advocated a more adequate means by which labor, farm groups, and management can be directly represented "in the formulation, administration, and the evaluation of over-all economic policies."[11] The CIO has proposed the formation of industry councils on which labor, management, and the government shall be represented, responsible for the direction of the industries in which they are formed. "No one knows to what extent a democracy can plan its future in advance. But it must at least make the effort. The CIO has a special responsibility because it is one of the largest organizations in the nation. We speak for a great group of citizens who will suffer most if powerful selfish interests pursue an uncontrolled course. We must make labor's voice heard in the councils of government and industry."[12]

The important fact is that unions are realizing that security cannot be achieved only in the firm but must also be realized through the national economy. They are fitting their negotiations, at least in the large bellwether corporations, into a scheme for national economic security. They may not be sure just what their own company's role should be—neither is management—but they are increasingly sure that the operations of the company must be keyed in some way to a national plan. The most forceful example of this attitude and belief has been offered in the 1945–1946 General Motors negotiations. In those negotiations the Automobile Workers embarked on an educational program to accompany the bargaining sessions, a program directed to their own members and to the public.

They suggested that the nation faced two economic alternatives, which they pictured[13] as:

[10] American Federation of Labor, *Postwar Forum* (1944), p. 4.
[11] AFL, *Postwar Forum*, p. 4.
[12] CIO, *As We Win* (1944), pp. 30–31.

LOW GEAR PRODUCTION—	HIGH GEAR PRODUCTION—
Sells at high prices Pays low wages Yields a high profit per unit on a few units	Sells at low prices Pays high wages Yields a small profit per unit on many units
Results: LOW STANDARD OF LIVING AND UNEMPLOYMENT.	Results: HIGH STANDARD OF LIVING AND FULL EMPLOYMENT.

In the hearings before the presidential fact-finding board, the union spokesman in justifying the demand for greater wage increases made clear that once the union had adopted the approach of "high gear production" it was committed to support not only high wages but also low prices and expanded production, the other two elements of its program. "We have said that wages and prices and ability to pay must have a relationship if we are to achieve a full production, full employment, full consumption economy. We have said that this is more than an ordinary wage argument, that it does transcend the narrow economic interests of the two parties because it gets to the heart of winning the peace."[14]

This union concern for security in the national economy has developed in at least some union leaders a keener consciousness of the effect of managerial decisions in the firm on the broader economic program which they have in mind. In the belief that in some manner the decisions of the firm must be harnessed to society's economic goals, if security is to be attained, lies a further reason why unions have sometimes felt the need for seeking a greater voice in areas of management from which they have been barred in the past.

If security is the first of the objectives sought by unions in intervening in the management of a business, it is not the only end in view. Accompanying it is a striving for recognition and self-expression. Sometimes this is stated as a desire for democracy in industry. In the words of one union official: "Workers want something more than the assurance of a full belly. Even if security is assured, they don't want to be pushed around. They

[13] Reproduced from Walter P. Reuther, *How to Raise Wages Without Increasing Prices* (UAW, undated), p. 20.

[14] *New York Times*, December 29, 1945. There is a difference in opinion in management circles as to the sincerity with which the union prosecuted this program. Some incline to the belief that it constituted only a clever maneuver to enlist public support. Others believe that at least some of the union leaders were genuinely concerned with the issues they raised. In linking ability to pay higher wages without increasing prices, the union, they feel, was attempting to place itself in a position where it could challenge management on a host of matters now considered managerial prerogatives whenever the corporation might plead inability to sustain or increase wages and employment.

want participation as well. If democracy means anything, it must come in industry to give any meaning to democracy in the political sphere. I wouldn't be here if I didn't think there was more to unionism than just bread and butter."

This desire of the worker for recognition as an individual in his own right, and for an opportunity to contribute constructively, has been set forth by one union in a manner which indicates the cause for some of its present resentment at the treatment of its members:

Underlying its aspirations for full participation in the job of production, is labor's basic position of equality. This is more than equality at the bargaining table. It is an intellectual equality. This contemplates abandoning the illusion, all too prevalent in industrial circles, that the human beings on management's side are possessed of greater intellectual faculties than are those among the working force. The idea that workers are intellectually inferior to management is the source of many of our difficulties. Years ago we used to believe that a woman was intellectually inferior to a man. Today we have admitted that we were wrong. The intellectual equality of management and labor is a prerequisite to the development of industrial relations along constructive lines.

Specifically, if management, instead of generously awarding to labor the possession of all the brawn while appropriating to itself the possession of all the brains, would come around to the point of conceding that labor possessed something besides strong backs, it would then be possible, by joint endeavor, for management and labor to reach a pinnacle of productive achievement never previously attained.[15]

Behind this aspiration for recognition and self-expression through participation lies, in part, a sense of frustrated power. Managers would be the last to deny that unions in America today have achieved a high order of economic power. In the postwar reconversion period, when strikes were epidemic, the critical cry was raised on many fronts that unions now wielded the authority to say whether coal should be mined, whether trains should run, whether automobiles could be manufactured, whether steel should be produced, whether a city should be granted the use of electrical power. Speaking before a meeting of the New York State Bar Association, the President of the United Hatters, Cap and Millinery Workers pointed to this accretion of power by the unions.

Fundamentally, nothing seems to have changed. The Constitution is virtually the same today as it was 150 years ago. The basic law is substantially the same. The courts and the legislatures continue to function under the same system which prevailed then.

What has changed, and is changing steadily, is the balance of strength and influence formerly in the possession of one and now in the possession of another economic grouping in our society. This process has been going on for some time but never was it more perceptible than during the past 10 or 12 years.[16]

This accumulated power, however, the unions have as yet been able to

15 Steel Workers Organizing Committee, *Organized Labor and Management*, pp. 13–14.
16 *The Hat Worker* July 15, 1946.

employ only defensively, in a real sense negatively. They can make demands upon others, but they cannot initiate. They may play a critic's role, but not the actor's. Behind their search for increased authority in the business sphere lies the realization that their great growth of power has not fully been recognized, for it is given no constructive role. It provides as yet an imperfect means of self-expression, for it is held in reserve to be exercised only when challenged or challenging. There is no continuous, affirmative, assigned, and recognized function which their organization may fulfill. A voice in the direction of business provides that function. It provides ground for recognition and opportunity for self-expression.

Occasional writers, among them some sympathetic to unions, have at times maintained that "the will of the worker to express himself has been somewhat overemphasized."[17] This may well be the case, but it would be incorrect to conclude that the desire for self-expression, accompanied by recognition, is not a real one. Every worker may not aspire to be recognized as a creative genius, and there may be many who have little aspiration at all for themselves. It would still be incorrect, however, to ignore the basic drive, which may be achieved not only by individual effort but by identification of one's self with an organization satisfying the desire. Recognition and a creative role for his union means, at least in part, recognition and a feeling of having his self expressed on the part of the individual worker. The boldness, daring, and tactical success of John L. Lewis bring a good deal of personal satisfaction to thousands of miners.

It remains to be seen whether the often-encountered statement of union leaders that they want no authority in the corporation providing the decisions and actions of management constitute no threat to the security of their members will square with this desire for recognition and a creative role. It may be that the development of powerful organizations, led by strong-minded individuals, supported by cohesive and numerous constituencies, will lead them of necessity into a more active seeking of business authority.

If we can accept, then, that the union is seeking, for itself and its members, security, recognition, and self-expression, we face an important conclusion. The union leaders and the union members, each in their own way, are seeking these goals *through the corporation*. It is not correct to view the union itself as the arena in which they hope to win their objectives. The union is an instrument, a tool, offering satisfactions of its own, it is true, but created for the basic purpose of influencing business decisions. It is not a social club, though it offers social pleasures. It is not a professional society, though its membership may have common occupational

---

[17] William Gomberg, "Union Interest in Engineering Techniques," *Harvard Business Review*, vol. 24 (Spring, 1946), p. 365.

interests. It is not an educational organization, though it may sponsor training programs. It is essentially an economic organ, meaningless without the business or industry in which it must function. Local 600 of the United Automobile Workers has no functional significance in the absence of the Ford Motor Company. If atomic power should replace coal, the United Mine Workers would cease to have organizational meaning. If the Firestone Tire and Rubber Company were to pass from corporate existence, Local 7 of the United Rubber Workers would pass with it.

As we have already seen, management too seeks its goals through the corporation. With the corporation as the single medium through which both management and the union strive to obtain security, recognition, and self-expression for themselves, there is opportunity for conflict. The contest between management and union for authority in the corporation is in part a contest for the satisfaction of one's personal goals at the expense of the other's. We may expect that the contest will continue until or unless both management and union reach an understanding which permits them to achieve their goals jointly.

DETERMINANTS OF UNION PENETRATION

We have discussed the purposes for which unions have sought to widen and deepen their authority within the corporation. We may now ask what are the organizational compulsions which have driven them in this direction? Is there a causation implicit in the very structure of unions which, apart from the goals sought, moves them to challenge managerial authority? If we view the objectives of the unions—security for themselves and their members, recognition, and self-expression—as exerting a pull upon the unions to seek an expansion of authority, is there anything in their make-up which provides a push? We shall here distinguish two such compulsions: a drive for organizational power, or the external politics of their situation, and a contest for power within the organization, or the internal politics of their situation.

A penetrating analysis of the will to power on the part of the unions comes from a man who has himself been associated with the union movement for more than 45 years. Writing in 1928, before the spectacular union advances accompanying the New Deal administrations, J.B.S. Hardman, then editor of the official organ of the Amalgamated Clothing Workers of America, observed that "in a social order in which groups and classes contend for power, trade unions cannot lead a vigorous, growing life unless they are powerful."

Generally and objectively speaking, *trade unionism is a sustained, systematic effort at power accumulation,* and this function of trade unionism is also its driving force. For power accumulated by an organized group or class of society cannot remain inactive, static. It must be put to certain uses as a result of which it spends itself and simultaneously generates new, greater power. The possession of power by a class or organized group compels action in the interest of further expansion, or doom is the inevitable alternative. Trade unions which possess no power do not have to decide not to lead a vigorous, expanding life. They could not do so if they would. Trade unions which possess power can not conveniently rest on their laurels. They are obliged to set out for greater stakes and cannot avoid transgressing the bounds of their immediate objectives.[18]

The union, says Hardman, is "openly and deliberately" erected on a class or group basis. Its power is class or group power. Class or group power is contentious and challenging, for power of this nature must necessarily grow at the expense of other social groups or classes. Class power is always a relative matter—it cannot *grow with* the power of other groups or classes, for its relative position would then remain static. "Thus driven by the logic of its own development, trade unionism proceeds from the prosecution of its immediate objectives to positions from which it menaces, if it does not directly attack, the balance of social power which is the foundation of the present social order." It is evident, then, that "it is not the subjective will of leaders but the objective logic of the situation which drives unions to contend for power and, under given conditions, to upset the social concert."[19]

Hardman recognized that in 1928 the "power attitude" had not been taken by most unions, but to the extent that this was the case it marked a division between unions with greater effectiveness and those with no effectiveness at all. The advance of unionism lay with those unions which capitalized upon their power to increase their power. Writing in 1946 Hardman thought he discerned a "trend" among unions to move away from the traditional dichotomy of union *versus* company toward an industry-minded orientation in which power would be exercised for "social-engineering" *leadership.*[20] The significance of such a trend, if it does exist, lies in its incentive to the unions to employ and simultaneously increase their power by widening their authority within the corporation and the economy, rather than confine its exercise to a deepening of control solely in the areas of wages and hours.

Management officials have long recognized the existence and impor-

[18] "Union Objectives and Social Power," from *American Labor Dynamics,* J. B. S. Hardman, editor (1928), p. 104. Italics in the original. The entire chapter from which this and subsequent statements are taken will repay thoughtful reading.

[19] Hardman, *American Labor Dynamics,* pp 109, 110.

[20] Hardman, "Dear Walter—An Unmailed Letter to Walter P. Reuther." *Labor and Nation,* April–May 1946, p. 5.

tance of the union's drive to power. They have appreciated that its organizational nature requires continued importunacy,[21] that is, a constant, persistent, demanding pressure for further gains. As one analyst has observed, in a great majority of cases the workers feel they have actually been denied the right of bargaining collectively unless they have obtained concessions from the employers.[22] The president of one company, then involved in negotiations, remarked in confidence, "We won't give the closed shop this year because we have to keep something to give next year."

Some members of management have gone so far as to maintain that the union's striving for power is necessary to hold to it a membership otherwise disinterested in organization. Workers join unions, they say, solely because of the promises on which they have been fed by union organizers. They retain membership because of new or repeated promises. The union must make good on these promises, at least in part, or its membership falls away. One company vice president expressed a firm and unshakeable conviction—"I know it, I am absolutely convinced of it"— that his employes had not organized in response to any actual need for organization, to any felt necessity, but solely as a result of "promises of the moon" given by union leaders. Said the industrial relations director of another corporation, "The 'union' is in reality a handful of leaders— and I mean a handful—who have drawn the others along by promises." If the union cannot secure the moon, it must at least draw down a few stars.

As a generalization, such a viewpoint condemns itself by its incompleteness. No one who has talked or worked with the rank-and-file members can fail to be impressed by the variety of reasons for which they have joined the union.[23] At the same time, it is quite true that the giving of "promises," the promulgation of slogans, and the portrayal of long-range objectives are effective techniques of maintaining organizational interest and solidarity. Thus in an early case coming before it the National Labor Relations Board had occasion to comment, "Where groups are to be organized and moved into action it is not unusual for the leaders to promise more than can be secured or to indulge in some exaggeration."[24]

[21] This importunacy, as the analysis will indicate, involves the creation of ever new demands upon the company. The word is used with no thought of stigmatizing unionism for such action. As will be shown, this demanding nature of the unions arises from the circumstances of their position, and can probably only be replaced by a cooperative relationship which it is not solely within their power to establish.

[22] William H. Spencer, *Collective Bargaining Under Section 7 (a) of the National Industrial Recovery Act* (1935), p. 32.

[23] An extensive discussion of this point is contained in Bakke, "Why Workers Join Unions," *Personnel*, vol. 22 (1945), pp. 37–46.

[24] *Matter of Rabhor Company Inc.*, 1 NLRB 470.

One union official in private conversation frankly admitted resort to such practice. Relating his experiences in an early organizing drive, he mentioned quite matter-of-factly, "There weren't very many men who belonged to the union then. They were spread pretty thin. So I had to do some lying to get them to join. I told them that no member of the union would ever be laid off."

A union is stamped as effective to the extent it can make good on its promises. It retains its vitality only to the extent it remains effective. The necessity of survival and growth lead to the marshaling of the strength of the membership around a campaign involving both immediate and long-range objectives. When one is achieved, another must take its place. To retain its power, the union must constantly strive to increase it. Power unused means a dropping away of the membership, stagnation, and possible disintegration. Power when used builds upon itself. The external politics of their situation thus provide a compulsion to the union to extend the range and the depth of their authority within the corporation and the economy.

Along with this drive for organizational power goes a contest for power within the organization. There are ambitious members who seek office in the union by appeals to the constituency for election. Since the effectiveness of the organization is a function of its degree of control over business decisions within the corporation where its members are employes, appeals for election are often couched in terms of the ability of the candidate to secure concessions from management, and the nature of the concessions to be sought. With two or more candidates competing for office there is a political compulsion upon each to promise more to the membership than his rivals. When elected, he labors under the necessity of fulfilling campaign promises or runs the danger of subsequent defeat by a disillusioned electorate. He can make good on his promises only by making demands upon the company. Inroads upon managerial authority may therefore be sought as a result of the political structure of the union.[25]

It is not only in the election campaign itself, however, that the basis for new demands upon the company is suggested or formulated. In anticipation of future elections, in a desire to demonstrate to the membership his capacity for office, a leader may provide a continual build-up for a drive to institute or modify some company policy. This political factor is never dormant. An office-holder neglects it at his own peril. One veteran newspaper analyst has summed up the situation in the following manner: "If any top-level labor leader should agree to a status quo, no matter how

[25] Interunion rivalry for representation rights may have the same effect.

favorable to labor it might be, he instantly would be attacked by ambitious rivals in the lower ranks of his organization."[26]

Looking at the drive for organizational power and the contest for power within the organization—the "push" behind union encroachment on managerial authority—management sees nothing of the idealism which has been said to characterize the union movement. For them the bare bones of realism and the opportunism of pragmatism are at the roots of both the external and internal politics of the union situation. But looking at the goals of the union and its members—the "pull" behind which the drive is focused—there is at root an idealist, reformist urge. The union's concepts are predominantly in terms of welfare rather than efficiency. It is true, of course, that a power drive may be pursued for other ends than the idealism which gave it its initial impulse. Internal factional feuds may weaken a union in the pursuit of its goals, personal ambitions may call for the sacrifice of the good of the whole. Such occasions divide and dissipate the strength of the union.

To concentrate exclusively upon the political determinants of the union's struggle for greater power within the corporation, however, ignoring the goals, or to focus solely upon the goals of union penetration of managerial authority, ignoring the political determinants, may lead either to a serious exaggeration or an underestimation of the union's potentialities. For if the push of circumstances conflicts with the pull of goals, less will be accomplished than one would expect by observing either individually. But if the push and the pull are synchronized, if the drives to power are squarely in support of the goals pursued, each will reenforce the other. It would be well, therefore, for the managers to look beyond their realistic appraisal of the external and internal politics of the union drive. They cannot afford to ignore at least as a major hypothesis the possibility that the power of the union lies as much in its idealism. In times when thinkers in many fields are deploring the absence of a unifying moral force, it is well to remember the ethical content with which the reformist program of the union movement is surcharged. It supplies the binding force which welds a multiplicity of organizations into a movement, behind a common cause.

THE MECHANICS OF UNION PENETRATION

Given the purposes and granted the drives behind the union's effort to achieve an expanding role within the corporation, what are the processes by which it is able to effect this result? By what techniques can the union

[26] Mark Sullivan, *New York Herald Tribune,* December 16, 1945.

draw to itself a greater measure of control over the decisions which govern the business?

The primary mechanism by which unions may share managerial authority in the corporation is collective bargaining, including both contract negotiations and grievance procedures, supported by the power of the strike. Management's concern with what it considers an encroachment on its prerogatives arises in the main from demands made, and sometimes won, at the bargaining table. Most of the penetrations of managerial functions revealed in the course of this study are embodied in collective agreements reached in negotiations, or have arisen as a result of interpretations of those agreements.

Management is well aware of this revolutionary aspect of collective bargaining, as are the unions. Both, however, have at times sought to obscure it for partisan purposes: management with the hope that it might successfully assert a "proper" definition of collective bargaining which would confine it within prescribed bounds, thereby limiting its challenge to managerial power; the unions with the intent of quieting the fears of those who resist changes in the social order. Thus in the 1945–1946 General Motors negotiations company officials declared that the union was more interested in laying the groundwork for a change in the economic and social system than in collective bargaining. It is doubtful, however, if collective bargaining can be divorced from such change. At the same time the union, which assuredly was attempting to blaze a trail to new areas of authority within the corporation for purposes of supporting an evolving theory of social rights and responsibilities, replied that it was simply following collective-bargaining practices as described in standard works on the subject. Management sought to deny that collective bargaining *in theory* was a revolutionary device. The union attempted to deny that collective bargaining *in practice* was a revolutionary instrument. Both, however, were aware of its threat to existing managerial power.

Despite the unions' often-repeated assertion that "the purpose of collective bargaining is to promote industrial peace,"[27] Professor Hoxie in 1921 could write that "Collective bargaining is not an instrument of peace primarily. It is a step in the process of control."[28] It is more than this, however. It is the very mechanism by which organized workers may achieve control and exercise it jointly with management.

More eloquent evidence of this fact than any testimony from top man-

[27] *UAW–CIO International Correspondence Course in Collective Bargaining* (1941), Lesson 5, p. 1.
[28] *Trade Unionism in the United States*, p. 275.

agement officials is supplied in the simple and straightforward replies of a shop foreman, one Richard Bone, to questions propounded by members of a senate investigating committee in 1945.[29] There is a quiet drama in his words which compels consciousness of the period of profound industrial change in which we live.

THE ACTING CHAIRMAN. What is your relation with the steward on disciplinary matters?

MR. BONE. We are in strict accord. We are instructed from top-flight management to cooperate with the union 100 per cent. There is never a move I make in the department that he doesn't know it. We talk things over, seniority, raises, movement of men. If the night shift is short a man, he even allows me to put an extra man in there, running, say, three men on two machines.

MR. MEADER. You say "he allows you to"?

MR. BONE. Well, he says it is all right, and he could say "No."

MR. MEADER. It sounded as though you couldn't do it without his permission.

SENATOR FERGUSON. He says he couldn't.

MR. BONE. We work together.

SENATOR FERGUSON. I mean you couldn't do it if he didn't want you to.

MR. BONE. He could order the C.I.O. man that he would take, you know, just ease along.

SENATOR FERGUSON. What could he do if he didn't want him to go?

MR. BONE. Well, that man on his machine, he has got to get his production out.

SENATOR FERGUSON. You wouldn't have any authority to change a man's shift at all?

MR. BONE. Not without consulting him.

SENATOR FERGUSON. Without consent, even.

MR. BONE. Yes.

SENATOR FERGUSON. What can you do without his consent? You say you are told to cooperate with him 100 per cent. I therefore assume that there is nothing that you can do without his consent. Is that right?

MR. BONE. Well, when a man is in the wrong, and I know he is in the wrong, I can go and take action and say, "I have done this, and this is it."

SENATOR FERGUSON. That is what I want to know. What can you do without his consent?

MR. BONE. All right. A man failed to get the production, and I docked them the time, and it stuck.

SENATOR FERGUSON. How many times did you do that?

MR. BONE. Well, we don't have that very often.

SENATOR FERGUSON. Then, you didn't have to go to him first? You didn't go to him first?

MR. BONE. I told him I was going to do it.

SENATOR FERGUSON. Oh, you told him you were going to do it? And what did he say?

MR. BONE. He went and got the committeeman.

SENATOR FERGUSON. What happened?

MR. BONE. Well, nothing, because I was in the right.

SENATOR FERGUSON. Well, the committeeman agreed?

MR. BONE. Yes.

[29] *Investigation of the National Defense Program*, part 28, pp. 13320–13321.

A shop represents only a small segment of a plant, and in many cases a plant is only a small segment of the corporation. Decisions in the shop involve the details of administration just prior to execution. They do not concern the decisions which guide the destinies of the business. The picture given by the testimony above is the picture of the collective-bargaining relationship at work in the shop. Yet it is safe to assume that unions seek the same relationship in every organizational frame of the corporation, right up to top management. They desire to reproduce at all levels, through the collective-bargaining relationship, the same conditions of joint control: "There is never a move I make . . . that he doesn't know it. We talk things over. . . . We work together."

While voluntary arbitration may be considered as simply one method of collective bargaining, it is worth independent consideration as a device by which the union may broaden its authority within the corporation. In any such consideration, arbitration of the contract issues themselves—the terms of the agreement—must be distinguished from arbitration of the meaning and application of those terms once agreed upon.

Resort to voluntary arbitration is of course the result of agreement reached through the collective-bargaining process. In very few cases does a collective agreement itself specify that disputes over the terms of a renewed agreement shall be subject to arbitration in the event of an impasse. A 1944 study of the Department of Labor found that less than one per cent of all agreements providing for any form of arbitration, out of a total of 1,254 contracts examined, authorized arbitration of disputes over changes in the terms of the contract.[30] Arbitration of these disputes of interests, as they are sometimes called, is generally undertaken only as the result of an agreement reached at the time of deadlock. When undertaken, the arbitrator substitutes his judgment for that of management, becoming the final directive authority in the corporation with regard to the issues in dispute. To the extent that his decision finds in favor of the union, whether in whole or in part, he becomes the instrument by which union power has been extended. Whether or not he finds in favor of the union, arbitration of the terms of relationship between union and management is a device by which the union joins in erecting an authority, responsible equally to it, which supersedes the authority of management.

The conclusion that resort to arbitration over such primary issues, for the resolution of which the arbitrator has no standards to guide him, constitutes an abdication of management has led to substantial resistance to its use, particularly in the large corporation.[31] In a number of cases the

---

[30] Division of Industrial Relations, Department of Labor, Bulletin No. 780, *Arbitration Provisions in Union Agreements* (1944), p. 13.
[31] For a representative management opinion on this issue, turn back to Chapter 2, pp. 16–17.

same objection has been raised to arbitration as a means of resolving disputes arising under the contract, or disputes of rights, as they are sometimes referred to. This attitude is evident in an exchange occurring at a collective-bargaining conference, as revealed in its verbatim record, where the seniority clause and methods of interpreting it were under discussion:

> Company representative: That's the reason I say the clause is ambiguous of and in itself, and will always be open to dispute by the men who are affected by it.
>
> Union representative: Your arguments show just why we should have an impartial man in the seniority clause. The seniority clause we presented to this company in our original presentation was a very simplified clause. It merely said that the man who could do the job in question in as good a workmanlike manner as the other men, that being true, the man with the greatest seniority should have the job. That's all we said.
>
> Company representative: Now, there you are—the same thing exactly. Can a man do a job? Yes, possibly he can. He can do the operation, but another man can do it much better. And in my opinion he could do it much better. In your opinion, he couldn't. The man's opinion is different. You've got to have somebody's judgment now. You have got to give that judgment to the management, who are responsible for the operation of the plant; but to give it to an outsider—the company's position is that it wants to operate its own plant. It wants to recognize seniority as far as it can, but first of all, operate its plant.

Nevertheless, in a number of the largest corporations in the country a system of arbitration of disputes under the contract has been installed. Through it has come a progressive delineation of the bargaining relationship in the company. At the same time, it is quite true that this application and interpretation of the agreement by an impartial agency has constituted a check upon managerial authority. Thus in the two-and-one-half-year period from October 19, 1942 to March 15, 1945, of a total of 170 arbitrated grievances respecting discharges or disciplinary layoffs imposed by the management of the General Motors Corporation, 55 penalties were modified by the umpire and 23 revoked.[32]

More than disciplinary measures were affected, of course. Under most grievance arbitration systems, all the provisions of the agreement, with few exceptions, are subject to final interpretation by an authority other than the legal management. The coverage of such decided cases is indicated by the subjects of the decisions in one important company over a three-year period: absences, apprentices, assignment of work, back pay, call-in pay, demotions, discipline, dockage of wages, fair day's work, grievance procedure, hiring-in, holidays, discontinuance of jobs, leaves of absence, lunch periods, merit wage increases, plant protection, premium pay, probationary employes, promotions, rates and classifications, representation of employes, safety rules, designation of seven-day operations, shifts, sick leave, supervisors, temporary employes, transfers, union ju-

[32] *Investigation of the National Defense Program*, part 28, pp. 13820–13821.

risdiction, vacations, and work week. The significance of decisons in these categories has been indicated in the discussion of the impact of the union on managerial authority in six industries, in the preceding chapter.

The rationale of such an arbitration arrangement is not now of interest to us. For the present we are concerned only with the fact that this "specifically devised, civilized method for the ultimate enforcement of labor agreements," as one umpire has referred to it,[33] is based upon a withdrawal of power from management by a recognition of equal authority of the union in interpreting the exercise of management as defined in the contract. The negotiation of the collective agreement is the process by which unions participate in the directive function. Resolution of grievances, including their arbitration, is the process by which unions participate sometimes in the administrative function but most frequently in testing compliance.

Less important than when exercised through the devices of collective bargaining and arbitration, but still significant, is the capitalization of a strategic position for direct action without discussion. Strike or threat of strike may be used to force management to rescind some decision or policy unilaterally established, or to require management to accept a union decision on which no negotiation is permitted. In some instances company officials assert that their orders have been countermanded by union representatives, with employes following the dictates of the latter. Schedules of production have been ignored through slowdown. These invasion routes to managerial authority, when employed, are generally followed by organized groups without official sanction, but at times such courses of action have been given full blessing by the elected officers.

Simply the process of organizing employes into unions may prove a means of placing greater control over management in the hands of the union. Most illustrative of this is the present drive to organize supervisory and confidential employes. Time-study observers have been traditional foes of the union man, but time-study observers are now being organized by the same parent unions that represent the production employes. Foremen have in the past been regarded as the tool of management, but foremen today are being enrolled in the union movement. It is impossible to overstate the concern with which most company officials view these organizing efforts, and their prevalent fear that managerial authority is being undermined simply by the union's technique of "raiding" their ranks for members. One corporation is probably speaking for American management generally when it says:

There is no other set-up at the present time in American manufacture for communicating the purposes and plans of management for making output, to the people in the

33 Harry Shulman, *Opinions of the Umpire* (privately printed, 1946), from the Preface, p. 1.

shops who do the work that the census calls the value added by manufacture, except the General Foremen and the Foremen.

If these General Foremen and Foremen, on whom management relies to see that work is done at the shops, are realigned so that instead of being the agents of management working in the company's interests, they become associated through labor associations with the workmen whom they are supposed to supervise, a change will be made that goes to the root of our present methods under which people work in manufacturing operations.[34]

Still another manner in which the unions are seeking to influence managerial decisions is through the assistance of governmental agencies. In the words of one industrial relations director, "There is a growing tendency on the part of unions to get their demands by resort to government rather than over the bargaining table." Agencies established for the purpose of assisting labor unions in achieving a protected status within the corporation are by no means the sole governmental resource of the unions. With varying degrees of success, they have been represented at hearings of rate-making commissions and more general regulatory agencies such as the Federal Communications Commission and the Interstate Commerce Commission. The United Mine Workers has been instrumental in the past in the establishment of government pricing and marketing controls, in the administration of which it participated. In the field of legislation, examples may be multiplied: in the railroad industry the eight-hour day came through the Adamson Act and a special retirement fund has been legislatively provided, to mention only two of numerous cases in this field; safety codes have been prescribed for a number of industries—the United Rubber Workers is now seeking one in the State of Ohio; the Fair Labor Standards Act, setting forth minimum wage and maximum hour provisions, had behind it a strong labor lobby, as did the Social Security Act. A further catalogue of such legislation would only add emphasis to the fact that unions "have come to look upon their government not only as their protector but as their benefactor."[35]

We have here been considering only direct and concrete pressures exerted by the unions in their efforts to expand their authority within the corporation or to control managerial decisions. They are able, of course, to bring pressures of a more indirect nature by other means, such as publicity or the election of friendly candidates to public office. This recital of the mechanics of union penetration of managerial authority within the corporation is not intended to convey the impression of an irresistible force sweeping all before it. Management has its own powers of resistance and its own mechanisms for expanding influence, of whose strength the unions are acutely conscious. That consciousness finds expression in the

[34] From an advertisement of Chrysler Corporation, *New York Times*, June 24, 1945.
[35] Steelworkers Handbook, *Organized Labor and Management*, p. 5.

thoughtful statement of one union representative: "Who knows? Ten years from now we may be back fighting simply for recognition."

THE PERSONNEL IN UNION PENETRATION

In an earlier section we observed that the goals of the workers could probably be reduced to security, recognition, and self-expression. The union—with its techniques of collective bargaining, arbitration, direct action, and political effort—is the instrument through which many have sought to further the pursuit of these objectives. It is a tool for those employes who attempt to gain their ends by their own efforts rather than through reliance on the goodwill or enlightenment of others. As an instrument or a tool, the union is subject to direction and manipulation. The personnel involved in the direction and manipulation of the tool of unionism is now the subject of our interest. What, for example, is the role of the general membership?

We may first take rapid notice that the members of the union are the employes of the company. This elementary fact becomes important only for the reason that both the union and the operating company are based upon the same group of working people. To the extent that the union and the management programs are in conflict, there must be appeals by each to the same basic group for support. Each attempts to identify the personnel of the business primarily with its organization. As one industrial relations executive remarked, "It is significant that we of management refer to the men in the shop as 'our employes,' while the union calls them 'our members.' " In this contest for loyalties, it is felt that one organization can win only at the expense of the other. Loyalty to one precludes loyalty to the other, or, at best, when the interests of one seem to conflict with the interests of the other, it is "loyalty" which determines whose interests are protected.

Second, there is an important managerial group which believes that the workers have been traduced by promises. This opinion was noted in connection with the determinants of union penetration of the functions and areas of management. Not only has the loyalty of the company's employes been undermined by the union, in the eyes of management, but often this has been accomplished by demagoguery, chicanery, and delusion. "It is absolutely inconceivable to those of us who have been with the company for a long time, who have come up through the ranks, that the loyalty of the employes could be lost within the brief space of four years without the use of propaganda and pressure techniques by outside influences."

Partly for the reason that they are thus satisfied by the optimistic injections of their leaders, partly from the natural disinclination of an electorate to undertake the trouble of participation, there is a considerable apathy among the members of a union. They are content to let others carry the load. It is management's belief and criticism that often those who "carry the load" are self-appointed leaders who have personal rather than group benefits in mind. This result can obtain, some of management say, because fundamentally the members are not interested; they are members only because they have been "sold." This view is expressed by two company officials thus: "The union doesn't have the support of the members. They show no interest. The union hall can hold no more than 200, while the membership now checked off is 5,500." "One difficulty in the union can be traced to lack of participation by the members. Only some ten to twelve per cent of union members are active, going to meetings, helping to run the affairs of the union. These are the 'firebranders' and they keep trouble stirred up. If the good element who are not now active would become active, maybe there would be better leadership."

It should be remarked in passing that this is not a problem peculiar to unionism. The difficulties of maintaining the interest and participation of the eligible electorate are common to any democratic form of government. The fact that unions are organized and led by "a small group of energetic workers" has been admitted by some union leaders themselves.[36] Organized activities are commonly conducted thus. More significant, from the standpoint of determining the influence of the membership in the union's program to extend its authority within the corporation, is its degree of control over the men who guide the union, the instrument or tool of that penetration. This involves the question of the political structure of unions, a subject to whose elucidation an entire volume could be addressed. The scant space dedicated to it in the present inquiry is no indication of the importance assigned it.

As a third consideration in assessing the role of the membership, then, we must at least take note of this question of the degree of control exercised by the membership over its leaders. Among some influential management representatives there are those who believe that such control is a negligible factor. Those, for example, who maintain that union demands arise only from a power drive by union leaders, while believing that the workers themselves at heart are "loyal" and "honest," explain that such a situation may exist because these "loyal" and "honest" workers are unable to overturn the intrenched officialdom. As one top-management representative stated his belief: "Members no longer have the power of 'vetoing' their leaders through withdrawal from the union, due to the

[36] Golden and Ruttenberg, *Dynamics of Industrial Democracy*, pp. 277–278.

union shop, the closed shop, or the government-imposed maintenance of membership. Nor can they make their influence felt within the union because the unions are not essentially democratic, except sometimes at the local level where they may have the same type of democracy that characterizes Ward 23 in Chicago."

By contrast, an industrial relations director in another large corporation of the same industry in the same locality declared that "there have been a few cases where a leader has seemed to be interested in personal prestige and power, but—as in the case of a recent local president—they have been turned out at subsequent elections." Indeed, in some industries, as in rubber, the complaint is far more frequently heard that the leaders are unable to control the membership, rather than the reverse. Thus in one large company where a slowdown in one department necessitated the layoff of workers in an affected department, a management representative explained that such a situation could develop only because of a factional split in the union, which made the local president's tenure insecure. "He can't press too hard for settlement or he'll find a revolt on his hands." A national official of the Automobile Workers admitted that local strikes were sometimes approved by the national office only because it was known they would be called anyway and would discredit the national's authority and diminish the prestige of its officers if called in the face of their opposition.[37]

Numerous other examples of the manner in which the membership of a union has controlled its leadership may be offered as offset to the equally numerous stories of a membership bound over to a dictatorial office-holding clique. There is here the same dual problem which confronts democracy everywhere, the reconciliation of membership control over the leaders with leadership's control over the members. Correlating these two positive exercises of control involves the power of the electorate to change leaders, a defined relationship between them, procedures for equitably enforcing the legal decisions of the leaders, and methods of challenging their decisions and actions as exceeding the bounds of the relationship agreed upon.

In those unions where the membership has lost the power of effective control over its leaders, the union's program may or may not have the support of the membership; there is no way of knowing. In those unions where the membership retains the civil liberties essential to criticism and opposition and an effective right of changing leaders, the union's program as formulated by its leaders must meet the approval of the membership. That is to say, the leaders lead until a majority of the membership has disapproved their leadership. This latter role of the membership in the

[37] *New York Times*, August 12, 1941.

union's drive to augment its authority within the corporation is therefore uncertain in incidence but important where exercised. In any event, we may readily recognize that it is the leaders, and not the general membership, who are responsible for formulating the union's program, whatever it may be, including the invasion of traditional managerial rights. It is to the leaders that we must now turn our attention.

Since initiative in the union stems from its leaders, it is their job to phrase in the form of programs those sentiments or aspirations which may remain largely inarticulate in the membership, and to formulate solutions to expressed grievances. This is a necessary art of leadership which management sometimes overlooks when it criticizes union officials for stirring up trouble by making demands which have never been heard from the workers themselves. It is the *business* of union leaders to articulate the formless desires of their membership. "Promises" may be made by the leaders of the union—but if they take hold it is because they express the previously unexpressed wants of the workers, at least in those unions whose memberships retain the power to change officials. This is true not only where the promise is of higher monetary returns but also in the case of most of those demands which have found their way into collective agreements as contractual terms or which are still being pressed. There is little question, for example, that the drive for the guaranteed annual wage derives directly from the leadership, but it has accumulated the strong support of the rank and file because it would provide one answer to their quest for security.

At the same time we should not gloss over the fact that the interests of the union leaders, with whom initiative rests, may at times diverge from the interests of the membership. We have said that the union is a tool or an instrument by which workers seek to achieve their personal goals. Once it has come into existence and acquired a set of full-time functionaries, it becomes something more. It becomes the tool or instrument by which the officials attempt to obtain their personal objectives. Again, it is important to note that this is not a condition peculiar to the unions but a characteristic of any organization. The drives of the membership and the leaders, in a democratic organization, must coincide in important respects, since the leaders may achieve security, recognition, and self-expression only insofar as they satisfy their constituency, where their tenure is actually at its pleasure. In subtle ways the drives may differ, however. The membership, for example, may regard the union as a means of easing tensions created by unsatisfactory working conditions. Officials may regard the union not only as the means of easing tensions but of creating them, if they are to demonstrate to the membership its continuing need for the organization and for their official services. In the face of this fact it is not hard to see why some management members feel that there can be no peace with the unions. This is a premature conclusion, but it points to one very necessary condition of industrial order.

If we can recognize and accept that the union has all the flaws and virtues which characterize organization itself, and that one of these characteristics is the necessity for its leaders to demonstrate their continuing value to the organization, it becomes an essential condition of industrial peace that union officials are integrated into the business structure in such a way as to permit them to demonstrate their value in constructive rather than importunate roles. If given a continuous responsibility of a positive nature, a responsibility within the corporation as representative of the organized workers, challenging their abilities and enabling them to "make a record" in the same way that the sales staff or the engineering department "makes a record," they will have a means other than militancy of demonstrating their competency to their constituents. It is not surprising that the men's and women's clothing industries have achieved a high level of industrial order, since the initiative of the union leaders in those fields has been channeled into industry planning and business participation, in which they have established reputations endearing them to their followers.

If this is one—perhaps a primary—road to industrial peace in a democracy, it can be followed only when the place of the union in the industrial framework has been better defined. "Participation" in the conduct of the business is not otherwise possible. The conflict over managerial authority and prerogatives, on the one hand, and union rights and responsibilities, on the other, now stands as one of the greatest barriers to such a definition.

In still another way do organizational requirements influence the selection and conduct of our labor leaders. While union officials may be "outsiders" to any individual corporation, they are not generally unfamiliar with the industry within which they operate. It is the rare official who has not come up through the ranks or who has not in the past worked at the trade. "Experts" are brought in from the outside only to fill specialized staff positions such as general counsel, research director, or journal editor, and even these are often industry-bred men. This inbreeding of the unions narrows the field from which officials may be drawn. A union does not, like a business, feel free to draft the services of talent wherever found. In the union, talent must come clothed in overalls or at least with lingering smudges from the greasepits as its stigmata. In view of this limitation, the development of the requisite leadership ability is often a thorny problem. Popular education for more than a hundred years has been one of the rallying points of all labor organizations in this country.

It is still a subject of deep concern to them, for the progress of their organizations depends upon the intellectual and cultural advancement of the working population from whom their membership and leaders are drawn.

It is thus not surprising that a recent survey of some 203 top-flight labor leaders—the presidents and secretaries of national unions and departments, state federations and state industrial councils—found that approximately 60 per cent came from laboring families, primarily repre-senting the skilled trades. An additional 16 per cent came from farm families. Only 14 per cent of this group had parents who were owners of small businesses—independent tradesmen, craftsmen, or owners of small retail shops. About 80 per cent of the grandfathers of these men had been either laborers or farmers. The absence of a white collar or professional background is marked.[38]

Considering these origins, the formal educational achievements of this same group are rather surprising. About 22 per cent of the total number went to college. Of those remaining, 41 per cent show high school educa-tion and another 36 per cent grammar school. Levels of attainment are markedly higher in the CIO, whose leaders are on the average 14 years younger than those in the older established unions. Thus some 32 per cent of their number are college men, though not all finished college; only 22 per cent failed to rise above the grammar schools, while for the older unions this figure increases to 45 per cent. "The labor leaders are def-initely better educated than the adult male population at large, but are probably not so well-educated as business executives."[39] Bearing out this conclusion, it was reported that of 2,700 delegates to the 1946 Steel-workers convention, 780 were college-trained men.

These educational and career achievements of our labor leaders raise interesting speculations. The number of *existing* managerial jobs is lim-ited. To begin in business for one's self requires some capital resources, and the prospect of a small shop may not be challenging in any event. Is the union's drive to participate in more and more of the areas of manage-ment in our corporations the opening of a new route to managerial posi-tions and a means of expanding their number? Managerial authority via this road does not come as a result of background or "connections." It is won through popular election by the employes. With the desire for par-ticipation in the business process—for recognition and self-expression—seemingly frustrated by limitations of numbers, if not for other reasons,

[38] C. Wright Mills, "The Trade Union Leaders: A Collective Portrait," *Public Opinion Quarterly*, vol. 9, Summer, 1945, pp. 163–165. Somewhat less than 20 per cent of these leaders have themselves been engaged in white collar work during some phase of their career prior to their union position. P. 172.

[39] Mills, *Public Opinion Quarterly*, Summer, 1945, p. 168; also pp. 166–167.

the union has offered a new path to these objectives for the most energetic of their members.

Something of this thought seems to lie behind the analysis of one observer:

Ascent for the bright working class boy, as well as for the educated middle class youngster, has perhaps of late been more likely within trade union channels than within the hierarchy of business. This is suggested by the greater proportion of men of lower occupational origins who are at the top in trade unions as compared with business (and probably governmental) positions of comparable income and power; by the younger age at which the trade union leader attains these positions; and by the lesser amount of formal education apparently required for the union career. Previously, and even today in many unions, a higher education was not seen as an asset for a trade union career. If present trends continue, however, we may expect that the climb to success in unions will require a better education, and we may expect more able young men to follow the trade union route. . . . Although existing information is meager, statistically speaking the CIO has offered young men of working class parents a faster road to a position of power than any other organization, except the Armed Forces, during the past decade.[40]

This statement seems valid as far as it goes. For our purposes, however, we may add that *union* power has functional significance only when exercised within or directed against the *corporation*. Union power means business power, in any functional sense. Achievement within the union is measured in terms of success in the bargaining relationship with management. If this view is accepted, then the "faster road to a position of power" which the union offers is not solely power within the union: it is also power within the corporation, within the industry, within the economy.

THE COMPETENCE OF UNION PENETRATION

The president of one of America's well-known corporations writes as follows:

An important corollary to the growth of great corporate enterprises, operating on a nation-wide basis, has been the formulation of exceedingly exact requirements which largely govern selection of these new professional managers. For example, the far-sighted major business executive of today must possess qualifications like these:

He must plan ahead with the vision of the engineer. In estimating prospective income and expenditure, he must be as accurate as the mathematician. He must have a knowledge of finance and law approaching that of the banker and the attorney. Like the research student in the laboratory, he must be keenly receptive to advances in technical knowledge. In directing his staff he must have the qualifications of the teacher, plus the psychologist's insight into human nature. If the business executive is to anticipate the ups and downs of the business cycle and make his decisions accordingly, he must be more than a rudimentary economist. He must also find time to keep abreast of the

40 Mills, *Public Opinion Quarterly*, Summer, 1945, p. 175.

literature of this new profession, which is already as voluminous as that of law or medicine, architecture or engineering.

And in addition to all these facets which must constitute today's executive, he must be acutely sensitive and adaptable to ever-changing social and economic thought. The tempo of the times is such that any static attitude carried over from the past becomes a positive handicap not merely in evaluating present-day conditions but in anticipating tomorrow's developments.[41]

These are exacting standards, but if anything they constitute an understatement of the professional competence which the top-management of our large corporations must bring to their jobs. The governance of a sensitive producing and distributing society of up to several hundred thousand population, engaged at specialized tasks requiring a high degree of technical and social coordination, working with specialized tools and equipment valued at up to two thousand million dollars, and integrated into a larger society in such a manner that shocks from without are registered within and changes within have their repercussions on the outside— the governance of such an industrial state requires a professional skill second to none.

The unions, through their leaders, are now participating in the control of these gigantic enterprises. They seek to expand their share of authority in these states within the state. They have become, to a degree which promises to increase in the future, co-managers of our large corporations. The same requirements of proficiency enumerated above for the professional managers apply to them. Reread those two paragraphs of requisite qualifications in terms of the union leader in the corporation. He too must plan ahead, estimate prospective corporate income and outlay, must know finance and law, be receptive to developments in technical knowledge, possess insight into human nature, anticipate cyclical fluctuations, keep abreast of theory and practice in his field, and be sensitive to his social and economic milieu, if he is to measure up to the responsibilities of his de facto profession. It is of no pertinence to say that some of the legal corporate managers are deficient in the listed requirements. Regardless of the remissness of any incumbent, the job of manager demands certain technical skills. This is as true of the labor men in management as of the chosen corporate officials. How well do the union representatives measure up to this challenge?

There is a fairly widespread belief in management circles that union leaders cannot master the intricacies of operating the business. A rubber executive speaks disparagingly of the "shop geniuses" who think they know more than company specialists about technical operations, and lets drop a reference to national union officials whom ten years ago he knew

[41] From Lewis H. Brown, "New Objectives of Management," in Bronson Batchelor, editor, *The New Outlook in Business* (1940), pp. 92–93.

as mediocre operatives on the assembly line. A steel official shakes his head at suggestion of a union-management cooperation plan and remarks that "they don't have much to contribute." Other executives have said, "We may as well recognize that management is generally best qualified by experience, training, and ability to exercise these rights."[42]

In some instances managements have gone further. Not only, they say, are union representatives incapable or less capable of learning the business, there is no real need for them to know it. In franker moments some may admit that too much concern with company operations may encourage union representatives to seek a deeper penetration into some area of managerial authority. "It is mainly important for them to improve their leadership in terms of responsibility, of living up to the contract."

It is scarcely necessary to suggest that the unions have disagreed with these views, but it is interesting to note that some management officials, too, have taken a contrary position. Thus one executive who has spent many years on problems of industrial relations in one of our largest corporations remarked: "The unions must develop leaders who are more experienced and knowledgeful of business and industrial problems, who have a management—that is to say, a functional—approach to problems, and who can be counted upon for a responsible performance. This is coming. I don't know how long it will take, but it is coming."

One of the most revealing aspects of this problem is the humility with which a significant number of union leaders assess their capability of exercising increasing managerial responsibilities. Behind the bravado of the bargaining table, there is often a deep and genuine concern. "The union must keep on working on its present gains, mastering the areas it has already penetrated," says one national president. "The leaders are little enough skilled in these areas, and with respect to other managerial functions they have virtually no training or competence at all. This is no reflection on their intelligence. They have the intelligence, but they have never been in a position where they could acquire the knowledge and experience which management has just by virtue of filling the job. In the long run the unions must and should get into more and more of the areas of management, but the timing will depend on the ability of the union leaders to prepare themselves for such responsibilities. But this is the catch—I don't know how the union people are going to acquire the training. I had hopes that the labor-management committees in wartime would provide a start, but they didn't work out satisfactorily in our industry. Now I don't know what the answer will be. I just don't know."

Another union representative remarked, "Union leaders must learn the language and the lingo of management. There must be communication,

[42] Hill and Hook, *Management at the Bargaining Table*, p. 58.

and communication requires a common language, so there is a tremendous need for greater training of union men." For every management representative who stresses the grave shortage of well-trained union leaders, there is a union representative to agree with him. The union leaders, or at least an important number of highly placed union officials, recognize their own deficiencies and those of their followers, but those deficiencies, they maintain, arise from lack of experience and training and not from incapability. Their answer? More training.

Some of the union leaders maintain that training should be offered by the unions themselves. "The unions should be responsible for training their own personnel, and this training should be thorough enough to permit them to meet management on equivalent terms."[43] Others have encouraged instruction through established institutions of learning. "May I point out that our land-grant colleges, supported as they largely are by public funds, could well become centers for the training of men and women for service in the labor movement. Short term courses of a few weeks, periodic institutes, research projects, and the like should be made as readily available to industrial workers as similar projects having to do with agricultural, manufacturing, or merchandizing problems are made available to farmers, manufacturers, and businessmen."[44]

In practice a combination of these two approaches has been most often effected. The union in cooperation with some educational institution, usually of college standing, has offered a planned course of instruction. The description of one such "labor institute" reads as follows: "All subject matter and courses of study have been jointly developed by the District Directors of the United Steelworkers in Pennsylvania and the faculty of the [State] College. It is intended that special skills in leadership may be broadened among members, and that related labor subjects be pursued both formally and informally in discussion groups so that current labor problems may be explored and understood more fully. Attention will be directed to the aims and responsibilities of the Labor movement. Through the facilities of the School of Mineral Industries broad courses dealing with the steel and aluminum industries will be offered. This course will concern itself with manufacturing processes by using modern steel-making equipment; the pricing problems involved, and the importance of the worker to the industry. . . ."

There is little doubt that a great deal of good will come from such training programs, by whomsoever sponsored. Without undervaluing their

[43] Gomberg, *Harvard Business Review*, vol. 24, p. 364.
[44] Clinton Golden, "New Patterns of Democracy," *Antioch Review*, vol. 3 (1943), p. 403. A resolution of the 12th session (1946) of the National Conference on Labor Legislation proposed the establishment of a Labor Extension Service in the Department of Labor to assist and promote the development of an informed union membership and competent union leadership.

contribution, however, we may reasonably question whether union leaders will ever attain in all areas of management the knowledge and experience of full-time management officials. The difficulties are obvious. Granting that management has no monopoly on brains, it does have a monopoly of the operating positions. The production manager who must meet and answer some very specific problems relating to output can be expected to have a broader and more refined knowledge than the union official who, if he hears about such problems at all, receives them at second hand. The sales manager who has studied, over a period of years, reports of product sales by area, income group, age group, occupational group, and by other population characteristics, is likely to give a more educated guess as to the effect of an increase or decrease of price than is the union official who has no opportunity for a similar concentration or application of effort. To repeat the words of the union president previously quoted, union representatives "have never been in a position where they could acquire the knowledge and experience which management has just by virtue of filling the job."

For several reasons, however, this basic disadvantage need not operate as an insuperable handicap to extension of union activity in the corporation. First, there exists the possibility that a union representative, while not specializing in a given managerial area within a single company, may devote his full time to a study and understanding of a specific phase of management within the industry, becoming in the nature of a consulting specialist. A comprehension of the problems faced in a number of companies with respect to production or sales, for example, may permit him to claim a competency which a member of management in an isolated corporation could not dispute. Second, the knowledge and experience of union representatives need not be competitive with the knowledge and experience of management, but may be supplementary. Speaking of the time-study program in the Cleveland women's garment industry, Professor Slichter declares, "Time and again the workers' committees, handicapped though they were by lack of technical knowledge, were able to point out omissions and mistakes in the standards."[45] With regard to wartime labor-management production councils, a union official writes, "The councils become successful to the extent that management and labor can mutually draw on each other's experience, knowledge and information."[46] The undenied contributions of workers' representatives in certain union-management cooperation programs testify to the union's ability, at least in certain areas, to complement management's skills.

[45] *Union Policies and Industrial Management*, p. 435.
[46] Julius Emspak, "Labor-Management War Production Councils," *Science and Society*, vol. 7 (1943), p. 91.

Finally, and perhaps most important, even in those areas where the union's competence is competitive with that of management, such competition may operate within broad areas of principles and policies, where specialized administrative ability and detailed knowledge are less requisite. For example, it is not difficult to imagine that the union leaders' knowledge of a firm's operations may become fully as respectable as that possessed by boards of directors operating on a part-time basis. Yet with the latter rests final directive responsibility for corporate policies. The union may find itself competent to participate in this directive function without contesting the wide latitude of management members in the functions of administration and execution, satisfied that a sharing in *final* authority will permit it to hold administrative and executive management to a standard of performance satisfactory to it. It is in this direction that the union-management relationship has actually, though somewhat randomly, been moving. Explicit recognition of this differentiation of the functions of management and the attendant possibilities of defining the union and management roles opens a new realm of thinking in industrial relations which we shall have occasion to explore more thoroughly in a later chapter.

Granting, then, that union officials may establish a level of competence in the conduct of corporate affairs, we must still face the question of whether they possess the facilities permitting them to exercise that competence. Are the sources of information necessary to informed judgment available to them? Do they have ready and continuous access to them? Corporations have developed extensive files of records and reports on every phase of their activity. These are at the command of the legal corporate officials. To what degree do union officials have similar command over the necessary data?

A highly placed leader expresses what appears to be the consensus of the labor representatives: "The union is handicapped by lack of information. It gets what it can from public records and the data it can work up itself, sometimes through its own members and their knowledge on the job. This is a long and difficult process. It is especially difficult insofar as management centers attention on cost, since the union doesn't have the cost data."

This situation obtains particularly in the large corporation. In industries of small businesses, the union has at times been able to acquire a command of knowledge superior to that of the company officials. This is notably true in the clothing industries. But in industrial enterprises of the size with which we are concerned, the union has sometimes been hard put to it to secure even elementary information on which to base its proposals. In other instances it can obtain needed data not by any right of access but only by petition to the company, and then perhaps will receive it, if at all, only after it has been screened and filtered by management.

Faced with this obvious handicap, the unions have set about to remedy it in several ways. First, they have sought freer access to company records. Here, without possibility of duplication for much of it, are contained the vital statistics of corporate existence. The union desire for an opportunity to penetrate the barriers now separating it from this information is evident in the plea—never published—of a committee of top-ranking union officials: "Both management and labor must realize the need for sound management policies and practices within their respective organizations. Furthermore, each has a duty to make available to the other full information on all factors which enter into the successful operation of the business." This "duty" has never been officially acknowledged, however. In the majority of corporations the unions must rely on little more than published financial accounts or official reports to governmental agencies for data on company operations. Even such matters as employe wage rates and productivity have been denied the unions on numerous occasions. Thus the research director of one national union described its relations on this subject with officials of one of America's giant corporations:

The company has refused to disclose information on the rates for particular jobs, and the job description. It takes the position that the wage structure is its own business and not the union's. The wages negotiated are consequently primarily in terms of increases to be applied to the existing wage structure. Of course the union can challenge a given wage rate through the grievance machinery, but as far as any over-all job classification and unified wage structure are concerned it has made little headway. Likewise, it can get no information from the company on its incentive rates. This attitude of the company means that the union is compelled to seek its information through its own members. This is a difficult procedure, however. In a company of thousands of workers it is difficult to assemble the needed data, in terms of job titles, job descriptions and rates of pay, and incentive rates. Moreover, in some instances the workers have difficulty in describing their jobs in similar terms. All this data the company now has, and the union sees no reason why it should not have access to it.

The resolution of the above difficulty provides an example of one way in which the union has met this handicap head-on. In 1946 negotiations this union successfully made an issue of the supply of the desired data, and the company is now obligated, by contractual agreement, to make this information available to the union. One union publication thus advises that "Labor would do well to include in its perspectives a demand for the right to inspect the books of managements, and to write into contracts a clause providing some such privilege."[47]

Additional assistance has come to the unions from the National Labor

[47] United Electrical, Radio and Machine Workers, *How Corporations Conceal Profits*, p. 12.

Relations Board. In a number of cases it has held that the refusal by management to supply certain essential data or to permit an independent examination of the company's financial condition, while contending that it was unable to grant wage increases, constituted unfair labor practices, and the federal courts have at times supported the Board in such determinations.[48] In one case coming before the Seventh Circuit Court of Appeals the Court asserted:

> Again we do not believe that it was the intent of Congress in this legislation that, in the collective bargaining prescribed, the union, as representative of the employees, should be deprived of the pertinent facts constituting the wage history of its members. We can conceive of no justification for a claim that such information is confidential. Rather it seems to go to the very root of the facts upon which the merits were to be resolved. In determining what employees should receive increases and in what amounts, it could have been only helpful to have before the bargainers the wage history of the various employees, including full information as to the work done by the respective employees and as to their respective wages in the past, their respective increases from time to time and all other facts bearing upon what constituted fair wages and fair increases. And if there be any reasonable basis for the contention that this may have been confidential data of the employer before the passage of the Act, it seems to us it cannot be so held in the face of the expressed social and economic purposes of the statute.[49]

This case concerned the availability of data in an area of management —wages—where union penetration has for long been accepted. The decision acquires further interest, however, when it is remembered that no adequate definition of the sphere of union interests has yet been attempted by legislature or courts. If a union believed that its interests required collective bargaining with respect to the price policy of a company and sought information from the corporate records for this purpose, would the Board and the courts likewise find that they could conceive of no justification for the argument that such information was confidential; that, rather, it seemed to go to the very root of the facts on which the merits should be resolved?

Several reasons have motivated management's reluctance to grant the unions ready access to company files and records. One is the fear that thereby unions may be encouraged to concern themselves with areas of management in which they now have no voice. Another is the belief that unions will only distort such information for argumentative purposes. Equally important is the feeling that where national union officials participate in negotiations, information made available to them may find its way to competitors, with unfortunate results for the company. Despite

---

[48] For example, *Matter of Pioneer Pearl Button Company*, 1 NLRB 837; *Matter of M. H. Birge and Sons Company*, 1 NLRB 731 (where the company submitted such data); *Matter of Sherwin-Williams Company*, 34 NLRB 651, enforced in *NLRB v. The Sherwin-Williams Company*, 130 F (2d) 255 (CCA 3); *Matter of Aluminum Ore Company*, 39 NLRB 1286, enforced in *Aluminum Ore Company v. NLRB*, 131 F. (2d) 485 (CCA 7).

[49] *Aluminum Ore Company v. NLRB*, 131 F (2d) 485, 487.

these considerations, a distinct minority of management members see no harm in making available to the union the company's accumulated knowledge. One says, "I think the union has a right to know the why of management decisions. It has a right to see the books and know all it can about the operation of the company. But this is quite different from the right to participate in management decisions. I recognize that the one may be just a step to the other, but I don't think such will be the case."

This belief is far from general, and the unions may expect to encounter strong resistance from management in any search for information on the basis of which they may make informed decisions in ever-widening areas of management. They are not discouraged, however. A union representative who has grown gray in the labor movement states with conscious emphasis that "Company records must be opened up to the unions—not just the 'books' but all the files and materials assembled by the company in its daily operations, if the unions are to make intelligent decisions and fulfill their functions adequately."

Lacking ready access to the company's informational facilities, many unions have fallen back on the development of their own. This constitutes, in some respects, a duplication of the facilities supporting managerial decisions, with the legal corporate officers and the labor leaders each developing their own. In the steel, automobile, and meat-packing industries the long-time goal is openly expressed of building the union research departments to the point where the union knows as much as management about the economics of the industry. "The normal process of negotiations and our progress toward a master wage agreement requires a strengthening of our research department. Of all administrative departments, it is the key to our collective bargaining relation and its work must be closely coordinated with all contract negotiations. It must have facilities and staff to insure that every union representative, local or international, is as well equipped with economic data and facts as the employer representative he faces across the bargaining table. If we are to participate in the solution of our basic economic problems, we must understand the economic facts of life within our industry. Economic facts, supported by economic power when necessary, make for effective bargaining."[50]

At present, however, these programs are in an inchoate state. In only a few of the larger and wealthier unions has substantial progress been made. The difficulties of establishing and operating an effective department of research are tremendous. First, there is the problem of educating even many of the leaders to the need for and use of such an enterprise. Second, there is the problem of coordinating the activities of the central office with the local unions—both as to supply and use of data. Third,

[50] Walter Reuther, *A Program for UAW-CIO Members*, p. 6.

there has been difficulty in staffing; in some instances the research department has become a political plum awarded to administrative favorites without special competence or imagination. Fourth and most important, in many unions the funds have not been available. The discouraged words of one national union president come to mind: "We fully appreciate the necessity of expanded departments of public relations, education and research. Our present departments are hardly shells. But for these purposes and for the general training of leaders the union has no money. There is no big reserve to draw on, current income is unable to provide much support for expansion. To some extent we can make second-hand use of other unions' materials, and we do, but we can't get far on that."

Largely barred from management's sources of information, faced with the slow and difficult process of building their own, the unions have in the main been forced to fall back on public facilities, primarily of a governmental nature. In some instances these have proven admirable for their purposes. The railroad brotherhoods have found the Interstate Commerce Commission an exceedingly valuable aid. In the words of one of the brotherhoods' outstanding research directors, "Because of the ICC, the union knows more about the financial and operating statistics of the companies with which it deals than is the case with most unions. It knows just about everything except what the general manager ate for breakfast." The Securities and Exchange Commission and the Federal Communications Commission have likewise been of assistance to certain unions. The War Labor Board was of temporary advantage. As one research director said, "The Board was a boon, since it could demand and secure elaborate data, which of course became available to the labor members."

The agency of most value to the largest number of unions is the Bureau of Labor Statistics in the Department of Labor. From it come basic data on wages, hours, cost of living, employment, production, and prices. Because such information is basic, it is primarily useful only as a means of comparison. It provides none of the required specialized facts on the operations of any single corporation. For information of this nature, a great many unions have nothing more on which to rely than the standard reporting services to be found in the public library.

The conclusion is inescapable that the unions have inadequate facilities to support their leaders, however competent they may be, in an expanding share of corporate authority. Indeed, it would be gross exaggeration to claim that their existing facilities are adequate to support their present role, if played with any other consideration in mind than relative bargaining strengths. At the same time it is more than likely that if the unions feel the necessity and possess the bargaining ability to continue to penetrate further into corporate operations, this present lack of data will constitute no strong barrier or severe impediment to them. For most of the needed facilities now exist, though in the possession of the company. And if the unions proceed far enough in their program, impelled by their goals and those of their members, propelled by their drives, provided with effective techniques of penetration, with mutual support of leaders and membership, they may be expected to try to open the doors to the companies' storehouse of knowledge in the same manner in which they have opened the doors to participation in an increasing number of areas of management.

Even assuming that the means exist for training competent union leaders and that ways may be found to support them with the necessary informational facilities, we must still face the question of whether these ways and means will be utilized. Past experience provides little basis for a prompt affirmative answer to this question. The number of union leaders or potential union leaders who have availed themselves of existing training facilities is not large. A vast number of them have been more preoccupied with their political competence within the union than with their managerial competence within the corporation. Many have made little or no use of such factual data as are now available to them.

From time to time employers have become exasperated with the union's lack of concern with details of corporate operation, an exasperation exampled in the outburst at one national bargaining conference: "You know, Mr. D——, it is too bad, it really is too bad, that more of your people do not have an opportunity to actually experience the problems that management has in disposing of its products and in keeping cost of production down to the place they can offer their merchandise at a competitive price with the other manufacturers, with the importers and with the non-union people, and that it is permitted or possible that such wild statements can apparently obtain belief among your people in the discussions that I presume come up in your local meetings, like that cost of production statement that Mr. H—— just made. A statement like that is so absurd and so ridiculous, Mr. D——, that it won't need any denial. . . . Every once in a while something comes out in some talk in the shop or something is said at these conferences, just like that statement of the total cost of production being down, and so on, without the remotest possible basis in facts. If you want the information on these things when there is any question about it, I think any manufacturer will gladly give you the facts in the case—as to what his labor is costing, and his material is costing, etc. We have it all here if you want to know it, but don't take any information from any source you know cannot be in any possible position to get at the facts—don't take those statements as facts. It disarranges your whole process of thinking."

Nevertheless, the conclusions which may be drawn from past union practice are at best uncertain. As yet we have failed to integrate the unions within the corporation, providing them with organizational procedures permitting joint decisions in areas of common interest. We have required them to rely on a method—the strike—to make their voice heard which has not been conducive to the development of leaders trained in managerial practices and expert in the use of underlying data. As one leader has expressed it, "High wages and better working conditions are not won by argument, but by the only weapon workers have—the right to strike. All the data and arguments presented don't convince the employer. The union is willing to show why it makes certain demands, but the basic question is not how strong a case the union presents in argument, but, Will my plant operate or will it not?"

The answer to the question of whether unions will resort to the ways and means, now existing or to be developed, of training competent leaders and supplying supporting facilities is bound up in the definition of union and management responsibility toward which we are slowly and painfully working, a responsibility which must be inherent in the corporate role and status of each. There has been a plethora of shallow talk about union responsibility. Emphasis has rested on the need for union observance of its obligations under the contract. This form of responsibility is obviously essential, but it is not sufficient. The managerial function of the union comes largely in the negotiation of the agreement itself, and it is here that there has been no adequate definition of union—or management—responsibility or provision of peaceful procedures within which such a responsibility, once defined, may operate. Unions now admit only one dominant responsibility—the advancement of their members' interests. Management now operates under an equally dominant responsibility—to the owners of the corporation. Beyond the compulsion on management to negotiate with the union, there is no mutual responsibility incumbent on these two cooperating protagonists. Their responsibilities to each other have never been stated by society. We shall have to defer for a time a further examination of this fundamental problem, but for our present purposes we need only observe that the present responsibility of the unions—to its own members only—requires little development of *corporate* leadership or adequate facilities to support such leadership. As long as this condition remains, it is futile to expect a widespread growth of managerial competence among union leaders. This is not, however, the fault—either mainly or entirely—of the union leaders. It is the fault of the organizational framework within which we have forced them to operate.

CHAPTER 6

Boundaries of the Union in Management

In what has gone before we have sought to understand the theory and the practice of the managerial function. We have attempted to estimate the degree to which unions have shared in the exercise of that function. We have tried to define the goals and drives, the techniques and abilities supporting the union effort to obtain a more powerful voice in the conduct of our corporate enterprises. We may now begin to come to grips with the puzzling problems which have been raised.

SHOULD THE UNION'S ROLE IN MANAGEMENT BE LIMITED?

The Views of Corporate Management

There can be little doubt that a majority of the ranks of management hold firmly to the view that some line of demarkation must separate the areas in which they have sole authority and those in which the union may be conceded the right to bargain. Management members of one committee of the President's National Labor-Management Conference of 1945 unanimously signed their names to a statement which read in part: "Management has functions that must not and cannot be compromised in the public interest. If labor disputes are to be minimized by 'the genuine acceptance by organized labor of the functions and responsibilities of management to direct the operation of an enterprise,' labor must agree that certain specific functions and responsibilities of management are not subject to collective bargaining."[1]

A spokesman for a steel company was voicing the views of most company representatives when he said, "The absence of such a line between management and the union means that there is no basis for program or policy on the part of the company—we don't know what to expect from the union in the immediate future. The biggest contribution the unions could make would be to perfect what they have now, stopping with the areas of authority they have already entered and setting the mind of

---

[1] *The President's National Labor-Management Conference,* pp. 56–57.

business at rest. It is better that we have definite, fixed limits to union authority, even though as respects a particular decision it may seem wrong to the rank and file, because over the long pull it will work out to the best interests of all. The assertion on the part of labor that a particular management authority ought to be canceled out in favor of joint operation because in that particular case the rank and file's interests may be better protected isn't as important as having a clear line of distinction."

So keenly have most business officials felt the need of "drawing the line somewhere," so touchy have some of them become on the possibilities of union penetration, that issues have been made of minor matters such as the union's access to bulletin boards. In the words of one union agent, "The company exhibits a fear that to give in to the union now on minor points might act as a precedent to future demands of greater importance." Illustrative is this excerpt from one major bargaining conference where the union was asking, for purposes of checking on the enforcement of seniority provisions, that service records and employment lists be supplied to a local president when he requested them, and the company was willing to concede only the right of the president to inspect the lists in the company office.

Asked a union representative, "What's the difference between whether you hand them to the local president or post them and have them copy them from the posted record?"

Replied the company's director of labor relations, "There may not seem to be very much difference to you, Otto, and you may be quite honest about it, but to the company there seems to be quite a lot of difference. I don't know how to explain it, but there is a lot of difference. This may be minor in one respect, but after all, the company is not committing itself to a sort of joint management of its employees. They would still like to retain their right to shift around their employees as they see fit, and subject to your criticism, if you don't like it, and as long as you can enter the office and ask for the records, as you know you can, the record of the man involved, why isn't that sufficient?"

Moreover, the "line" which management would like to see drawn is not of interest only to the individual company. Concessions granted in one contract may make resistance to similar concessions more difficult in other negotiations. The power of the precedent and the principle of the entering wedge are feared by management. It is a line of general applicability which most company officials would like to see demarking the spheres of joint interest from those of management's single interest.

What reasons motivate management's resistance to the union's drive to share authority in the corporation and prompt its insistence on a definition of spheres of interest? They are numerous. Without an understanding of them we shall fail to appreciate the magnitude of the problem of industrial relations which we face today.

1. Management fears that union penetration threatens business organization itself by destroying unified final authority.

A vice president of one of America's great corporations who has achieved a high degree of understanding of the union's aims and sympathy with their objectives makes the statement that "the power of decision may be hedged about with limitations as to its exercise, but somewhere, in some hands, must lie the authority for saying yes or no on a given question." It is this necessary authority which management feels is being attacked by the unions' program.

The corporate system which management represents rests on a final authority which is exercised by officials chosen for that purpose. It is a single line of authority. It operates within a legal framework which spells out its powers, obligations, and limitations. Wherever the union penetrates, this authority becomes bifurcated. Final authority is exercised only by agreement which must be accomplished outside of the legal corporate framework. The union does not recognize the same obligations and limitations. Its power is derived from a different source. By the same tactics which allow its initial penetration, management fears that its authority will become compelling.

"How are the contracts rights, 'the management of the works and the direction of the working forces,' which are vested exclusively in the Company, to be given any effect if the determination of how work is to be done can only be resolved after there has been Union approval on the subject?" ask the officials of one company.[2]

Says another management representative: "Authority in the corporation must be centralized. It is something which should be held in the hands of the management, to be delegated by them as necessary. But in such delegation there is always the power to take it back. Now when unions come into the picture, any power which they secure from management they view as an outright grant which will never and can never be retrieved. Once given, it is gone for good. Management cannot resume it if it wills. This is an impossible situation."

The ways in which unions have challenged unified final authority have been numerous and insidious, in the estimation of many of the managers. They point out that there has been the frontal attack by trying to win contract concessions covering areas of management heretofore under the company's sole purview, subjecting them to joint decision. ("The union is attempting to breach the whole line.") There has been the counterat-

---

[2] Quoted from the company's brief in *Timken Roller Bearing Company and United Steelworkers of America*, NLRB Case No. 8–C–1815 (August, 1946).

tack through the grievance procedure, in which the unions have sought to enlarge the scope of the agreement, subjecting management decisions to review by the union. ("The union is constantly probing in an effort to expand the boundaries of the contract.") Union representatives have overruled the instructions of management. ("In some instances our orders for overtime have been countermanded by union officials.") Employes have been led to regard the union as the source of final authority, rather than to accept the orders of management. ("But the union is attempting to dictate the kind of telephone service the public should have and has encouraged operators and supervisors to look to it for direction and to interfere with management's efforts to furnish good service."[3]) Some unions have sought to bind management to union-originated bylaws and rules. ("The issue is simple. Is the publisher of a daily newspaper to be forced in any way to accept, without his consent or agreement, any rules adopted by the International Typographical Union for the operation of a part of the plant to produce newspapers?"[4]) The organization of foremen has split the very ranks of management. ("We are convinced that it would be impossible for a foreman to follow both management and union leaderships at the same time, and under those conditions to carry on all his duties as they now exist. All elements of management must have a common objective."[5])

Even when managements have sought the participation of unions through cooperation programs there has been a firm insistence that final authority shall not be disturbed. In the much-publicized Eric Johnston plan establishing a "junior board of directors" manned by employes it was stated, "That invitation did not, of course, mean that management renounces its right to manage or to make the final decisions. Final decision, we felt, properly lies with management . . ."[6]

2. Management fears that union penetration prevents the discharge of its responsibilities.

Since the basic motive behind the stockholders' association is to seek profits, obviously the Management of a business must devote itself to this single purpose. Their authority is given them for no other reason.

The investments of a business in machinery, buildings and goodwill, by their very nature, can only be recovered over long periods of time, and thus the Management must take a long-term point of view in the conduct of its affairs, that is, it must use as its yardstick on its actions, the enlightened long-term best interests of its investors. . . .

[3] From an advertisement of the Chesapeake and Potomac Telephone Company in the *Washington Post*, January 5, 1946.
[4] From a statement of the American Newspaper Publishers Association, *New York Times*, July 23, 1945.
[5] From an advertisement of General Motors, *Washington Post*, April 9, 1945.
[6] Eric Johnston, "Labor Should Have a Stake in Capitalism," *New York Times Magazine*, February 24, 1946, p. 50.

To sum up, society has determined certain rights called "property rights." In a corporation, the stockholders have delegated some of those rights to the Management and holds the Management accountable for the preservation and development of their best long-term interests. The Management of a business, therefore, is accountable primarily to the owners from whom it receives its authority. . . .

The very act of accepting authority constitutes an agreement to exercise it in accordance with the aims and interests of the person from whom it is obtained, and the use of this authority in a contrary manner is a violation of the terms of its acceptance. . . .

The Management, in its delegation of authority, is bound to make certain to the best of its ability that the authority will be used only in accordance with the interests of the business. This precludes it from delegating authority to anyone whose interests may be in conflict with those of the owners of the business. These are the principles that are involved in so many of the labor controversies of the moment.[7]

It was on this ground that General Motors based its refusal of the union's offer to arbitrate differences in the negotiation of the 1945–1946 contract. "Stripped of its deception, the union proposed that General Motors relinquish its rights to manage its business. This was not an offer of arbitration but a demand for abdication. General Motors, of course, rejects such a demand. Actually your proposal means that an arbitration board would assume the responsibilities of management; that it would assume responsibility for determining what is a sound financial and economic policy for General Motors; that the presently constituted management would relinquish functions which have been assigned to it by the owners of the business—the stockholders; that the duly elected officers of General Motors would surrender their functions and responsibilities to outsiders including a representative of the union."[8]

Its legal responsibility which runs solely to the stockholders thus precludes it from granting concessions which dilute that responsibility, in the opinion of management. Its protection of final authority and its concern with the discharge of its responsibility are thus two sides of the same shield. For authority comes only as a resultant of its responsibility, and its responsibility can take on meaning only with the exercise of authority. In the institutional framework in which they are thus set, most managers see no other feasible course of action but to resist the union drive to weaken authority and responsibility. They feel compelled to such resistance by the law and logic of their position.

3. Management fears that union penetration endangers the efficiency of its industrial organization.

In the words of one writer, "While there may be exceptions, it can generally be assumed that the aim of the executive can be summed up in one

[7] From *Authority and Responsibility in Industrial Management*, an address before the Institute of Public Affairs, University of Virginia, July 14, 1934, by S. M. DuBrul, now director of the Labor Economics Section of General Motors (mimeo.).

[8] *New York Times*, November 24, 1945.

word, 'Control.' An expansion of this definition might be stated as, 'The regulation and government of a manufacturing plant, its equipment, its personnel and its functioning, so that proper quantities of the proper products of proper quality will be produced at the proper time at the lowest possible cost consistent with continuation or expansion of the business.' "[9]

This aim of management is based on efficiency concepts, in which the functioning parts of the business organism—including of course the personnel—have their assigned roles. In the business organism there can be only one mind and one nerve center if the various parts are to be coordinated into a harmonious whole. The union, however, constitutes a second center of authority, which speaks in terms of welfare rather than efficiency.

"Unions are not good for management," says one corporate official. "It interrupts our efficiency to have to be in a constant state of defense against the threat of the use of force. We have to divert management and men from their real jobs of production to straighten out difficulties between management and the union. You would be surprised at the amount of money we have paid to union men and management just to straighten out these difficulties with no relevancy of such payments to the operation of our productive machinery."

And from another manager, "We worked for years to eliminate chance in our operations—now here it comes back in a big way. A new and unpredictable element has been injected into our business."[10]

The power of the union in the corporation has its effect on management's ability to raise needed capital, to set aside reserves for expansion, to introduce new technologies, to improve productive methods, to meet sales commitments, to lower costs, in fact to do any of the things which management's drive to efficiency would prompt it to do and to do as expeditiously as possible. The effect, management feels, is more often for worse than for better.

4. Management objects to union penetration because of a lack of union responsibility.

As management sees it, the unions are seeking greater authority without concomitant responsibilities. One of their number states the problem as follows. "As matters stand now, management is responsible—with its job as forfeit—for a good showing of the company. The union can press for a wage increase or some other concession, perhaps a change in depreciation policy, which will have its effect on the company's operations in

[9] Walter F. Titus, "The Kind of Information an Executive Needs to Operate a Factory," *Journal of the American Statistical Association,* vol. 31 (1936), p. 43.
[10] This and the preceding quotation are from Bakke, *Mutual Survival: the Goal of Unions and Management,* pp. 48 and 39.

ten or twenty years. The union leader may not even be around to shoulder any responsibility for that action, even if he would. He might even get a higher office for having done a good job on management. And if the company goes broke or has to retrench or cut wages or take some other radical step as a result of the concessions forced from it, the union always has a stock answer—'bad management.' There's such a thing as bad unionism, too. Some means have to be found of making the union and its leaders take the responsibility for their actions."

An industrial relations director of a large steel corporation continues with the charge. "Many issues raised in union relations involve a responsibility which the union will not assume. Thus in safety, for example, the company has a financial liability for accidents. Under its present program, which has been eminently successful, it conducts investigations and hearings to fix the responsibility for accidents, then metes out any necessary discipline. The results have been phenomenal. Now, however, the union wants to sit in on these hearings, but as I see it only for the purpose of preventing discipline and not of preventing accidents. They don't wish to share the responsibility which the company itself cannot avoid."

In important measure, complaints such as the above are only another aspect of management's single responsibility to the corporate stockholders. Because the union does not share in that responsibility, management views it as having no commensurate duties or obligations. Even when the union's political responsibility to its membership is explicitly recognized by certain of the managers, they find no comfort in the thought that this is at variance with the requirements of their own position. It is little better than no responsibility at all.

There is another way in which management regards the union as lacking in responsibility. Most commonly mentioned of all the union's faults is its failure to live up to the agreement, particularly by its failure to prosecute a grievance by established procedure rather than by strike, slowdown, or intimidation, and by its attempts to enlarge the area of a signed agreement through constant pressure. Says one company official: "Granted that the union has a different type of basic responsibility than the company has, once having signed an agreement both have the same immediate responsibility—to live up to that agreement. Adherence to the contract involves permitting the company to discipline those union members who violate it. It involves the union's use of discretion as to what grievances it will process. The grievance that cannot be supported by a contract provision should not be presented by the union, but be screened out. I recognize that the democratic and political nature of unions makes this impossible in all cases. I appreciate that sometimes union leaders are 'forced' to process a grievance because it is presented by an important constituent or bloc, and in such cases they prefer to have an arbitrator, rather than themselves, decide the lack of merit of the case. This is unfortunate but perhaps it can be accepted as a necessary part of the problem. Nevertheless, the unions should do all within their power to see that the agreement means something."

It is what they consider a poor record of such observance of collective agreements that managers have most often in mind when they charge the union with "irresponsibility" of conduct. There are mixed feelings as to whether this condition will be corrected. Some express optimistic belief that unions will discover the benefits of strict adherence to the contract. There are others, however, who believe that irresponsibility is rooted in the very political framework of the union, with aspirants for power capitalizing on belligerency or importunacy to further their political ends.

5. Management opposes union penetration because it believes that union leadership is inadequate.

One representative lists this as perhaps the primary reason for management's resistance to sharing authority with the unions. Another says that the company must bargain on important issues of vital concern to the company with men whom they would not hire for their shops. A union agent corroborates this frequent management attitude. "They still consider us as inferior in brain power," he says, "and are unwilling to accept us as equals."

It is true that many managers have a healthy respect for the bargaining and tactical abilities of the union leadership. But in the conduct of business enterprise they are not prepared to admit that men who have risen from the ranks by political preferment show any competence warranting participation in expanding areas of decision-making.

6. Management suspects the motives behind union penetration.

This is not true of all businessmen, but the suspicion that there is "something" behind the union's effort to "worm" its way into managerial authority is sufficiently widespread to be significant. Thus one corporate officer says with earnest conviction, "It is their intent to keep matters stirred up in the plants and in the shops so as to provide a setting for their insidious infiltration. The union is setting out to spread its gospel among the teachers, preachers and others in positions of influence, to win converts to its cause. It speaks in the name of Democracy, thus winning with this catch-word many who think softly. It is sometimes able to identify 'democracy' with democracy-in-industry, or labor management, or socialism, even communism of the Russian brand. A great deal of harm has been done by the do-gooders—the college professors and ministers and other socially minded citizens, who have spread the gospel of the dignity of the individual and the thought that if we would only treat each person as an individual and not as a number all problems would be solved. This is a lot of bunkum. The problems run much deeper than that, and the unions know it. They don't believe this soft-headed nonsense, but they make good use of it and encourage it, turning it to their own purposes."

What are these purposes? Personal power, selfish gain, political ends, say some representatives of management. It is worth instant notation that at least in individual instances there can be little doubt of the sincerity with which they hold this belief. It is sometimes stated with an earnestness that is arresting. Two management officials, responsible for the industrial relations of two of America's great corporations, privately expressed their convictions as follows:

Behind the union's effort to encroach on management's authority are two things, which merge into one: a lust for power and a movement towards some form of socialism. Both are very strong. The union is only incidentally a vehicle for the welfare of the workers and primarily a mechanism for achieving these two goals.

Unions seek to expand their authority within the corporation solely because of the greed of the union leaders for personal power. In some cases this may be coupled with the thought of power under a communistic system. How can Yale University or any other academic institution analyze that sort of thing? We who face the union people know it to be true. But how can you dissect it? How can you analyze motivation except in terms of psychopathic, neurotic behavior? Is there any academician left who is still so naïve as to believe the rot spread by the unions that they are motivated solely by consideration for the interests of the workers?

7. Management fears the end result of union penetration.

A vice president who holds one of the most strategic positions in American industrial relations makes the following analysis:

"The American economy is in the throes of a cosmic drift which had its real beginning or impetus back in the period of the first World War, approximately dating from the sweeping demands of the I.W.W., many of which have since been assimilated by industry and found not so bad, some of which have been very difficult to adjust to. This drift was supported by the political atmosphere and legislation of the last decade, which has speeded things so rapidly that it has been more and more difficult for industry to digest the changes. What the future holds I won't attempt to predict, except possibly in these general terms. The political complexion will determine the speed of change, but the drift will probably continue regardless. Factors such as the leadership of labor and industry will also be important, and the general economic condition of the country. But the success of the unions has bred a self-generating force which will be extremely difficult to stop, if possible to stop at all. Management must continue to resist the encroachments of labor by all the power within its means, attempting at the same time to work out such compromises as will be workable. But over the years management will continue to have to buy labor off with concessions that will mean the end of free enterprise as we know it. The end result will probably be internal revolution. I see no prospect and know no way of achieving a peaceful cooperative resolution of the long-run conflict. Unions are insidious in their ability to worm their way into situations. They are masters of the lever principle. One concession becomes a lever by which a greater concession is sought and obtained. They are never satisfied. They keep stirring up discontent by which they can further their power. Within our management family we have our difficulties too. Sometimes we have worse fights among our own people than we do with the union. But whenever we have such difficulties, we can sit down together and thresh things out, and ultimately right prevails. But you can't do that with the unions."

The industrial relations director of another large corporation declares, "The legitimate areas of collective bargaining must be defined. Until that time, management is in the position of an army retreating and regrouping. At some point it will have its back to the wall and there will be no further retreat—without a new economic system, possibly along socialistic lines."

If the privately expressed opinions of a number of management officials in the six industries examined in this study are representative, a significant proportion of our legal managers share this belief that unions are leading the country on the road to socialism or some alternative form of collectivism. There is not only the harsh charge of the propagandist or the critical cry of the unwilling; among some of the managers who have reached the years of philosophical maturity there is at times almost a resigned acceptance of a changing order: "The unions are motivated by two objectives in encroaching on management's functions: one, a search for security; two, a drive for a new economic system approaching socialism. Of course there is a place and a necessity for collective bargaining in American industry—but the ultimate result of it will be socialism of a sort." The eventual soundness of any of these predictions is not of immediate concern to us. The important fact is that such beliefs motivate some of our managers.

In 1937 *Fortune* conducted an "anonymous symposium" of businessmen, and among its findings was the following: "It is of course impossible to speak for *all* businessmen, and in attempting to speak for even a few one runs into insuperable difficulties in social terminology. . . . Here we can only say that in general, as the businessman sees it, this is a free country, with jobs open to all who can get them and the rights of private property inherent in every economic fiber. He has on the whole no 'objection' to the organization of labor provided that this will not impede his free action as an owner (or representative of owners) of private property; provided he can hire and fire as he sees fit; provided his individual employees can work when they want to; provided, that is to say, that traditional labor relations are not materially changed."[11]

Not only are the traditional labor relations materially changed and changing, they are moving in a direction which threatens the businessman's concept of private property. To preserve the economic system which he knows and loves, he feels the necessity of holding the line somewhere against the unions.

The safeguarding of unified final authority, the discharge of imposed responsibility, protection of efficiency, lack of union responsibility, inadequacy of union leadership, suspicion of union motives, and the fear of a changing economic system—these are the principal stated reasons why management has sought to limit the sharing of authority in the corporation. It will be noted that none of these is inconsistent with the others. They mutually support and reinforce the determination of many managers to call a halt to the expansion of labor's spheres of interest. In addition to these given reasons there are others which are generally left unsaid. As was observed in an earlier chapter, the union's program carries a threat to the personal goals of the managers—their security, recognition, and self-expression—which are attained through their position in the corporation. It challenges their essentially realistic philosophy. These unstated reasons lend further support to an intent to hold the line.

As a result of the wearing contest for authority in the corporation, many managers, as we have seen, have reached the conclusion that it is desirable to end the struggle by drawing a line of demarkation between matters of mutual interest to unions and management, and those of sole concern to management. Some feel that such a distinction is more than desirable: it is necessary if industry is to be granted the conditions requisite to its effective operation. Management and the unions can never work together if there is constant suspicion, continuing threats, and brief periods of uneasy peace, they say. Let us draw the line somewhere, they urge, so that we may devote all our time to productive work rather than to defensive preparations.

This view that a definition of spheres of interest should be attempted is common among the managers, but it is not universal. There is a minority who opposes it. Within this group the reasons for objecting to demark-

11 "The Industrial War," *Fortune*, November, 1937, p. 105.

ation are frequently at variance with each other. There are not the same consistency and mutual reinforcement of views that characterize the proponents. We may briefly note their opinions.

1. A few believe that the union may play a constructive role. The most outspoken expression of this belief came from a staff member of a trade association. Speaking of one large corporation he said, "It could fire every vice president on its rolls and the company would still go on. They don't do the work, they don't make any contribution. It's the workers down in the shop and the supervisory people who make the wealth. The vice presidents aren't making their $50,000 a year. They don't know what they're doing, they never had oil in their nose and that's their trouble. If the union can bring in some ability, why shouldn't it have a chance at the job? I think it might be able to make a real contribution."

2. A number of managers voice the belief that "you can't stem the tide or stop the moon," and express a certain willingness to go along with social trends. Coupled with this is sometimes a feeling that the union's drive is a part of a broader democratic movement.

A high official of one large corporation foresees that unions will continue to penetrate more and more into managerial spheres until we have reached some form of a complete labor-management system, or socialism. "This may not be a bad thing, it is impossible to say now, but the important consideration is that it should be reached only by evolutionary procedure, with the speed of progress dependent on how quickly both labor and management officials become trained for such a program."

From the industrial relations director of another large business comes the statement: "I think I speak for our management generally when I say it is not so much objection to the nature of union requests which characterizes our company, but objection as to the timing. We think the union should digest what it has chewed off and establish its responsibility in those areas where it already has authority before seeking to add additional authority."

Others have expressed similar views:

Some sort of syndicalism is on the horizon. It may be good or it may be bad. If properly developed it will probably be for the good. But before we get there, as a necessary prelude to any development in the labor relations picture, there must be a stable relationship. This means contract responsibility.

This drive to socialism must be properly timed, we must make way slowly and learn to operate as we go. Take the guaranteed annual wage, which will probably be the most important union demand of the immediate future. We sympathize with its purpose. We feel, however, that in its usual statement it is inapplicable to many businesses and industries, and if there is an effort to fasten it wholesale to industry there may be business failures and eventual unworkability, followed by general discontent. So we would like to move up to it gradually, and we are trying to work out something which over a period of years would operate to stabilize employment. Making progress slowly. And we have no dogmatic views as to the desirability or undesirability of some of these matters. For example, we oppose unionization of foremen at the present time, but we feel we are going to have it, and we know that in some industries it has worked all right. So the big thing will be to oppose it long enough and introduce it gradually enough so that when we have it it will work smoothly. And at that time we may find it is better than our present arrangement, that it may be all for the good.

3. A very few management officials believe that there is no need to attempt to confine the union's areas of interest because they see no real threat to managerial authority. "With respect to union encroachment on management functions, I see no problem—either now or in the future. It is the last of my worries. The political nature of the unions will prevent it. Their leaders want to be able to criticize management, not to be placed in a position of having their members ask *them* to explain *their* part in a management decision that went astray."

4. Some managers think that criticism of the union for "interfering" with management is beside the point. "The union necessarily limits managerial authority and impedes its functioning by its very existence, but that doesn't mean that unions aren't needed." These officials believe that the desirability of union penetration cannot be discussed outside of a given framework of union responsibility in the areas penetrated, a responsibility which has not yet been adequately defined.

Says one steel company official: "I see no difference between the areas where authority is already shared and those not yet penetrated by the union, so far as the basic question is concerned. Responsibility is the key in both cases. In such traditional areas as wages and hours, for example, union irresponsibility may lead to results as disastrous as if the unions were to have a voice in deciding how to use the corporate reserves, without assuming any responsibility for the success or failure of the company. What about the union movement for the 30-hour week? Does the 20-hour or 10-hour week lie beyond it? What about the union's constant demand for higher and higher wages, with the real danger of pricing the company's products out of the market? The question is not what areas the union shares. It is the degree of responsibility which the union must assume. We must not blur the decisive issue."

5. There are those in management circles who object to an attempted definition of spheres of interest on the ground that it inevitably means greater government control of industrial relations. If existing labor laws, particularly the National Labor Relations Act, were repealed or at least modified, and if government would remove itself from the field of industrial relations, these managers would allow the issue of the degree of union authority in the corporation to be settled over the bargaining table,

on the basis of relative bargaining strengths. "Give us a chance," they say, "and leave us to ourselves."

One significant point stands out from this expression of views of those who oppose an effort to demark the managerial areas of sole interest to the company from those subject to collective bargaining. None of them evidences a hearty welcome to the union to come and share managerial authority. Even those who profess to see present or potential advantages in an expanded union role are firm in their insistence that the union must earn, by demonstrated capacity and responsibility, its right to more of a voice. Some have said that they will fight the union on its attempted advances just to insure that the growth of union power comes slowly enough to be assimilated by the labor leadership, by business organizations, and by the economic system. And some who would attempt no definition of spheres of influence adopt such a view out of an opposition to unionism as fundamental as that expressed by the managements who favor demarkation of interests.

THE VIEWS OF UNION LEADERSHIP

"The first thing to remember is that the function of management is to manage and the function of the union is to protect its members. Any local union which makes the mistake of taking over functions which belong to the management will get nothing but headaches for its trouble. Let a shop steward picture the difference between telling a union member the following about how his grievance came out:

"No. 1. '*We* talked your case over, Joe, and *we* decided that *we* can't give you more job evaluation points to get you upgraded.'

"No. 2. '*I* tried to get you a higher rating, Joe, but *they* turned you down.'

"The union member receiving No. 1 answer naturally will put the blame on the union for not getting him upgraded. He should. The union has abandoned its rightful function—that of protecting the worker—when it participates in management's function."[12]

This advice to shop stewards comes from the United Electrical, Radio and Machine Workers. It is paralleled in many unions by similar protestations that labor has no intent of invading the field of management.

"To relieve the boss or the management of proper responsibility for making a success of the enterprise is about the last thing any group of employees—organized or unorganized—would consider workable or even desirable. The unions are on record in numerous instances as recognizing

---

[12] *UE Guide to Wage Payment Plans, Time Study and Job Evaluation* (1943), pp 97-98. Italics in the original.

that in the last analysis management has to manage, if any concern is to be a success financially or in any other way."[13]

"The job of railroad labor, it should be pointed out, is that of manning the railroads. Railroad labor is content with this lot, and is not disposed to assume management functions."[14]

Such professions as these have not served to allay the fears of the business leaders, however. They know that whatever the intent it is belied by the practice, and from union statements in other contexts they are even quite certain that assurances such as the above are little more than camouflage and seduction. They believe that the unions are converging upon their intrenched position with a triple offensive.

First, the unions are emphasizing the workers' interest in the conduct of the corporation as citizens and members of the public. Thus one highly placed union official asserts that "even if price policy has no place in negotiations, our members have a legitimate interest in it as part of the public, and can exert their influence through public pressure. The same is true of the guaranteed annual wage and full employment. We can do something along these lines in collective bargaining, but the biggest job will have to be done on a broader front, through government, which our members can influence as voters." To the extent that the unions promote such measures through political pressures, rather than through direct bargaining with the corporation or industrial associations, they are attacking the scope of managerial authority by public rather than private means.

Second, the unions are demanding the right to be informed about and to criticize management policies. "The time has passed when a labor leader could say that he had no interest in the methods by which a business was financed and managed. An artificial legal person, which is called a corporation, is the sort of employer which most American industrial workers now have for a boss. If we are to have a fair distribution of income between Capital and Labor, it will be necessary for business agents of unions to become familiar with the financial statements of corporations. The corporation is the agency through which the laborer sells his service to the consuming public. He has a direct interest in knowing whether it is an efficient middleman."[15]

Of more immediate concern to management than either of the above approaches, however, is labor's outright or implied assertion of a present

[13] Cooke and Murray, *Organized Labor and Production*, p. 84. The co-author is Philip Murray, president of the CIO and of the United Steelworkers of America.
[14] Railway Labor Executives' Association, *The Wages of Railroad Labor—1938*, p. 26.
[15] "The Distribution of the Income of Corporations," *American Federationist*, vol. 39 (May, 1932), p. 549.

or reserved right to participate in expanding areas of decision-making within the corporation. In few cases is the assertion made with such absence of qualification as characterized the declaration of one union official: "We are always trying to encroach on the managerial prerogatives."[16] Nevertheless, candor has not been lacking. One of the management members of the President's National Labor-Management Conference following World War II reported subsequently: "Labor wouldn't even agree to an effort to define the functions of management, although we made a real effort to get that issue settled. We drew up a list of some thirty-odd specific acts, such as the determination of prices, accounting procedure, and so forth, which it seemed clear to us must be reserved to management. Labor refused to accept a single one, and we were told officially by one of the labor delegates that the reason they had refused was that at some future time labor may want to bring any one of these functions into the realm of collective bargaining."[17]

Such inconsistency of attitudes—the denial of a desire to assume management functions, as earlier noted, on the one hand, and the declaration of the possible desirability of further participating in management functions, on the other—is not attributable to the differing viewpoints of individuals. It reveals a basic irresolution within the union movement which has contributed either to the bewilderment or the cynicism of many managers. Examples of the unions' dilemma are not lacking.

The labor members of one of the committees of the National Labor-Management Conferences of 1945 declared in their report, "The function and responsibilities of management must be preserved if business and industry is to be efficient, progressive, and provide more good jobs." Three paragraphs later they stated their unwillingness to define the functions and responsibilities which "must be preserved" because "to do so might well restrict the flexibility so necessary to efficient operation."[18]

At the hearing before the presidential fact-finding board in the General Motors dispute of 1945–1946, the president of the United Automobile Workers made the statement:

"We have not at any time challenged management's right to manage the plants.

"We have at no time raised the question of sharing managerial functions."

And then, with no apparent recognition of inconsistency, he went on:

[16] Matthew Smith, secretary, Mechanics Educational Society of America, testifying before the Special Senate Committee in *Investigation of the National Defense Program*, part 28, p. 13245.

[17] Ira Mosher, then president of the National Association of Manufacturers, as reported in the *New York Times*, December 6, 1945.

[18] *President's National Labor-Management Conference*, p. 61.

"We have said that wages and prices and ability to pay must have a relationship if we are to achieve a full production, full employment, full consumption economy. We have said that this is more than an ordinary wage argument . . ."[19]

In championing union-management cooperation programs, two labor leaders make the following assertions, which most businessmen would regard as a remarkable instance of non sequitur: "In no way does management surrender any of its prerogatives. Before anything can be done under union-management cooperation, the consent of both parties must be obtained."[20]

It is not surprising, then, to find one company representative voicing the complaint, "They say they don't want to tell you how to run your business, but in the next breath they complain that such and such a matter should be decided or acted upon jointly." The key to this seeming inconsistency is perhaps contained in the words of one national union president, "I don't believe it is the desire of any Union to take from Management the right to conduct a business in the most efficient manner possible, but do believe that when a contract is entered into any change in the manner of operations that will affect the working conditions, job security or promotional possibilities of employees covered by the contract should and must be subject to collective bargaining if industrial peace is to be maintained."

There is thus no desire to challenge managerial authority *as such,* but a firm insistence that where the interests of the workers are bound up in the exercise of authority in a given area of business operations, the unions must be granted a voice. As expressed by one agent, "There is no field over which the union will renounce jurisdiction if the welfare of its members is directly concerned." This welfare of its members, as we have seen in the previous chapter, embraces security, recognition, and self-expression, all broadly defined. It is at this point, however, that the paradox is reintroduced. For there is a growing consciousness on the part of an increasing number of labor leaders that there is scarcely an area of business operations in which managerial decisions do not affect these interests of the workers. This belief is still in its formative stages and has not yet crystallized to an important degree, but it is becoming more widespread. Thus one national labor official has suggested the possibility that at some future date the union may become vitally concerned with the selection of management itself, since the choice of corporate officials may determine the conduct of the business.

It is perhaps fair to say that with few exceptions the union leaders have

[19] *New York Times,* December 29, 1945.
[20] Golden and Ruttenberg, *Dynamics of Industrial Democracy,* p. 293.

not fully thought through the implications of their stated position. It is a safe prediction that as the issues are formed more concretely they will be led irresistibly to the conviction that the preservation of management's undivided authority and responsibility is incompatible with the logic of their objectives. This process has already proceeded to the point where few labor leaders would willingly consent to a demarkation of the union's sphere of interest. Their words speak for themselves.

The carefully framed statement of the labor members of the Committee on Management's Right to Manage of the 1945 Labor-Management Conference read:

"It would be extremely unwise to build a fence around the rights and responsibilities of management on the one hand and the unions on the other. The experience of many years shows that with the growth of mutual understanding the responsibilities of one of the parties today may well become the joint responsibility of both parties tomorrow.

"We cannot have one sharply delimited area designated as management prerogatives and another equally sharply defined area of union prerogatives without either side constantly attempting to invade the forbidden territory, thus creating much unnecessary strife."[21]

A union representative declares, "Any attempt to draw a line between areas subject to collective bargaining and others subject to the sole discretion of management is an attack on collective bargaining itself. It is not feasible nor desirable in a democratic society—collective bargaining is democracy at work."

The views of probably a majority of union leaders are well summed up in a statement drafted though not released by a committee of their own number:

Management and labor are both vitally interested in full and efficient production and each has functions to perform to attain the common objective. At the present time, some of the functions can best be performed by management alone without any participation on the part of labor. Among these functions we may include for instance the type and size of the plant, the determination of the type of product, and the engineering and commercial phases of its manufacture and sale. Labor likewise has functions which are peculiar to itself. All these exclusive functions must be integrated into the good of the whole.

As to the other functions that lie in the middle ground, labor can make an outstanding contribution if invited to participate in an advisory capacity. In still other functions genuine progress can be made only with labor's fullest cooperation on a partnership basis.

This is as far as labor is willing to go in any process of demarking areas of joint and single interest. It refuses to tag any specific area of decision with the permanent label of managerial prerogative, but it is

[21] *President's National Labor-Management Conference*, p. 61.

willing to recognize that "at the present time" there are operations which can "best be performed by management alone." These areas and operations are not fixed. Some future occasion may demonstrate the desirability of shifting them to the category of decisions in which labor plays an advisory role, or to that category demanding "labor's fullest cooperation on a partnership basis."

It is clear that in any effort to draw the line between areas subject to collective bargaining and areas of sole concern to management, businessmen will proceed unaided by the unions.

THE BARGAINING STRENGTH OF CONVICTIONS

The arguments of management and labor with respect to the union's role in the corporation are being brought to bear not only on each other but also on the American people generally. In seeking a resolution of the issue they are using their beliefs as bargaining weapons directed against each other, but each realizes that it is simultaneously engaged in a continuing bargaining session before the public as arbitrator. The public as yet has shown no disposition to decide the matter, but has preferred to reserve judgment pending the course of events. This attitude has on the whole been favorable to the unions, but it does not necessarily betoken the nature of the final decision. Without regard to the merits of the dispute, we may here take note of one important fact affecting the relative bargaining strengths before the public of the convictions of the two contending parties.

The objections of management to extending the scope of union authority in the corporation primarily rest on legal and technical considerations. These are frequently challenged by indicating the possibilities of new—and perhaps more desirable—legal and technical arrangements. The union's arguments for extending its spheres of interest in the corporation are, on the other hand, grounded almost exclusively on ethical considerations. This appeal to social morality provides the basis on which a new legal and technical order has been defended. In this debate management is at a disadvantage, for the logic of law and technology have never provided a satisfactory answer to an ethical challenge. Our legal institutions are only a reflection of the prevailing social morality, and as that morality changes so too—with a lag—do our laws. Prevailing technologies have sometimes seemed to control the ordering of our social institutions, but it is widely recognized that technology can and should be the instrument and not the master of men; within the same technological framework social arrangements can and do differ, over time and geography, depending upon their ethical content.

There is no need to weigh the relative merits of conflicting moral judg ments in order to assert their importance in deciding basic issues of group interests. There is no necessity at this stage of our investigation to assess the ethical claims on which the unions rest their case. We are interested now only in the fact that unions have chosen to base their insistence on a voice in corporate affairs on the broad ground of construed justice and rightness, while the managers—accepting as implicit the ethical grounds of their own position—have urged the rejection of the unions' claims primarily on the legal and organizational supports of their ethical system.

Consider the implications of this subtle fact in weighing the probable effects of the respective arguments on public response to them.

Management contends that it requires unified final authority and opportunity to discharge its responsibility, a responsibility for which the unions have no counterpart. Final authority and responsibility there is certainly need for—but the hands in which they have concentrated have changed from time to time in the course of human history. Such concentration must be defended on ethical grounds, and the unions challenge the ethics of our present corporate system.

Management charges that the union program will endanger industrial efficiency. It defends its principles of rational commercial engineering because these serve the interests which, under the law, it is compelled to serve, because these show up on the profit score by which its success is marked. Neither "management" nor "efficiency," however, is synonomous with commercial engineering. Both are required whatever the aims of the business—whether maximum profits, satisfaction on the job, peak production, or high employment. The unions challenge the aims of business —a challenge based on moral grounds. "It is conceivable that goods may possess an ethical value which is assessable in no ratio whatever to their economic value. The ethical value of goods produced under 'sweated' conditions, or of goods deleterious to the well-being of the community, may indeed be in inverse ratio to the economic value of those goods."[22] The same may be true of production in which the workers are controlled but do not control.

Management argues that the end result of the spread of union authority may be a different economic system than that we now know. Their prevision may be accurate, but a "system" evolving slowly on lines indigenous to this country may provide an increasingly effective instrument for the attainment of social aims, which are necessarily ethical norms. Social change there has always been, and it cannot be condemned on its face, simply because it is change.

Management maintains that union leaders are inadequate to the authority which they seek. They have yet to prove that, given authority—

[22] Sheldon, *The Philosophy of Management*, p. 78.

and responsibility—in a business framework in which other motives than profit are recognized, the union leadership may not ultimately prove competent in the fulfillment of its assignment within such an altered framework.

Reversing the field of argument, the unions contend that increasing their corporate role is desirable in the attainment of the workers' objective of greater security, including not only material advancement but also a share in the control over their own working lives. This ethical argument carries immense appeal to a nation devoted to a mass sharing of control over its political institutions. Can it be combated by the legal proposition that this threatens unified final authority and responsibility, when under our present corporate laws that authority and that responsibility run only to the stockholders?

The unions assert that the expansion of their corporate authority is necessary for that participation of the workers in the enterprise on which depends their opportunities for adequate self-expression and recognition. Can the assertion of a moral right of an individual, through his selected agency, to develop his personal capacity and to render his maximum contribution be overridden by the contention that this threatens technical efficiency?

It is thus probably the case that the unions have some advantage over the managers in the presentation of their views to the public, in view of the fact that their appeal is to moral consciousness rather than to a code of laws, that their standard is justice to men rather than the requirements of engineering efficiency. At the same time we must recognize that it is of course not true that the arguments of management have no ethical basis. Actually they find their justification in the ethical concept of the right of private property. In a practical sense business spokesmen find difficulty in making use of this appeal, however. For *as management* the strength of their position is in a legal addendum to private property and not in private property itself. It is not their own rights they are defending, but those of absentee owners. It is not their own interests that are rooted in the legal system of authority and responsibility in which they must operate, but those of a shifting body of stockholders.

Moreover, in the large corporation the property rights which they are thus defending as paid agents have long since ceased to retain much of their private character. Our large corporations have become in a real sense public institutions. This has been recognized in certain of our laws, and even in forum statements of the managers themselves. We shall later examine expressions of management's self-assumed responsibility to their employes and to the public, a responsibility which, while perhaps in part designed to answer the ethical claims of the union, in a sense only recognizes those claims. Yet even with management's assumption of such larger responsibilities, it is clear that its authority, the responsibility from which that authority derives, its efficiency concepts and its criticism of union motives and competence are rested on its dominant legally imposed responsibility to the business owners. For the present we are interested primarily in the fact that the managers are employing, to oppose the ethical stand of the unions, only an arsenal of legal and technical considerations which in the contemplation of the law and the public have lost much of their force.

This is not the whole story of the relative bargaining strengths of the two parties before the public. It is worth taking specific note of two other factors.

1. The conduct of the parties in the pursuit of their objectives may be important if not decisive. For example, management's suspicion of the union's motives—a belief that it is a vehicle for selfish gain and personal power—may spread to the community, but it will probably do so only if its spread is justified by union conduct. In this area the unions are at a decided disadvantage, for we have placed in their hands as their only effective means of attaining their objectives within the single corporation a weapon—the strike—which by its very nature is disruptive of industrial peace and suggestive of mass holdup.

2. The stress on ethical aims does not deny the necessity of giving careful consideration to the legal and technical structures within which those aims are pursued, and the unions may be charged with insufficient attention to such matters. Indeed, we may go further and say that the strength of the union's position will in large measure be determined by the desirability and feasibility of the legal and technical institutions it proposes to achieve its ethical ends. The latter do not operate in a vacuum. However attractive a goal, we are justified in exercising caution as to the choice of means to attain it. Communism may well claim to rest on the same moral motivations, but the American people as a whole are convinced that the means adopted have been self-defeating.

Despite these considerations it remains true that most management members have failed sufficiently to appreciate that the legal and technical defenses which they have so carefully erected will provide little bulwark if the case before the bar of public opinion is conducted on an ethical front which they have largely ignored.

CAN THE UNION'S ROLE IN MANAGEMENT BE LIMITED?

In addition to the question of the desirability of attempting to draw a line demarking the spheres of joint interest from those of sole managerial competence, there remains the further question of whether such a line can in fact be drawn.

There are some management people who feel that such a separation of interests can and must be made. One who holds to this view adds that "if such a line can't be drawn and held we might as well turn the common stock over to the union and let them run the business." Another maintains that the union's contention that it is willing to concede full authority to management as long as the welfare of its members is not involved provides no adequate stopping place to the union's drive, as "the union can arrange facts to prove that the employes' welfare is concerned in almost any type of management decision." A line can and should be drawn on another basis, he feels, perhaps on a distinction between direct effects on wages and working conditions and indirect or remote effects, with the union conceded no interest in the latter.

Mere belief in the feasibility of a separation of spheres of interest is insufficient. The advocates of such a policy must assume the burden of demonstrating where such a line of demarkation may be drawn and how it may be held. Proposals embodying these details have been made, and it is these suggested approaches which we shall examine here.

1. "The law should define the area which is the proper subject of collective bargaining; it should prohibit all bargains which extend beyond the area as defined."[23]

This suggestion of a legal definition of spheres of interest has perhaps had its ablest expression by Robert M. C. Littler, an attorney who has specialized in problems of industrial relations. We may use his plan as a model of this approach. It involves legislation resting on a number of simply stated principles, the most important of which may be summarized as follows:

The law should define the proper area of collective bargaining as that which includes wages, hours, and conditions of labor, that which bears directly upon the employment and collective-bargaining relationship. No other area of union interest would be recognized.

Union action to penetrate the forbidden territory should be treated as an improper exercise of concerted pressure.

There should be a clear statement of the public interest and public policy with respect to all types of union restrictive rules.

Enforcement should be left to an administrative agency, which would be empowered to investigate and make public report upon the nature and consequences of those restrictive rules which are not subject to

[23] Robert M. C. Littler, "The Public Interest in the Terms of Collective Bargains," *American Economic Review*, Papers and Proceedings, May, 1945, p. 220. The subsequent quotation is from p. 222.

specific prohibition, and to issue "cease and desist" orders for violation of the statutory provisions.

As for a definition of the permissible and forbidden areas of collective bargaining, "Generally speaking, the transactions of the employer which precede the performance of work by his employees and those which follow the completion of that work are not the business of the employment or the union relation. To exclude them from the scope of collective bargaining would almost automatically proscribe those collective bargains which restrain trade and attempt to control the general market."

Since the object of this proposed legislation is more the protection of the public than of management, it is especially concerned with "restraint of trade" and "make work" rules imposed by the unions. While the former would be prohibited outright, proponents of this type of legislation recognize that the latter category includes contractual provisions which at times have some justification. This category would not therefore be outlawed, but the floodlight of publicity would be thrown upon such practices by the administrative agency, so that the public would be better able to judge the good and the bad. Regardless of this public rather than private basis for the proposed legislation, the process of delimiting the union's legitimate sphere of interest might serve as that line of demarkation which many of the managers desire.

The effect of the legislation as outlined would be to establish an allowable area of collective bargaining. All else would be beyond the union's pale. Other legislative proposals have reversed the field by attempting a definition of a proscribed area, outside of which union interest would be unchecked.[24] Thus it would be considered a violation of the antitrust laws "to induce or require any employer to impose or adopt unreasonable restrictions or conditions upon the use of any material, machine or equipment," subject to the proviso that restrictions of this nature are not to be considered unreasonable "if they are directly and appropriately related to the wages, hours, health, safety, or working conditions of the employes." Such legislative proposals are not an attempt to define the areas of union interest, nor have they been so intended; they are, rather, an effort to forestall certain agreements which might otherwise be reached in given areas. While a union would be forbidden to bargain for an "unreasonable" restriction on managerial authority in the area of methods of production, for example, it would not be barred

[24] As for example in the two bills introduced in the House during the first session of the 77th Congress, one by Representative Walter (H. R. 5218), the other by Representative Munroney (H. H. 5259), from which quotation is made below. Both bills were supported by the Antitrust Division of the Department of Justice at the time when it was pressing for the extension of the antitrust laws to embrace certain union practices.

from all interest in that area. Nevertheless, the effect would be to limit, if not to define, the union's sphere of interest.

To contend that either legislative approach—to define by principle the union's permitted or prohibited influence in the corporation—is probably unworkable is not to argue that union actions may not be controlled in the public interest. It may fairly be assumed that action considered antisocial by management is equally antisocial when practiced by the unions, in the absence of any proof to the contrary. It may reasonably be maintained that unions possess no characteristics entitling them to a privileged position in our society. Nevertheless, it seems probable that attempts to draw the line demarking the union's legitimate interests at those issues which "directly" affect the employes' wages, hours, and working conditions are foredoomed to failure, and that efforts to confine the union to matters of "reasonable" relation to traditional areas of collective bargaining will bog down in controversy. It is more than a problem as to whether such a demarkation is desirable, it is more than a question as to the ethical ground on which management may claim an inviolable right to single competence in broad areas of business decision. It is equally a matter of the feasibility of the proposed segregation of interests.

For "on closer inspection the pattern dissolves at the edges. The line between wage and nonwage issues, and between issues that do and do not bear a direct relation to 'wages, hours and conditions of labor,' could probably be drawn no more satisfactorily and precisely by a legislature than it has been drawn in practice at the bargaining table and by labor relations boards."[25] We are indebted to countless industrialists for the dictum that prices and wages are indissolubly related. Financial and accounting policies may likewise bear directly upon the setting of wage rates.[26] The introduction of technological improvements concerns the techniques of production; it concerns likewise the job security of the individual. As those managers will readily agree who see no identifiable "line" in the union's profession to be concerned only with matters affecting the welfare of their members, a claim can be made that will embrace any or all areas within that definition.

The possibilities of building a legislative fence to circumscribe the union's interests would be limited, then, by the continuous necessity of defining the area enclosed and excluded; the progressive definition of

[25] James J. Robbins, *American Economic Review*, Papers and Proceedings, May, 1945, p. 226.
[26] As in a case occurring in New York City in 1940, in which a 5 per cent adjustment of wages hinged upon the question, submitted to arbitration, of whether certain items charged to operating expenses were properly charged to such accounts.

that area would necessarily be shifting and uncertain. The definition of today would give little promise of resemblance to the definition of the future. The resolution of the union's role in the corporation would be at best postponed; it would not be answered. More important, the questions of the union's proper authority and responsibility, which lie behind the question of its spheres of interests, would remain to be solved.

2. "If labor disputes are to be minimized by 'the genuine acceptance by organized labor of the functions and responsibilities of management to direct the operation of an enterprise,' labor must agree that certain specific functions and the responsibilities of management are not subject to collective bargaining."[27]

This effort to define the boundaries of union interest by joint agreement of management and union leadership has been tried many times, most notably in the Labor-Management Conference of 1945 convened at the President's direction. For a period of several weeks a committee of twelve sought to reduce to writing a definition of interests on which all could agree. The result was fruitless, and independent reports were issued by the labor and management groups composing the committee. The former would agree to no specific limitations on the subject matter of collective bargaining. "The extensive exploratory discussions of the committee have brought forth the wide variety of traditions, customs, and practices that have grown out of relationships between unions and management in various industries over a long period of time. Because of the complexity of these relationships, the labor members of the committee think it unwise to specify and classify the functions and responsibilities of management. Because of the insistence by management for such specification, the committee was unable to agree upon a joint report."

The divergence in views was made more obvious by the separate report of the management members. Two classifications of decisions were drawn, the first comprising "those matters which are clearly the functions and responsibility of management and are not subject to collective bargaining." Illustrative items in this category were set forth as follows:

The determination of products to be manufactured or services to be rendered to customers by the enterprise; and the location of the business, including the establishment of new units and the relocation or closing of old units. (When it becomes necessary to relocate a unit, or close an old unit, or transfer major operations between plants, management should give careful consideration to the impact of such moves on the employees involved, and discuss with them or their accredited representatives possible solutions for the resulting problems.)

The determination of the lay-out and equipment to be used in the business; the

[27] From the statement of management members of the Committee on Management's Right to Manage, *President's National Labor-Management Conference*, pp.56–57. Subsequent quotations are from pp. 58–61 of the same report, which includes the labor members' views as well.

processes, techniques, methods, and means of manufacture and distribution; the materials to be used (subject to proper health and safety measures where dangerous materials are utilized) and the size and character of inventories.

The determination of financial policies; general accounting procedures—particularly the internal accounting necessary to make reports to the owners of the business and to government bodies requiring financial reports; prices of goods sold or services rendered to customers; and customer relations.

The determination of the management organization of each producing or distributing unit; and the selection of employees for promotion to supervisory and other managerial positions.

The determination of job content (this refers to establishing the duties required in the performance of any given job and not to wages); the determination of the size of the work force; the allocation and assignment of work to workers; the determination of policies affecting the selection of employees; establishment of quality standards and judgment of workmanship required; and the maintenance of discipline and control and use of the plant property; the scheduling of operations and the number of shifts.

The determination of safety, health, and property protection measures, where legal responsibility of the employer is involved.

The second category developed by the management members comprised those matters in which management would exercise the authority to make initial decision, but where the decision or its consequences would be subject to review by the grievance procedure. Illustrative of this classification were "discharge of employees for cause, the application of seniority provisions of contracts; penalties imposed as the result of disciplinary action; and such other matters as may be mutually agreed upon."

The conflict of views, with the resulting impossibility of agreement, is readily apparent when one contrasts management's list of issues not subject to collective bargaining with some of the practices presently prevailing in the industries previously analyzed in this study. Job content, size of work force, allocation and assignment of workers, hiring standards, discipline and control, scheduling of operations and shifts, safety and health standards—the unions have already established their influence in these areas. Specific unions in specific localities in specific industries and specific companies have penetrated many another of the items on the list.

If not joint agreement generally throughout the economy, can joint agreement be achieved in the single corporation or industry? We already have the answer. In almost all cases contract clauses now set forth the reserved powers of management, agreed to by the union. Such expressions, however, must be read with the reservation that they may be elsewhere modified in the contract. They constitute no barrier to the spread of union authority within the corporation from year to year, as the contract expires and is rebargained. The fact that management is still concerned with union penetration in the face of these "reserved rights" indicates that they indicate no more than a temporary line of separation of interests. It is difficult to reach any conclusion other than the infeasibility of establishing a line of demarkation by a process of joint agreement.

3. If not by legislation, if not by joint agreement, one other method of limiting the union's role in the corporation has been suggested—a self-definition by management. In the words of one company official, "If we were free to pursue our own course, we would not indulge in any recrimination against individuals, but we would fight to the last ounce the union." Some managers have made no secret of this willingness to draw their own line, prepare their own defenses, and have it out with the union—if the government would step out of the picture. In one company where the union is threatening to make an unfair-labor-practice charge of the company's refusal to bargain over retirement benefits, an official says with grim earnestness that "my company will tell the government to take over our plants before we will concede on this issue. A stop has to be called somewhere."

Of all the proposals for confining the union's interest, this is perhaps the most feasible if the premise of governmental nonintervention is granted. It is true that it would operate unevenly. Strong unions might continue to invade fields defended by management, in the pursuit of the goals of their members and under the drive of their political nature. But strong corporations, of the type with which we are concerned, might prove more than a match for unions bereft of any support but their own. If we concede, however, that governmental support of the collective-bargaining process is here to stay, and that the political pressure of 15 million organized workers and their families cannot be shrugged aside, then here too there is no possibility of the rearing of an effective barrier to further union penetration.

We are thus brought to a conclusion which a number of the managers have themselves reached—that no feasible way has yet been suggested by which a line of demarkation may be drawn separating matters of interest to the union from those of sole concern to management. "Our industrial relations department feels the futility of attempting to draw a separating line. Issues and relationships are evolutionary, and no such line would hold for longer than from one contract period to the next." "The Labor-Management Conference approach of attempting to spell out management prerogatives is not only inappropriate but impossible. It is impossible ever to draw up a complete list of management responsibilities and functions. They can't all be put down because they are so numerous and complex and because they are subject to change. The only feasible approach is to leave the settlement of such questions up to collective bargaining itself." "It's impossible to draw a line which will hold good generally. It is a problem for each company individually, and there is no set rule which can be applied within any one company. Where the line is to be drawn is dependent on the general situation, economic conditions, union responsibility, and other such factors." "Such a line might be drawn today—it is set out in the contract—but it would not hold for long. It is a floating line, and there is no possibility of tying it down with an anchor."

This is the view of union officials as well. Few will commit themselves to a statement of areas of management which they believe it necessary for the unions to penetrate, beyond the immediate program of the union. They speak of winning a retirement plan next year, of "tightening up" the seniority provisions in the next contract negotiations, of "going all out" for a guaranteed annual wage when the agreement is reopened for bargaining. There is no consciousness of invading managerial prerogatives. By the same token, there is no area of management which most of them would hesitate to put on "next year's list" if they felt the interests of the union were involved. In the words of one, "You *can't* pin the union down. Unionism, like society itself, is dynamic."

CHAPTER 7

The Historical Perspective of Union Interests

"The question of managerial prerogatives is age-old. It is at least as old as the days when Jacob hired workers to tend his flocks."

This observation of an official of one of our large public utilities is worth remembering, for it emphasizes that the challenge to managerial authority did not originate with the unions. Wherever the relation of employer and employe, master and servant, owner and slave, exists, wherever, in fact, authority is present, there is occasion and opportunity for those bossed to challenge the bosses. It has been at few times and in few societies, however, that groups have been permitted to organize for the very purpose of challenging vested legal authority.

Without organization, the possibility of resistance to intrenched authority is meager. It was for this reason that employers, with the support of public authority, bitterly fought for so long the right of laborers to form unions and to engage in concerted action aimed at compelling changes of managerial decisions. Legislatures and the courts united in condemning such attempts as infringements on the right of owners of private property to direct the use and disposition of their property as they saw fit. Until the past century such efforts by workers were banned, broken by force, and punished by sentence. The National Industrial Conference of 1920 could still report that "It was not, however, until within the memory of men still living that it ceased to be a penal offense, under the laws of England and in some of our States, for two or more workmen to combine to quit work, in order to secure increased wages or improved working conditions."[1]

There is no need of tracing here the long and bitter road to legalization of the right of workers to organize and press for improvement in working conditions—that is to say, to seek changes in managerial decisions. Suffice the recollection that each step along that road has been impeded by those who have contended that such organization to challenge legally constituted authority is inimical to society's interests as expressed in its existing laws and institutions. This the unions have not forgotten. Few

[1] Contained in the *Eighth Annual Report of the Secretary of Labor* (1920), p. 252.

158

organizations have treasured their history and traditions more than they, inculcating them in each succeeding generation of leaders. The legends of triumphs over such obstacles are part of the lore of the profession, and they have inured labor leadership to charges which might make another man cringe. Is he called revolutionary? His predecessors were so called when they fought for the 12-hour day. Is he charged with sapping the foundations of economic society when he seeks to influence prices? His predecessors were so charged when they sought to influence wages. Is he accused of challenging managerial prerogatives when he appeals for a voice for labor in the standards and methods of production? His predecessors were so accused when they petitioned for the right to bargain collectively about working conditions.

.. They talk about our challenging management's prerogatives. That issue is as old as management itself. . . . The right of men to band together in free association in trade unions to better their conditions—that challenged free enterprise.

If you go back into history, to the dark history of industrial England, you will find that when the coal miners in the coal pits around Newcastle said that there should be a law in England to abolish the sixteen-hour day for children and women, it was said that that would destroy free enterprise and that that was an attack upon the prerogatives of management. These are the old slogans that have been thrown in the way of social progress ever since man has organized to advance himself.[2]

Despite the persistence of these "old slogans," labor unions have grown in power and effectiveness, indeed to such an extent that the problem of industrial relations is now conceived of in terms of management and the unions, though as recently as World War I the unions were not often recognized as bona fide expressions of employe interests. The growth of power has been erratic, it is true, but there is little question of its continuity and acceleration. From the Emergency Ordinance of Laborers in the England of 1349, fixing the conditions of employment and set in a common-law background where unions were considered antisocial conspiracies, to the Combination Acts of 1824 and 1825, legalizing union activity but only for certain purposes, was a tortuous march of 475 years. From the latter combination acts to the days when a labor government was supreme in England required less than 125 years more. In America, the taint of conspiracy which had been applied to unionism by the English common law was first removed by the 1842 decision of Chief Justice Shaw of the Massachusetts Supreme Court in the case of *Commonwealth* v. *Hunt.* Despite the gradual development through a process of death and rebirth of effective national unions during the remainder of the nineteenth century, however, it was not until the present

[2] Walter Reuther before the Truman Fact-Finding Board, *New York Times*, December 29, 1945.

century that they had become strong enough to command an attention and political deference which facilitated their growth. We may briefly note certain of the more important manifestations in the last few decades of a growing public recognition of union interests.

The pace of labor's advance began to accelerate in 1913 with the establishment of the Department of Labor with a Secretary in the President's cabinet, culminating an agitation that had begun in 1865. Created in the interest of all wage earners, whether organized or not, the new Department quickly found that "official intercourse with individuals as such has practical limits which organization and representation alone can expand," and turned to the unions for its contacts with working groups.[3] In marked contrast to earlier governmental attitudes, a conciliation service was formed within the Department whose sole function lay in assisting employers and organized employes to reach *mutually* satisfactory working agreements.

The pace quickens with World War I. In 13 months of active existence, the National War Labor Board made its impact upon the industrial scene. Acting upon principles laid down by the War Labor Conference Board, consisting of both labor and management representatives, the Labor Board through its decisions established "the right of workers to organize in trade unions and to bargain collectively through chosen representatives . . ."[4] Provision was made for choice of representatives through secret election. Representatives so chosen might or might not be union-affiliated, but unless recognition had been granted to the union previous to the war employers were not required by the Board to recognize the union as such. "What they are dealing with is committees of employees and not with the union." Indeed, in the absence of prior practice the employer was not obligated to deal with any representative who himself was not an employe in the company affected. This, we must remember, was not much more than 25 years ago. Small concessions? Perhaps, but the workers' committees so elected were empowered to bargain with their employers on subjects which, under the Board's directives, included the following: uniform classifications, job content, discharges without sufficient cause, holidays, weekly work periods, piecework rates, payment for special services, health standards, establishment of an apprentice system, and of course wage schedules, hours, and overtime.

The hurdle of conspiracy had thus been left in the past—but as the postwar tripartite National Industrial Conference revealed, the doctrine of managerial prerogatives was still very much alive, though a little

[3] *Eighth Annual Report of the Secretary of Labor*, p. 26.

[4] *Report of the Secretary of the National War Labor Board* (1920), p. 52. Subsequent quotation and information will be found on pp. 52–67.

bruised from the war. The Conference broke up when employers refused to concede "the right of wage earners to organize without discrimination, to bargain collectively, to be represented by representatives of their own choosing in negotiations and adjustments with employers in respect to wages, hours of labor, and relations and conditions of employment." A second Industrial Conference was thereupon convened by the President and succeeded in coming forth with a report elaborating suggestions for employe participation. Anticlimactical, it made little impact, but interest attaches to one of its paragraphs. After pointing out that "for the most part causes of [industrial] unrest are not the result of the war; they have been accentuated by it," the report continued:

"There is, however, a feature of the present industrial unrest which differentiates it from that commonly existing before the war. It cannot be denied that unrest today is characterized more than ever before by purposes and desires which go beyond the mere demand for higher wages and shorter hours. Aspirations inherent in this form of restlessness are to a greater extent psychological and intangible. They are not for that reason any less significant. They reveal a desire on the part of workers to exert a larger and more organic influence upon the processes of industrial life. This impulse is not to be discouraged but made helpful and cooperative. With comprehending and sympathetic appreciation, it can be converted into a force working for a better spirit and understanding between capital and labor, and for more effective cooperation."[5]

In the prosperity years of the 1920's the "restlessness" and "aspirations" of the workers were not so readily discernible, partly from discretion. Union membership declined and company employe representation plans mushroomed. Nevertheless, the "march of labor" continued. The feeble protection of railway labor in the Transportation Act of 1920 gave way to the Railway Labor Act of 1926, further strengthened in 1934, and upheld by the Supreme Court in 1937. The right of railroad employes to organize in unions of their own choosing, the obligation of the employer not to discriminate against employes for such action or otherwise to impede their efforts, and the requirement upon the employer to bargain collectively with his organized employes—these were all set forth. The power of railroad employes to organize to effect changes in managerial decisions was thus recognized and protected by law. The Anti-Injunction Act of 1932 provided further support by removing an important weapon with which management had resisted the unions' most forceful efforts to affect its decisions. With the National Industrial Recovery Act of 1933 and subsequently with the National Labor Rela-

[5] Report of Industrial Conference, in *Eighth Annual Report of the Secretary of Labor*, pp. 234–235.

tions Act of 1935 came the grant to all employes in interstate commerce of the same rights previously extended to the railway workers only. In the country which scarcely a hundred years before had held unions to be conspiracies, a strong arm of government was now raised to assist them in their struggle to take from management the right of unilateral decisions at least in certain areas of the operation of a business.

With World War II was born a second National War Labor Board, which fulfilled many of the same functions as the first, except that the existence of the National Labor Relations Board relieved it of problems of certification of employe representatives and allowed it to concentrate primarily on the resolution of disputes over contract issues between management and unions. Once again, as awards traversed numerous areas of management, the cry was heard that managerial authority was being rashly diluted. A public member raises the question "whether or not the Board was bucking, riding along with, or getting ahead of the great surge in the organization and mobilization of the power of the wage workers which was in progress when the war started and which the war did not interrupt. On a question of that kind, the opinions of the Board members would surely have split three ways. The Labor members would contend that the Board bucked the tide. The Industry members would no doubt say that it tried to speed it up. It would be my impression as a Public member that the Board moved along with the tide. . ."[6] There was no question, however, that the tide was still running. In management's mind there was only a question of how far it would go.

Even so summary a review of organized labor's forward march in little more than the last quarter century reveals the acceleration of its accretion of influence in the business life of the nation. This is by no means the whole story, however. For along with this growth of power by the union movement has gone an expansion of power on the part of the component unions, a significant trend which we cannot afford to overlook. This expansion has proceeded primarily in two ways—the concentration of union authority in the hands of national organizations and the spread of union jurisdictions over broader industrial groups. The autonomy of local organizations has given way to control by parent unions. Crafts organized singly have been caught up in amalgamations and mergers. Within recent years the earlier established industrial unions, such as those existing in clothing and coal, have been joined by industrial unions in the mass production fields, such as steel, automobiles, electrical equipment, glass, rubber, uniting in a single organization all wage workers in the industry irrespective of occupational skills. Something of the

---

[6] Dexter Keezer, "Observations on the Operations of the National War Labor Board," *American Economic Review*, vol. 36 (1946), pp. 255–256.

same effect has been achieved by certain of the older craft unions, which have banded together into departments, such as the building trades, metal trades, railroad, and the more recently established maritime department of the American Federation of Labor.

The nationalization of union power has been spurred by several strategic considerations. It has permitted a greater standardization of the conditions of employment on those jobs within the union's jurisdiction. To this extent it has removed conditions of employment from the field of competition. It has made the strike a more potent weapon, since the resources of the national organization may be mobilized in support of member locals, and since direct action against all employers of the union's members may prove more effective than isolated, individually directed action.

The spread of union jurisdiction to embrace an entire industry, a movement which has gone on to some extent concurrently with the nationalization of union power, has likewise had compelling motivations. Skilled craftsmen can rely on their strategic position within a company or an industry to insure that their voices will be heard and respected by management. Production workers whose requirements of skill have been reduced through introduction of automatic machinery and new production techniques have no such bargaining power, however. If the workers in one shop walk out, the possibility of their replacement by other production workers, capable of training on new assignments within a brief period of time, threatens the success of their action. It is only through the organization of all the production workers in an entire company, leaving no pool of workers to be reassigned to other jobs, that bargaining power may be achieved.

With an increasing adoption of technological improvements in this century there has been such a progressive deterioration of skills. It is worth remembering that with the advent of Taylorism, with its emphasis on a reduction of a complex job to a number of simple processes or movements no one of which required the worker's former ability, there was an outburst from the unions against this transferral to management— through a production device—of the skill and knowledge of the worker, which were his only capital. Despite the stormy protest the specialization of labor has proceeded. In industries where this has been true, an industrial union was found to be the only protection for many production workers. All the employes of a company were banded together into a single organization, and such local units were welded into a national organization as had been true of the earlier crafts.

This greater emphasis on the industrial form of worker organization has immense significance for our study. It is apparent that in a single corporation where organization proceeds on a craft basis, with a number of unions bargaining only for their memberships, it is impossible for such individuated unions to establish terms applicable to all the employes of that company. They are concerned only with terms for the craft. Wages, hours, working rules, and occupational standards they can bargain for, for their own members. But on matters affecting the operation of the company as a whole no one union has any more standing than the others. Can the carpenters attempt to influence the price policy of a company when twenty other craft unions hold contracts as well? Can the machinists ask for joint control over a company retirement plan in which members of other unions have an equal interest? Can any one of a number of unions assert an interest in any managerial decision which cuts across occupational lines and affects the operation of the entire company? This limitation of interests does not apply in the case of a company-wide union, or council of unions, however. Representing all the production employes, it may speak authoritatively in the interests of all. It may, if it wishes, seek to affect the company's price policy, its retirement plan, or any managerial policy in which it feels the welfare of its members is involved. And beyond the company, it may seek collective bargaining on an industry-wide basis, asserting the interest of all or most of the organized employes in the general policies or trade programs of that industry.

It is not surprising, then, that the question of union participation has risen most importantly where unions may speak on behalf of all the employes in the company or industry. Company-wide and industry-wide bargaining represents a growth of union power within the union movement, for it permits the union to exercise greater influence in broader areas of management if it so desires. It is from the industrial unions primarily that one hears and reads statements to the effect that "Labor relations have now advanced to the stature of industry-wide problems, to be discussed in the light of conditions in the industry as a whole," and, "We must replace our present system of carrying on hundreds of isolated and uncoordinated wage negotiations in plants and corporations throughout our industry with wage conferences of the entire industry, where the full power of our union can be expressed and translated into an industry-wide agreement for our entire membership."[7] It has been with the entry of the CIO, with its predominantly industrial structure, into the mass production industries that the question of managerial authority has become such a pressing one.

[7] The first statement comes from Philip Murray, in an explanation of his industry-councils plan, *Steel Labor*, April 18, 1941, p. 11. The second from Walter Reuther, in his *Program for UAW-CIO Members* (1946), p. 4.

The nationalization of the union movement and the broadening of union jurisdictions to coincide with the business unit have thus been evolutionary developments permitting a more effective challenge of existing corporate control. It is too much to expect, as many managers have expected, that with such a growth of power unions should be content with its exercise within prescribed and unchanging boundaries. The belief currently gaining wider expression in business circles that the union's expanding influence will lead ultimately to socialism represents both a dawning and a growing consciousness that labor's interests, along with its power, are broadening and will brook few confines.

This belief in a trend toward socialism is significant for still another reason. It constitutes an implicit recognition that while unions are primarily economic institutions, the union movement may be an instrument or vehicle for the transmission of political philosophies. Moreover, the size, the power, and the strategic position of unions constituent to the movement, coupled with their internal cohesiveness, contribute to their effectiveness in this capacity. The fact that in America they have shown a reluctance to challenge the traditional two-party system and even to favor one party over the other should not blind us to the fact that within both of those parties they have been consistent purveyors of a political philosophy. It would be difficult to define that philosophy with any precision—few philosophies can be so expressed. Perhaps a description not far amiss would be that it consists essentially of a modification of the utilitarian principle of the greatest good of the greatest number, in which the unions have readily identified themselves with the greatest number and have *on that ground* insisted on a right to determine the greatest good. One thing, however, is clear: it is a credo which they seek to apply throughout society, in the economic as well as in the political sphere, and this universality of application distinguishes it from the philosophy characteristic of the managers.

This difference in viewpoint is marked. For the most part management representatives are firmly convinced that in industry someone must give the orders and others must obey him. This is the relationship of the corporate officials to the employes, of the managers to the managed. In their opinion to challenge or control that authority is to destroy the basis of industrial order. At the same time, on the political side, they profess the same democratic beliefs as do their labor adversaries. The union representatives, on the other hand, would make little distinction between the political philosophy underlying the state and industry. In both spheres they see a necessity of controlling authority in the interests of those who take the orders. Industrial democracy is more than an empty slogan to them; it expresses their firm conviction that those in control must be themselves controlled, that authority must be made responsible to those over whom it is wielded.

In recognizing this distinction in philosophical outlook we must avoid any suggestion that the managers are motivated by insincerity, or cherish mutually contradictory philosophies accommodated to simple self-seeking. The managers do not deny the necessity for responsibility as a concomitant of their authority—but they view their responsibility as running essentially to those from whom they derive their authority, the stockholders, and not to those over whom that authority is largely exercised, the employes. This is indeed the legal requirement of their position. Moreover, while the lineal descendants of those business interests who championed capitalistic democracy, and themselves staunch defenders of the democratic faith in the politics of the state, they consider the extension of democracy to the politics of industry, in the sense of controls by the workers over those in authority, an unworkable system which would bog down in sheer inefficiency and disorder, threatening the stability of the democratic state itself. It is worth repeating that these convictions are honestly held and with few exceptions do not represent a subtle manipulation and accommodation of political philosophy merely to suit personal ends. This sincerity of conviction is matched in the unions by an equally sincere belief in the applicability and desirability of democratic controls by the workers—not the denial of authority nor the subjugation of authority, but some means of enforcing the responsibility of that authority to those over whom it is exercised.

The idealogical conflict is not confined to expression in the bargaining relationship. As we have seen, the arena has become much wider; these distinctive philosophies are competing for recognition in society as a whole. And important to any historical perspective of the struggle over managerial authority is the fact that the history of our society has been written in terms of a developing political democracy. The unions have found strength in and have lent support to this movement. Regardless of the merits of the managers' opposition to the extension of democratic procedures to industry in any literal sense, such an extension has an appealing consistency with our philosophy of the relations of the government and the governed. The unions have themselves been an important instrument for the championship of the democratic doctrine from which they derive their support, and an effective vehicle for the dissemination of the political and philosophical principles whose logical extension constitutes a challenge to managerial authority in the operation of the corporation.

That is to say, the conflict over managerial authority cannot be viewed independently of the historical development of political ideas. The unions, in effect, are simply carrying forward the dominant political idea of our time, though it originated in another context by other interests. The rise of the large corporation, so often referred to as an industrial empire, has lent point to their efforts to apply that dominant political philosophy in the economic sphere. It is this historical coincidence of the rise of political democracy and the rise of large corporations which explains if not the very existence of the modern labor unions at least their present nature, their growth of power, and the form which their challenge to authority assumes. For, as we have seen, the challenge to authority is old and persistent, recurring throughout history; but that it operates in this country through a demand to participate in a contractual definition of the terms of operation of the business, in those areas of interest to the workers, and through agents chosen by election, is a reflection of the spirit of our laws and institutions.

In this respect our political and industrial development has many significant resemblances to parallel developments in England and Sweden. Indeed, the pertinence of their systems of industrial relations to our own was evidenced in the appointment in 1938 of a presidential Commission on Industrial Relations in England and Sweden. We may note with interest, then, the following statements of two writers in this field bearing upon the point at issue.

"The demand for industrial democracy is nowadays defined, in Sweden at any rate, as the struggle of the workers to obtain some share in the technical and economic management of undertakings or to give effect to their points of view and interests in this respect."[8]

"The spirit of democracy, the spirit of control by persons other than capitalist managers, is merely the final step up to the present time in English industrial development . . . Such a continuous movement as this, so analogous to the movement for political democracy, so wide in its extent, cannot be expected to stop short of some great epoch-making change. It obviously has all the characteristics of evolution in human society. It is part of the organic growth of the community."[9]

Both these observations were made in the early 1920's, since which time the socialist sector of the mixed economy of Sweden has grown under the impact of labor's political influence, and in Britain a Labor Party has come into office frankly committed to socialist objectives. One may question with good reason whether a pattern of development for the United States is indicated by these events, or whether the socialist system pro-

[8] Ernst Wigforss, "Industrial Democracy in Sweden," *International Labour Review*, vol. 9 (1924), p. 668.
[9] E. P. Cheyney, "The Trend Toward Industrial Democracy," *Annals of the American Academy of Political and Social Science* (July, 1920), pp. 8-9.

vides in itself that participation which labor seeks. Nevertheless, the march of events in these countries in our time is not wholly without significance to us. The weight of predominant political philosophy in our own country, as in England and Sweden, is on the side of increasing rather than static participation by representative unions in the operations of industry. It is not a matter of the importation of foreign ideologies but of the application of our own.

If this conclusion is valid, then managers who seek to confine unions to "traditional" areas of collective bargaining are fighting not only unions as economic organizations but also the historical continuity of a still developing philosophy—a philosophy, it may be remarked, which they themselves have accepted as desirable in the political sphere. Union participation must then be viewed not simply as a device for satisfying the goals of employes, unrelated to other social phenomena; it is encouraged by a prevailing social philosophy which has deep historical roots and which is still growing. In a sense, the direction which unions have taken has been guided not by self-choice but by the democratic philosophy of the society of their origin. It is this philosophy and not the areas of collective bargaining which is "traditional."

Those who speak of the traditional areas of negotiation would be hard put to it to define that term. They talk of wages, hours, and working conditions. But the miners were concerned with the price of their product as long ago as 1869. Unions in the mechanical trades of the daily newspaper field have organized foremen since at least 1889. Clothing workers throughout the industry assist in setting the standards of production and this has become one of their recognized areas of interest. Does time, continuity, or prevalence constitute tradition? And if so, in only the company or industry affected, or in the economy as a whole? If only in the company or industry, those now not organized would be barred from any union penetration whatsoever, since no tradition exists. If in the economy as a whole, no area of management would be free from penetration, since at some time or place unions have negotiated on subjects embracing virtually every area of management. The fact is that tradition is on the side of an expanding union influence, not of its constriction. And this expansion of employe participation through a representative organization is consonant with and fulfilling of an historical developing philosophy of social and political organization.

Too sweeping an inference must be avoided, however. We may remind ourselves that our dominantly democratic philosophy does not commit itself to any specific form of organization—either business or union—or to its own perversion for ulterior objectives, or to the accumulation of power in the hands of any group, smaller than society itself, which uses that power irresponsibly. Our political philosophy is conducive to union growth, but only insofar as the unions show themselves trustworthy of the power which their association brings. If the unions' challenge to management becomes at the same time a challenge to society, that same democratic philosophy will provide ground for checking their power, for democracy immunizes no one from responsibility.

This evolutionary view of union-management relations and historical perspective of their function is found frequently among the labor leaders, but it is also found among a smaller group of management officials. One union representative says, "Collective bargaining is only a transitional phase, leading into cooperation programs where the union will work out business matters with the company continuously, and not merely in fields specified in the contract, not merely as adjudication of rights established annually." A vice president of one large corporation expresses a similar thought. "We are approaching labor-management conduct of an industry, with the speed of its arrival dependent on the type of leadership we develop. I believe that industry will adjust itself to this evolutionary change, just as it has adjusted itself to the advent of collective bargaining and to the spread of the areas in which it operates. There are some executives who will not concede this, I know, but deep down in their hearts many business leaders are reconciled to it or will become reconciled to it, phase by phase, with something of a lag. As to the precise manner of labor-management directorship of the industry, that will work itself out as it develops. As of now, 1946, management opposes and must oppose union encroachment on managerial power, because the unions are not prepared to assume the necessary leadership. As of 1966, with new union leadership, the area of management opposition will be very much narrowed. The unions will have made further gains. Management will never, at any date, willingly say, 'Tomorrow we will go all out for union-management cooperation.' But bit by bit, they will approach that stage. Final authority in the large corporation will then be exercised within a different framework, surrounded by different restrictions than now obtain."

The industrial relations director of another large company, with numerous plants, laughs "at the suggestion that we can ever return to 'the good old days.' " He says, "Some time ago the president of our company asked me what I considered my outstanding accomplishments of the year just past. I told him they were the things I had been fighting the year before. We fought the checkoff—it is now in the contract. We are now fighting the union shop——" His sentence remained unfinished, but the implication was apparent. He was convinced that he was fighting only for time.

There is nothing inevitable in the course of human events, it is true, but it is likewise true that the present and future build upon the past. Historical perspective is needed in the interpretation of social developments. We can only say that in the light of the past there is no reason to read a future in which the union's challenge to managerial authority will become less pressing, less persistent, or less successful.

C H A P T E R **8**

The Legal Perspective of Union and Corporate Interests

Disputes over rights and disputes over interests have commonly been differentiated. The former are viewed as concerned with the application of the law, and conflicts of this nature may be resolved by an appeal to the rule—existing in legislation, equity, or the common law—which governs the disputants. It is thus conceived that disputes of rights may be settled by judicial action which establishes the manner in which the operation of the law affects the parties. In disputes of interests, however, such a method of settlement is not available precisely because there is no standard or rule of common application: that is to say, there are no "rights" enforceable by one against the other of the disputants under sanction of the law. Such a statement of the distinction rests emphasis on the existence or nonexistence of a law which validates the claim of one of the participants as against the other or others. Strictly speaking, this is not an accurate distinction and it will be instructive for our purposes to give it a refinement more in keeping with legal tradition and philosophy.

A conflict over interests may arise and continue only because the assertion of contending interests is possible *under the law,* or under institutional practices recognized by the law. If this were not so, then the asserted interest which ran contrary to law would be squelched by action of the law—as were early efforts of workers to join in unions for concerted action—and the conflict would thereby be extinguished. The circumstances under which this condition would not obtain are when a group is seeking the legalization of previously unlawful action and has achieved such widespread sympathy with its aims that its assertion of unlawful interest is not put down under the law but is overlooked, condoned, or rationalized. These circumstances would prevail at a time when previously unlawful action was in process of receiving the hood of legal respectability. Again, the fight by workers for the right to organize in unions for concerted action provides a forceful illustration.

Conflicts of interests do not, therefore, arise outside of the law, or mean that law may not be pertinent, or necessarily imply that no rights

171

have been established. They indicate merely that laws establishing some order of "rights" exist in one form or another to support the claims of the disputants, and are of relatively equal applicability and force, so that neither claim may be considered to take precedence over the other. The operation of this principle is strikingly illustrated in Mr. Justice Brandeis's dissenting opinion in the Hitchman Coal Co. case of 1917,[1] involving the legality of union action to secure a collective agreement in the face of employment contracts individually executed between workmen and company binding the former to abstain from union membership—the so-called "yellow-dog" contract. Said Brandeis, "Both plaintiff and defendants insisted upon exercising the right to secure contracts for a closed shop. The plaintiff sought to secure the *closed non-union shop* through individual agreements with employees. The defendants sought to secure the *closed union shop* through a collective agreement with the union. . . . In other words, an employer, in order to effectuate the closing of his shop to *union* labor, may exact an agreement to that effect from his employees. The agreement itself being a lawful one, the employer may withhold from the men an economic need—employment—until they assent to make it. Likewise an agreement closing a shop to non-union labor being lawful, the union may withhold from an employer an economic need—labor— until he assents to make it."

In view of the *equal* claim of both company and union to seek the type of contract which it favored, Brandeis would have allowed the actions of both as legal, leaving the contest of interests to the parties themselves *under the law*. The only means by which such conflicts of interests may be extinguished through a substitution of "rights" for "interests" is by extinguishing all prior existing legal claims in the very process of creating new rights. This means that the respective canons of the law on which the disputants lean for support for their interests must be eliminated as not any longer pertinent, and in their place must be reared a chapter of the law recognized as governing both or all the disputants in the area of conflict. It is such a law which we then commonly regard as establishing enforceable rights. It must be noted, however, that if all the legal bases for a conflict of interests in the given area are not satisfactorily extinguished in the process, the newly established rights will not adequately perform their intended function of resolving the conflict.

These considerations are significant for our study. It is desirable for us to turn our attention to the law underlying the question of managerial authority and the union's challenge to it. From the above observations we may assume, a priori, that the managers have legal support in their resistance to union penetration—but that the unions have likewise a legal

[1] *Hitchman Coal Co.* v. *Mitchell,* 245 U. S. 229.

freedom to pursue that objective. There is here a conflict of interests which have a legal component, which we shall try to understand. We shall also be interested in the extent to which, if at all, the National Labor Relations Act, so frequently considered to have modified legal "rights" in this area, has in fact modified the fundamental contest of legal interests.

We may begin by examining the relevant provisions of that Act. Most importantly, it proscribes certain types of managerial actions. Managers are forbidden to interfere with or restrain employes in their self-organization and choice of representatives for the purpose of collective bargaining. They are forbidden to dominate or interfere with the formation and administration of a union. They are forbidden to discriminate among employes with the purpose or result of encouraging or discouraging their membership in any union, except that within the terms of the Act they may agree to a union shop. They may not discriminate against an employe because he has filed charges or given testimony under the Act.

In addition to forbidding these actions, the Act prescribes that management must, at the desire of its employes, engage in collective bargaining with their chosen representatives with respect to "rates of pay, wages, hours of employment, or other conditions of employment."

It will not be necessary for us to examine here in any detail the progressive delineation of the meaning of these requirements by the National Labor Relations Board. We may concern ourselves only briefly with the obligation to bargain collectively, the full purport of which is not quite so readily discernible. The Board has held that under this provision management must negotiate in good faith with the union with the intent of reaching an agreement on the terms of employment, and that when such an agreement is reached it must be reduced to writing if the union so requests. Negotiations in good faith involve more than listening to the union's demands and then rejecting them. Although the Board has repeatedly insisted that the Act does not compel agreement, it has also repeatedly urged that management should demonstrate its intent to bargain through the presentation of counterproposals to the union. Good-faith bargaining requires an earnest effort at compromise, permitting agreement. Union offer should therefore be met with counteroffer. This attitude of the Board has prompted management to complain, in the words of one of their number, that "As matters now stand, the unions can make ever new and greater demands, and unless the company makes some concession it stands in danger of being held in violation of the N.L.R.A. The unions, supported by the government, thus extend their powers and prerogatives at the expense of the company."

The Board has also ruled that good faith in collective bargaining precludes management from taking unilateral action in any matter which is properly the subject of collective bargaining. "Where employees have designated an exclusive bargaining agent, that agent should be consulted before revisions are made in the employees' terms and conditions of employment. That the representative may not be averse to the contemplated revision, or, indeed, may even welcome it, does not obviate the necessity for consultation."[2]

A clear expression of this view came in a case where the union had asserted an interest in merit wage increases, an interest which the employer refused to admit though he was willing to conclude and in fact did conclude a collective agreement with respect to other matters. In this instance the Board majority ruled: "Upon these facts, we agree with the Trial Examiner that the respondent has not fulfilled its obligation to bargain collectively with the Union. We find no merit in the respondent's contention that merit increases are a prerogative of management. Like the Trial Examiner, we are of the opinion that merit increases are an integral part of the wage structure, and as such, constitute a proper subject for collective bargaining."[3]

Such a ruling provides a suitable introduction to one of the thorniest problems in the administration of the Act and one directly pertinent to our interest, the definition of "a proper subject for collective bargaining." The Act requires negotiation on rates of pay, wages, hours of employment, or other conditions of employment. But what may "other conditions of employment" include? What is it that the Board has in mind when it says: "The collective bargaining process is inevitably one of give and take in which each party gives in on certain demands and positions in order to gain assent on others, thereby achieving a satisfactory compromise. While the Act does not impose an obligation on an employer to agree to a union's demands, it does impose an obligation to discuss any *proper* subject of collective bargaining in a good faith effort to reach an agreement when requested to do so by the bargaining representative. To say that an employer may require a union to surrender one demand as a condition to a discussion of its other demands, is obviously inconsistent with an unconditional obligation imposed by the Act on an employer to bargain on request with respect to any *proper* subject of collective bargaining. Such procedure would make impossible the ordinary give and take which is the essence of collective bargaining."[4]

When the Automobile Workers demand that General Motors shall bargain with respect to its price policy, is this a "proper" subject of negotiation which the company may not avoid? And if so, is any area of man-

---

[2] *Matter of Todd Company*, NLRB Case No. 3–C–752 (October, 1946).

[3] *Matter of J. H. Allison & Company*, NLRB Case No. 10–C–1725 (August, 1946).

[4] *Matter of Winona Textile Mills, Inc.*, NLRB Case No. 18–C–1176 (June, 1946). Italics added.

agement excluded from the "proper" subject matter of collective bargaining?

The Board has given no clear indication of its position on this controversial issue. At times it has studied the union's demands as if in an attempt to determine whether they fell within the scope of legitimate subject matter for negotiation. For example, it has said: "The type of supervisor under whom an employee works is of direct concern to the employee and may be of vital importance to him. The conduct of a supervisor may affect an employe's well-being as much as low pay, long hours, or other unsatisfactory conditions of work. A dispute involving the discharge or demotion of a supervisor objectionable to the employee is, we think, a dispute concerning a condition of employment."[5]

At other times the Board has spoken as though it was not concerned with the subject matter of negotiations. Thus in one case where the union sought to bargain on the composition of the board of directors it declared: "Respondent's theory that the labor dispute involved in this case was simply a plot to seize control of the organization renders advisable a brief statement of the position of the National Labor Relations Board in such a matter. The Board has no power under the Act to decide upon the subject matter of substantive terms of a union agreement. For this reason attempted seizure of control through the medium of collective bargaining negotiations is not within the cognizance of the Board. Again, highly improbable as it is to say that a union might be able to effect a change of management by means of the collective bargaining machinery of the Act, a union could never seize control unless such 'seizure' were acquiesced in by the employer. By the Act, the terms of agreement are left to the parties themselves; the Board may decide whether collective bargaining negotiations took place, but it may not decide what should or should not have been included in the union contract."[6]

It thus appears that the Board has yet to make its position clear. Its reluctance to undertake a definition of the phrase "conditions of employment" is entirely understandable and may readily evoke sympathy. For two differing interpretations are possible of defense. On the one hand, "conditions of employment" may be taken to mean the equivalent of "working conditions," the immediate industrial environment in which employes carry on their tasks. On the other hand, it may be used in the sense of any term on which employment may be made conditional. In the first case, the field is considerably restricted, and with the adoption of this

[5] *Matter of Aladdin Industries,* 22 NLRB No. 101.
[6] *Matter of Consumers' Research,* 2 NLRB 57, 74. It may be fairly said that in this case the Board has confused the distinctly separate issues of whether the subject matter of negotiations limits the Board's jurisdiction, and whether the Board's jurisdiction extends to the subject matter.

meaning the Board would be placed under the onerous obligation of ex
amining all union proposals on which an employer had refused to bargain
to determine whether it fell within this definition of the proper subjec
matter of collective bargaining. The second definition would provide n
limitations whatsoever, but would place the Board in the position of hav
ing to require management to bargain on any issue which the union pre
sented—leaving the definition of the area of negotiations subject only to
a union's discretion. It is not therefore surprising that the Board ha.
dodged this issue.

As may be expected, practitioners in the field of collective bargaining
have been less reluctant to define the term. There is an unequivocal ex
pression from most members of management that the phrase "conditions
of employment" must be restricted in meaning to working conditions
This is no more than a reflection of their view, which we have already
encountered, that some line of demarkation must be drawn between mat
ters of joint interest and those of sole concern to management. Union
representatives, though sometimes expressing doubt as to the intended
meaning of Congress, have no hesitancy in advocating the broad inter
pretation of including in its content any matter on which they may make
the employment of their members conditional. This too reflects their opinion that no line of demarkation can be drawn.

What is the significance of this controversy over a definition? Where
does it—and the Act which evokes it—fit into the broader legal framework? Let us drop the National Labor Relations Act for the moment and
turn our attention to more basic considerations.

Our society has as its legal base a system of rights, privileges, legal
powers, and immunities, granted to and enjoyed by individuals or groups
as a result of certain institutions or processes.[7] It is often difficult to un-
ravel these or to state them with precision. Even an incomplete attempt
to indicate the most pertinent of these manifold relationships in the sphere
of industrial relations may serve to point up the issues, however. Let us
consider some of the relationships involved, for example, in the 1945–
1946 General Motors negotiations when the Automobile Workers sought
to bargain on the price policy of the company but were rebuffed with the
charge that management could not consent to an abdication of its legal
responsibilities to the owners.

In this situation management acted as the agent of the stockholders.

---

[7] It is scarcely necessary to add that this method of examining our legal institutions derives
primarily from Wesley N. Hohfeld, who provided the framework in his *Fundamental Legal
Conceptions,* published in book form in 1923 and edited by Walter Wheeler Cook. Max Radin
has added to its refinement, as for example in "A Re-statement of Hohfeld," *Harvard Law
Review,* vol. 51, p. 1141 (1938), and "The Endless Problem of Corporate Personality," *Columbia Law Review,* vol. 32, p. 643 (1932).

In such an agency relationship it acquired the legal capacity to exercise all the authority delegated by the owners and conferred by the corporate laws under which the charter was granted. It likewise possessed the legal power to conclude agreements binding upon the owners except in certain reserved areas not of present significance. Included in its received authority was a privilege of determining the company's price policy. This privilege, it will be noted, did not create any duties on the part of anyone else nor did it erect any claims against anyone else—for example, the union. At the same time, by the existence of this privilege—which management would call a prerogative—the company enjoyed a freedom from any claims which might be put forth by the union. That is to say, because management enjoyed the privilege of defining its own price policy, the union had no rights which it might assert in this area.

On the other side of the bargaining table, the Automobile Workers, through their union, enjoyed a similar privilege of determining the conditions on which they would agree to work for General Motors. This privilege carried with it no grounds for them to make claims or impose duties on any other person—including General Motors. It simply permitted them to conclude the terms on which they would agree to work, free from interference by any outside agency. That is to say, because the union possessed the privilege of defining its own terms of employment, the company had no rights which it might assert in this area.

It is evident that if the union, in the exercise of its privilege of stating —unilaterally—the conditions on which it would consent to the employment of its members, stated conditions which were in the realm of the company's privilege to determine unilaterally—a voice in price policy, for example—and the company was unwilling to consent to these terms, an impasse would result. This is actually what happened. The effect was the unemployment of the workers and the suspension of operations by the company—in more common terminology, the strike, an action which is only an outgrowth of a conflict between the recognized privileges of both the parties. The only means by which this deadlock could be resolved was through the voluntary surrender by either or both parties of its privilege of unilateral determination, and compromise on a bilateral agreement. Depending upon the feeling of urgency weighing on each of the parties, the resulting bilateral agreement could be expected to constitute a retreat by the union on its conditions of employment—a willingness to give up its price demands, perhaps, or a retreat by the company from its insistence on declaring its own price policy as the cost of reaching an agreement with its workers. Either course of action would have been "legal." In the bilateral agreement or contract which resulted, these respective privileges and freedom from claims would be converted into rights and duties—a right of the company to the labor of its workers on the terms agreed and the duty of the workers to work, if at all, on those terms, or a right of the union to a voice in the price policy of the company and a duty of the company to recognize the union's right of such participation. In this case, it was the union which yielded on the price question.

In such a conflict, in addition to the rights and duties which emerge from the contest over privileges, each party may accept a disability of further changing the terms of relationship by granting the other immunity from pressure for such changes for a specified period; or on the other hand, each party may place the other under the liability of contract termination by reserving the legal power to terminate the contract on notice.

Now this line of reasoning applies to all of management's so-called prerogatives, whether they are based upon rights or claims, such as its right to the use of its property without trespass by others and the correlative duty of others not to trespass (a right involved in the sit-down strike, for example) or upon privileges, such as its privilege to determine unilaterally its price policy, depreciation, financial, or even wage policy. Management is thus legally justified in asserting such "prerogatives," but having asserted them it may exercise them only if the union is unable or disinterested in securing their compromise or abandonment through the exercise of its own privilege of refusing to permit its members to work except upon condition of their compromise or abandonment. And here management is not logically justified, in any legal sense, in claiming that the union has no "right" to "invade" its field of prerogatives. It is true that the union has no right in the sense of a legal capacity to compel a duty on the part of management, and no right directly to intervene in management's exercise of its "prerogatives," but it does have a privilege of refusing to work, except upon its own terms, against which management can assert no controlling right. Until or unless the privilege of strike action is modified or removed, management's own rights and privileges—in any area of its management—will remain subject to challenge. Thus when management says the union has no right to invade the managerial field it is in effect saying that the union *should* not. Its defense cannot rest on legal grounds. It must rest, if at all, on logical grounds concerning the nature of the managerial function or of the private property system of which the union may be subject to persuasion.

As the workers' privilege of concerted action—the so-called right to strike—has become established, the courts increasingly have accepted the above reasoning. They have said that "the courts have not been constituted arbiters of the fairness, justice or wisdom of the terms demanded."[8]

---

[8] *J. H. & S. Theatres* v. *Fay*, 260 N. Y. 315, 317–318, 183 N. E. 510 (1932); *Interborough Rapid Transit Co.* v. *Lavin*, 247 N. Y. 65, 159 N. E. 863 (1928).

". . . The fact that the contractors are forced to do what they do not want to do is not decisive of the legality of the labor union's acts. That is true wherever a strike is successful."[9] "Economic pressure may eventually compel the acceptance of mechanical changes, but there seems to be no legal reason why those who may be injuriously affected thereby may not meanwhile make lawful and orderly efforts to prevent or lessen the extent of the injury to themselves. It is well known that employers do not always use the latest technological improvements where such improvements might lessen their opportunities for profits or destroy large capital investments; and no one claims that they owe anyone a legal duty to do so."[10]

We may summarize, then, by saying that management possesses the privilige of managing the business at its discretion, within the boundaries of the law, one of those boundaries being a legal compulsion to act for the benefit of all the stockholders. But in the exercise of this privilege it can claim only freedom of discretion for itself—not compulsion of duty on the part of anyone else. On the other hand, unions enjoy a similar privileged position of determining in their own discretion, within the boundaries of the law, the terms on which their memberships will accept employment. In the exercise of this discretion they can impose no duties on the part of others, with reservations soon to be noted.

Collective bargaining is the process by which the privileges of both management and union are modified, but again it is a matter of discretion with both parties as to how much of a modification they will accept. The privilege of neither party extends to compelling a duty on the part of the other. If "prerogative" is understood in this sense, there is no legal castle to which either management or the union can retire to defend its "rights." Where collective bargaining prevails, neither management nor union may exist independently; one is functionally impotent without the other. Yet neither controls the other. Each is privileged to stand on its own decisions, but the preservation intact of that privilege is useless if thereby the function of each is destroyed. Where collective bargaining prevails, it is correct to say that production goes forward, that managers manage and workers work, only if there is some recession from privileged position. The degree to which each will recede is the subject of collective bargaining.

Now we may raise the question as to whether the National Labor Relations Act has modified this legal relationship.

That Act, as we have seen, restricts the discretion of management by proscribing certain types of actions, such as discriminating among employes on the basis of union membership and interfering with the forma-

---

[9] *Pickett v. Walsh*, 192 Mass. 572, 584, 78 N. E. 753 (1906).
[10] *Opera on Tour v. Weber*, 258 App. Div. 516, 523–524, 17 N. Y. S. (2d) 144 (1940).

tion and administration of unions. These requirements, however, are basically nothing more than part of the legal framework within which management must operate—just as are state factory sanitation codes, safety regulations, antitrust legislation, and maximum hours laws. They withdraw certain matters from the realm of privileged decision without modifying the remaining privileges of operating the business at management's discretion. While this modification of the legal framework within which management operates constitutes the essence of the Act, and as we shall soon see is responsible for the intensification of union-management conflict over corporate authority, *in itself* it affects but little management's discretion as to how its business shall be conducted.

Is the requirement to bargain collectively, with the attending controversy as to the proper subject matter of collective bargaining, to be viewed in a different light, however? Is this a compulsion which attacks the whole structure of managerial privilege? If one can place emphasis on the Labor Relations Board's declaration that management is compelled to reach no agreement with the union, it would be difficult to conclude other than that the duty to bargain does not modify management's central stronghold of privilege. For even in the absence of a duty to bargain and with the existence or nonexistence of any definition of the appropriate subject matter of negotiations, the unions would be free to challenge management's privilege of unilateral determination of business policy with their own privilege of unilateral determination of the conditions on which their members would consent to be employed. These opposing privileges could then be reconciled only by bilateral agreement, or collective bargaining, unless management was successful in destroying the organization of its employes, thereby eliminating all opposition to the exercise of its privilege, or unless the union was abandoned by its own members.

It is clear, of course, that without direct attack upon the union a management through dilatory bargaining tactics and bad faith could so weaken the confidence of employes in their union as to secure its dissolution. In this manner the contest of privileges might be resolved by a process other than either direct attack or collective bargaining. But as long as one accepts that the Act is designed to *protect* the workers' privilege of organization and bargaining through claim-duty relationships formulated *for that purpose,* and to do only that, even a requirement of procedural forms of negotiation involves no greater surrender of managerial privilege than is involved in the absence of a duty to bargain. For the degree of surrender of management's privileges still remains in its discretion, even under the Act, in theory and to a considerable extent in practice.

Only because union organization was weak in many instances and the wishes of management so powerful an influence on individual employes was the requirement to bargain included in the Act—belatedly, as an afterthought—and has it become important. And even so it has become important only by a progressive delineation of that obligation establishing corollary claim-duty relationships of union and management running in favor of the former and designed to preserve the very organization of the union. Thus the right of the union to know the facts on which an employer's inability-to-pay argument is based cannot be subsumed in the privileged area which the Act was designed to foster on behalf of the union, nor can any of the other indicia of good-faith bargaining, unless one looks at them from the viewpoint of efforts to preserve the integrity of the union—an oxygen tent, as it were, to sustain organizations many of which could exist only in a somewhat more rarified atmosphere than that pictured in the Senate hearings on the Violation of the Rights of Labor. Such requirements cannot be viewed as independent rights imposing duties without removing them from the context of the Act or without changing its whole tenor, and they are not so construed by the well-informed, including corporation lawyers.

The importance of the National Labor Relations Act, then, does not lie basically in any large-scale withdrawal of privilege from management, nor in any attack upon such privilege which is contained in the Act itself. Its significance rests almost exclusively in its guarantee to employes of the privilege of concerted action in determining the terms on which they will work. That protection has permitted and sustained the development of unions, some of them now organizations of great power. That these organizations, so protected, should challenge managerial privilege on so wide a front may or may not have been within the intent of the framers of the Act. But it is difficult to arrive at any conclusion other than that the Act has not significantly affected the underlying legal relationships of rights, privileges, powers, and immunities *except insofar as it has protected and fostered the growth of champions of labor to exercise preexisting privileges.*[11]

That in the administration of the Act the attempt to preserve to labor the privilege of concerted action should have been transformed into a

[11] Thus in the Board's report to the Senate Committee on Education and Labor at a time when that Committee had before it proposed amendments to the Act, it pointed out that "prior to the passage of the act the legal rights and economic strength of employers and employees were drastically out of balance," and then went on to declare: "The purpose of the act was to relieve, at least in part, this glaring inequality. It did so simply by forbidding the employer to use his economic power to interfere with and destroy the right of self-organization of his employees. The act thus merely placed employer and employee upon a plane of equality in one limited respect—freedom in law and in practice to organize for collective action. None of the other legal rights of employer were taken from him . . ." From *National Labor Relations Act and Proposed Amendments*, Hearings before the Committee on Education and Labor, United States Senate, 76th Congress, 1st session, part 3, pp. 476–477 (1939).

right of the union to be consulted may or may not have been inevitable. Even so, the Act requires no abdication of discretion by management as a result of such consultation. It is the existence of unions and not of the Act which is responsible for any concessions which management may make. It is the power of the unions and not of the Board which carries the challenge of further union penetration in the areas of management. To the extent that unions owe their existence and power to the Act, and to that extent only, has the Act served to modify the privileges and pre-rogatives of management in determining its operating decisions and policies.

Such a conclusion should not serve to lessen the significance of the National Labor Relations Act for our purposes, however. For even though the Act itself may not require any important abnegation of managerial discretion other than to compel a good-faith acceptance of unions, that requirement constitutes a departure in corporate law and philosophy of the first magnitude. It supports the legal interest in the corporation of a group other than stockholders. That interest, as we have seen, rests on the union's privilege of stating the terms and conditions on which its members will consent to their employment, an interest which while con-sonant with the underlying common-law relationships is difficult to square, except in a technical and superficial sense, with the statute-law require-ments that the corporation shall be managed solely for the benefit of its owners. It is this fundamental conflict of legal interests, a conflict which the Act promotes, which is unquestionably responsible for the reluctant acceptance of the Act by the managers. By supporting the workers' priv-ilege of determining the terms on which they are to be employed, the Act in effect assures that management must bargain on the terms of surrender of ever-widening portions of its delegated authority.

As matters now stand, management is governed by our corporation laws which define its responsibilities as running exclusively to the stock-holders. On some occasions some of the legal managers have spoken of a responsibility to their employes and to the public, but such a responsibil-ity has never been elaborated. It has never been spelled out in terms which are enforceable, or even widely understood and accepted. Where specified at all, it is in such piecemeal legislation as the Sherman and Clayton anti-trust acts, the Securities and Securities Exchange acts, and the Fair Labor Standards Act. Outside of these, a general definition of such a re-sponsibility and procedures for enforcing it has never been attempted. On the other hand, the National Labor Relations Act has given the unions enforceable rights guaranteeing their integrity and effectiveness. These rights have been used in support of their privilege of determining the con-ditions on which their members will accept employment. In determining those conditions the unions have challenged management's exercise of authority on behalf of the stockholders and have asserted a right to share that authority on behalf of the workers.

Neither the National Labor Relations Act nor any other act compels management to relinquish its delegated discretion in the operation of the business, except to compel its acceptance of a majority union. No affirmative managerial action is required except negotiation. Agreement on or compliance with any specific terms of business operation—the clauses of a collective agreement—is not provided for in any legislation. Corporation officials, operating under corporation laws, charters, and bylaws, have good reason, therefore, for believing that their obligation to the stockholders requires as little dilution of authority as is necessary to continue in business or to operate it effectively. Management is thus left in a position where if it surrenders or shares its delegated privileges it may be charged with inadequately representing the stockholders' interests. But in preserving such privileges, under requirement of the law, it is faced with the challenge of unions whose position is protected in law and who demand a share in them.

Without fully realizing it we have permitted the simultaneous development in recent years of two conflicting philosophies and their legal supports. The law of the land compels management to bargain with the unions with a view to sharing its authority with them, while saying nothing as to the nature of such sharing. The laws of the states, however, place all authority for corporate decisions in the hands of the managers, thus providing no organizational basis through which union participation in the corporate processes may be made effective.

Managements concertedly have charged the unions with garnering corporate authority without assuming correlative responsibilities. They have been quite right in perceiving that responsibility is the problem issue at the heart of the union-management relationship. They have assumed, however, that the redefinition of responsibility must run only in terms of the union. Such an assumption understandably arises from the belief that the responsibility of management is already fixed in law, while that of the unions is not. That assumption misses the point at issue. For as long as management is faced with the perplexing problem of the effect of its responsibility to the owners upon its sharing of authority with the union, the nature of its own responsibility will remain in doubt. Redefinition of corporate responsibilities there is needed, but quite likely not solely in terms of the union. Management's own traditional responsibilities are no longer consistent with the changed legal and social framework. Moreover, those responsibilities cannot be questioned without at the same time questioning the basis of its authority, for authority and responsibility are inseparable. Try as we may, and regardless of our sympathies, we cannot escape the fact that the rise of strong unions as legally protected associations has reopened for examination the nature of the corporation as a business instrument.

At bottom we have here a conflict of interests, interests which while conflicting are both legally protected. As we noted at the start of this legal perspective, resolution of the conflict—if it is to be resolved—calls for extinguishing the legal interests in conflict by erecting new legal relationships governing the parties joined in issue. This is the redefinition of corporate authority and responsibility which both management and unions seek but fear. They admit, indeed argue its necessity, but at the same time they fear its coming. For neither is sure that the outcome will be to its liking.

Institutional Perspective of Corporate Interests

In 1939 the Congress of American Industry, sponsored by the National Association of Manufacturers, drafted a platform which included the following paragraph: "Industrial management in America is equipped to contribute effectively, in its own sphere, to a constructive solution of the problems the nation faces. The maximum result will be attained with sound governmental policies and with all elements of the economy—industry, agriculture, labor, distribution, transportation, banking and finance, and the rest—striving to serve the public good. It must be made clear to the public that industry's enlightened self-interest is linked inextricably with the welfare of all of these other elements and with the welfare of the nation as a whole."[1]

The unspoken as well as the spoken assumptions of this statement command attention. "Industry" is considered as something distinct from "all of these other elements" of the economy, including labor. Its "enlightened self-interest" conduces to the welfare of the nation. But who or what, then, is this "industry," and what is its "self-interest"? If we substitute for this word of doubtful referent the names of our large corporations we will probably retain the meaning intended by the framers of the platform while pointing up the issues pertinent for our purposes. We may say by paraphrase that "U. S. Steel's enlightened self-interest is linked inextricably with the welfare of all of these other elements [from which it is thus distinguished] and with the welfare of the nation as a whole." Once again, however, we would have to inquire, Who or what is U. S. Steel, and what is its self-interest? Considered as an operating agent, is it something apart from labor, for example?

There is little doubt that the representatives to the Congress of American Industry were concerned with "industry" as a legal institution, with the corporation as it exists in the eyes of the law. As we saw very early in our investigation, such a legal perspective identifies the corporation with stockholders, "industry" with the owners. The more evasive statement of the Congress representatives can be replaced, without loss

[1] *New York Times,* December 8, 1939.

of meaning, with the less equivocal words of the President of the Studebaker Corporation: "After all, it is the job of a corporation to make money for its stockholders. And it so happens that it is good business to be humane and that decency pays dividends."[2] Other managers have privately expressed consistent views. "There is only one purpose to business, and that is to make money for the owners. Any other purported motive is a false one. Corporations aren't eleemosynary institutions and they can't be run as such." "A management that consented to give the unions a voice in all operating decisions could be attacked by the stockholders in court and thrown out on the ground that it violated its fundamental trust. Businesses don't come into existence to give employment. They are formed to make money."

Perhaps no more positive assertion of the nature of corporate interests, under the law, has been made than that by A. A. Berle, Jr., an assertion which indeed goes somewhat beyond the bounds which many lawyers and managements would recognize: "It is the thesis of this essay that all powers granted to a corporation or to the management of a corporation, or to any group within the corporation, whether derived from statute or charter or both, are necessarily and at all times exercisable only for the ratable benefit of all the shareholders as their interest appears. That, in consequence, the *use* of the power is subject to equitable limitation when the power has been exercised to the detriment of such interest, however absolute the grant of power may be in terms, and however correct the technical exercise of it may have been. . . . And that, in every case, corporate action must be twice tested: first by the technical rules having to do with the existence and proper exercise of the power; second, by equitable rules somewhat analagous to those which apply in favor of a *cestui que trust* to the Trustee's exercise of wide powers granted to him in the instrument making him a fiduciary."[3]

In such views as these no doubt can be discovered. Corporate interest, at least in the legal sense, is expressly confined to the owners of the corporation. Yet law remains only one of our institutions. Our legal framework must itself derive its strength and support from other institutions. Any social institution, including the corporation, is given reality by *all* the elements of society which contribute to its form and functioning, and not merely by one of those elements, such as law. An institution acquires meaning and commands acceptance because it is fitted

---

[2] "The Corporation as a Social Instrument," from Batchelor (editor), *The New Outlook in Business*, p. 108.

[3] "Corporate Powers as Powers in Trust," *Harvard Law Review*, vol. 44 (1931), p. 1049.

within the philosophy and practices, the desires and needs of a particular society, and not because it is sanctioned by only one of their manifestations, such as the legal code. If, then, we consider the whole cluster of social usages, the complex of procedures, conventions, arrangements, and organizations, the total range of values and habits which characterize our society, and examine the nature of corporate interests from such a broader perspective, we may arrive at quite a different answer from that which the law presently allows.

To the view expressed by the Congress of American Industry that the owners constitute the industry, labor has posed a challenge. So precise is this challenge that on one occasion the president of a large national union came forth with the statement that "The worker is the industry."[4] While other union officials have seldom adopted so strong a stand, they have been as one in asserting that workers as well as owners have an interest in the conduct of the corporation. They are not speaking of legal interest. They are referring to a moral and economic interest arising from the institutional framework in which workers, particularly in the large corporation, find themselves, an interest so patent that it overrides what they regard as narrow legal definitions. Their position is expressed in an exchange which took place during collective-bargaining negotiations at one manufacturing plant.

Said the company representative: "You will find our figures to be exactly the same as in our published statement—over $5,000,000 invested and some $200,000 profit. The stockholders got $180,000 in total out of this business and that is a very trifling ratio."

Said the union representative: "These men have their lives invested here."

Organized labor's spokesmen who would thus enlarge the concept of corporate interest do not deny the legal interest of owners in the conduct of the business. Recognizing this property right, they nevertheless counterpose an equivalent right—nonlegal—earned by the workers through their contribution of "human capital." The issue which they join has been well stated by a member of the management of one large corporation: "The early industrialists failed to recognize that they did not merely own land, buildings, machinery and power, but also a working environment in which men earned their livelihood."[5] In effect the unions are saying

---

[4] Sidney Hillman, then President of the Amalgamated Clothing Workers, quoted in H. M. Kallen, "Responsibility," *Ethics*, vol. 52 (1942), p. 369.

[5] Robert B. Wolf, *Pulp and Paper Mill Management in the Pacific Northwest Under the N. R. A.* (Reprint from Technical Association Papers of the Pulp and Paper Industry, series 18, no. 1, 1935), p. 6.

that a business is bigger than just the owners of its tangible and intangible property. "Industry" is more than the stockholders. The working force is fully as essential and integral. How can it be said, then, that the corporation must be managed only in the interest of the owners?

The rise of large corporations has contributed to the development of this belief. Few people seem more removed than the owners from the actual operation of such businesses. Their ownership is of a paper share, traded back and forth upon a stock exchange, rather than the possession of any physical assets to which they alone, as individuals, hold title. Shall men be severed from their jobs and cast adrift because new machinery may take their place, in the interest of owners who may not even be aware of what is transpiring? When depression threatens, shall employes be dropped without power of protest as no longer contributing to the profit of owners, some of whom themselves may be threatened with loss of job and principal earning power, in another corporation, for the same ostensible reason? Shall corporate policies, of whatever nature, be directed to the increase of the return to transient owners unconscious of the policies pursued on their behalf and assuming no responsibility for them? Regardless of any legal structure of corporate interests, organized workers refuse to assent to an affirmative answer to such questions. And in a manner they have been encouraged in their stand by a society which has supported their organization to combat the sole claims of the owners.

If labor insists that a corporation cannot be considered simply as the property of its owners and has asserted an interest of its own, similar claims have been made on behalf of an even larger community, society itself. The question has been raised as to why management should operate a business on behalf of the owners only, or even on behalf of owners and employes, if larger economic interests are involved—interests of the public as consumers, of the public as members of an economy whose effectiveness is dependent in important measure on the actions of our industrial giants. To the extent that labor has felt its interests identified with those of the public, it has joined in this chorus. Thus one union representative asserts that "the age of private business is dead, in the sense that it is operated by a few people for the benefit of special groups. All business is a matter of public interest."

This opinion has found voice in a number of thoughtful theorists and practitioners. The power of the modern corporation has been pictured in such terms as to question the wisdom of confining the exercise of such power to the behalf of only a segment of the community.

"The economic power in the hands of the few persons who control a giant corporation is a tremendous force which can harm or benefit a multitude of individuals, affect whole districts, shift the currents of trade, bring ruin to one community and prosperity to another. The organizations which they control have passed far beyond the realm of private enterprise—they have become more nearly social institutions."[6]

"The private profit-making business corporation soon loses, if it ever really had, its status as an enterprise subject to the uncontrolled will of its owners. If it operates a 'public utility,' which is in fact any enterprise upon which the community is highly dependent, it must furnish the service required by the community. The owners of the telephone company cannot decide suddenly that they choose not to provide telephone service tomorrow morning. They do not have the same sort of right to do what they like with their property as they have when they decide whether to wear their hats or throw them away. It is evident enough that the business corporation which operates an important enterprise, employs large numbers of workers, is indebted to a multitude of bondholders, is owned by a multitude of shareholders, is operated by salaried employees, is controlled by men who only in theory represent the shareholders—that such an organization is no one's private and personal enterprise."[7]

"It is a responsibility [of the U. S. Steel Corporation] that, willy-nilly, leaps over its corporate boundaries to include responsibility for the way of life, not just of its own 196,000 employees, but for the way of life, the security and happiness, the improving standard of living of millions of Americans."[8]

"Our industries can no longer be operated to serve private interests where those interests conflict with the public need. Initiative can find its most useful outlet, greatest recognition and highest reward when exerted in the public service."[9]

The above comments come from a joint statement of a professor of law and a professor of economics, from a journalist, from a business magazine, and from a labor union. The diversity of sources is readily apparent. More significantly, however, we may go on to add to such a symposium expressions remarkably similar emanating from business sources.

"Industry must accept its responsibility for the national welfare as

---

[6] Berle and Means, *The Modern Corporation and Private Property*, p. 46; by permission of The Macmillan Company, publishers.
[7] Walter Lippmann, *The Good Society* (2nd edition, 1943), pp. 305-306.
[8] "The U. S. Steel Corporation: III," *Fortune*, May, 1936, p. 94.
[9] *The UAW-CIO Post-War Plan* (April, 1944), p. 14.

being an even higher duty than the successful operations of private business."[10]

"In this evolution of a complex industrial society the social responsibility of management has broadened correspondingly. Management no longer represents, as it once did, merely the *single interest* of ownership; increasingly it functions on the basis of a *trusteeship* which endeavors to maintain, between these four basic interlocking groups, a proper balance of equity. Today the executive head of every business is accountable not only to his stockholders, but to the members of his working organization, to his customers, and to the public. . . . The full implications which flow from this new concept of trusteeship have not been completely grasped by industry, and certainly not by worker and public. The traditional private status of industry has been supplanted, under changing social concepts and regulation, by a quasi-public status. For instance, the secrecy which was the inevitable accompaniment of an intense competitive struggle for markets has given place to klieg lights beating mercilessly upon all business activities. The result is that decisions on industrial and economic policies, which once were made solely from the standpoint of private interest and profit considerations, must now be evaluated in terms of *consequence*—not merely to one individual company, but to an entire industry of which the company may be a comparatively minor unit. And these decisions must take into account a new factor of increasing significance—that of *public* relationships."[11]

"The consumer must get an adequate product at fair price. The employee must get steady employment at a fair wage. Finally, only, may come the fair return to stockholders, and this primarily to assure the flow of capital necessary for new enterprises. . . . It is not a very palatable doctrine to put the stockholder last among the obligations of the enterprise. . . . Yet today I think we will all agree that top management has problems of a totally different character from the problems that occupied top management fifty years ago."[12]

"In my judgment the corporation in the future may recognize a broader responsibility—to include not only stockholders, but labor and the consuming public. In the annual report under such circumstances, the number of days of employment, the regularity of employment and the income per worker would be reported in addition to the profits for stock-

[10] C. M. Chester, Chairman of General Foods, cited in J. Walter Dietz, "Controlling Factors in Industrial Relations Administration," from *Channels of Dealing With Workers*, American Management Association (1937), p. 37.

[11] Lewis H. Brown, President of Johns-Manville Corporation, "New Objectives of Management," in Batchelor (editor), *The New Outlook in Business*, pp. 95–96.

[12] Statement of William L. Batt, President of SKF Industries, quoted by John R. Steelman in an address before the Ohio State Federation of Labor, August 4, 1938 (mimeo), p. 4.

holders. At the same time the corporation might publish or have available records showing its relation to the consuming public. In reality, the responsibility of a corporation runs in three directions—to the stockholders, to its employees and to its consumers. This is being recognized by the leading corporations in America to a degree unequalled elsewhere in the world."[13]

Examining the institution of the corporation in its relation to society, numbers of thoughtful men have thus felt the need for a change in the concept of corporate interests. Relying on the expressions of businessmen, such as those just given, others have pointed to the need for new standards by which corporate conduct may be judged. "As capital recedes from actual participation in the day-to-day affairs of industry and management extends its sphere, the motive of profit alone becomes increasingly remote and archaic. As the primary partners in the conduct of industry become increasingly untrammelled by the interference of capital in the conduct of industry, the need for a motive and an ideal, which will adequately interpret the fundamental purpose for which industry exists, becomes a common necessity. The profession of the manager is becoming a public one; he is beginning to sense his obligation to the community. We are indeed witnessing the entry into the direction of industry of ethical considerations as a determining factor in policy, at least equal to considerations of profit or personal advancement. Such considerations assume rights held by the community, not only over the products of industry but over its methods. They assume industrial responsibilities with regard to the conditions which the community may impose."[14]

"The proposition that the sole function of business organizations is to produce the maximum profit for absentee owners is not only one which cannot, in the nature of things, appeal strongly as a code of professional ethics to the managers; it is also one which no longer appeals strongly to the community as a social policy."[15]

Sensing this evolutionary development many managers have gone along with it, and by an assumption of social obligations have sought to justify their position as industrial leaders in a society which asserts the involvement of other than stockholder interest. By a voluntary broadening of their personal and corporate responsibility they have attempted to qualify for leadership in a new era. In some cases this effort has found

---

[13] Frank Gannett, publisher, in a statement before a subcommittee of the Committee on Finance, United States Senate, 75th Congress, 3rd Session, Hearings, *Survey of Experiences in Profit Sharing and Possibilities of Incentive Taxation* (1939), p. 204. See also the statement of Owen D. Young previously quoted on page 19.

[14] Sheldon, *The Philosophy of Management*, p. 76.

[15] Dodd, "Is Effective Enforcement of the Fiduciary Duties of Corporate Managers Practicable?" *University of Chicago Law Review* (1935), vol. 2, p. 205.

expression in the formulation of suggested codes of conduct and articles of faith.[16]

One need not question the conscience of such industrial leaders nor the soundness of their conclusions, however, to question the effects of their initiative in adopting these views as a guide for action, rather than merely as a proposal for reform. For as matters now stand there is only one clearly specified standard of conduct to which the managers may be held accountable—operation in the owners' interest. There are no well-defined standards or tests for fostering public or employe interests. "Certain minimum claims on the part of employees and consumers can and to an increasing extent are being given legal formulation, but they do not substantially alter the basic principle. A duty to pay a legal minimum wage or to charge no more than a legal maximum price is not a duty of loyalty to employee or consumer. It is, as a general rule, a duty owed by the enterprise as a whole rather than by the managers personally. It is merely a modification of the rules of the game for the benefit of certain classes—a modification which does not affect the principle that the management is to play the game as representatives of another class—the investors. However much modern corporate executives may like to think of themselves as trustees of an institution rather than attorneys for the stockholders, the law furnishes them with no guiding principles in accordance with which such trusteeship can be conducted."[17]

Indeed, there are some who see danger in permitting, by silent concurrence, managers to assume broader responsibilities than the law now countenances. "When the fiduciary obligation of the corporate manage-

---

[16] A good example is the following draft of Lewis H. Brown, as President of Johns-Manville Co., published in Batchelor's *The New Outlook in Business,* pp. 101–102:

"We who are responsible for the management of business in supplying the needs of the public for goods and services and who recognize our obligations to stockholders and employees believe

"THAT we should constantly seek to provide better values at lower costs so that more of our people can enjoy more of the world's goods.

"THAT we should strive to develop the efficiency of industry so as to earn a fair return for the investing public and provide the highest possible reward for the productivity of labor.

"THAT we should stimulate the genius of science and utilize the methods of research to improve old products and create new ones so as to continuously provide new fields of employment for the present and coming generations.

"THAT management should encourage fair trade practices in business which, whether effected by competition or by cooperation, will be so shaped as to be for the best interest of our customers and of society as a whole.

"THAT it is management's duty to be alert to its own shortcomings, to the need for improvement, and to new requirements of society, while always recognizing the responsibility of trusteeship.

"THAT business in this country has never been what it could be and never what it yet will be.

"THAT business, labor, government and agriculture working hand in hand can provide jobs and the opportunity for all to work for security without loss of our liberty and rights as free men."

[17] Dodd, *University of Chicago Law Review,* vol. 2, pp. 205–206.

ment and 'control' to stockholders is weakened or eliminated, the management and 'control' become for all practical purposes absolute. The claims upon the assembled industrial wealth and funneled industrial income which managements are then likely to enforce (they have no need to urge) are their own. . . . Now I submit that you can not abandon emphasis on 'the view that business corporations exist for the sole purpose of making profits for their stockholders' until such time as you are prepared to offer a clear and reasonably enforceable scheme of responsibilities to someone else."[18]

Management itself has been most insistent that authority and responsibility may not be separated. Yet those managers who have voluntarily assumed responsibilities to the public and to their employes have failed to appreciate that their authority derives *solely* from a group to whom, by its own profession, it accords only a partial responsibility; that they have admitted a responsibility to those who have had no voice in determining their authority. This split of the basis for authority and responsibility is in part the cause for the challenge which has been raised to management, by unions as well as by the government representing the public. As an institution, the corporation must be accountable to broader interests than the owners. As a legal relationship, it is representative only of the owners.

When management resists the union's attempted participation in the conduct of the corporation, it is relying upon its legal position of authority and the narrow responsibility—to the owners—which stems from its delegated authority. It is protecting that position. But the unions are concerned more with the institutional than with the legal view. They know they have interests, whether legal or not, which are bound up in the corporation. They have heard those interests championed not only by theorists and reformers but by management itself, in its public professions. In raising their challenge, they are seeking to enforce a responsibility on management which its authority does not permit, and they are seeking to empower an authority—on their own representatives, if need be—commensurate with the responsibility they feel is owed to them. Where institutions and the law conflict, can boundaries of interests be drawn and held?

[18] Berle, "For Whom Corporate Managers *Are* Trustees," *Harvard Law Review*, vol. 45 (1932), p. 1367. Berle uses "control" in the sense of "that individual or small group of individuals who are able to mobilize or cast sufficient votes to elect the corporate management."

CHAPTER 10

The Need for Functional Integration

The penetration by unions into the functions and areas of management has created a problem of organizational stability. The operation of most large corporations depends upon agreement between management and union. In the absence of such an agreement, the corporation of stockholders with their managerial representatives, and the union of employes, become functionally meaningless and impotent. Neither can operate without the other. In the face of this admitted mutual dependency, management members for the most part believe that the requisite organization cannot be achieved if the business enterprise becomes a setting for internecine struggle for controlling power. Because the unions have shown no willingness to draw a line demarking their sphere of influence some of our managers see no ultimate basis for resolving the continuing contest other than complete victory by one or the other of the contestants. Pending such an outcome, they believe the enterprise must move forward as best it may, with management fighting the internal opposition of its organized employes and the external opposition of the government expressed through regulation.

Management's relationship with the union, in the view of these men, consists of an endless struggle marked by occasional armistices which take the form of collective-bargaining agreements. Business under fire, however, is not conducive to efficient operation. The uncertainty of the future makes planning difficult at best. Management is thus prevented from doing a whole job. It must divert some of its energies to preserving its position. Those managers who do not warm to a fight, and those who see no possibility of peace with unions in the absence of agreement on the areas in which their influence will be felt, have acquired a rather bleak outlook on the future of their companies and the business system as a whole. One manager when asked if he saw any reason for optimism in the industrial relations scene replied, "None whatsoever. In fact, the situation is getting worse, and at an accelerated rate. We can always hope —I suppose there is always room for optimism. But if you mean, do I have any *grounds* for optimism, does our experience provide any *basis* for hope, the answer is No. I don't know what the solution can be."

If any conclusion is to be drawn from the analysis of the preceding pages it is that such solution as may come will certainly not arise from any demarkation of areas of interest. Aside from any question of desirability, no feasible method of outlining boundaries of union influence has been shown. Our historical, legal and institutional excursions indicate no reason for supposing that the union movement can be held at any line of advance on the broad front of the operating areas of management.

If boundaries of subject matter cannot be set to confine union activity, and if unions are to be allowed to continue their vital existence, there remains only the possibility of a functional integration of the union within the business enterprise. In the words of Justice Brandeis, "Some way must be worked out by which employer and employee, each recognizing the proper sphere of the other, will each be free to work for his own and for the common good, and that the powers of the individual employee may be developed to the utmost."[1] This does not mean that competing interests will not arise within the corporation. It does mean that organizational procedures must be provided to resolve differences which threaten the integrity of the business unit.

This is no easy task. It involves the acceptance of existing economic and political institutions which are socially respected and which are thus modifiable only within fairly narrow limits, to meet the pressing needs of the moment. At the same time it involves a recognition of underlying problems which such modifications may only touch without solving, and the focusing of attention upon them so that broader changes which time and crisis may require at some future date may then be acted upon on their own merits, with an intelligent appreciation of why such action is required. In searching for solutions we must thus keep two time periods in mind: one, the short run, involving adaptations of institutions and behavior which are possible under existing conditions; two, the longer run, when more basic reformation may be necessary and for which adequate preparation must be made. In both cases, it will be our underlying assumption that the objective is to modify present institutions no more than is needed to meet the issues posed. There is value in institutional continuity for its own sake, aside from the fact that respect for habits of thought and action bodes better for the success of the desired change.

Against the background of the earlier portions of this study it is possible to establish certain organizational requirements of the large corporation in which the union has been integrated. Building on the analytical foundations which we have laid, we may now inquire as to what arrangements are needed if, under collective bargaining, union and man-

[1] *Business—A Profession* (1914), p. 17.

agement are both to play meaningful and mutually accepted roles. On the basis of our previous investigation, we shall examine the requirements of a functional integration of union and management which will preclude that impotence which each singly must experience. In the light of the preceding analysis we shall attempt to understand in what respects present procedures or institutions make integration difficult, the extent to which existing practice may be improved by action of the parties themselves, and the degree to which such voluntary improvement may still leave unanswered basic problems requiring institutional changes beyond the power of the parties themselves to undertake. The estimates contained in the following pages concerning the degree to which unions and managements measure up to requirements imply no criticism. It is a matter of facing facts.

THE FUNCTIONAL ROLE OF THE PARTIES

Functional integration requires a clear understanding of the role each participating organization must play or may play in the business enterprise. In terms of the managerial functions which we have previously isolated and defined, this requirement involves a statement of the union's part in direction, administration, and execution.

It will be recalled that direction establishes what is to be done, and speaks with final authority; administration determines how it shall be done, while execution sees that it is done. In these terms we may come to immediate grips with the question of what constitute managerial prerogatives. Starting with the frame-within-frame organization of the corporation, we may recognize that management in all frames exercises one or more of these three managerial functions. Directive management operates within a framework supplied by the corporate charter and by-laws, the state corporation laws, and the general laws of the society in which it exists. Administrative management, in addition to operating within this same framework, must operate within the bounds prescribed by directive management and administrators in the frames above it. Executive management must operate within the limits set forth by directive and administrative management. The prerogatives of management—regardless of whether its function is direction, administration, or execution—are the total bundle of discretion which is permitted to it within the framework in which it operates. That framework may change, and with it the prerogatives.

Management is thus considering legal, not functional, issues when it says that its existing prerogatives must be preserved undiluted if it is to function as management. Within the managerial structure, the prerogatives of management are constantly being changed—by management itself, as well as by state and federal legislation. Legislation limits directive management in its freedom of action, but likewise directive management, on its own initiative, limits the discretionary area of administrative management, and the latter restricts the prerogatives of executive management. The framework of prerogatives is thus subject to constant change, but within that framework management retains freedom of discretion.

The union is challenging vested interests but failing to recognize organizational functions if it says that management has no prerogatives. It may itself assist in determining what are the prerogatives which management may exercise, but following upon such determination it cannot avoid leaving to management an area of discretion, of freedom of decision and action, which constitute managerial prerogatives. It may join with management in establishing a directive framework which includes rules governing, for example, the selection of production employes for advancement, but within that framework administrative and executive management have freedom in the application of those rules, subject only to the union's (or higher management's) check upon proper compliance with them.

In the earlier corporations, the owners of the business took an important part in determining the area of freedom to be permitted their managers, which is to say that they defined, within the law, the prerogatives of management. Berle and Means have provided us with an excellent portrayal of this practice:

"We have the picture of a group of owners, necessarily delegating certain powers of management, protected in their property rights by a series of fixed rules under which the management had a relatively limited play. The management of the corporation indeed was thought of as a set of agents running a business for a set of owners; and while they could and did have wider powers than most agents, they were strictly accountable and were in a position to be governed in all matters of general policy by their owners. They occupied, in fact, a position analogous to that of the captains and officers of a ship at sea; in navigation their authority might be supreme; but the direction of the voyage, the alteration of the vessel, the character of the cargo, and the distribution of the profits and losses were settled ahead of time and altered only by the persons having the underlying property interest."[2]

The situation today is remarkably different in a number of ways from the conditions so pictured in corporations of a century or more ago. One

[2] *The Modern Corporation and Private Property*, p. 135, by permission of The Macmillan Company, publishers. These writers hold that this picture "probably was not unfair up to, say, 1835."

of the most important respects in which circumstances have been altered is in the introduction of strong unions, capable of insuring a hearing for their views in the conduct of the business. Along with the owners and the government, they assist in establishing the conditions under which management must operate, in defining the area of management's discretion, in determining managerial prerogatives. This change in business operation has been summed up by one analyst thoroughly conversant with the industrial scene in the statement, "Modern business management must expect to operate within the framework of a system of industrial jurisprudence."[3]

This industrial jurisprudence, which consists of the collective-bargaining agreement and its interpretations, accepted practices which are not subject to unilateral change, and understandings which are jointly respected, thus constitutes part of the framework defining management prerogatives. Within that framework management retains freedom of operation. The important question remaining is the nature of the union's participation in the processes of industrial jurisprudence.

We have previously said that the union's participation is itself the exercise of a managerial function. The union leaders are actually de facto managers. They are to be distinguished from a legislature which passes general laws forming part of management's framework of prerogatives, and which is not management, in that their decisions with which we are concerned are decisions made *within* the corporation of which their members are employes. They are concerned with specific problems of specific corporations in which they play a continuing role. The unions, moreover, join in the establishment and operation of certain corporate processes, such as the compliance system. Where collective bargaining prevails, the continuity of business operations is dependent upon their collaboration.

To the extent that the union participates in forming controlling policies and joins in making final decisions, it is participating in the directive function of management. This is commonly true in negotiations leading to the collective-bargaining agreement. That agreement constitutes part of the framework within which administrative and executive management must operate, and, in the subject matter which it covers, bears the stamp of final authority. None of the policies or decisions of the agreement is subject to modification, for the life of the agreement, by any authority other than the joint conference from which it originated.

Within this directive framework, however, administrative management remains free to operate. Its decisions as to how the objectives of the collective agreement are to be realized remain within its discretion. This

[3] Sumner Slichter, *Union Policies and Industrial Management*, p. 2.

area of discretion may be narrow with respect to some areas of operation, and wide with regard to others. In the matter of layoffs, for example, it may be rigidly bound by seniority provisions but in all other respects retain freedom of decision. Faced with a need for economy due to declining sales, administrative management may thus be eligible to determine how many employes shall be laid off (an administrative decision as to how economy is to be effected), but once having determined the number it will be controlled in the designation of such employes by the seniority provisions of the agreement (a directive policy since emanating from final authority, establishing what shall be done under the stated circumstances). The essence of direction, it will be recalled, is the finality which cloaks it and not the importance or generality of its decisions. The latter are frequent but not necessary accompaniments. The collective-bargaining conference, in its directive capacity, may attend to such minor matters as the use of company bulletin boards, just as the Congress of the United States may decide whether John Jones shall be paid $300 compensation for injuries sustained when struck by a post-office truck. The union participates in this directive function whenever it joins in a decision which is not subject to reversal by any higher authority.

The operation of a large corporation is a complex business. Its manifold activities require a continuing stream of decisions, emanating on a day-to-day basis. A wide latitude of discretion is required if flexibility is to be retained in meeting the problems which each new day brings Such decisions are the province of administrative management in its determination of how the objectives set forth by directive management are to be accomplished. This is what one corporation official has in mind when he says that "A broad purpose and a broad decision require fragmentation of purpose into detailed purposes and of principal general decisions into detailed subsidiary decisions."[4] In this steady flow of administrative decisions the union cannot play the *same* role as in the directive function if the requirements of flexibility, expedition, and organization are to be met. It participates in providing the framework within which administrative discretion is to be exercised; it cannot participate in the *same* manner in administration itself without sapping the vitality of the business enterprise.

This does not mean that the union can play no part in the function of administration, however. It merely means that its administrative role is governed by considerations not present in its directive capacity. In the frame-within-frame organization of the corporation the union frequently participates in decisions at every level of organization, within all the frames. Administrative participation is particularly evident when

[4] Barnard, *The Functions of the Executive* (1938), p. 206.

local plant negotiations supplement a company-wide contract, but it is likewise present when the foreman consults with the steward. The factor which distinguishes such administrative participation from the union's role in direction is the absence of final authority on the part of its representatives as well as those of management.

Each frame of the corporate structure operates within a framework which defines the discretion permitted to management at that level. It cannot exceed those bounds, which are prescribed by the successive policies and decisions handed down from the frames above. The union may participate with management in the administrative process subject to the limitation that it is bound by the same framework of discretion within which management must operate. It may play an important contributing role by providing administrative management with factual information and a point of view which might otherwise be lacking. Good administration requires an examination of all facets of a problem before a decision is reached. The union can assist in that examination, and seek to influence administrative decisions in which it feels its interests are involved. It cannot, however, bring its influence to bear in an attempt to secure a decision which transcends the area of discretion of the frame within which it is operating without endangering the organizational structure of the enterprise.

The union joins in final authority only in the directive frame. In all subsidiary frames the decisions which it seeks must be reached within an area of discretion which is not complete and which is not final. It must accept as an organizational absolute that *it cannot exercise final authority on administrative matters,* as it does in direction. Two considerations are wrapped up in this organizational necessity of the union's recognition of the function and sphere of administration.

First, the absence of final authority in any administrative frame and the limitations on the freedom of action of management in that frame imposed by authorities in the frames above it mean that its decisions and actions are circumscribed in a manner which is beyond its control. This is a principle of organization which the unions readily recognize within their own structures, but they are sometimes less willing to accept it within the business enterprise. In a number of instances, as management will testify, they have operated *within an administrative frame* as though management in that frame held final and complete discretion as to its course of conduct. They have sought agreement on a matter which management at that level was powerless to consider, and have accepted its explanation of this fact only as a stall or a run-around. They may, of course, legitimately question whether such management should not be given the authority which it lacks, and they may take action in higher administrative frames or in the directive process to attempt to confer such authority on it. But until the area of discretion in that frame is redrawn, their issue cannot be settled there. It may be settled only in a higher frame where discretion is present. As a prerequisite to their participation in the administrative process, then, the unions must accept the given frame-within-frame structure of the enterprise, with the respective areas of discretion. They must operate, administratively, within the boundaries prescribed.

As a second consideration stemming from the fact that participation in the administrative process involves operating within a framework where discretion is neither complete nor final, the union must be prepared to see its administrative agreements reversed by higher authority. This harsh requirement cannot be avoided. Joint agreement in the administrative process cannot serve to bind the directive or higher administrative officers of either union or company unless the whole concept of final authority and its delegation is to be discarded. Joint agreement on an administrative matter may indeed be reached, and frequently is, but it may stand only so long as the higher officers of both union and company accept it. The union can participate in administration, but it cannot impose final authority in administration. Final authority rests only with direction.

The nature of administrative decisions, even within a framework, can never be fully predicted. The range of possible choice can never be wholly foreseen, and if higher authority—either of union or company—finds unacceptable a decision reached in a lower frame, it remains free to reverse the decision. A union which joins in the administrative process must necessarily accept this hazard.

If the union may participate in direction and in administration, may it likewise participate in execution? The answer to this question has been given in an earlier chapter. Little in the way of discretion rests with executive management. It is the function of execution to see that the job is done in the manner which administration has decreed, to organize and direct personnel in the performance of a prescribed task according to prescribed methods. In the absence of a discretionary area, there is no room for sharing authority in this task. The union may be given executive responsibilities which it alone is charged with fulfilling. It may assist executive management in the performance of its function. It cannot, however, share the same executive responsibility with management without introducing confusion. In the executive responsibilities of the shop, the union steward may assist the foreman, but he cannot share equally his authority.

In terms of the first criterion by which the functional integration of the union with the large corporation may be tested, we may say then that the union may participate in the direction of the enterprise; it may likewise participate in its administration, accepting the requirements of operating within the discretionary boundaries of each frame and of recognizing that higher authority may overrule it; it may not share in the function of execution, though it may be delegated executive responsibilities.

Is there at the present time a clear understanding on the part of both union and management as to the nature of these functional roles of the union? It is difficult to say, but the answer is probably in the negative. In some instances management in an administrative frame has been reluctant to share its authority with the union, despite the example set by its superiors either in higher administrative brackets or in the directive process. Though possessing the discretion to act, it has sometimes hesitated to reach an agreement with the union. In some cases this reluctance may be traced to a fear that agreements may be frowned on by a higher management not desirous of extending the influence of the union. A freer exchange of views between management and union representatives in all the administrative frames has thus been retarded.

On other occasions the union has failed to recognize the limitations of participation in administrative matters, and has refused to accept as datum the area of discretion within which management in a particular frame must operate. It has sought to bring to administration a final authority, and has sometimes struck when agreements reached on administrative levels have been overturned by higher authority. It cannot be denied, however, that it has sometimes found this method the only one capable of securing for it an audience with management in a frame possessing adequate authority to settle the issue involved.

The charge is frequently voiced by company officials that stewards in the shops have usurped the foreman's executive role, countermanding his instructions or issuing orders of their own. They cite instances when workers under the foreman's direction have challenged his executive capacity.

These are all either examples of a lack of understanding of the role which the union may play, or of a failure to translate such an understanding into practice. It is clear, however, that this deficiency in the collective-bargaining relationship is one which the parties on their own motion may overcome. No institutional changes are required to encourage this aspect of functional integration. Only a more thorough appreciation of the organizational processes of the business enterprise, as they relate to the union, is needed, along with a genuine desire and willingness to act in such a manner as mutually to accommodate each other's role while jointly preserving the business structure. In some quarters there are signs of an explicit acceptance of the function of the union as here outlined, though the terms employed may differ. There is ground for optimism when a representative of a powerful national union explains that "The Union wishes to share the policy formulation through annual negotiations culminating in a contract between labor and management. Insofar as policy execution is concerned, the Union wishes to reserve the right to challenge the company through the grievance machinery, if the Union feels the executive policy to be in contradiction with the contractual provisions."

Application must follow profession before we may feel satisfied, of course, but an understanding of the union's role in the managerial function is a prerequisite to its application. Union and company officials seldom discuss the role of management except when engaged in controversy over a specific issue, and then only in terms of the assertion of "rights" by one which are denied by the other. It is worth speculating on the advantage to both parties of entering into an exploration, free from partisanship and theoretical in nature, of the managerial function in the large corporation, designed to clarify for both the requirements of that function and the manner in which the union may be brought within its terms. It is easy to ignore the fact that collective bargaining has materially changed the form of our business organizations. Worthy of attention of the best minds of company and union is an examination of the business procedures required by that change.

INTEGRITY OF THE PARTICIPANTS

Functional integration requires the integrity of each of the participating organizations. This involves an acceptance of the organization and its purpose by those it is designed to represent and by those with whom it participates. There must be such a respect for each of the participating organizations that its security is unchallenged and its representative nature is unquestioned.

The relation of this criterion to functional integration is apparent. The participating organizations are representative in nature, and their integrity as representative organizations is essential if they are to discharge this aspect of their function. If mutual acceptance is understood not in the sense of a resigned assent, but of affirmation and acquiescence, the proportions of this requirement are readily recognizable. In this study we can do little more than reach a nodding acquaintance with the issues attached. Our interest has been chiefly centered upon the parties in collaboration, rather than upon the parties which collaborate, a focus which unfortunately but necessarily restricts examination of problems which while pertinent can only be satisfactorily treated by more exhaustive and direct analysis.

Acceptance of each of the participating organizations involves (1) acquiescence in the organization and its purpose by those represented; (2) opportunity for change of leadership and methods by those represented; (3) conformance of the constituency to the legal decisions of its leaders; (4) opportunity for those represented to challenge abuse of power by their leaders; and (5) recognition of the organization by those with whom it deals, involving not necessarily acceptance of its point of view but of its right to a point of view, as well as of its privilege of functioning and of its methods of operation. These criteria are equally applicable to the employes and their representatives and to the owners and their representatives.

1. Acquiescence in the organization and its purpose by those represented involves support of the group objectives and of the organizational means jointly established to secure them. This does not preclude the possibility of amendment and modification through democratic procedures; it does require a good-faith acceptance of the organization and its goals as they exist at any given time, even at the moment that some may be seeking change.

In the case of the union, a process of boring from within on the part of factions to capture the organization for camouflaged objectives is inimical to achieving this requirement. So likewise is a refusal of dissident employe groups to recognize the representative status of a majority union, even though accorded the privilege of declining membership in it and of seeking its defeat in a subsequent election.[5] In the company, attempted seizure of control by an organized bloc for its own interests is condemnable on the same ground, as is an attempt by management to foster independent objectives unrelated to owner interests.[6]

2. Opportunity for change of leadership and methods by those repre-

---

[5] An example of the negation of this requirement is afforded by a 1945 strike at the Detroit plant of the United States Rubber Co., where a minority faction caused suspension of operations affecting 6,000 employes for more than two weeks. This faction struck not against the company but against the representative union. Charges of Communist, Trotzkyite, and white-racial group objectives were freely made, indicating a confusion of purposes. Detroit newspapers for the period July 13–August 1, 1945 provide accounts of this episode.

[6] These evils are particularly to be found in, but by no means exclusive to, reorganization proceedings. An excellent statement of the dangers involved to the interests of investors as a group is given by William O. Douglas in "Lawyers and Conflicts of Interest," *Democracy and Finance,* pp. 230–240. Gardiner C. Means and C. F. Ware, in *The Modern Economy in Action* (1936), pp. 50–51, amplify the statement that "many stockholders have found that their board of directors is most adept at keeping the company's earnings from reaching them." A. S. Dewing, in *Financial Policy of Corporations* (1934), pp. 694–697, speaks of personal motives of management in the conduct of corporate enterprise which may run counter to the interests represented.

sented may be restated as a democratic control by the constituency over its leaders. Not all unions nor all managements can come into court with clean hands in this particular. A recent report of the American Civil Liberties Union, while frankly admitting a bias in favor of unionism, declared: "As this survey indicates, the majority of unions satisfy reasonable requirements of democratic practice, though few are entirely free from criticism for lack of it in one respect or another. The chief complaints by rank and file members concern lack of opportunity for full participation in the conduct of a union's affairs, tending to the perpetuation in office of entrenched officials; the difficulty of organizing an opposition to the leadership; the lack of adequate machinery for review of expulsions and suspensions; the penalties imposed by varied means on critics of the leadership; the lack of control over expenditures and assessments in many unions; discrimination in assignment to jobs; and exclusions from membership based on race, sex or political connections."[7]

Information vital to a member's participation in his union's affairs may be lacking to him. The vice president of a large corporation reported that in negotiations then current the membership had not been informed of either the union's demands or the company's offers. "How can there be democratic control of the leaders in such a situation?" he asks.

From the company's side, the situation, conservatively speaking, is often no better. The divorce of ownership and control has been too well publicized to require emphasis or dramatization. The ability of management to retain corporate control is rooted primarily in the dispersion of stock among thousands or hundreds of thousands of investors, no one of whom customarily possesses a sufficient block of stock to encourage an active interest, nor an effective means of enjoying his ownership rights if he were so inclined. Here too there is a lack of information on the organization's affairs. "It has been suggested that at every stockholders' meeting at the back of the platform there should be a sign carrying Tennyson's words: 'We have but faith, we cannot know.' "[8]

3. Conformance of the constituency to the legal decisions of its leaders is a necessary corollary to the mere fact of organization. Without this requirement there would be anarchy. The problem here has been chiefly confined to the unions, perhaps indicative of a greater control exercised by corporate leaders over their constituency but also of the differing nature of the organizations themselves. Revolt, by disobedience of constituted authority, is possible to a greater extent in the organizations of workers than in the organizations of owners.

[7] *Democracy in Trade Unions* (1943), p. 68.
[8] John M. Hancock, as chairman of the stock list committee of the New York Stock Exchange, quoted in the *New York Times*, April 27, 1940.

The issue has been raised primarily over wildcat strikes, and examples might be multiplied. Management speaks of the membership's failure to conform to procedures legally established by their leaders and usually ratified by the members themselves as "union irresponsibility." The industrial relations director of one large corporation related how five women presented a grievance, asking for payment of wages which they believed were due them under a clause in the contract. The foreman refused the grievance. Without attempting to follow the prescribed procedure for appeals, the women laid down their work and walked out. The foreman asked five other girls to take over their jobs, but was met with a refusal. Despite the fact that the union steward supported the foreman in his insistence that the normal grievance procedure be followed, before long some 50 employes in the department had joined in the walkout. Regional union officials were called into the picture, but the difficulty was not finally resolved until national intervention was forthcoming. From this example, the industrial relations director reached two conclusions: one, that the union was unable to control its own members; and second, that the union membership lacked sufficient self-control to follow procedures which its organization had joined in establishing.

There is basis for such complaint. Whatever the provocation to anger, employes in all enterprises where there is a union now have agreed-upon procedures for pressing their claims. In those companies or industries where umpires are supported, they have certainty of a final impartial ruling on their grievances. Failure to rely upon such procedures, to which their union is party, involves a nonacceptance by the members of their union's organization and authority. Acceptance cannot be fostered by "control" from top officials of the organization, however, though it can be encouraged by them. It can come only through a greater degree of self-control and organizational responsibility in the rank and file.

4. Opportunity for those represented to challenge abuse of power by their leaders is the counterpart to conformance of the constituency to the legal decisions of their leaders. Officials of both owners and workers are circumscribed by limitations of their organizations' charter, constitution, bylaws, and resolutions. Removal from office of officials who fail to conform to these limitations constitutes one check upon them. By itself it is insufficient, however. Illegal actions may be difficult to retract after the lapse of time pending election, and may serve the interests of incumbents seeking reelection. Moreover, such actions may have been taken in good faith, on an interpretation of permissible authority, and the constituency may seek the restraining of what it considers unwarranted action while unwilling to discard the elected officers responsible for it.

In the case of both union and company, the powers of the leaders are frequently loosely drawn and at the same time sweeping. Guides for official conduct are nevertheless provided. While no generalization can be made as to the respect accorded such limitations on the exercise of authority, abuse has sometimes been flagrant. In one union whose official records were independently studied, illegal actions undertaken by its leaders over a three-year period included unauthorized disbursement of funds; the passage of "emergency legislation" with the apology that its legalization "through the regular channels shall be undertaken as soon as possible"; the increase of officers' salaries, amounts of which were specifically provided for in the constitution and bylaws; extension of terms of representatives; the amending of the constitution itself by other than prescribed procedures; the negotiation of agreements violating a constitutional injunction against members' belonging to employers' associations; and the refusal to call membership meetings which the constitution required. The interpretation of the union's laws customarily rests with the president or the general executive board. There is often futility in appeal against an interpretation when it must be made to a tribunal which is composed of those officers themselves responsible for the interpretation.

The situation of the owners shows no improvement. "The whole effect of the growth of powers of directors and 'control' has been steadily to diminish the number of things on which a shareholder can count; the number of demands which he can make with any assurance that they must be satisfied. The stockholder is therefore left as a matter of law with little more than the loose expectation that a group of men, under a nominal duty to run the enterprise for his benefit and that of others like him, will actually observe this obligation. In almost no particular is he in a position to demand that they do or refrain from doing any given thing." "A set of legal rights which can hardly be enforced, constituting claims on an economic operation from which the individual shareholder is separated by so many barriers, present an appearance of satisfactory legal relationships to the enterprise, which in practice have little significance to the individual investor."[9] As with the union, the interpretation of the enterprise's laws rests with the officials who administer them, and there is no appeal within the enterprise to any other set of functionaries.

In this situation, there has been no genuine recourse for constituents who challenge the legality of actions undertaken by their officials other than to the courts. On the whole, the courts have been less reluctant to provide equitable relief for owners than for organized employes. In the latter case constitutional provisions explicitly granting officers the power

---

[9] Berle and Means, *The Modern Corporation and Private Property*, pp. 277 and 287, by permission of The Macmillan Company, publishers.

to promulgate conclusive determinations of the meaning of laws which define their own powers have sometimes been upheld,[10] while with corporate actions the courts have shown greater willingness to penetrate beyond the technical exercise of power to perceive whether the result fairly protects the interests of the owners.[11] In the case of both organized owners and employes, however, restraint of official action by suit is a costly and delaying process.

5. Recognition of the organization by those with whom it deals involves their acceptance of its privilege of functioning and its methods of operation. Without such recognition the integrity of the organization is imperiled and its participating role is called into question.

By this criterion the deficiencies of the existing union-management relationships are quite apparent, with notable exceptions. For the most part, such exceptions occur in corporations and businesses of smaller magnitude than those with which we are concerned in this study. The relative harmony of the men's clothing, women's garment, hat, and hosiery industries, of an occasional small steel company or meat-packing concern, is not generally duplicated in the large corporation.

On the part of the union, the feeling of nonacceptance is eloquently voiced by a composite statement of five leaders of the organized employes at one vast plant of a giant corporation. Without prompting, their feeling of hurt spilled out, with one taking up where the other left off.

"We were supposed to have a labor-management committee here during the war, and it received a lot of publicity, with famous movie stars and radio performers coming out to the plant to be photographed with the workers. Actually it was kept down to such things as war bond drives, blood bank campaigns, community chest programs, Red Cross drives, with the union doing the work and the company getting the glory. We had the feeling that the company was taking advantage of us during the war by slipping through variations in production methods, job standards, and so on, with the union raising less objection and often consenting on the basis that sacrifices should be made for the war. But there was increasing bitterness among the members as time went on, with a tendency toward the end of the war to fight back at management, even though war production was still involved, because we thought we were being taken advantage of.

"Since the end of the war, the company has been tightening up on its enforcement of the contract, squeezing every little technicality out of it that it possibly can. We've had to file a lot of grievances, but the company won't settle them in the plant unless it's an open and shut matter. They

---

[10] "Disputes Within Trade Unions," *Yale Law Journal*, vol. 45, p. 1260.
[11] Berle and Means, *The Modern Corporation and Private Property*, p. 275.

prefer to take them to arbitration. We don't have a very good record in arbitration, but we don't think that means we're in the wrong. It's simply further evidence that the company is seizing upon technicalities, and has persuaded the arbitrators to consider technicalities, so that the decision may be technically correct but actually it's at variance with the spirit and intent of the contract provision.

"Within the last ten years or so, more and more jobs have been created by the company in the field of industrial relations. They take the bright young men who have training in personnel matters and make them personnel assistants to the superintendents of departments, with a staff relationship to the superintendent of industrial relations. These men have undertaken to train the foremen in their responsibilities as part of management, but so far as we can see all the company is trying to teach its foremen through the program is how to be diplomatic in chiseling the worker.

"Along with this industrial relations program, the company has been going over the head of the union to the workers, like the case of a general foreman who has been calling in the key skilled workers and talking to them in a father-to-son manner. 'I know something is wrong among you fellows in the shop. I hear some talk about no more overtime work by you fellows. What's it all about? We want to do everything we can to help you boys out. Instead of taking everything to your steward, why don't you bring it to me? My door's always open. I'm always glad to see you and talk over any problems. Your steward's got plenty to keep him busy, so bring it to me, and if it's something I can't do anything about we'll go right to the superintendent. His door's always open too. And if he can't help, we'll take it right to the plant manager. We want to work with you guys.' Naturally we resent this deliberate attempt to circumvent the union.

"We feel our relations with the company are bad and deteriorating. The company is returning to its old attitude of not dealing with the union unless it's forced to. The plant management has little authority to settle many local issues, being bound by 'corporation policy,' as they tell us. The foremen have no authority to settle any grievance of any importance. They have to refer the matter to the superintendent of industrial relations, who writes out the answer for them. In one case a foreman wrote out his own reply to a grievance, but before he could deliver it another official saw it, forced its withdrawal, asked the union to submit another form on the excuse that the original had been lost, and that was sent to the industrial relations department for reply. Until recently we were able to settle many grievances verbally, right in the shop. Now the company has been insisting on writing up grievances in strict conformity with the contract, which means that the industrial relations department is in on more and more of them, hewing to the line and delaying action. Literally months elapse before a final decision is handed down. There is purpose behind their waiting out the full permissible time of answering grievances.

"What's behind it all? The company has never really accepted the union, for all the lip service it pays to collective bargaining. They feel they have been forced into relations with the union, first under the Wagner Act, then by the War Labor Board. They are out to smash the union at the first opportunity they get. Right now they are tightening up on their relations with the union, conceding as little as possible, sparring with the union, making it tough going for us, jabbing as they can before the big showdown."

It must be remembered that this is a partisan statement, to which company management took exception, but at the same time it is an honest representation of sentiment in one union. Perhaps more illustrative of a nonacceptance of the unions are such statements, from management representatives themselves, as the following: "The fault is not entirely with the union. There are the 'bright idea boys' among management who think they can play the veterans off against the union." And from one vice president, "We are admittedly anti-union, but we like our workers." It would be unfair to imply that such an attitude characterizes the managers of large corporations generally, but the union's belief that it does is an effective determinant of its reactions.

On the part of the management representatives of the organized owners, this sentiment finds it counterpart. It is evidenced in the prevalent belief that socialism lies at the end of the collective-bargaining road, and the corollary that unions give only lip service to the private property system and would willingly assist in its passage from the social scene, either by direct removal or by so circumscribing it as to render its rights and privileges meaningless. They point to statements from labor leaders asserting that "private ownership of monopolistic industries must be replaced by forms of social ownership"[12] as sufficient indication that the unions have not accepted the privilege of functioning and methods of operation of the organized owners, that they challenge the integrity of the owners' very organization—not simply nor necessarily the business enterprise, but the owners' participation, through the corporate form, in that enterprise. If management has sometimes slighted the interests of employes and the status of their union, say some company officials, how much more flagrantly and frequently have the unions ignored the interests of the stockholders—even at times to the extent of seeming to deny the existence of any rights accruing to ownership. In their

[12] Victor Reuther, "Look Forward, Labor," *Common Sense*, December, 1945, p. 8.

experience, the union and its leaders regard stockholders as members of a moneyed aristocracy and the recipients of unearned income. "Private profit" are words which can be used as a lash. With such union attitudes, how can the organized owners and their representatives feel secure in their position—not intrenched in their privileges, but only recognized and accepted by the union as a desirable partner in the enterprise?

By some cyclonic twist of events, owners and management are now fighting for recognition by the unions in the same manner that unions have long been fighting for acceptance by management. The organizations of which they—the owners and managers—are, or have been, such important and essential parts are being remolded around them in such a fashion as to threaten their long-run if not immediate existence. There is a feeling of being compelled to participate in self-obliteration. If ownership rights are removed or sequestered, the nexus upon which legal management relies for its authority will be destroyed, and there is no assurance that it will continue to share in the management function on another basis. The rise of a socialist government in England has strengthened their fears. Union pressure for industry-wide bargaining, crossing corporate lines, sounds like only a way-stop to collectivism, in one form or another. Whether justified in their belief or not, many managers are convinced that the institution of private property, at least in business, is endangered by the union program. They and the owners whom they represent feel that the union has not genuinely accepted the integrity of their organization, founded as it is upon private property in business.

Functional integration, we have said, requires the integrity of each of the participating organizations. This involves acquiescence, by those represented, in the organization and its purpose; opportunity for change of leadership and methods; conformance of the constituency to the legal decisions of its leaders; opportunity for those represented to challenge abuse of official power, and recognition of the organization by those with whom it deals. We have sought to examine the deficiencies of present union-management relationships, and in so doing have painted a picture which perhaps overstates the negative aspects of their connections, but which at the same time lays bare the problems in this area. What means are available to resolve these issues?

It is perhaps unsatisfactory to leave this phase of our investigation with the remark that the cure lies with the parties themselves; for the opportunity for self-application of remedies has never been absent though it has not been widely resorted to. Perhaps more persuasive encouragement of such a widely recommended nostrum is called for, for the fact remains that it gives greatest promise of relief. Particularly in the case of the unions is it true that few organizational difficulties stand in the way of their improving democratic procedures, stimulating membership participation, requiring membership conformance to proper decisions, offering a genuine opportunity to challenge abuse of official power. Again, acceptance of each other's organizations is such a subjective process as to be peculiarly susceptible to voluntary action—not only through a willingness on the part of one party to make a place for the other, but also through a striving by that other to make itself acceptable.

The diffuse and unequal representation of the shareholders presents special problems of ownership organization, which ultimately may demand more complete answer than can be given by their independent action or that of their managerial representatives. Here public action may yet be required to protect the integrity of organizations of owners, as it may also be required—in the face of continued union inaction—to protect the integrity of organizations of workers. Such public action would relate to requirements for elections, civil liberty guaranties, and adequate judicial remedies within the organization. It would have for its purpose not restriction upon the union or upon the corporation, but a strengthening of those organizations for the fulfillment of their functional roles.

Responsibility and Authority in Functional Integration

An appreciation of the nature of the corporate managerial functions and of the need for the organizational integrity of each of the parties participating in those functions constitutes only a point of departure in exploring the requirements of integration. Basic to the problem, and providing its most difficult aspects, is the statement of the responsibilities and authority residing in each of the parties by reason of its corporate role.

RESPONSIBILITY

Functional integration requires understood, common responsibilities of the cooperating parties.

"We of management have a responsibility to the stockholders which the union does not share. Can we be asked to share our authority with an organization that does not recognize the same responsibilities?"

"The union has a responsibility for the welfare of its members. Management, too, often talks about its responsibility to the employes, but I ask them, where is your responsibility to your employes when you lay them off?"

These expressions of opinion, one from a director of industrial relations, the other from a national union president, are representative of widely held views of management and labor, respectively. Both groups speak of the other's "irresponsibility," of its failure to assume "responsibility," but they are not speaking of the same thing. Actually, their charge is not that the other is irresponsible, but that it recognizes a responsibility foreign to their own. Management *does* own a responsibility —a legal one—to the stockholders. Union leaders *do* accept a responsibility—a political one—to their constituencies. There is, however, no mutuality of responsibilities.

If both labor and management are to be integrated functionally, neither of these present responsibilities can be slighted. But more is needed. There must be a *system* of responsibilities which is understood

213

and accepted by the cooperating parties. Obligations which are now divided must be shared, in a system which is real and not merely formal. The parties who join together in agreement must be joined together in responsibilities.

The outlines of such a system of responsibilities are now fairly discernible, though with discontinuities and an imprecision which have rendered it peculiarly susceptible to partisan use. Its degree of acceptance is uncertain and there are few compulsions requiring its acceptance. Yet here lies the central root of many of our present industrial relations problems, including the question of the union's role in managerial authority. The painting in broad sweeps of a system of responsibilities, as we shall do here, is only to suggest the nature of an issue whose dimensions challenge the capacities of our ablest public and private leaders.

1. Each of the bargaining parties—the union and the legal management—owes responsibilities to its own constituents, the union to its membership, the legal management to its stockholders. These responsibilities are of two kinds, internal and external. The internal responsibilities involve the preservation of the integrity of the organization, as discussed in the preceding section. The external obligations are the standards by which it governs its short-term actions and sets its long-term course. They may involve, for example, economic gain for the constituents. While there remains some uncertainty as to the exact nature of these internal and external responsibilities of both union and management to their respective followings, there is a general awareness of their implications. Their more precise definition suggests no formidable obstacles.

2. Each of the bargaining parties—the union and the legal management—owes responsibilities to the other. This is not a requirement of altruism but one of necessity. As we have seen, in an enterprise where collective bargaining is operative, neither party has any functional significance in the absence of the other. Legal management may proceed unmindful of the union only after the process of collective bargaining has been abandoned. The union may ignore its relations with management only if it has forgotten its economic rationale. The interdependence of the two organizations, where collective bargaining prevails, imposes the necessity of mutual obligations if only in the interest of self-preservation.

These responsibilities primarily concern the actions of one vis-a-vis the other. We are not now speaking of a duty simply to comply with the terms of a joint agreement. The responsibility which is suggested is one implicit in the total operation of the business. It arises in the process of a continuing relationship and may concern the efficiency of collective bargaining as a method of management, the desirability of proposed decisions, or compliance with those terms jointly agreed upon. However, neither of the parties may be viewed as owing a responsibility to the other for its internal affairs unless these should affect the performance of its responsibilities in the bargaining relationship.

There is less understanding and acceptance of this phase of a system of corporate responsibilities than there is of the first proposition, which we stated as a responsibility to one's own constituents. The legal ties of management to stockholders have led some of the former to recognize only a single line of responsibility. Such an attitude has in some instances driven the union into a defensive position from which it counters with an equally single responsibility to its members. Nevertheless, among many of the managers the concept of a responsibility to the union is no novel doctrine. A highly placed representative of one large corporation, not noted for a prolabor policy in union circles, states with obvious conviction that management's responsibilities to its employes include payment of a fair wage, provision of an adequate, pleasant, and sanitary working environment insofar as the nature of the business permits, opening up opportunities for promotion and advancement, and cooperating in programs of retirement, group insurance, and health and welfare. In return, he feels, the employes and their union must keep the welfare of the company in mind. Another corporate representative remarks that the company is obligated to its employes for their economic security, but that the size of wage payments and extent of employment benefits are limited by the corporate income, for which the employes must accept a responsibility. Nevertheless, he continues, the employes are not solely responsible for corporate income. A purchasing agent's mistake may cost the company millions of dollars and wipe out all the hard efforts and loyal support of ten thousand workers. If this is so, then our responsibility to the employes is not limited simply by the results of their efforts. If management's decisions are of such importance to the welfare of our employes, then management must be responsible to its employes *for all its decisions.* "Why shouldn't our employes have a right to expect that?" he asks.

The reciprocal responsibility of the union to management, and through it to the stockholders, is perhaps more difficult of encouragement. While the representatives of the owners—management—live with the employes, to whom they are asked to admit a responsibility, the employes come face to face only with the representatives of the owners —management—and seldom so much as know the identity of the owners themselves, or knowingly ever come in contact with them. A feeling of responsibility is thus never imminent. Moreover, the more so-phisticated union leaders have become informed on "management con-trol," and having achieved a belief that management itself is not always responsible in the performance of its trust, see no reason why the employes should be held to standards of responsibility not fully recognized by the owners' representatives themselves. This is a matter which challenges the integrity of the organization of owners—which ques-tions its representative character and refuses it genuine acceptance. To the extent that the challenge is justified, the integrity of the organiza-tion of owners must be restored and rehabilitated.

It would be difficult for the unions to deny that a responsibility to the suppliers of capital is owed, however. Unless the employes are prepared to furnish the sum total of the assets required—an obvious impossibility in the large corporation—capital must be forthcoming from some other source, and there must be a responsibility to its suppliers. When the source is a congregation of private individuals and institutions, the responsibility runs to those private suppliers. When the source is a public treasury, as in the case of TVA, the responsibility is to the gov-ernment as owner. In exactly the same manner as management must recognize a responsibility to its employes and their representatives, so too must the employes, through their union, recognize a responsibility to the owners and their representatives.

3. Each of the bargaining parties—the union and the legal manage-ment—owes responsibilities to the public. More than the welfare of the immediately participating parties is bound up in the operation of the large corporation. No system of corporate responsibilities would be complete if the public interest were omitted from consideration. That interest lies in part in the nature of the internal affairs of each of the parties. It is questionable if a democratic society can claim indifference to the impact of autonomous groups upon their component individuals. Though according the maximum scope for freedom of association, it may find it difficult to admit no concern with the effect of association upon the person. At a minimum it will afford the protection of its courts to those who charge personal injury through violation of the constitutional or contractual terms of association.

At least as importantly, and perhaps more certainly, the public in-terest is bound up in the relationship between the parties—in the con-tinuity of vital services which they may perform, in such decisions as have direct incidence on the public, primarily through price, and in the impact of both these factors upon the effectiveness of the economy as a whole. To some extent these latter responsibilities have been recognized by both management and union representatives. "Certainly the concept of collective bargaining cannot be regarded as limiting the parties to the mores of the marketplace. We have reached a stage in our national development when the concept of collective bargaining must be enriched by an appreciation of the social obligation of both sides to the nation as a whole."[1]

These three sets of obligations of the bargaining parties—to their own constituencies, to each other, and to the public—probably must form the basis of any *system* of responsibilities to be held in common. The problem, while one of moment, is scarcely susceptible of ready resolution. The statement of *related* obligations of which we are in such compelling need is one sufficiently specific to permit judgment of their performance. It is worthy of further note that the standards which are ultimately fixed need have no connection with abuses of power—whether from management or union—which have been experienced. They will simply affirm the operating requirements of the large corporation in a business economy. We can, moreover, be reasonably certain that the question of corporate authority to which this study is addressed is incapable of solution until the prior question of corporate responsibilities, the basis of authority, finds its adequate answer. Here indeed lies an insufficiently explored area—a wilderness through which we must expect to thread our way before arriving at any Promised Land of industrial peace.

There is little doubt that actions of labor and management representatives themselves to introduce a system of mutual responsibilities could be undertaken with considerable success, if both sincerely were willing. There is reason to doubt, however, that a genuine system of reciprocal responsibilities could be introduced short of legislative or social sanction. The law of the states still binds management to the stockholders, as its single interest. The only standards by which managerial decisions can now be subjected to judicial scrutiny are to be found in the requirement that they be undertaken for the good of the corporate owners. *Some* standard of managerial conduct cannot be dispensed with; if this is to pass, another must take its place. Law may not be required to create such a change, though it may prove necessary

---

[1] *Brief submitted by the United Packinghouse Workers of America to the Panel of the War Labor Board* (Case No. 111-5544-D), p. 114. For management expressions equally forceful see Chapter 9.

If obligations are to be shared and reciprocal, however, and if a responsibility is owed to the public, it seems equally clear that the public must itself assume a secondary responsibility to both owners and employes. Concern for low-priced products should not constitute permissible ground for defense of inadequate wages or denial of ownership returns. The immediate exploitation of technological advances, though seeming to conduce to the public welfare, may involve excessive costs of displaced workers and capital made obsolete. Only if there is a public responsibility to the participating parties can the public ethically demand their responsibility to it.

to support it, but some *general* acceptance of *recognizable* standards is needed.

AUTHORITY

Functional integration requires an understood common authority, adequate for decision.

We are sufficiently familiar with the proposition that power to make decisions, resolving conflicts of opinion, must reside somewhere in the corporation. Not only must there be a known source of final authority binding upon all participants, but also accompanying and accepted procedures permitting decision when decision is needed. An impasse has no place in a healthy business. Varieties of opinions may be represented, and indeed their expression may be encouraged by frequent resort to committee action, but a process of refining opinion into decision and for translating decision into action cannot be avoided. This is true not only of final authority, but of management in all its frames and centers of coordination. In each frame, at each center of coordination, authority for decision and action must reside.

If the union is to achieve functional integration within the corporation, this requirement cannot be avoided. Authority within the corporation must be known and recognized by all participants. It must have the power and means for effective resolution of all conflicts of opinion among participants. It must function with the consent of all the cooperating parties. These are rigorous requirements, but if integration is desired they cannot be escaped. Bifurcation of authority, with no effective means of insuring decisions when decision is needed, is hardly consonant with organization. Quite the contrary, it is likely to prove a disorganizing force.

If we may accept on principle that a common accepted authority is required by functional integration, there is a further principle to guide us in the designation of that authority. It has found frequent expression by the managers, and effective statement by Alfred P. Sloan, Jr., chairman of the board of directors of General Motors: "One of the most essential principles of sound managerial technique is that authority should not be separated from responsibility."[2]

There is a dual significance to this familiar proposition. It asserts, first, that authority must be adequate for the discharge of imposed responsibility, and, second, that responsibility must serve as a restraint upon authority. A possible but troublesome corollary to the second meaning of this proposition, perhaps most often encountered in demo-

---

[2] *The General Motors Strike,* A Special Message to General Motors Stockholders, 1946, p. 28.

cratic societies, avers that if responsibility is to serve as a restraint upon authority, then authority must derive from those to whom responsibility is owed. We may consider these requirements in turn. In doing so, however, we shall labor under the handicap of correlating authority to a responsibility which is still in process of definition. We shall therefore assume that corporate responsibility, when defined, will embrace that system of obligations to owners, employes, and public which we have, though sketchily, just examined, and it is to some such system of responsibilities that corporate authority will be equated.

If the bargaining parties share between them, in some measure, the managerial functions, and each owes a responsibility to its own constituency, to the other's constituency, and to the public, then each requires an authority for the discharge of this triple responsibility which is adequate both as to scope and effectiveness. Neither now possesses such authority, though legal management is perhaps less handicapped than is the union. Moreover, the authority of each must be welded into a *system* of authority matching the system of corporate responsibilities.

Management now possesses an almost plenary authority, certainly an adequate one, to discharge its present legal responsibility to the stockholders whom it represents. In point of law, however, it may be questioned whether the scope of its authority is sufficient to meet those responsibilities—undefined—which it admits to its employes and to the public. It is confined by legal restrictions to single responsibility to the owners, and though the strictness of such confinement may be doubted its existence remains. The mark of management's performance is still the profit position of the company, and the latter is tied to stockholding interests.

If the union is to be bound to public and ownership interests—in some undefined sense—as well as to the welfare of its members, the union too is without adequate scope of authority. The issue is clearly pointed by a national union leader responsible for the collective-bargaining relationship in one important corporation: "Assume two companies, one losing 20 per cent on a certain type of production and the other making 30 per cent. In the former case the workers may be working every bit as hard as the workers in the latter case. The operating results in the first instance may be due to poor management in one or a number of areas, or to less efficient production techniques or machinery, or to some other consideration *beyond the power of the union to correct*. We could make recommendations—but we would have no authority to back them up. What would be our responsibility to the stockholders here? To take a wage cut?" It has been management which has urged upon the unions a responsibility to the stockholders; but if authority and responsibility cannot be separated, with such a union responsibility must go a union authority which management has been seeking to restrict. At what point should the union's responsibility—and authority —end?

In one important manner does the absence of a common system of authority adequate for the discharge of responsibilities make itself felt in the modern corporation. Legal authority in the corporation is now established in the hands of management. Collective bargaining is a process by which one of the participating parties—organized labor—is free to challenge that established authority, at its pleasure. The collective-bargaining conference, rather than legal management, has become the directive force in important business areas. By legal sanction, we have supported this challenge to existing corporate authority. As we have seen in this study, there are no apparent limits to that challenge.

At the same time, the bargaining process, because of its equal and bilateral composition, provides no means of resolving differences of opinion between the parties in interest. Differences of opinion thus may—and sometimes do—create stalemates of authority, in some instances leading to a total or partial suspension of corporate operations during which period of impasse the participating parties bring economic, social, and political pressures upon each other to force agreement.

Without passing upon the desirability of retaining, unchecked, the *right* to strike and lockout, it seems clear that the *use* of these pressure devices is inimical to functional integration. Their use involves a breakdown of organization. As procedures for reaching decisions, they may at times require a denial of responsibility to one or more of the parties to whom responsibility is admitted. They provide specific example of the absence of an adequate common authority in the conduct of an enterprise. These deficiencies in the placement of authority in the large corporations are sufficiently well appreciated by both labor and management representatives that earnest efforts have been made by both parties to find alternative means of settling differences of opinion, though without relinquishing the ultimate sanction of strike or lockout.

The most prevalent method of attempting to prevent a breakdown of authority is the resort to services of outsiders known as conciliators, men having no connection with the enterprise itself but offering a skilled service of reconciling conflicts of opinion. Wielding no authority themselves, they seek to cajole the management authorities and the union authorities into reaching a temporary compromise settlement permitting the continuity of operations of the business on which both of the parties are dependent. In some instances, relatively few in number in the large corporations, outside interveners have been voted the power to make decisions which are accepted as binding upon both contestants. In these cases of voluntary arbitration, the outsider becomes, for the time being and only in defined areas, the understood common authority of the business. In other instances the third party to whom labor and management have both owned responsibility, the public, acting through elected representatives, has itself exercised an ill-defined authority to break the stalemate and compel decision. Such public authority, unless conferred by the bargaining parties themselves, however, is frequently neither understood nor common, and sometimes it too is inadequate for decision.

If there is difficulty in the placement of corporate authority adequate to discharge responsibilities, there is a correlative difficulty in the assertion of responsibilities adequate for the restraint of corporate authority. This requires more than the definition of the obligations resting upon the bargaining parties, a matter we have already examined. It involves as well a method of enforcing or insuring the responsible performance of those in whom authority has been vested. If this is indeed a requirement which cannot be avoided, we are faced with a problem of such enormity that its resolution promises a profound revolution in business organization and practices. No adequate answer has yet been suggested; none will be attempted here. Only the nature of the issues will be suggested.

In an earlier chapter we found that management officials in a number of our large corporations are now professing a threefold responsibility—to the owners, to their employes, and to the public. Some have gone so far as to post the interests of the owners last in a hierarchy of responsibilities. Even assuming what is not presently the case, that there is achieved a satisfactory definition of the *standards* governing the discharge of such a triple responsibility, no headway will have been made on the further problem of the means of assuring the fulfillment of such obligations. By whom may and can be enforced these responsibilities, which should constitute the basis for authority? To raise a pointedly simple question, could employes or their union, or could government officials, appeal to the courts if they believed that corporate authority was not being employed to discharge the responsibilities which management owns to employes and public, or was being employed in a manner which threatened those interests? If some control over corporate authority, designed to insure the performance of recognized obligations, is not provided, their performance is conditional solely upon the integrity, intelligence, and judgment of those who are the managers. They will be accountable only to themselves.

As matters now stand, only one of the parties to whom legal management admits responsibility, the stockholders, is provided with means of enforcing that responsibility in all areas of operation of the business. Neither employes nor the public, through their respective elected representatives, are similarly served. In certain areas of business operation, however, union officials, as de facto managers, are positioned to force in some degree the discharge of corporate responsibilities to the employes. But even in these areas, again the public is ineffective to safeguard its interests, however defined, even though such interests are admitted by both bargaining parties.

It may thus be seen that the problem of managerial authority is not one which the unions have alone forced upon us. It is an issue which the managers of some of our great corporations have themselves raised. It has been the leaders of management who in recent years have been insisting upon a modification of their responsibilities—witness their statements in a preceding chapter—to embrace other interests than those to which they are now legally bound. On their own organizational logic that responsibility and authority are inseparable, such a modification requires means by which their authority may be made dependent upon the discharge of their obligations. What shall be the standards governing their conduct, and how shall they be enforced?

It was earlier observed that the proposition that responsibility must serve as a restraint upon authority may have as a possible corollary the requirement that authority emanate from those to whom responsibility is owed. This corollary we have accepted in the political institutions of our local, state, and federal governments. We may anticipate that it will be suggested as a possible solution to the problem of controlling authority in our large corporations. It may logically be proposed in some quarters that the base for managerial authority in the large corporation be broadened; that along with a board of directors responsible to the stockholders there should be, with equal authority, a similar board of union officials responsible to the employes, and public officials responsible to society at large; that these three groups, representative of all major corporate interests, shall discharge the directive function within the corporation, and shall jointly name the high administrative and executive officials of the business who shall be charged with an impartial management of corporate affairs within the framework of discretion thus permitted them. Such a proposal may consistently derive from the broadened corporate responsibilities which many managers have avowed, but at the same time it would raise problems of its own. It suggests, too, the potentially explosive aspects of the issue of managerial authority, an issue which has been loosed not solely by the unions but by management officials as well, and which—now loosed—must ultimately find its answer. The nature of that answer we cannot now even dimly discern.

One important conclusion, however, we can draw. The questions raised by the unions' challenge to managerial authority would not be answered even should management discover some feasible means of drawing a line of demarcation beyond which union interest would not be admitted. The challenge to managerial authority runs far deeper and spreads far wider than is evidenced in a union's assertion, at the collective-bargaining table, of a desire for participation in areas of business formerly of concern only to management. The challenge to managerial authority is inherent in the changed nature of social institutions and the changing recognition of social values, changes which the managers themselves have publicly recognized—even though they have been reluctant to admit the further consequences.

Since no satisfying solution to these underlying problems of corporate authority is yet at hand, we may perhaps appropriately close this phase of our discussion of the functional integration of union and management in the modern corporation by reverting to an earlier conclusion. A system of clearly defined authority must attend a system of clearly defined responsibilities. As yet we have scarcely progressed to the definition of the parties in interest. There has been no definition of the scope of their interests. The organizational need for an understood, common, and adequate authority in the large corporation is indeed pressing, but the need cannot be met in the absence of an adequate constitutional basis for authority. The old constitutionalizations embodied in state corporate laws and charters are insufficient if not actually ineffective. The responsibilities there defined have been disavowed by some of the managers themselves, though periodically resurrected as convenient argument. In the National Labor Relations Act new corporate authorities— the union leadership—have been given express legal sanction, but without a statement of correlative responsibilities. There is widespread recognition of the corporation's responsibility to the public, but the nature of that responsibility has been left unsaid, and there is consequently no recognized public authority to support it.

We are in the process of transitions which bear witness to the revolutionary aspects of freedom of association. It is to be expected that the balance of power among organized groups within our society will shift with the passage of time. The rise of the large corporations and other industrial concentrations itself contributed to the birth of organizations of workmen whose growing power challenges that which brought them into being. But if their demand for recognition and authority cannot be evaded, it must be channeled along constitutional lines which impose accompanying responsibilities.

The managers have been right in seeing responsibility as the basic issue in the development of industrial order. They have been slower to perceive, however, that the placement of responsibility involves the grant of authority. The unions, on the other hand, have been insistent upon an accretion of authority, with a greater reluctance to accept the hard fact that the conferring of authority carries with it the premise of responsibility. There is need now for a harmonization of viewpoints. As management accedes to a sharing of authority, the unions must accept an imposition of responsibility. The nature and degree of such sharing is still uncertain, but it is unlikely that management, for long, will be permitted to insist upon defining its own authority, nor will the unions be allowed to limit their own responsibilities. The role of public representatives is equally uncertain, though simply on organizational principles one may question whether a party to which both management and union speak responsibility will remain without authority over business operations adequate to insure the performance of corporate obligations to it.

How far the parties themselves may go in reestablishing an effective system of understood common authority in the corporation is dependent, to an important degree, on their ability to establish understood common responsibilities of corporate action which will prove socially acceptable.

THE ORGANIZATIONAL STRUCTURE OR COMMUNICATION SYSTEM

Functional integration requires an organizational structure held in common. This may be expressed, alternatively, as an understood communication system or as accepted lines of authority. The structure of which we are speaking is nothing lifeless or abstract—it is men with grades of authority and the relationships connecting them.

The purpose of the structure or communication system is to funnel information to the authorities requiring it for decision, and to transmit their decisions, for compliance, to those designated to effectuate such decisions. In the large corporation, these requirements pose a traffic problem of no little magnitude. With the introduction of the union the problem has increased enormously. Failure of the communication system to function efficiently and of lines of authority to hold has been responsible for some of the difficulty of the union-management relationship.

The organizational structure is basically designed on the frame-within-frame system with which we are already familiar. Within each frame there is at least one coordinating center, and there is always one such center which exercises the full authority of that frame. The manner in which these centers are tied together determines the effectiveness of the flow of information and the passing of orders. An exhaustive analysis of an organizational structure which satisfies the requirements of functional integration will not be attempted, but brief attention may be fastened on five criteria. We may then examine their relevance to our subject.

1. There must be proper identification of those in the line of authority. They must be recognized and accepted by all as constituting links in the official system of corporate communications. This means that union officials, when functioning in such a capacity, must be recognized and accepted as fully as management's own designees. It means, on the other hand, that when not so functioning union officials may not claim the authority of the line.

2. There must be cohesion in the organizational structure. From this follow two necessary consequences. First, only a single system of communication and authority may be tolerated. If duplicating systems are permitted, the least result to be expected is that one will threaten the reliability and acceptance of the other. A management system and a union system of authority, competing in the same areas, will permit a choice of conformance with the consequence that at least one of the systems, if not both, cannot be depended on. Second, all phases of the company's operations must be serviced by connected channels. There must be no blind alleys or dead ends preventing the flow of information or the passing of orders to any segment of the business *from* any segment.

3. If there is to be a single system of authority and communication, each of those who, as a coordinating center, functions in that system must discharge his responsibilities to the others in the system. The frames of the company must be properly tied together. This involves (a) screening the information which is to be passed either up or down the line, to superior or subordinate, so that the arteries of communication do not become clogged with unessentials, but all essentials are forwarded; (b) reliably and expeditiously transmitting to another frame the information or orders which emanate from those above or below in the line of authority; and (c) taking necessary or appropriate action on information received from above or below, and on orders received from above, within the framework of permitted discretion.

4. Each of those who functions in the system of authority and communication must adequately discharge his responsibilities to those for

whom he serves as a center of coordination. In this capacity he ties together groups of individuals *within* a frame. By virtue of his position *in* the line of authority and communication, he must service those who themselves are not part of the line but are dependent upon him for access to it, representation in it, and understanding of what comes from it. This involves (a) his passing of information concerning their needs and interests up and down the line, to those who are in position to act upon it; (b) his transmission to them of all information received which may be of value or interest; and (c) his coordination of them to accomplish such tasks as are set for him by those in frames above. Particularly in the shop, but elsewhere in the corporation as well, have these necessities brought increasing emphasis on the role of union officials such as shop stewards, department committeemen, and plant chairmen. Since union members frequently look to these latter representatives for the satisfaction of wants *on the job,* for instructions *on the job* and for information *concerning their job,* the effective functioning of the management official designated as a center of coordination requires close collaboration with these union officials. This may involve a sharing of some administrative authority, and in some instances the corresponding union official may actually join him as a joint center of coordination, but on other occasions the union officer may simply be recognized as the source of effective assistance, as a management aide.

5. The position of each of those in the system of authority and communication must be respected by those who have defined it. The system is the channel through which the administrative process functions. As we have previously noted, administrative decisions must be subject to reversal by higher authority, since final authority rests only with direction and with no lesser frame. Nevertheless, if the line of authority and communication is to be effective, the reserved power to overturn subordinate decisions must be used sparingly. If allowed discretion is not respected by those above (and below) in the organizational structure, the administrative arteries will become congested at those points where its exercise is challenged. Decisions at those centers may be made with hesitancy and uncertainty; they may be regarded diffidently by those to whom passed for action until affirmed by a higher frame than that in which originated; they may even be held in abeyance until approved by that very authority which has purportedly granted the discretion necessary for their issuance, producing redundancy of managerial action. The flow of information through the channels of communication, necessary to efficient administration, may be similarly checked at certain centers in the face of such official intimidation. If administrative decisions at some point in the line of authority are found consistently objectionable,

one of two courses may be pursued: the officials responsible for them may be removed or improved, or the area of their discretion may be narrowed or made more precise to preclude the possibility of such decisions.

This requirement is important in integrating the union into the system of authority and communication. Since management officials in various administrative frames, in order more effectively to service those for whom they serve as a coordinating center, may find it expedient and even advantageous to share their authority with union representatives or to seek the assistance of union representatives, the area of operating discretion must be defined with a view to indicating the permissible extent of such sharing. Attention to this requirement will minimize the need for reversing joint decisions reached by management and union officials in a frame, within their allowed discretion, an event always disruptive of harmonious relations.[3]

If, then, there is to be a cohesive, identified system of authority and communication in the conduct of the business; if each official in that system is to discharge his responsibilities to others in that system and to those whom he serves as a coordinating center; if the position of each official in the line of authority is to be respected by those who have defined it, proper provision must be made for the union. With the advent and growth of collective bargaining, the system of authority and communication previously prevailing must be overhauled if these criteria of its satisfactory performance are to be met. Basic to the realization of these requirements is a single ultimate source of authority and information and a single channel of flow, but concomitant with union participation.

[3] An example is perhaps in point. For our purposes we may assume, without accepting, the correctness of the facts as related by an official of the United Automobile Workers. "We had a problem in the Guide Lamp plant in Anderson, Ind., where they had worked out verbally and had in operation for years a shift preference understanding, whereby the oldest workers in the plant, providing they could do the job, could pick the shifts. In other words, the younger fellows would have to work the unpleasant shifts. We finally said, 'Well, you have to get all your seniority provisions in writing, so the umpire can administer them,' because the umpire will not administer verbal agreements because he cannot know what the people meant. So they wrote it up down in the Guide Lamp, management and the local committee, signed it, and sent it to the corporation, but the corporation said, 'No; we won't ratify that. It can't become effective.' Why? Because at that time we were trying to get them to agree to shift preference as a corporation policy and they knew that if they O.K.'d the Guide Lamp agreement that we would say 'Well, if it is practical here, why isn't it practical in other plants if they meet these certain stipulations?'" *Investigation of the National Defense Program*, part 28, p. 13175. If the union's story is founded on fact, there is some justice in its complaint, for management and the union in the Guide Lamp plant had presumably acted within the framework of their discretion only to have the result denied by those in a higher frame. If the example given represents a true statement of circumstances, the management of the Guide Lamp plant might justifiably contend that its managerial prerogatives had been attacked by higher management.

The collective-bargaining process, with its resultant agreement binding upon management, has required the latter to operate within something of a double framework, to perform something in the nature of a double function. As representative of the owners, management is free to operate within the framework of discretion which they, the owners, have established. The discretion allowed has permitted it to conclude collective agreements with the union, governing certain areas of business operation. At this point it is no longer free to operate within the discretionary framework supplied by the owners, however, except in those areas not touched by the agreement. Except for these latter areas, it must operate within a framework established by the agreement itself. That is to say, on those matters covered by the joint contract, the discretion given to management by the owners ceases to be an *operating* discretion, and the agreement itself becomes the measure of the operating discretion permitted to management. Within the first framework, the interests of the owners remain single. Within the second, the interests of the owners and employes alike must be protected. Within the first framework, authority derives from the owners alone. Within the second, it derives from both owners and employes. Operationally, however, the two frameworks cannot be separated; they form in fact a composite framework. *Structurally, they must be united to prevent an overlapping of lines of authority and a duplication of communication systems, with consequent confusion.*

The nature of the resulting organizational structure is diagrammed in Figure 2. Top union officials negotiate with the directive officers representing the owners to reach a collective agreement, which establishes the framework of final authority in the areas of operation covered. (These areas are indicated by the shaded portion in the directive management frame of the diagram.) In all areas of operation not governed by the agreement, the final authority of the owners' representatives supplies the framework. Within this composite framework, general management retains complete administrative freedom. This freedom may permit it to negotiate with union officials on its level to reach supplementary agreements, but such agreements must lie within its own discretionary authority as well as within the power of the union officials in the subordinate union frame. Such supplemental agreements must also lie within the area of discretion permitted by the *collective* agreement. In the frame of divisional management and throughout the remainder of the structure the same considerations hold.

The union may thus seek to influence managerial decisions within the framework of discretion permitted at a particular level. Where such influence is sought, the line of authority and communication may become blurred. What is the status of the union representatives in the structural organization of the enterprise? Does the line include only management members or must it embrace union agents as well? Failure on the part of both union and management representatives to face up to these questions has sometimes resulted in administrative confusion. The union has sometimes accused management of failing to consult it in the effectuation of joint agreements. Management has often accused the union of robbing it of its rightful authority and discretion in the administrative process.

LINES OF AUTHORITY IN THE CORPORATION UNDER COLLECTIVE BARGAINING

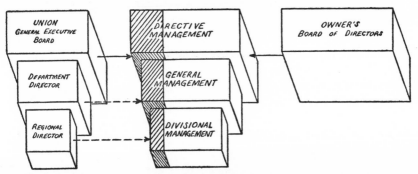

FIGURE 2. Owners' and workers' representatives join in a collective bargaining agreement constituting the final authority in certain areas of operation (indicated by the shaded portion of directive management). All other final authority is exercised by the owners' representatives alone. Successive frames of management must operate within areas of discretion permitted by the double framework of joint and owner-management delegated authority.

Part of the answer to these questions is bound up in a distinction between consultation and negotiation. Good management requires full information, and this in turn may require consultation with union representatives preliminary to reaching a decision, the sort of committee action which we have seen is normal to the decision-making process even where the union is not involved. In such a consultative proceeding, the union agents have no place in the line of authority, fulfilling only an advisory function. They assist management officials in the performance of the function of coordinating center, within the frame.

In other instances, however, the framework of discretion within which management—and the union—must operate, in any frame, may necessitate not only consultation but negotiation. In such cases management does not carry sole authority to reach a decision, but shares its administrative authority with union representatives. For such purposes, union agents do become links in the chain of authority, part of the communication system responsible for the transmission of orders. They exercise not only the authority of their union position, but an administrative authority within the structure of the business enterprise. An example of such a situation has been given in an earlier chapter. In large corporations it is not infrequently determined, at the directive level, that seniority agreements shall be negotiated locally, that is, at the individual plants of the company. This is a delegation of administrative authority to *both* the management and union officials in the plant management frame, and for purposes of carrying out this order the authority of both sets of officials is required. In this case, the designated union officials become part of the line of authority, an integrated element of the organizational structure.

It is this fact that union representatives in the administrative frames sometimes are part of the system of authority and communication in the corporation, and sometimes are not, which has been responsible for their vague status. Perhaps to some extent this confusion is unavoidable, but some clarification between the parties is possible. Such clarification can take the form of a more careful and explicit drafting of the area of discretion accorded management in the successive lower frames of the business. Where authority for the administration of a decision handed down from the frame above is rested solely with management, the union must recognize that it may play none except a consultative role. Management may, however, find it advisable, if important union interests are affected, to employ the committee action which has become an accepted managerial technique, inviting union representatives to participate in the committee. Nor need union interests be endangered by such a recognized delimitation of the function of its representatives in the line of authority, for in the phrasing of any joint directive decision, within whose general framework all administrative decisions must be reached, the union may, if it feels strongly the need, seek the provision that administration shall be by negotiation, rather than consultation. Excessive resort to administrative negotiation may be avoided, however, if both parties accept in good faith an organizational proposition to which we have earlier alluded.

We have said that in the administration of the collective agreement management finds itself serving the interests of both owners and employes. Within the areas of operation covered by the agreement, it derives its administrative authority from the organizations of both these groups, and as a result owes a responsibility to them both. That responsibility consists of the fair and impartial effectuation of the terms and spirit of the agreement. If this "neutral" role of management in the areas of agreement is fully recognized and accepted by both management and the union, there should be less reluctance by the union to accord management full authority to carry out the agreement. If management accepts this role of dual responsibility, fewer instances will arise when the union will feel the need of insisting that its agents participate directly in the system of authority and communication in the administrative frames. Especially will this be the case if management is receptive to consultative advice from the union representatives, employing them as administrative assistants. The desirability of thus restricting the role of the union insofar as possible to consultation rather than negotiation in the line of administrative authority lies not in any lesser ability on its part, nor in any absence of "right" to authority, but simply in the need for flexible and expeditious operation of the business in its day-to-day affairs.

It thus appears that a genuine acceptance by all parties of management's dual responsibility to both owners and employes for a fair and impartial administration of the collective agreement carries the greatest promise for preserving the requisite freedom of administrative action required by the business organization. In the absence of such a mutual acceptance of management's dual responsibility there is an ever-present danger of that same division of authority in the lines of administration as necessarily exists at the directive level. In such a neutral administrative role management personnel will likewise find their best prospects for survival, regardless of the extent of union participation in the direction of the business. The process in which the union has been engaged has been the widening of the areas of the joint agreement, encompassing more and more of the operations of the business. If the time should ever arrive, as even some managers believe it may, when the union exercises coordinate authority with the owners, the role of administrative management will necessarily be confined to a neutral effectuation of the terms of their joint directive decisions.

In what respects have the parties failed to achieve a mutually recognized and accepted organizational structure of the nature suggested? In some instances there has been an inadequate definition of the area of discretion of the respective administrative frames, and an imperfect understanding of the degree of authority permitted in the effectuation of decisions handed down from the frame above. Both effective consultation and negotiation between union and management officials have been thereby impeded, in these lower frames. The union has sometimes failed to distinguish between a consultative role and the exercise of authority in the administrative process. It has sometimes, through lesser officials operating without sanction, sought to assume an unwarranted position in the line of authority, as occasionally when a union agent has counter-manded or vitiated an administrative order emanating from proper au-thority. On the part of management there has frequently been reluctance to accept its dual responsibility in the administration of the collective agreement, and a regard for the agreement as establishing rights which can be pushed to their limit, rather than as providing a framework within which it must operate to secure the best results envisioned by both sig-natories.

For the elimination of such deficiencies, only action by the parties themselves is required. It is entirely within their power, without outside assistance, to correct such defects as may now exist in their common organizational structure.

Further Requirements of Functional Integration

In rejecting union demands for the inclusion in collective contracts of clauses detailing such matters as transfer and promotion practices, managers have sometimes stressed the need for "flexible procedures" permitting adjustment to the needs of each situation as it arises. In refusing to commit themselves to any specific line of demarkation of managerial and joint interests, union officials have sometimes emphasized the necessity of retaining freedom of action to safeguard the welfare of their members as they see it. This insistence by each of the parties on "flexibility" to preserve its own advantages is understandable; what is to be hoped for in addition, however, is a flexibility of *thinking* on the part of the leaders of business and labor which will encourage objective examination of the mutual requirements of their functional integration. It is from those rare individuals with accumulated experience in the conduct of economic affairs who at the same time offer moral and intellectual leadership that we may hope for a progressive refinement of the precepts and practices which will govern the future conduct of corporate enterprise. Without any pretense, therefore, of *completing* a statement of the requirements of functional integration of union and owner-management, we may nevertheless consider certain additional necessities if that objective is to be achieved.

THE COMPLIANCE SYSTEM

Functional integration requires an understood common procedure for insuring compliance with joint decisions.

Directive orders setting forth what shall be done must be followed by administrative orders establishing how it shall be done. The administrative process may involve a progressive detailing of procedure, with each frame in the administrative structure successively narrowing the problem and passing it to the frame below for further action. In some frame the administrative process will be completed, leaving the executive responsibility for seeing that the job is actually performed, and in the manner prescribed. In all this series of steps the necessity of compliance is apparent. Administrative officers must comply with directive decisions, and each official in the administrative process must likewise comply with orders coming down to him from higher administrative frames (orders

233

which, as far as management in any frame is concerned, partake of the nature of direction). In the same manner, executive agents must comply with administrative decisions. Unless compliance is actually forthcoming, decisions may be changed in substance by those responsible for fulfilling them, either intentionally or unintentionally. To guard against such an eventuality, it is necessary to establish some procedure for insuring that decisions are in fact complied with. In the case of decisions involving the collective agreement, this procedure must be a joint affair.

In the collective-bargaining relationship, the compliance machinery operates through the grievance procedure. With exceptions in the case of some few companies, both union and management have access to this procedure to ascertain whether the other has acted within the limits of jointly agreed authority or has measured up to a jointly defined responsibility. Since determination of compliance is dependent upon an interpretation of the meaning of joint decisions, there must first be an understanding as to what action was required or permitted under the joint decision, and secondly a finding as to whether the action taken conformed to the requirement.

There are at least two additional purposes, other than ascertainment of the fact of compliance, involved in this procedure. One is the assurance of redress of any wrong done to individual or group as a result of failure to comply with some joint decision. Most commonly such redress takes the form of the restoration of a job to an employe improperly dismissed, or the payment of lost wages to an employe disciplined for insufficient cause or unjustly refused a promotion. That is to say, redress when granted commonly runs in favor of the employe or the union, a result which stems from the fact that it is generally management who exercises the authority abuse of which is alleged. While relatively infrequent, cases of the opposite nature do occur, however, and employes have sometimes been required to work overtime at straight-time wages for an illegal assumption of authority to declare a holiday, or have been required to return excessive wages paid under an improper administrative decision in which their representatives participated.

The second additional purpose of the compliance system comes as a resultant of this assurance of redress of wrong. Because provision is made for the correction of abuse of authority or responsibility, even, if necessary, months after the abuse has occurred, a peaceful procedure is thereby established to eliminate the need for threat of strike or lockout, or other unilateral action, to enforce compliance. The need for direct action to insure observance of the terms of joint decisions or to make restitution for loss incurred as a result of noncompliance is avoided. Continuity of business operations is therefore assured, even in the face of charges by one that the other is subverting the intent of the collective agreement, with the full understanding that if the charges are substantiated redress will be made.

These are the purposes of the compliance system. The effective functioning of that system is far from automatic, however, and involves certain obligations on the part of both management and union. At least three may be mentioned.

First, the compliance system must be respected for what it is. The difficulties of this requirement stem from the fact that the grievance procedure, through which the compliance system functions, is frequently employed for the resolution of controversies not covered by the agreement—where compliance is not therefore in issue. This latter purpose is sometimes extended to include as well the changing of joint administrative decisions, and it is here that the problem arises. There are those who earnestly and sincerely believe that the grievance procedure may be effectively used to modify joint decisions as the needs of a particular case may dictate. They emphasize the working relationship of the two parties and the need for resolving differences which arise between them in the course of the day-to-day operations. They believe that if the resolution of such differences is better served by changing a joint decision rather than requiring strict compliance with it, the overriding consideration of harmonious relations should dictate the former course. This is an argument which cannot be lightly brushed aside. At the same time its danger should be admitted, for if the grievance procedure is employed to alter joint administrative decisions from case to case, there may cease to be any effective standard by which compliance may be judged. Joint administrative decisions would then be looked upon as something not controlling the actions of the parties, but as the dictates of expedience, of so loose a nature that noncompliance may be justified by ex post facto decision.

It is difficult to take a dogmatic stand on these two conflicting views. And perhaps no stand is required, as long as both parties recognize that, for whatever else the grievance procedure may be employed, one of its essential purposes must remain the insurance of respect for jointly placed authority and responsibility by testing their correct exercise.

Respect for the compliance machinery involves other considerations of a less debatable nature. Despite assurance of ultimate redress if wrong is proved, the series of steps in a grievance appeal, detailed in an earlier chapter, should not be protracted to delay an unwelcome decision. The presumption must always be that *both* parties desire compliance, however unrealistic that presumption may be in individual cases. Nor should the grievance procedure be employed simply as a harassing weapon, piling case upon case, however justified or unjustified, to overwhelm the other party in the hope of securing favorable settlement of some proportion of them. This is the practice of some "percentage experts," who operate on the basis of a belief that a certain percentage of the cases will be decided in their favor, and who multiply cases in the expectation of receiving an absolute increase in the number of favorable verdicts. Nor should the grievance procedure be employed for partisan political purposes, by charging violation of the agreement simply to incriminate the other party in the minds of those who accept charges without substantiation, or by pointing an accusing finger to counter more legitimate charges directed against it.

In addition to an acceptance of the compliance machinery for what it is, a second obligation rests on the parties to insure that the system does not crack from overuse. This is more than a matter of resorting to it only in good faith, the aspect touched on above. It involves a discriminating use of its procedures to the end that it may function efficiently. Petty grievances may be overlooked not because they are unjustified but because more important matters must be given priority within the limitations of time and personnel. If attention is too much directed to the satisfaction of personal complaints which, while technically justified, may reasonably be relegated to that class of annoyances which is every man's lot, or to the consideration of grievances which have no basis at all, the business of the enterprise will suffer. There are management people who contend, with some reason, that the compliance machinery has "gotten in the way of doing business" and has become excessively burdensome. They point to the proportion of complaints dismissed as unfounded as evidence of a too ready resort to the grievance procedure. Aside from the waste of official time, such a practice threatens the procedure itself, for important compliance cases warranting extensive consideration may be given only brief attention because of the case load which officials must carry.

Union representatives have not hesitated to affirm their responsibility for sifting the chaff from the wheat in the presentation of grievances, but the basis for their judgment is not altogether clear. One union has cautioned its committeemen, "Do refuse to handle unjustified grievances. There are two kinds of unjustified grievances. First, the grievance that is not covered by the contract. Usually grievances not covered by the contract should be corrected, but you cannot do anything about it unless your contract covers it. Secondly, there is the grievance that is not supported by facts."[1] An official of another union has declared: "Sometimes the workers don't understand the contract and they appeal to us because they don't understand it and we do understand it and we analyze it carefully and if we think there is a possibility of winning the grievance, it is a border line, we always give the worker the benefit of the doubt. That is what we are paid to do."[2] Such an attitude stamps the union as, first, an at-

---

[1] *Handling Grievances*, Steelworkers Handbook (undated), p. 23.
[2] Walter Reuther, in *Investigation of the National Defense Program*, part 28, p. 13172.

torney for its members, resorting to the convenient grievance procedure as a lawyer would to a court wherever there is "a possibility of winning the grievance." This attitude is further demonstrated by the advice given in a publication of the same union: "The steward's greatest difficulty will come on grievances which do not appear to be covered by the terms of the contract. . . . In practically all cases where a worker has a legitimate complaint it will be possible to find some clause of the contract which, with a little pulling and hauling, can be made to cover the situation. Lawyers have been able to use a Constitution written over 150 years ago to cover the complex issues of modern life. A bright steward should be able to do just about as well with his contract."[3]

This union approach is understandable. Carrying a statutory duty to act as the representative of *all* employes in the bargaining unit, it may reasonably feel an obligation to press such complaints as have any intrinsic merit. Relying on the continued support of its constituency for its strength, it may sense a political necessity to process all grievances having any contractual basis. At the same time, there is room for recognition that this policy may react against the union by weakening the compliance system, whose strength is an important union safeguard. Adequate consideration of the interests of the employes as a whole may lead to the conclusion that an overburdening of the grievance procedure by the presentation of cases of slight importance or insubstantial ground may limit its effectiveness in cases of more vital concern. The number of grievances which some unions have supported may in a measure be responsible for that slowness of the procedure which unions have often protested.

There is sufficient ground for the union to justify greater selectivity of the cases which it argues. As itself a party to the contract, it possesses an interest in maintaining the vitality of the compliance system which is at least as great as the individual employe's interest in seeking redress for personal injury. This position has been effectively advanced by Professor Harry Shulman of the Yale Law School who, from a varied background of arbitration experience, wrote in one grievance decision: "When the Union processes an employee's grievance, it acts in the dual capacity of representative of the employee and party to the proceeding. It is not merely in the position of counsel for the employee. It is itself a party in interest. . . . It is the Union—not the employee—which has the authority to process, and to determine whether to process, appeals from dispositions in the lower steps of the grievance procedure." Guaranties that this course of action will in fact be discriminating as to cases selected, and not discriminatory, must lie in the steps taken to preserve the integrity of the union organization, as respects its relations with the membership.

[3] *How to Win For the Union,* UAW–CIO Handbook (undated), p. 25.

A third obligation resting on the parties in the conduct of the compliance system is the provision for an impartial decision where joint settlement cannot be reached. Since both union and management are parties in interest and the collective agreement runs jointly in their names, neither possesses an unqualified right to insist upon its peculiar interpretation and application. If a joint determination as to whether or not there has been compliance with the agreement is not forthcoming, the issue is of a nature which is susceptible to resolution through an impartial, judicial agency. The contract itself provides the standard for judgment. Increasingly unions and managers are joining in establishing a final court of appeal in the grievance procedure, presided over by an umpire, impartial chairman, arbitrator, or board of arbitration. There has been growing recognition that if the compliance system is to discharge one of its functions, that of permitting continuity of production by the assurance of ultimate justice, neither party can insist upon a right of unilateral interpretation.

If these are the purposes and obligations of the joint compliance system, what, if any, are the inadequacies of present practice? It is probably a safe generalization that the grievance procedures, at least those providing for ultimate disposition through an impartial agency where joint settlement is not possible, have been the most satisfactory phase of existing union-management relations. Nevertheless, certain defects which appear in one corporation or another, at one time or another, may be noted. For the most part they require little elaboration.

At the top of management's list of criticisms is placed the failure of the union to make use consistently of the grievance procedure, preferring at times to resort to direct pressure through walkout or slowdown. Wildcat strikes have been frequent enough to lend point to this complaint. The compliance system cannot function if it is not used. On the other hand, unions have on occasions retorted that management has prompted direct action by employing the grievance procedure for delay rather than settlement. To secure settlement, pressure must be applied.

Despite the widespread publicity accorded wildcat strikes, however, there is reason to believe that the situation is improving. There has been an increasing employment of permanent umpires, and these officials have waged an effective educational campaign, involving indoctrination by decision and direct contact, to impress upon the parties a respect for the procedure which they have jointly established. National union officers have assumed greater responsibility than have local officers, and in some instances have taken over local unions in receivership where their leaders have refused to follow prescribed procedure. Even those managers who complain of union "irresponsibility" will sometimes testify to an improvement in union conduct. One who protests the disregard for the established system—itself a refusal to comply with the terms of the agreement—goes on to add, "But the situation has improved perhaps 70 per cent in the last five years, and on this basis I have hope that the union will ultimately grow out of this stage. It is still a young union." And another who hammers away at the need for responsibility, and between whom and the unions there is no strong affection, nevertheless reports, "The union is making progress. It has had a big educational job on its hands. Most of the trouble we experience is now localized in just three of our 15 plants, and we are looking into those to make sure that it is not a lack of responsibility on the part of our own people which is at least partly the cause of the trouble there."

Perhaps at the head of the union's bill of complaint is the charge that management officials in the lower stages of the grievance procedure either lack authority or refuse to accept authority in the disposition of grievances. The ground for such criticism is evident in one grievance decision of an umpire:

"The first stage disposition of each of the grievances in this case was, 'Refer to L.R.O. [Labor Relations Office].' This is not a unique instance of such a disposition. In some units and with some foremen this disposition seems to have become routine and habitual. . . . The foreman in the first stage of the grievance procedure is not merely an automatic conveyer of the grievance to the Labor Relations Office. It is his duty, as it is the duty of representatives in the subsequent stages of the procedure, to make a sincere and determined effort to dispose of the grievance. He may not abdicate that responsibility."[4]

In addition to failure to resort to the prescribed procedure and a re-

[4] Decision A-229 (June 11, 1946) of Harry Shulman, for the Ford Motor Company and the UAW-CIO. A partisan statement of the union's difficulties is contained in *Investigation of the National Defense Program*, part 28, pp. 13387–13388:

THE CHAIRMAN. It is my understanding that the grievance is first of all brought to the attention of the foreman by the steward. Is that it?

PLANT COMMITTEEMAN. That is right. He checks it.

THE CHAIRMAN. Is there anything to the statement that we have learned from the foreman that he isn't in authority, has very little to say?

PLANT COMMITTEEMAN. He refuses to accept the authority, or is deprived of that authority. However, our grievances are checked and passed on.

THE CHAIRMAN. To whom? What are the steps?

PLANT COMMITTEEMAN. To the district steward, and the district steward in turn deals with the personnel man who I indicated by a cowcatcher. He brushes them aside. Then they come to us and management walks out on us, as they did the other day.

THE CHAIRMAN. When you say "they" who do you mean?

PLANT COMMITTEEMAN. The top bargaining committee.

THE CHAIRMAN. And do they have a counterpart to deal with your committee?

PLANT COMMITTEEMAN. They have a management committee. They have a buffer who also checks it to the next guy. It is a constant series of checks. It is one of confusion.

THE CHAIRMAN. Then above the committee do they have any court of appeals?

PLANT COMMITTEEMAN. You go to the president and he says, "The guy under me has the answer." You go back and it goes back and forth. There is no answer.

SENATOR FERGUSON. You have no umpire?

PLANT COMMITTEEMAN. No.

fusal of some officials in the compliance system to assume their authority and responsibility, deficiencies of present practice in some companies include a reluctance to provide a final impartial office of appeal. In other instances, the grievance procedure has been employed for political purposes, such as the publicizing of unfounded charges. Finally, one of the thorniest problems which has emerged in this area of union-management relations has involved the status in the grievance procedure of unionized foremen. Almost universally under present practice the foreman represents management in the first stage of the procedure. Management is now expressing concern whether his affiliation with a union does not bias the foreman in favor of his unionized men, leaving management without proper representation at this step. At least with respect to foremen affiliated with the same union which represents the production employes, some union officials have admitted the reasonableness of such fear. In explaining the basis for his union's refusal to accept foremen as members, one official of the United Automobile Workers has asserted, "I don't think you can represent both labor and management at the same time."[5]

There is no evident solution to this problem at the present time. A solution certainly does not lie in refusal to foremen of their right to organize, for if organization is badly enough desired the same continuing overt conflict between foremen and higher management would be likely to emerge as characterized the employe-management feud in an earlier day. It is not even clear at this point whether the danger envisaged by management will actually result from the unionization of their supervisors. The difficulty is, however, that management is understandably reluctant to wait to test results, on the hypothesis that if their fear should prove justified the problem will then be too far advanced to permit of favorable answer.

The issues here run deeper than merely the question of compliance. They involve the structure of the business organization and the relations of its component parties. On this basis one stand of the managers appears fully justified. A union of production employees should hold no power of disciplining foremen as it might discipline its members. For the most that the union can ask is that the foreman accept the role of neutral administrator and executor of the terms of the collective agreement, charged with applying the agreement with justice to all interests involved. This role the foreman cannot play if he is subject to the disciplinary control of a union of his men. But the same may be said as well for disciplinary control of foremen by a management responsible only to the stockholders, once other corporate interests are admitted. The status of the foreman involves the same question of corporate authority which we have already examined though without conclusion.

[5] *Investigation of the National Defense Program*, part 28, p. 13173.

If these are the deficiencies and problems of the joint compliance system as now practiced, how may they be met? Once again it is possible to conclude that their resolution lies within the power of the parties themselves. No outside intervention is needed to secure functional integration in this respect, if the parties undertake to do their own job. The requirements are clear, except for the status of the foreman in the system, a problem which demands much further examination.

SUPPORTING FACILITIES

Functional integration requires adequate supporting facilities.

In functional integration, the roles of the participating organizations are important to each other. Where both union and management are dependent upon one another, neither can assert a right of independent action unlimited by a recognized responsibility to the other and to the enterprise as a whole. Poor union performance or poor managerial performance may equally act as a dragnet upon the business. Each party owes an obligation to the other, as well as to its own constituency, to develop supporting facilities adequate for its own needs and for the needs of the business, and to encourage the similar development of supporting facilities by the participating party even though it may frequently regard the latter as an antagonist. The supporting facilities to which attention may perhaps best be directed are two: leadership training programs, and adequate data on which to base decisions.

We have previously noted the demands which corporate leadership makes upon those who assume that role. The conduct of our large corporations, carrying with it immense potentialities for good or evil in our society, imposes a burden of responsibility which, though still ill-defined, calls for its shouldering only by those adequately trained for the task. Equally evident is the fact that no double standard running in favor of the unions is here permissible. Considering the degree to which they have shared authority in important managerial areas, even in the absence of any further expansion of their authority they cannot escape judgment for their actions any more than can our legal corporate officials.

The problem here is twofold. Technical proficiency is obviously an asset of immense value to the business leader—not solely a knowledge of the mechanics of the company's operations but also an organizing and administrative capacity. At the same time there is the urgent necessity for developing qualities of morality supporting a claim to leadership status. The development and fusion of these two characteristics are the purpose of leadership training. The obligation to undertake such training rests upon management and the union both.

There is little question that inadequate consideration has been given by both organizations to the need for such a training program and to its requirements. Yet in this area lies one of the brightest hopes—and greatest dangers—of the perfection of the union-management relationship. Indeed, so little attention has been given to this subject that it would be mere presumption at this stage for anyone to state with conviction the course such training should take. There is intense need for a thorough exploration of the field by and between the parties.

Progress has of course been made through the greater spread of advanced education throughout society generally. As noted in an earlier chapter, college degrees are no longer rare in union circles. Beyond such liberal education, however, there is need for specialized training. It is still uncertain whether this need can best be met by the development of new university instruction, by the broadening of existing graduate schools of business administration, by programs undertaken within industry itself, or by some combination of these approaches. Only the urgency is sure. "Organized labor, in seeking fuller participation in the affairs of industry and government, will have to be prepared through an all-out program of leadership training. Events in the near future may prove this to be one of the most crucial problems facing labor unions."[6]

The second support to successful union-management cooperation which is worth special attention is the availability to both parties of pertinent factual information.[7] Any casual reading of conference records, or conversation with union or company negotiators, reveals that with few exceptions the facts which have been injected into their meetings have been brought in by one of the parties as argument to bolster its position, and have seldom been introduced by both parties as the basis for arriving at agreement. It has been said by representatives of unions and management that both sides regard data as arguments which they are reluctant to give up, that facts are bargaining cards to be played as tactical considerations warrant; that there is no attempt on the part of the bargaining parties to agree on factual data, but rather to explode each other's facts; that facts are used only argumentatively, principally to befuddle the other fellow. It is not too much to say that such research facilities as have been developed by both company and union have been prevented from accomplishing much in the agreement-making process by this attitude toward the data with which the parties work. Material which has been available to the conference has been often designed not to provide a basis for agreement but a point of attack.

[6] Golden and Ruttenberg, *Dynamics of Industrial Democracy*, p. 67.

[7] Most of the material in the following paragraphs on the use of economic data has been drawn, with permission of the American Council on Public Affairs, from Neil W. Chamberlain, *Collective Bargaining Procedures* (1944), chap. 6.

The disadvantages of the prevalent system of factual argumentation have not gone entirely unnoticed by those immediately involved, however. Because the need for economic data as a basis for negotiation is so great, attempts have sometimes been made to reach agreement on the pertinent facts of a situation. By this process of factual accord, the bargaining parties reduce the area of conflict, expediting and facilitating agreement on issues of interests. Such determination of fact may take the form of attempts to reconcile conflicting sets of data prepared by the parties independently, agreement on a source of data to be accepted as authoritative, establishment of joint fact-finding commissions either permanent or ad hoc in nature, or the joint employment of impartial third-party investigators. It is clear, however, that the success of any of these procedures rests upon the availability of the information which is sought by *each* of the parties. This requirement is not always met.

Management has frequently condemned the union for its disregard of factual considerations in the drafting of its proposals and in subsequent negotiations, with the plain implication that it would welcome proposals finding their support in economic considerations. Some managers, however, have failed to recognize that this attitude on their part obligates them to supply the union with such necessary information as may be found only in company records. "Factual" proposals cannot otherwise be drawn, nor can agreements grow out of the facts of the issue.

Moreover, some members of management are coming to recognize that to the extent unions develop research facilities for an effective and adequate analysis of company operations, unions may become increasingly critical of accounting procedures and policies which in their estimation bias the enterprise's financial showing. They may demand independent critical analyses to provide impartial judgment as to the nature and effects of company accounting practices. Management may thus be faced with the dilemma of encouraging a union practice—the factual approach to collective bargaining—which threatens to undermine one of its own cherished privileges, determination of accounting policy. It is quite possible, however, that the problem here posed will be solved on another front. The increasing recognition of public interest in large-scale business activity is bringing with it a norm which promises to become a rule, that accountants will become more independent of management. "It may be that we are reaching the time when there should be a new emphasis on the *public* aspects of the *public* accountant's work. Perhaps, it will before long be recognized that he is, indeed, a quasi-public official."[8]

If the independent accountant does in fact become recognized as ful-

---

[8] Jerome Frank, speaking as S.E.C. chairman before the Controllers' Institute of America, October 10, 1939 (S.E.C. mimeographed release, p. 11).

filling a public function, it is likely that in the future the statement he prepares in examining the company's operations will be more nearly the critical analysis sought by the unions. It would seem the part of wisdom for management, in the light of this independent development which it probably cannot stay, to continue to encourage unions to establish capable research agencies, and *as they do so* to provide them with the company information which they seek, securing the benefit of dealing with unions possessing the basis for responsibility. The desirability of such treatment must of course be weighed in the light of the attitudes and practices of the union with which the company is dealing. Little can be done by either party—and much needs to be done by both—without a sympathetic response from the other.

Mere availability of data means nothing if the data are not used and respected. The training of management and union executives, with which we have previously been concerned, will necessarily include the development of a knowledge of the purpose and use of pertinent facts. There is no basis for an assumption that only the union leaders are presently deficient in these respects. One attorney who has represented numerous companies in negotiations says that the unions usually have only a "very rough idea" of company operations from which to draw their conclusions and phrase their demands. What they should have, he asserts, is a complete picture of operations and policy: the competitive situation; the profit position; the basis on which dividends, management returns, and workers' wages are computed; the effects of price increases, and similar information. Yet he reports that his experience has been that *companies themselves frequently do not possess this information.* In one instance where he requested a company to provide him with such data and analysis for his own preparation of the company's case, he was advised that such a procedure was impracticable, as weeks of elaborate study would be necessary to comply with his request.

The obligation here is therefore dual. Management, which holds the key to much of the required facts, must consider how best to unlock these treasures for its own use, and ultimately too for the use of the unions. And the unions, if they are to earn access to information which they profess to desire badly, must improve their agencies of research and analysis. Equally important, they must embark simultaneously on educational programs designed to improve their members' understanding of the economic problems underlying collective agreements. As long as the rank-and-file membership retains the right of approval over any agreement reached, which is to say the right of veto, it should not be politicized into expecting what cannot economically be obtained, or into believing that progress always lies in the direction of sweeping demands and continuous importunacy. If this result is to be obtained, however, it requires assurances of the integrity of each organization, and it requires likewise an opportunity for the union to demonstrate its value to its membership in ways other than pressure for higher earnings without regard to their source.

The need for training and research facilities to support functional integration can be met without remaking present institutions. It can be achieved within our existing institutional framework, and it is possible of attainment by action of the parties themselves. Whether the need will be satisfied without prior resolution of the problems of authority and responsibility is problematical, however.

EFFECTIVENESS AND EFFICIENCY

Functional integration requires satisfactory opportunity for the participating parties to realize their social and personal goals through the enterprise.

One of our most thoughtful managers, Chester I. Barnard, has come to the conclusion that "the persistence of cooperation" is dependent on two conditions: its effectiveness and its efficiency. Effectiveness is a measure of the success of an enterprise in accomplishing its purpose, a purpose which is social and nonindividual in nature. Efficiency is a measure of the success of the enterprise in satisfying the aspirations of those who compose it, aspirations which are personal and individual.[9] Translating this into example, union-management cooperation in the coal industry will and can continue only as long as it meets the double condition of producing the country's needed coal and satisfying certain personal goals of those who make up the "coal industry." Failure of either condition will lead to a breakdown in cooperation. More than the machinery of industrial peace is obviously needed to insure the mining of coal; there must be an incentive to employ that machinery, and that incentive is present only when the goals of the participating parties are served by cooperation.

The goals of which we are speaking are subjective factors, and therefore difficult to isolate. Though personal, they spring from the social environment in which each individual finds himself. The medium through which they find expression is a product of institutions. As institutions and conditions change, the opportunities for and means of achieving those goals likewise may change. This has been notably true in the case of large corporations.

The rise of the large corporation constituted a changed condition affecting the efficiency of the enterprise in the sense of its capacity to satisfy

[9] *The Functions of the Executive,* p. 60.

the personal objectives of those who composed it. The managers who grew up with these industrial giants failed to an important degree to recognize that the change which they had wrought required further change—adjustments to increase efficiency, again in the special sense of their ability to satisfy the goals of those who made up the corporations, including the employes. The individual in these expanded institutions became submerged in their bigness, losing a sense of belonging and participation and acquiring a feeling of being used for the advantage of others. Nor did the older craft unions recognize the need for change, except for the handful which reached out through amalgamations and mergers to embrace jurisdictionally *all* the workers in a business or industry, rather than only the skilled few. The advent of the CIO in the 1930's constituted a long-delayed adjustment to the change introduced by the rise of large corporations. Whether it provided the most desirable adjustment is disputed by many, but it was indisputably a conscious effort to provide for the workers in mass-production industries the opportunity and means for the achievement of goals which had been neglected. Ironically enough, the CIO was thus from the start designed to improve the efficiency of the large corporations—efficiency always in the sense of capacity to satisfy the personal goals of all those who compose the enterprise.

The rise of large-scale industrial unions itself constitutes a change of the first moment, demanding adjustments if the efficiency and effectiveness of our business institutions are to be preserved or improved. For the goals which must be served are not solely those of one group, even as large a group as the production employes. The goals of the managers cannot be ignored if they are to contribute their maximum efficiency. Moreover, efficiency, the satisfaction of the personal goals of all who compose the enterprise, cannot be gained without effectiveness, the satisfaction of the production purpose of the enterprise, a social matter. These considerations the unions may ignore at their own peril. If they fail, as did management of an earlier day, to recognize the need for adjustment *which they themselves have created*, they are themselves erecting a threat to the continuity of their own organizations.

The vital nature of personal goals is thus apparent. They are not the imaginary or synthetic products of a social worker's armchair dream; their satisfaction is essential to the well-being and perpetuity of institutions. Barnard has rendered a contribution of tremendous potential importance to the body of thinking on social relationships in industry, by relating the *efficiency* of the enterprise to the satisfaction of personal goals. For the concept of efficiency has significance only in terms of the objectives sought. It is therefore essential that the objectives of those who compose the enterprise be identified and defined if the concept of efficiency of enterprise is to have meaning at all. The efficiency which guides the conduct of a business directed solely to the maximization of profit for the owners has a different content from the efficiency which characterizes an enterprise including among its objectives not only profit —the goal of only one component interest—but satisfaction of the goals of management and employes as well. If efficiency in business is to be given a realistic—not idealistic—content, then, it is imperative that the goals of those who compose the business first be recognized and understood. Unless this procedure is followed, it will be pure coincidence and sheer good luck if a business enterprise acquires efficiency. And because of the interaction of efficiency with effectiveness—the measure of productive results—it will likewise be fortuitous circumstance if the latter gives satisfaction.

Professor E. Wight Bakke, Director of the Labor and Management Center at Yale University, has been preoccupied with the identification and definition of the goals of workers and managers for a period of years. A summary of his conclusions to date is as follows:

In our studies we have identified goals of two sorts. First, men want to have the experience of security, progress, and justice. Second, these goals are realized or not as experiences in attempting to reach the following six goals:

1. *Respect of fellows*
   The desire to play a socially respected role.
2. *Creature sufficiency*
   The desire to have that degree of creature sufficiency (food, clothes, shelter, health, etc., and the means to provide them) enjoyed by the most favored of one's customary associates.
3. *Increasing control over one's own affairs*
   The desire to have one's decisions and actions effective in shaping the course of his own life and to reduce the control exercised by others.
4. *Understanding*
   The desire to comprehend the forces and factors that operate in one's world, to "know the score."
5. *Capacity performance*
   The desire to utilize in living the full range of capacities possessed, both actual and potential.
6. *Integrity or wholeness*
   The desire to experience consistency within one's self, among the parts of one's world, and a significant relationship to that world.[10]

It is recognized that the force of these objectives and their specific content may vary among individuals and among groups, and indeed within the individual and group over a period of time, but there appears to be a significant persistence of these motivations. In this study, for purposes

---

10 E. Wight Bakke, *Adaptive Human Behavior in Industry* (preliminary draft mimeographed, 1946), p. 6.

of simplification, we have reduced these goals to a more general statement of the objectives as security, recognition, and self-expression, while preserving the same content.

In the course of this investigation and analysis it has been observed that in the case of both management and workers these objectives are sought to an important degree through the corporation in the course of business life. It is thus apparent that the enterprise cannot rely, for its efficiency, on the satisfaction of the major objectives of its workers and managers *outside the enterprise,* as it may reasonably do in the case of owners with respect to all their goals except creature sufficiency, or in the terms of this study, security. Parenthetically, it may be noted that this very ability of the stockholders to seek the satisfaction of their goals outside the corporation contributes to some of our problems, lessening as it does their interest in and concern with the conduct of the business, thus rendering their effective representation a question more difficult of solution.

If business efficiency can be achieved only in terms of the personal goals of those who compose the business, it becomes essential not only to recognize the goals which are sought but to analyze them. It is necessary to know how both workers and managers seek to achieve their ends within the corporation, the specific means and medium through which they work. The vital nature of this aspect of the study of goals is easily demonstrable. There is clearly nothing inconsistent between the goals of management and of the employes, since they are in fact the same goals. Conflict between employes and management within the corporation must arise, then, if it arises at all, in the manner by which each of these groups seeks to attain its objectives. If the employes, through their union, seek their security in a manner which threatens the security of management, it is not the goals but the means of securing them which conflict. As a corollary we may say that there should be no inconsistency between the specific content of the goals of each if conflict is to be avoided. Self-expression for management should not mean less opportunity for employes and their representatives to participate creatively in the conduct of the enterprise. Recognition of the union leaders should not involve a loss of esteem for management by either the employes or the community. This is more than an acceptance of the integrity of the other's organization. It involves a functional integration in which all participants, through cooperation, may seek their goals consistently with each other. The desired cooperation will be at its maximum when the participating parties believe (preferably with some reason) that not only can each achieve its objectives within the framework of cooperation, but can do so better than it could outside of such framework.

Not only must there be identification of goals and a consistency of means of achieving them if the enterprise is to be efficient; there should also be some method of ascertaining the *degree* to which goals are satisfied. The idea of measuring satisfaction is at present as skeptically regarded as was once the idea that manual efficiency could be measured, prior to the advent of Taylorism and scientific management. The measurement that is needed is not some psychological probing into the mental recesses of the individual, but some objective test of the degree to which the individual possesses potentialities, within the corporation, for the satisfaction of his personal goals, and his capacity to capitalize on those potentialities. If we are to profit from Barnard's insight that business efficiency must be considered in terms of its ability to satisfy the personal goals of those who compose the business, we can scarcely rely on faith or circumstance to realize efficiency. It must be earned by plan and design directed to the efficiency we seek, and there must be adequate means for testing the success of the planning. Such a test does not lie in production per man-hour or the total productivity of the firm, for despite an interrelationship these relate primarily to social effectiveness rather than efficiency in promoting individual objectives.

The potentialities of this approach have been sensed by only a very few people, despite the widespread discussion of "social engineering," "human engineering," and "human relations in industry." These terms have often been used to embrace a wide range of welfare sentiment, without adequate understanding of what is sought. The manager who answers that his business is not an eleemosynary institution is justified in his criticism. The same manager, however, may be quick to champion the necessity of business efficiency in terms which are all but obsolete. The successful creation of opportunities *by and for all who participate* and the satisfactory use of those opportunities is the business efficiency which must be sought. To seek it rationally the ends to be served must be identified, the means to achieve them must be made specific, and methods of measuring the degree of business efficiency must be found. This is a program of staggering and challenging proportions. It requires content and not slogans, detail and not generality, perception and not preconception, procedure and not emotion, action and not pontification. It calls not for social workers but for strong leadership of the type found in large corporations and national unions. It calls not for soft thinking about "human relations" but for objective and dispassionate analysis of business efficiency and effectiveness defined in terms of concrete personal and social objectives.

Efficiency, then, relates to the capacity to satisfy the goals of all those who compose the enterprise. Without this efficiency the survival of institutions, including the business corporation and the union, is threatened. The old commercial engineering content of this concept as used in the corporation springs from the legal theory that the stockholders *are* the corporation, and efficiency, related to their objectives, dictates the maximization of profit. We are now suggesting that the corporation is greater than the stockholders. Even more directly involved are the managers and the employes. The content of efficiency must therefore be broadened to embrace the pursuit of their interests. Efficiency, however, is still required; it measures the success of the joint efforts of all the participating parties.

If functional integration requires satisfactory opportunity for the participating parties to realize their personal and social goals through the enterprise, this is a need which can best be met by the parties themselves. They may be assisted by others outside the corporation, as the federal government has aided employes in organizing into unions for the pursuit of their goals within the corporation. They may be encouraged and supported and joined by others in the making of opportunity, but it is they who compose the enterprise who are ultimately responsible for the efficiency of their organization.

MUTUAL INTENT

Functional integration requires mutual intent, faith, and cooperation. We have said that the criteria of functional integration include a clear understanding of the role each of the participating parties is to play, the preservation of their organizational integrity, understood common responsibilities and authority, an organizational structure held in common, a satisfactory compliance system, adequate supporting facilities, and opportunities for all those who compose the enterprise to achieve their goals. It has been evident that in all these respects the needs of integration can be met, to an important degree, by action of the parties themselves. Except probably for a modification of responsibilities and authority, except possibly for the preservation of the integrity of the organization of owners, no outside intervention is necessary, and even in these areas the parties can if they will give direction and supply purpose to the required changes. If these objectives are to be accomplished, however, there must be a *mutual* intent by the parties, *mutual* faith in each other's sincerity of purpose, and cooperation to achieve the desired ends. There is little need to belabor this proposition. It is all too evident that functional integration is at best difficult and at worst impossible if one or both of the parties do not wish to be integrated. If individual victory rather than mutual accommodation is sought the outlook for industrial order is dark indeed.

A good case could be made for the thesis that it is not so much an underlying and inevitable conflict of interests which is responsible for the tenuous and disorganized relationship of management and union as it is a deep-seated doubt of the other's intent and a lack of faith in the other's sincerity. Many managers are convinced that there is subversive purpose in the union program. Many unionists are certain that management would welcome an opportunity to crush their organizations. There is still a widespread belief that loyalty to management and loyalty to the union are mutually exclusive categories. In disputes over issues it is customarily the motive which is attacked.

Management's distrust is characterized by its despairing question, "Where will it all end?" The unions' doubts are contained in their query, "Does management think it can go back to 'the good old days?'" Neither feels sure of the other. Representatives of both management and labor will admit that proposals emanating from the other are seldom indeed received without suspicion. They are searched for catch phrases, weasel words, disguised motive.

It is this atmosphere of mutual distrust rather than mutual faith which has bred pessimism as to the possibilities of joining union and management in cooperation. Of what value is the delineation of needed courses of action if both parties draw back because unconvinced that the other will not seek an unfair advantage when the guard of suspicion is lowered? Of what point are joint statements of good intent when neither is sure that the other really intends anything more than a tactical exercise to win public support or lull the other into a false sense of security? In such a hostile climate, what *can* be done to stimulate mutual faith and cooperation? If mutual intent is a prerequisite, what hope is there for functional integration?

The outlook may not actually be so gloomy as such queries might indicate, and for a number of reasons. Even prior to mutual intent there must be a conviction held by each of the parties of the desirability if not necessity of joint accommodation. The fact is that *both* management and unions now include in their leadership many who believe that they are fighting simply for survival. Management is seeking recognition from the unions in the same manner that the unions have been seeking recognition from management. It is possible to conclude that out of this bitter struggle may come nothing but disorganization, but it is also possible to conceive that as the conflict persists there may be born an increasing understanding that attrition will benefit neither and that both will profit from an entente in which each plays its meaningful role. It is thus possible that *because* of the industrial conflict the parties will be driven by sheer necessity to that integration of which we have been speaking.

Moreover, the integration of management, owners, employes, and union is something which need not and indeed cannot blossom full-blown overnight. Progress towards this end is even now taking place. In many enterprises the joint compliance system, for example, is already reaching a high state of efficiency. Progress along the other indicated avenues may proceed at an uneven pace, but as long as there is movement in the desired direction there is ground for optimism.

The increasing frequency of contact and interchange of information and opinions between union and management representatives is another encouraging sign. Union leaders and those company officials responsible for industrial relations frequently agree on the efficacy of these devices. A vice president of a large company who has been occupied for many years with relations with unions says without hesitation, "The more a company official comes in contact with the union and hears the union's arguments, the more amenable he is to its persuasion. I would generalize by saying that the executives who have little or no dealings with the union are very often the ones who oppose the union most, while those who have to deal with it are more receptive to its arguments. One fruitful possibility for resolving this conflict between unions and management seems to me to bring together more and more the union and business leaders so that they can understand each other's points of view. Understanding of this sort is one of the real promises of industrial peace. Like responsible leadership, it will not come overnight, however. It may take years to work out, but if we can get started on the road there is no need to worry about the outcome." Another company representative, subscribing to the same opinion, adds by way of explanation that "The people we like are the people we know."

In public office, in private conference, in academic gatherings the men of management and the men of labor have been meeting each other with growing frequency in recent years. In not all instances has there been evidence of congeniality between them, but it would be hazardous to assume that the results have been purely negative. Widening the area of understanding through personal contact may be an important preliminary to widening the area through agreement.

Still further ground for hope is to be found in changes of leadership and the force of example. In the words of one company official, "One basis for optimism is that the new and younger leaders of both unions and management can start from the present and do not have to repeat the experiences of the past." As the older leaders pass from the scene, carrying with them memories of the seeds of former conflict, the younger men who take their place accept as part of their social framework practices and arrangements which were bitterly contested in an earlier day. It is doubtful if the younger Henry Ford was conscious of the anxious hope with which his rise to the presidency of the Ford Motor Company was viewed by labor leaders both within and outside the automobile industry. In him they saw the possibility of a new corporate leadership which would start from a position of further advancement than that which had previously characterized the company's management, and the force of whose example would be felt in other companies and industries. Other rising leaders in both company and union bring similar hope of desirable change. Moreover, in virtually every industry there is at least some one company whose relations with the union, while not wholly happy, represent an improvement over the union relations of its competitors, and whose practices exert some influence, however slight, tending to raise the general level of union-management cooperation in the industry. This force of moral leadership cannot be ignored.

Finally and perhaps most important, public pressure may compel the parties to undertake the functional integration which is so essential. Public pressure, it is true, is at best a doubtful force, difficult to arouse and uncertain of direction. It is nonetheless potent. If the drive to mutual accommodation is lacking in the parties directly in interest, and is deemed sufficiently essential to guarantee the effective operation of the economy, it is possible that popular support may move the parties to take the needed action, by pressure brought either directly upon the unions and the managers, or operating through legislation. As in the case of good faith in collective bargaining, as construed by the National Labor Relations Board under the act which it administers, good faith in functional integration may for a time be artificially forced, by applying to it the yardstick of objective indicia with the expectation that in time it will take natural root. It is to be hoped that such recourse will prove unnecessary, for it is a poor substitute, but neither management nor the unions may proceed on their independent ways in stubborn oversight of broader interests than their own without courting compulsion. For if integration becomes imperative, ways *will* be found to supply the vital spark, even if it involves the unseating of recalcitrant leaders of either faction and the guidance of government. Viewing such moves with less than enthusiasm, we will prefer to lend our encouragement to a voluntary conciliation of legal management and the unions. If either or both should consistently fail us, they will, however, lose claim to indulgence.

ACCEPTANCE BY OTHERS

Functional integration requires its acceptance by others.

To this point we have been proceeding upon the implicit assumption that whatever the sentiments of the parties in immediate interest, the desirability of functional integration of union and management was accepted or could be presumed to be accepted by all others. The validity of this assumption is open to question. It *may* stand as a generalization, but its proof is in doubt. If functional integration is to be achieved, however, there is no doubt that its acceptance by others is requisite. The "others" who are involved are not only the public generally but also lesser groups whose cooperation and support are necessary to the success of the enterprise.

Little argument is needed to establish the fact that popular approval of the form of industrial organization we have been discussing is essential to its birth, growth, and survival. At least in the areas of responsibilities and authority, change from existing legal theory is involved. As has been suggested, it is possible that the required change may come through other than legislative means, though it is doubtful if it could completely escape the necessity of legislative sanction. Even should this prove to be feasible and evolution should relieve the parties of the need for a statutory blessing, judicial approval would be forthcoming only if there was evident public support for responsibilities running to and authority emanating from other than the stockholding interests. The integrated business enterprise must be accorded public approval, if only of a passive nature, if it is to prosper in its social setting.

More than approval of the general public is necessary, however. It is essential that other organized groups in our society which are in a position to affect the cooperative efforts of the integrated parties should also accept their organizational form. Acceptance involves a willingness to recognize the integrated enterprise as the legitimate expression of its corporate interests, and as a working member of the business community.

The importance of this requirement lies in the fact that the sort of mutual accommodation with which we have been concerned in this study will probably not develop in all companies or industries at a simultaneous rate of progress, nor even concurrently. Varying degrees of opposition to it may be expected in one area or another of the economy. If this opposition takes the form not only of staying its progress within the company immediately concerned but also of discouraging its development in other companies through pressures brought upon them, a threat to its evolution may emerge. Both management and the unions will attest to the difficulties of fostering organizational stability when under fire.

Threats of this nature may arise from actions both by managers and by unions other than those in the affected enterprise. In an earlier chapter was noted the variety of external influences to which management is subjected—influences from important suppliers of materials, important customers, primary sources of capital. Even granting that these influences may not deter the management of a particular corporation from working with the union to establish an integrated enterprise, it is possible that they may be used to undermine its business position. Flows of needed materials may be diverted to less "radically" minded managements, customers may shift their orders, capital may not be forthcoming when wanted, or only at high rates of interest. A general business boycott of the company may be instituted. The possible rationale of such actions is discernible. We have seen that there exists among the managers a widespread belief that the unions are leading us along the road to socialism. If there should be a growth of opinion that functional integration constituted only an important way-stop on that road, the basis for strong opposition at least in some managerial quarters is evident. At the same time the success of such opposition would be problematical, not only because we have been concerned solely with the large corporations, most of which are in a strong individual business position capable of defensive tactics, but also because any opposing managerial interests would themselves be subjected to public pressure if their actions should threaten a system of industrial order which had been given popular approval.

A more direct threat to the integrated business form is likely to arise from unions other than that immediately involved. Some unions have shown remarkably little restraint in their use of the strike and other types of direct action for jurisdictional purposes. Even the Labor Board's certification of a union as the majority representative of the employes has not inhibited some unions from bringing pressures, either primary or secondary, to secure the unwilling disavowal of the certified agency, destroying that integrity of the employes' organization which we have seen is essential to the success of integration. In a case by no means unique, a trial examiner of the National Labor Relations Board reported that the president and general manager of an electrical supply company "stated that he had not been told directly by any of his customers why they had suspended their orders, but, running through his entire testimony is the inference that the reason for the withdrawal of his former business immediately following the election, is the fact that his employes are represented by the CIO while those of his customers are represented by

I.B.E.W. or one of its affiliated locals, and that they are faced with a threat of reprisals from those organizations if they attempt to utilize materials originating in Respondent's CIO shop. In the light of experience in the field of labor and its controversies between rival unions contesting for representation in the same occupational area, a realistic approach to the conditions found to exist here leads directly to such an inference. No other reasonably can be drawn."[11]

No conceivable threat by management to the development of the integrated enterprise is more direct than such action by the unions. It constitutes a challenge to the organizational stability of the business. Such a refusal by unions to accept the functioning of union-management cooperation where it is found involves a denial of the very interests which are their sole valid reason for existence. The successful integration of all corporate interests into a unified enterprise cannot possibly come until they, as a whole, have accepted a responsibility and an obligation which are already implicit, if not explicit, in the law and in our democratic morality.

In this last criterion of functional integration, its acceptance by others, we have come to a requirement which the participating parties in the single enterprise possess no means of fulfilling by their own actions, except insofar as their actions may invite acceptance. The response of other organized groups and of the public is beyond their control. Since acceptance by others is necessary to the success of the union-management relationship, a weighty responsibility for the eventual outcome rests in varying degree upon us all. By encouragement or discouragement, by withholding or according approval, we assume, in the measure of our respective influences, an accountability for the eventual issue. This responsibility we cannot dodge. It is ours by the very fact of our existence in a democratic society.

[11] *Matter of Lakeshore Electric Manufacturing Corp.*, NLRB, Case No. 8-C-1875 (April, 1946).

C H A P T E R **13**

Final Considerations

The primary conclusion of this study is that the roles of management and union in the large corporation cannot be defined by a differentiation of spheres of mutual or exclusive interest in the operation of the business. Solution of the problem of union-management relations must be based on a functional integration which conceives of the enterprise as composed of its various interest groups and builds its organization around them and encompassing them. We have examined in some detail the needs and requirements of such an integrated organization. Our study has, however, left unconsidered certain questions which some will feel require answers in any investigation of this nature.

In this analysis we have spoken of "the" union in the corporation. This is a simplification which is, of course, remote from fact. Even in those industries where so-called company-wide bargaining is practiced by an industrial union there are numerous additional unions which represent fragmentary groups of other employes—in some instances the skilled crafts, such as electricians, carpenters, plumbers, painters, or steamfitters, or in other instances some group which simply possesses a longer history of bargaining unity or whose strategic position accords it greater bargaining strength than is possessed by the rank and file of production workers, such as the Teamsters, or in still other cases a group of workers whose occupational interests may be quite removed from those of all other employe groups, such as the maritime workers employed by a steel company to move its freighters. Not infrequently the plants of a single company may be organized by different unions, with or without similar jurisdictional claims. The Automobile Workers and the Farm Equipment Workers represent the production employes at different plants of the same company, as do the Automobile Workers and the United Electrical Workers, and the American Communications Association and the Commercial Telegraphers Union. One large corporation maintains collective-bargaining relationships with more than 130 unions, only a fraction of which are locals of the same international organization. We cannot, then, realistically speak of relations between the management of a company and a single union when we speak of their functional integration. What bearing does this fact have on our problem?

The splintering of the body of employes of a company into a number of unions creates serious difficulties in achieving a genuinely integrated enterprise. The difficulties are not encountered in the negotiation of terms covering conditions which are peculiar to a group of specialized workers. They arise in the discussion and settlement of matters of more general company policy. If unions come increasingly to possess an effective voice in the determination of broad issues of business operation, affecting the interests of all employes, how can one union speak with authority when other unions also claim a representative status?

If integration of owners, employes, and management is what we seek, to establish an organizational framework within which the component interests may be adequately represented, there must be a collective representation of the employes just as there is collective representation of the stockholders. In matters involving the interests of all employes, employe representation by leaders of up to 130 unions, each with potentially differing viewpoints, is infeasible. In such matters employes can best be represented by a single organization harmonizing the interests of them all. This does not necessarily mean that authority must rest with only one of the many affected unions, however. It is possible that all unions in the company may join in a common council empowered to represent the total working force in matters affecting the interests of all. This is a practice which has been developed by certain international unions in the American Federation of Labor: negotiations are sometimes conducted by the building trades council on behalf of a number of separate unions, and similar cooperative programs have been developed by the metal and printing trades unions.

While such council action is practicable it seems unlikely, at least for the present, in view of the strong jealousies existing between unions, particularly between those affiliated with rival federations. It is improbable, however, that the failure of interunion cooperation will be allowed to stand in the road of increasing union participation. It is more probable that the dominant union in the company, representing a majority of the rank-and-file production workers, will invoke the doctrine of majority representation as the basis for a right to speak with authority on issues affecting the interests of all employes, in distinction to issues relating to special occupational or group interests represented by minority unions. This pattern of action is already evident in the automobile, steel, and other industries. While fractional representation has created difficulties, it has not halted the unions' drive to increasing participation.

If the existence of more than one union in the corporation does not act as a barrier to functional integration, it may nevertheless endanger its success. For as long as minority unions in separate units are recognized for bargaining purposes but are beyond the control of the dominant union, there is always the possibility that independent action by the former, backed by strike, will render meaningless all the cooperative efforts of the management and the principal union. This problem is a real one, but it is not likely to persist; for if it is found seriously to threaten industrial integration its challenge will be met, through public action if this should be necessary.

The division of workers into numerous bargaining units in a single company is a problem of more concern to the unions than to management in the working out of cooperative relations. Indeed, though it can scarcely be proved it is more than probable that this division along occupational lines has spared management from more expansive labor demands in the past. Rather than the problem of small-scale bargaining units, many managers have been concerned with the concentration of many into one, with their increasing size and continued growth, in a number of instances now promising to spread beyond the company itself.

Consolidation of a number of companies into an industry-wide bargaining unit has in the past been undertaken chiefly where small businesses predominated. In some few instances, such as the coal and railroad industries, large corporations of the magnitude of those with which this study is concerned have been included. Expansion of the bargaining unit has customarily, however, been a device employed to standardize costs if not prices in industries which in the absence of union regulation would be characterized by intensive competition and a high rate of business mortality, and this has generally meant its confinement to industries of small units. In the early years of the industrial unions there was even some question as to the desirability of a unit broader than the company, the belief being championed by some union officials that any large corporation possessed sufficient influence by way of example that the best conditions or terms wrung from each might be pressed upon all. In this manner, it was believed by some, progress might be swifter than if the large firms were united in negotiations, with none granting more than was jointly agreed among them.

This question of union policy has largely been resolved, so far as union sentiment is concerned, and in favor of industry-wide negotiations. An invitation to the important automobile companies to participate in such conferences has already been extended by the United Automobile Workers. A partial agreement has been jointly negotiated with the Big Four of the rubber industry. In the electrical and steel industries management confidently anticipates developing union pressure for industry-wide agreements. In the flat glass industry a joint agreement with the two dominant corporations is already the practice. The National Federation of Telephone Workers is seeking a national agreement covering all subsidiaries of the American Telephone and Telegraph Company, which is to say, the telephone industry. Beyond these separate movements, the CIO has formulated a general program for industry-wide councils. While there has been no attempt to blueprint this plan in detail, an eight-point statement reflecting "the thinking that is going on at the present time," prepared unofficially but by officials of the CIO in response to a series of questions, indicates the nature of the movement toward industry-wide organization in some quarters.

1. The first authority vested in the industry council would, of course, be that of collective bargaining as to wages, hours and working conditions. Eventually, the council would pass upon all matters having to do with the operation of the business, specifically, planning and improvement of product; pricing; trade practices; division of the proceeds in rent, interest, profits and wages; correlation of the business operation to the rest of the economy.

2. The council plan contemplates setting up an over-all industry council, representation on which would come from the individual plants.

3. The right to strike would be retained, just as would the corresponding right of management to withdraw its investment. The whole theory of setting up the council is to reach agreement, not to arrive at disagreement.

4. Most likely the council within the individual business would function at periodic intervals, or as occasion demanded. The over-all council for the specific industry would, because of its volume of work, function continuously.

5. The public representatives would be appointed by government and presumably serve as long as they wished to serve and carried out their functions properly. The whole industry council plan contemplates moving economic and political interests closer together.

6. Management would choose its representatives as it pleased, just as would the union.

7. Inasmuch as one of the functions of the individual plant council would be to correlate the plant with the rest of the economy, there no doubt would be a trend to industry-wide bargaining. There likewise would be a trend toward the single union. No doubt in such a scene we would continue to have rugged individuals among workers. In the overwhelming majority of current cases these people are in the minority. It is somewhat hard to assume that a minority would arise powerful enough to decide against full employment, guaranteed annual wages, fair prices and a steady continuous rise in the standard of living. The union shop most definitely fits into the council plan.

8. There no doubt would be individual corporations and unions which would object to accepting council decisions. They would, of course, be permitted to retain their sacred right to starve to death if they so chose. In the very nature of the case such characters could not survive the competition of quality, plenty and price, coming from the industry operating on a cooperative basis under the council plan.[1]

This movement from unions within the separate industries as well as

[1] From private correspondence of June 12, 1946.

from at least one of the major federations of unions has been meeting with increasing opposition from management. While some, indeed, have indicated a willingness to consider it on its merits when the union leadership has demonstrated its competence in bargaining units of present size, others have been gathering support for the idea that the industry-wide agreement carries with it such a threat to present economic institutions and to the independence of management that it cannot be tolerated.

Neither an international union nor a national trade association is as well qualified to discharge the full responsibilities of collective bargaining as the particular union and employer directly concerned. These are the people who know the specific problems and conditions first-hand. Therefore, we believe the new national labor policy should lodge the responsibilities for collective bargaining in a union exclusively representing the employees of a single employer. This would build responsibility for stable relationships and put it where it belongs. It would permit the working out of agreements on a basis mutually satisfactory to the parties directly covered by the collective-bargaining contract. Executives and staffs of international unions would provide economic research, reporting, technical, public relations, and advisory services to their autonomous union members. This policy would make unions, which are parties to collective-bargaining contracts, as responsible and as autonomous as the other party to the contract. . . .

It is clear that industry-wide collective bargaining is a major step toward the corporate state and cartelization of American industry. . . .

With separate industrial unions bargaining with separate employers, both fully responsible for their acts, the management-labor relationship that must exist if we are to obtain improved productivity during the war and a higher standard of living following the war can come into full force and effect. How can this cooperative management-labor relationship, at the employer and plant level, best develop? Can it develop permanently as long as management is dealing not with the present powerless representatives of its own workers but with officials of industry-wide or international unions? How can it develop when the officials of these international unions are rapidly increasing their ability to bring the full political and economic power of 6 million workers to bear on a single employer of a handful, a few thousand, or a hundred thousand workers?[2]

There thus exists a deep-seated disagreement as to the desirable unit of collective-bargaining negotiations. Particularly among those of management the opinion may be held that until this controversy is settled the question of integration must be held in abeyance, or alternatively that the resolution of this matter is an essential part of the integration problem. The view adopted in this study is that the two questions may be held separate. The same requirements for functional integration which have here been applied to the single enterprise can and must be applied to industry organization *if* that should develop. Whether our economy shall function along lines of company or industry organization is a question which must be settled on the broader grounds of economic and political

---

[2] From the statement of the Automotive Council, in *Investigation of the National Defense Program*, part 28, pp. 13572, 13574.

philosophy, and thus ultimately on the basis of that public acceptance which is one of the requirements for the integration of corporate interests.

This study has been concerned solely with the large corporation, and even more narrowly with those large corporations in which unions have gained an important functional status. This limitation has centered discussion around the large manufacturing concerns and public utilities and has permitted the avoidance of an issue which is now looming and which will yet require examination. The organization of employes into unions for bargaining purposes is now spreading from the fields of manual labor and encompassing white-collar workers in all occupational lines. Already there are unions recognized as bargaining agents in banks, insurance companies, stock exchanges, and newspapers, for example. As we have seen, there are now no defined limits to the coverage of collective agreements, and no evident feasible means of confining the subject matter of agreements. As an alternative to such efforts to spell out the legitimate areas of union activity, this study has suggested a functional integration which builds the corporate organization around and inclusive of all the interests importantly involved. But can such a solution be made applicable to institutions of the type just enumerated? Can unions in their respective companies be permitted, if they will, to speak with authority on the standards governing bank loans, on the nature of insurance investments, on the regulations governing the stock exchanges, on the editorial content of newspapers?

Once again we find ourselves face to face with the revolutionary aspects of freedom of association. But we shall arrive at no satisfactory answer to our question if we are led into swift judgment without reflection. There *are* no ready answers here. It is possible that upon examination we may discover that the conduct of large corporations in the special fields mentioned, and others raising like issues, must be treated in a different manner from our major manufacturing companies, and that the conduct of the union in those corporations must similarly be governed by different standards than apply in the mass-production industries. There is no *a priori* reason why they should be treated the same. In any event, these cases should be considered upon their own merits, without prejudgment based upon a false sense of the need for uniformity of treatment.

The developing problem of the role in our society of institutions such as banks, insurance houses, and stock exchanges, and the accompanying problem of the role of the union in those institutions, emphasize the growing challenge to our established ways of thinking. If the unions have accomplished anything, they have driven us perforce into an examination of the basis for private authority and the nature of private responsibility in important economic and political areas now largely removed from state control. We cannot for much longer avoid the reconsideration of old faiths and cherished tenets which now show less consistency than formerly with the changed character of many of our institutions.

There may be benefit in such a reconsideration, and in the restatement of political and economic norms which develops from it, but there is also a danger. It is not always the old doctrines which are most harmful; sometimes it is the new dogmas which carry gravest threat to the continuity and improvement of our social and private ways of life. Apart from all other considerations, we may recognize, for example, that socialism in itself is no answer to labor's quest for recognition and self-expression, or even security. Governmental managers may ignore the interests, desires, and aspirations of workers in a given plant fully as much, if not more so, than any of our present managers. Even under socialism, a procedure and an organization built for employe participation in the individual company would still be required. And to the extent that the public believed that in political elections labor had a sufficient voice in determining its conditions and terms of employment, socialism might prove a far greater threat to genuine employe participation than democratic capitalism. The answers which we seek are not therefore available for instant use as part of a doctrinaire package, but must be originated as we go.

It is now widely recognized that the growth of unions into bodies wielding power not incommensurate with that of our great corporations has posed organizational problems of the first magnitude. We are faced with the necessity of integrating these two groups for the benefit of society as well as for their own mutual advantage. More than simple restriction of power is needed; there must be a channeling of power to cooperative ends. The solutions which we seek must grow out of an analysis of the circumstances, building wherever possible on existing foundations. This objective has guided the present study. It is hoped that the conclusion as to the need for functional integration of owners, management, and the union in the large manufacturing and utility corporations has stemmed logically from the requirements of the situation.

The functional integration which has been suggested rests upon a redefinition of corporate interests in our giant businesses to include the employes and the public as well as the owners, a development which has as its harbingers many of the legal managers themselves. Growing out of a recognition of this principle, which has already been received in fact if not in law, a *system* of corporate responsibilities is needed to replace the single-line flow of responsibility to the stockholders. The enterprise must be organized and must operate to discharge recognized obligations to the public, to the owners, and to the employes. This undertaking the parties cannot complete alone. Social sanction is wanted to make the conversion possible, but there can be little doubt as to the readiness with which such sanction will be forthcoming if there is evidence of sincerity by explicit definition of intended purpose and procedure, by both the parties.

If a system of responsibilities is to be made definite and effective, the authority of both legal and union management must *rest upon* their adequate performance. Failure of the bargaining parties to discharge admitted responsibility to the public may provide cause for the assertion of public authority as well, in the corporation.

It is logically conceivable, on the further organizational premise that authority should derive from those to whom responsibility is owed, that within some unspecified time the managerial function of direction may be equally assumed by representatives of owners, employes, and public. If this time should ever arrive then corporate management as we know it today will play its vital administrative and executive roles in neutral fashion, seeking only to effectuate with impartial justice the decisions of final authority. Employes through their union representatives would still participate in the administrative function through consultation and negotiation—justifiably, since so much of their lives is bound up in their jobs—but such participation would still proceed, as it must now, with an acceptance of the framework established by higher management, right up to the directive level of authority. Prior to this development, if it should ever come, corporate management will better serve the expanded interests which it represents by accepting a joint responsibility to owners and employes in the administration and execution of the collective agreement, seeking the effectuation of its terms to the mutual advantage and impartial benefit of both participating groups.

To insure that joint decisions, once reached, are effectuated, a compliance system is required. Since neither party may claim the right of unilateral determination of the fact of compliance in areas of joint interest, there is needed, for ultimate resolution of controversies on such matters, an impartial determination by a jointly established authority, as has already been provided in numerous companies. If the compliance system is to operate effectively, the areas of managerial discretion in all frames of the corporate structure must be sufficiently defined and respected.

The supporting facilities required by integration of the cooperating parties will include training programs to foster the growth of those, including the unions' representatives, with whom authority and responsibility are lodged, those upon whom rest the conduct of our large corporations, upon whom the demands of competence in technology, organization, and morality are made without reserve. The supporting facilities required will include, too, adequate factual collection and analysis, which in the areas of mutual interest must be available to all those charged with decision-making. The training of competent leadership will prove fruitless if the information on which decisions should be based is unavailable or unused.

The effectiveness of the enterprise which integrates its participant groups will be measured by its ability to serve its social purpose of production. Its efficiency will be gauged by its capacity to satisfy the personal goals of those who compose it. The content of the concept of efficiency must thus be redefined if the corporation is to serve interests broader than those of the stockholding group to which it is now legally attached.

In this system of shared responsibility and authority, the integrity of the participating organizations of owners and employes must be preserved against internal and external abuse. There must likewise be the growth of mutual intent and mutual faith if the cooperative end is to be achieved. In these respects the public is entitled to more than hope. It may reasonably require performance, and those leaders of either management or labor who fail in the test must be hurried from the scene by the force of opprobrium. This means the assumption of individual responsibility and authority by all who compose the public, for in the last analysis it is their acceptance, as expressed through their actions and organs of opinion, which will determine the nature of the industrial order. In translating their often inarticulate desires into concrete statement, the burden will rest chiefly upon their public representatives, whose integrity and resourcefulness are thus challenged, as they must always be in a democratic society.

In all this we cannot expect perfection, nor should we avoid caution. There is, however, an urgent need for the best that is possible. No man knows how much time we have allotted to us to perform the needed task before crisis shall test the results of our efforts. There is sound sense in the view of a group of thoughtful managers that change is needed, that it must come, but that the timing should be dependent on the capacity of union and business leadership to accommodate themselves to the change, a capacity still in the process of development. Still, the years of slow and peaceful change are behind us. We are living in times so dynamic that it is difficult for the best of us to keep pace with the present. Crisis, whether economic or political, international or domestic, is part of our age. Pressing needs are generated which are met by whatever expedient means lie at hand. We can no longer be sure that we have time for the luxury of extended reflection or the satisfaction of slow adjustment.

In this atmosphere we may weigh well our problems of industrial integration, and consider them soundly; we may proceed with caution. We will be ill-advised, however, if we refuse *now* to meet them squarely and accord them the consideration which is their full due. These are our *present* responsibilities. To shift them to the future may foreclose a solution which we would find preferable to one which is suddenly adopted under emergency pressure that cannot be denied.

A P P E N D I X A

Union Penetration of Managerial Areas: Automobiles

In analyzing the automobile industry we shall concern ourselves principally with those few large corporations which are classed as assemblers of final products. The union involved is the United Automobile, Aircraft, and Agricultural Implement Workers of America (UAW-CIO). In this and the following industry surveys, the outline of "Areas of Management" on pages 46–47 will be followed.

The important contracts in this industry, as in many other industries, set forth general limitations upon the union's sphere of interest by clauses preserving to the legal managers their sole authority in stated areas. Examples of such clauses are this from the General Motors 1946 agreement:

> The right to hire; promote; discharge or discipline for cause; and to maintain discipline and efficiency of employes, is the sole responsibility of the Corporation except that Union members shall not be discriminated against as such. In addition, the products to be manufactured, the location of plants, the schedules of production, the methods, processes and means of manufacturing are solely and exclusively the responsibility of the Corporation.

and from the Chrysler 1946 contract:

> The Union recognizes that the Corporation has the exclusive right to manage its plants and direct its affairs and working forces.

The corresponding clause in the Ford contract is most detailed, consisting of eight sections.

In connection with such "management clauses," we must note, however, first, that they are valid only for the duration of the contract and do not bind the union at the time of negotiations for a new contract; second, that the rights enumerated are subject to any limitations imposed in the remainder of the agreement; and third, limitations not contemplated in the agreement itself may be imposed during its lifetime by means of grievance proceedings, by actions not contemplated in the agreement, or by outright violations of the agreement.

FINANCE

The union does not now share managerial authority in this category, which includes the areas of raising capital and determination of the capital structure; dividends; reserves; amortization and depreciation; accounting procedures; insurance; and budgeting. It must, of course, influence certain of these decisions by virtue of its wage demands, however.

In the 1945–1946 General Motors negotiations, the union's interest in the company's profit position (directly affecting its dividend and reserve policy among other matters), became itself an issue between the parties. "The Union constantly reiterated its willingness to reconsider its 30 per cent proposal if the 'arithmetic' of the Corporation's financial condition showed such a wage boost would necessitate price relief or undue

267

profit cuts. It refused to eliminate from the negotiations the consideration of the effects of its wage demands on prices and profits and requested Corporation data to show what these effects would be."[1] The union's expressed interest in certain financial policies of the companies has not yet resulted either in its securing a voice in those decisions, however, or even in its making official demands for the right to participate directly in them.

PERSONNEL

It is in this category that the union has made its greatest penetration, for the time-honored spheres of union interest are involved here.

Type of Personnel. The union has concerned itself with aspects of personal characteristics and professional competence. With respect to the former, its general policy, as expressed in one contract, is that "The Company shall not discriminate against any person because of race, sex, political or religious affiliation, or nationality." Its official statements have always emphasized equal job opportunities for Negroes and for women. With respect to skill qualifications, it has in some instances participated in apprenticeship programs. In the General Motors Corporation, an Apprentice Committee of three union members may be appointed at each plant, to meet with local management, under an Apprentice Plan, to discuss the training of men for journeymen trades.

Size of Force. No desire has been shown by the union to participate in determining the actual total number of workers to be attached to a given plant or company. A more general interest has been displayed in two ways, however. First, the union's recent attention to corporate price policy has as one of its roots a belief that the automobile industry and the individual component companies must "do their part" in supporting full employment. This responsibility to employ some indefinite segment of the working force can be accomplished, it believes, only if the price of automobiles is set to attract the largest possible market. As a corollary, one of its leaders has proposed a flexible pricing policy designed to lessen seasonal fluctuations and maintain a level work force the year round. (This matter will be discussed further under price policy.) Second, to *maintain* the attachment of as many workers to the company as is feasible in times of business slump, the union has sought and secured the business policy of reducing hours from the normal work week of 40 to one of 32, prior to layoff of seniority employes. This policy results in maintaining the size of the work force while permitting a reduction in manhours worked.

A tie between the number of workers on a given operation and the rates of operation has been effected in some contracts, as for example, in the following clause:

> When, on account of breakdown or shortage of stock, it becomes necessary to increase the speed of a conveyor beyond the normal speed that is required to attain the established production it will be necessary to add adequate manpower to the group to offset the increase in conveyor speed.

Hiring. Contract provisions have been secured guaranteeing that in hiring new employes a company will give preference to workers who have been previously laid off without expectation of being returned to their former jobs. In some cases this guarantee applies not only to those who have worked at a given plant, but also to those who have

---

[1] From *Report of the National Citizens Committee on the GM-UAW-CIO Dispute,* published by the union, December, 1945. This issue was part of the complicated "ability to pay" argument in which the union's sincerity was questioned as a result of a subsequent statement by the leading union negotiator, Walter Reuther, that it had been adopted solely for tactical purposes. While some believe this was the case, others in the automobile industry incline to the view that Reuther's later statement was occasioned by the political contest for union office in which he was then engaged, and that as negotiators rather than politicians union officials were genuinely interested in the corporation's profit position.

worked at any plant of the same company. It likewise may apply not only to expansion of force in an existing plant but also to the building of a work force in a newly established plant. Other contracts provide that before a new man is hired, any employe in the works may make application and receive prior consideration for the job being filled.

In rehiring following layoffs, employes are generally taken back in the reverse order in which they were dismissed. Exceptions to the practice may be made only by agreement with the union, or subject to union objection via the grievance procedure.

Layoffs. The union counts as one of its greatest achievements the elimination of alleged favoritism in the laying off of workers at times of low production. A prescribed order of dismissal now appears in every contract. Provisions vary, but in general the pattern is one of reducing the force first by dropping probationary employes, then by dropping permanent employes on the basis of seniority. Union officials are given preferred status in such layoffs; thus one contract provides that "Chief Stewards shall, in the event of a layoff, be continued at work as long as there is a job in their district which they are able to do and any of their respective constituents still are at work. . . ." Local union officials are given corresponding protection. In the event the agreed order of layoffs is not followed, the company must make up loss of pay to the aggrieved employe by offering additional work, or failing this, by payment of back wages for time lost. In one arbitration case a worker dropped from the roles by a mistaken omission from the seniority list, while probationary employes remained at work, was awarded lost wages for the three-and-a-half-month period which had elapsed before the error was discovered.

In the event the reduction of force is one affecting a number of workers (in one contract defined as 20 per cent of the employes with seniority dating to June 20, 1941) or one promising to continue for an extended period of time (in another contract, defined as four weeks), work-sharing down to 32 hours a week is provided for, below which figure dismissals on the basis of seniority begin.

Some companies have accorded to union representatives the right to review scheduled layoffs before they become effective. Others have agreed to notify the employe and his steward 24 hours prior to dismissal. The union has gone on record as maintaining that the 24-hour notification is insufficient and may be considered only as a step in its long-range objective of "adequate notice." It may also be noted that arbitration in one company has established the principle that failure to give the prescribed notice must be compensated by pay for the equivalent time. Such payment was ordered even though the employes involved had been at work on a government contract, immediate termination of which had been ordered by the government. The impartial chairman ruled that since the company had entered into the contract with foreknowledge of the requirement to provide workers 24 hours' notice, it had had the opportunity of protecting itself in its contract with the government or by special arrangement with the union. "The Chairman finds that the Union cannot and should not be limited in its rights under the Agreement by contracts subsequently made by the Company to which the Union was not a party, and about the details of which it had no knowledge, and had given no consent."

More recently the union has contested the power of a company to dismiss its employes at age 65, to make room for younger men. The union's position is that men at age 65 should be allowed to continue on the job as long as they are physically capable of performing their tasks adequately. It cannot be said, however, that the union fails to recognize the need for some modification of this position. It, as well as the companies, is aware of the need for bringing young blood into the industry; it recognizes the problems accompanying the increasing average age of the automobile workers. Its officials frankly admit to contesting the authority of the company to dismiss men at age 65 only until what they consider a satisfactory retirement plan has been established by mutual agreement.

Allocation. In general, the contract provisions in the industry contemplate, in the words of one impartial chairman, "that management shall instruct the employees as to the work to be performed and that . . . the employees shall perform the work which they are instructed to do. If an employee, or his representative, feels that the instructions are improper, then he must proceed in an orderly manner as contemplated by the parties and provided for by their agreement"—that is to say, by protesting through the grievance procedure. Despite this general provision for assignment of the working force, specific clauses in the agreements limit management's freedom in making transfers. Examples of such limitations are these:

Transfers from one plant to another plant may be made only with the signed consent of an employe and his committeeman.

In the event that employes are "loaned" from one classification within a unit to another classification in that unit, or from one unit to another within a plant, or between plants, the employes with the least seniority are those who shall be "loaned."

In the event an operation is transferred from one unit to another, employes shall be transferred to the new unit, taking their full seniority with them except under certain circumstances. For partial transfers of an operation, the method of transferring employes is subject to local negotiations.

In case of the permanent discontinuance of an operation, the employes affected shall be transferred to a similar occupational group in the plant within five days.

Employes transferred due to layoffs in the department in which they were originally employed will upon request be retransferred to their original job whenever production warrants, providing their seniority entitles them to be transferred.

It is fair to say, and the above clauses indicate, that the union has sought to govern transfers—both to better or to worse jobs—on the basis of seniority. This limitation has been resisted by the companies, who prefer greater freedom of allocating workers, and was one of the important issues in contest in the bitterly fought 1946 General Motors negotiations.

Although top union officials have never sought to restrict the freedom of allocation on any other basis than seniority, lesser union officials have at times used their power to frustrate or countermand the work assignments of management representatives. For example, a district steward removed a man from a job assigned to him and returned him to his former operation. In another instance, management representatives charged that a shop steward, a department steward, a building steward, and a local union president successively refused to permit the retransfer of three women employes who had not proved satisfactory on the job to which assigned. Other cases may be cited, matters of record, in which individual union members, relying on the strength of their union, have refused to accept work assignments. The only form of official union approbation of such actions consists in the prosecution of their cases through the grievance procedure. It would be inaccurate to charge the international union with sponsoring these challenges to the system of work allocation now in effect. At the same time it is fair to observe that these challenges would unquestionably not have occurred in the absence of the union.

Discipline. In no area has management felt its authority more strongly challenged than in the imposition of disciplinary penalties. The depth of the union's penetration requires a rather lengthy statement even in a condensed survey. Corporate officials in several of the major companies agree that it is at best difficult for a foreman to maintain discipline within the shop. This situation, they maintain, results from two fears on the part of the foreman: (1) that the organized workers will strike against the imposition of a penalty on one of their number; and (2) that any penalty imposed may be reversed by an impartial chairman or umpire, lessening the foreman's status in the eyes of his men. On the strength of these fears, say these company officials, foremen are more inclined today to overlook actions that merit discipline on the argument that it is better policy to keep the shop operating and to forego a contest over authority which may only serve in the end to lessen that authority. Another management representative makes the statement that "most companies in this industry wouldn't dare to fire a union steward no matter what he did."

On the union side of the problem, the claim is made that management originally resented *any* limitations upon its complete disciplinary authority, and that that resentment has only slightly diminished with the years. They list as one of the achievements of the union that whereas workers were once afraid to bring up grievances, now the "UAW fights to have wrongs redressed."

The contract provisions themselves only suggest the important voice which the union has gained in the exercise of discipline. A general clause commonly contains some statement such as the following:

The Company retains the sole right to discipline and discharge employees for cause, provided that in the exercise of this right it will not act wrongfully or unjustly or in violation of the terms of this agreement. Complaints that the Company has violated this paragraph may be taken up through the Grievance Procedure provided in this agreement.

One of the major contracts contains a system of penalties which has been jointly negotiated and which may be "abrogated, changed or substituted by mutual agreement between representatives of the Company and the Union." This code lists conduct which is subject to discipline and the penalties which may accompany such conduct "when completely established and determined through the Grievance Procedure."

Theft from fellow employees or from Company.	Discharge.
Assault of fellow employees, brawling or fighting on Company property.	Minimum—two weeks' layoff to discharge for men involved.
Any act of threat.	Two weeks to discharge.
Disobedience to proper authority.	One day to discharge.
Working under assumed name.	Subject to discharge.
Possession of illegal weapons on Company property.	Discharge.
Malicious or careless destruction of Company property.	Three days to discharge.
Soliciting on Company property without permission.	Reprimand to discharge.
Habitual garnishments.	Discharge.
Careless making of unnecessary scrap (spoilage).	Reprimand to three days' layoff.
Smoking where or when prohibited.	Three days to discharge; Reprimand to three days first time; second time—two weeks; and third time—discharge.
Influence of liquor.	Three days to discharge.

Leaving department or building during working hours without notifying foreman or without reasonable excuse.	Reprimand to three days.
Washing or preparing to leave before proper time or idling before time clock before quitting time.	Reprimand to three days.
Wilfully ringing clock card of another.	One week to discharge.
Gambling on Company property.	Reprimand to two weeks—first offense; discharge second.
Drinking or possession of intoxicating liquor on Company property.	Two weeks to discharge.
Engaging in carnal acts or relation with employees of the opposite sex on Company property.	Discharge.
Constant breach of safety rules.	Reprimand to discharge.

Constant and habitual breach of Company rules may result in discharge.

The types of conduct penalized in the above code are those which primarily are objectionable to the company. Occasionally the union has been able to secure agreements that discipline shall be meted out to those engaging in conduct objectionable to it, as in the clause that "The Company shall take appropriate disciplinary action including discharge in any case of an employee who on Company time carries on anti-union activity or who seeks, directly or indirectly, to interfere with the status, membership, or responsibilities of the certified Union." Such a clause would seemingly apply to managerial personnel as well as the working force.

A more direct control by the union over discipline of the working force, though not of managerial personnel, is made possible under a union shop. This arrangement exists in only one major automobile contract, that with Ford. It provides that in order to retain their employment with the company workers must be members of good standing in the union. Thus expulsion from the union, as penalty for some action either connected or not connected with their behavior on the job, may require their dismissal by the company. This is not an absolute requirement, however. Its limitations have been well stated in a case coming before the umpire, involving the union's demand for the discharge of two employes who had been expelled from the local union. The company, contending that the expulsion was grounded solely on the objection of fellow workers to the speed with which the offending men worked, "spoiling" an easy job, refused to make the discharges. While ruling that protection of union members against unjust expulsion in general is not the function, privilege, or duty of the employer, the umpire nevertheless held for the company. Such discharges, he asserted, were not required in cases "in which the expulsion infringes rights assured to the Company by the contract and in which the cause for expulsion is concededly not proper cause under the [UAW] International Constitution." Since the contract required "a fair day's work," prohibited restrictions on production, and justified discipline for employes violating this prohibition, the union could not be conceded the power to compel discharges for reasons which made these provisions a nullity. The union's right to effect a man's discharge by expelling him from the union is thus limited by the requirement implicit in the collective agreement itself that this right shall be exercised in good faith. Even with this limitation, however, the union shop, or provision for maintenance of membership, remains an effective disciplinary tool in the hands of the union.

A common provision in the important agreements of this industry requires that the chief steward or committeeman be promptly notified of disciplinary action taken against an employe, at least of discharges for discipline. A time period of 24 hours is sometimes specified. In addition, at least one contract provides that before a penalized employe leaves the plant he has the right to summon his committeeman to discuss the penalty with management officials. The strict insistence on this notification procedure is evidenced in one case arising before an impartial chairman in which an employe had been discharged for alleged thievery. The company attempted to inform a union official of the discharge orally, but no written notification was delivered to a union representative for eight days. Though the union did not deny the allegation against the employe, the company was ordered to pay back wages for the eight-day period between the date of his discharge and the date of written notification to the union.

This case is some indication of the important role played by the impartial chairman or umpire in the enforcement of the contract. Such an officer is the agent of union and management jointly, and is responsible to both. His function is chiefly to interpret and apply the collective agreements, and in this capacity he becomes the instrument for defining the nature and extent of union and managerial authority under the contract. In matters of discipline the umpire's role varies among the companies, however. Thus in some instances he is empowered to pass upon the merits of the conduct which invited discipline, but finding discipline warranted may not pass upon the justice of the penalty imposed. In other companies he is further empowered to determine whether the penalty imposed was justified. This latter power has been defined by one of the industry's umpires in the following manner:

The Umpire is not expected to substitute his own judgment for that of management. His power is to review the penalty and determine whether it is reasonable under the circumstances. Management has considerable discretion in the imposition of discipline. That discretion has not been transferred to the Umpire. His power is to modify only when the penalty is beyond the zone of reasonableness. Where several penalties are all reasonable, the Umpire cannot alter the one selected by management, even though, were he in management's shoes, he might have selected a different one. The reasonableness of a penalty depends, of course, on all the circumstances of the case: the nature of the offense, the prior record of the employee, prophesy as to his future behavior, effect on discipline and morale in the plant, and so on.

In the course of numerous decisions involving disciplinary action imposed by management, protested by the union, and passed upon by the impartial chairman or umpire, certain principles have gradually evolved. For the most part, these have not been explicitly set forth in any official document, nor do they necessarily prevail in all union-management relationships in the industry. They are, however, invoked with sufficient frequency to warrant consideration of them *as* principles. At the same time, they perhaps represent the point of furthest penetration on the part of the union in sharing, through one medium or another, formal control over discipline in the large automobile company.

1. Employes must have prior knowledge of the causes for which disciplinary penalties may be imposed. While offenses may be established by practice or common understanding, increasing emphasis is being placed upon written rules. Thus from one ruling:

It is clear that there was here no effort to survey the field and to prescribe knowable and enforceable rules. The matter was left largely to idiosyncracy of circumstance and of persons in authority. This is not the way to prescribe or enforce rules of conduct.

In cases where work directions are disobeyed, the directions must be shown to be specific before discipline will be upheld.

There is no evidence that the men would have refused these requests or orders if they had been made. They were not given an opportunity to choose. All that appears is that on the second night they reported and quit at the old time. Their claim is that they understood that they were entitled to do so under their arrangement for a trial of the new shift. Nothing was done by supervision on that night to question or correct their understanding or to lay a foundation for the charge of disobedience. It was made quite clear at the hearing that the discharges were a hasty, ill-considered act not warranted by the men's conduct.

As a corollary to this principle that the cause for discipline must be known, it has likewise been established that previous offenses overlooked at the time of their commission may not be used at a later date as a basis for discipline.

But it is true that disciplinary action, if taken, must be taken fairly closely after the commission of the offense. Not all shop offenses are made the occasion for disciplinary penalties; many are, for one reason or another, permitted to die without consequence. If an offense is not followed by disciplinary action fairly promptly, it becomes part of the great past, an incident to be recalled as a missed opportunity or a lucky break. It cannot later be revived as the occasion for current disciplinary action.

At the same time, it has been accepted that offenses for which an employe is warned may be considered along with subsequent offenses *of the same nature* in imposing penalties. For, as one umpire stated, this "is not a case in which past sins are suddenly sprung on a man without prior warning."

2. Along with knowledge of the cause for which discipline may be imposed, there must be a reasonably certain knowledge of the penalty attached to the offense. Such knowledge may arise from mutual agreement upon a range of penalties for prescribed sins, as in the code of conduct reproduced earlier in this section, or it may arise from past practice. Illustrative of the operation of this principle is the extract from the following decision:

The Chairman finds that the company has the right to discharge an employee for leaving the plant before his shift is completed, contrary to management's proper instructions, providing there is no unfair discrimination and the employee was properly put on notice.

In this case Y left the plant after conversations with two of management's representatives. There can be no question but that his actions were improper and that he knew them to be so. There is no basis to claim that he was unfairly discriminated against, at least by the assistant superintendent.

However, the general practice of the company in cases of this kind when employees walk out appears to be to limit discharges to ringleaders only. Unless Y was first put on notice that if he disregarded management's instructions his discipline would not conform to that usually given under the circumstances, it would not be proper to apply discipline so considerably in excess of that normally given.

Assuming the statements of management's representatives to be correct, the most they both said was "You will be subject to discharge." In the Chairman's opinion this did not put Y on notice that if he left early he would be discharged. It would have been reasonable for him to have assumed that he would probably receive the same discipline normally given, and although this in no way justified his action, it did permit him to act without a fair realization of what the penalty would be.

On the basis of the above reasoning, the impartial chairman ordered the reinstatement of the offending employe, but without pay for the period during which he had been without employment.

3. Adequate evidence must support the charge. Thus when a chief steward was dis-

charged for cursing a foreman, the impartial chairman hearing the case ruled that since evidence, including the affidavit of the assistant foreman, failed to establish the alleged facts, the disciplinary action should be rescinded and the steward reinstated with back pay.

Similarly, in the case of a worker discharged for fomenting an unauthorized work stoppage, the umpire ruled:

D worked on the afternoon shift. The stoppage started on the day shift. According to his testimony he had come to work at his regular time and found that the stoppage was in progress with no one working. He went to the committee room, spoke to the committeeman there for about 15 minutes and then left by the side door. The only evidence against him is the statement of a foreman that one of his men told him that D had been sitting in the lunchroom and was there to see that the men stopped work. D denies that he was in the lunchroom at all on that day. And in that he is supported by the testimony of the committeeman and by circumstantial evidence. No one before me testified to seeing D do anything whatever in the way of inciting, encouraging or being otherwise active in the stoppage. On the evidence before me, then, I must find that D is innocent. He is to be reinstated without loss of seniority and with compensation. . . .

4. Any disciplinary penalty imposed on the employe must conform to the charges. There may be circumstances mitigating the employe's action and hence considered in extenuation when penalty is imposed. There can, however, be no circumstances which make an employe's action graver than is charged, for if this were so the employe would be in no position to render a defense. The operation of this principle is shown in the following extract from the decision of an impartial chairman.

In the instant case the Company specifically limited the reason for discipline to insubordination for refusal to give the production count. Therefore, the Chairman must view the penalty from this standpoint. Had the Company chosen to include in its basis for discharge other factors set forth by it [restriction of output], as heretofore recounted, and established its case thereon, the discipline assessed probably would not be open to question. However, the Company did not choose to act on this basis and therefore the penalty must fit the basis used for discharge—refusal to give a production count.

In another sense, this principle also is designed to assure that the punishment imposed is not an "unusual" one. Thus in the case of two men who had left their shift half an hour early, though warned by the foreman not to do so, and who were thereupon given a disciplinary layoff of one week, it was ruled:

[Management] fixed the penalty of one week on the premise that the men were guilty of "disobedience to proper authority," for which the penalty is "one day to discharge." That rule, however, must be applied with care. It is only one of some twenty rules listed in Exhibit A of the parties' contract. A violation of any of these rules can be called disobedience to proper authority. Obviously, however, that one rule is not intended to embrace all the others. For example, distinct first, second, and third offense penalties are provided for "smoking where or when prohibited." By definition, smoking when prohibited is a disobedience to proper authority. But the smoker must be punished under the smoking rule, not under the disobedience rule. Where a specific rule is provided for the particular misconduct, it is inappropriate to disregard the specific rule and deal with the misconduct as a violation of the general mandate of obedience.

Relative to this case, Exhibit A provides that the penalty for "leaving department or building during working hours without notifying foreman or without reasonable excuse" is reprimand to three days. And the same penalty is imposed for "washing or preparing to leave before proper time." The men here left work before the proper time without reasonable excuse. To be sure, that is a form of disobedience, but it is a form of disobedience for which Exhibit A prescribes a penalty of not more than three days. The foreman's request or order that the men work through their scheduled time was a request that they do that which they were already bound to do. It added nothing to their duty or to their misconduct. It can add nothing to their penalty. Accordingly, my award is that the lay-off be reduced to three days and that the men be compensated for the time lost in excess of three days. . . .

In addition to the restrictions on management's power of discipline imposed in the contracts and their interpretation by the impartial chairmen of the industry, direct action by unofficial groups of organized workers sometimes serves as an additional limitation. The circumstances recited in an arbitration case reveal the possible complications:

On August 29, 1944, the Labor Relations Supervisor met in a special meeting to discuss the X grievance. As a result of the discussion X's discipline was reduced to one day. The meeting lasted from 9:30 A.M. until approximately 11:00 A.M. At 1:00 P.M. fifty-seven employees in the Tool Room walked out. The Company states that this walk-out was in protest of the discipline given X. The Union states that it did not have to do with the X case, but resulted from the objection of the employees to the action of a Tool Room foreman . . . regarding the discharge of a Chief Steward and the removal of another man from the plant. At approximately 6:00 P.M. thirty-three Tool Room employees on the second shift, including X, walked out. The Company states that it does not know the reason for this action other than that apparently it was because the first shift had walked out. The first shift did not come back to work on August 30th; the second shift did.

Illustrations of this type of concerted group protest of managerial discipline, operating outside and in contravention of the established channels of protest, might be multiplied. The union is not unmindful of the situation. Any action which it sponsors to remedy the situation, however, is not likely to lead in the direction of restoring more authority to management in this area, but of further limiting managerial freedom with the intent of eliminating the irritants now considered to be the cause of such illegal and unofficial group protests. The union's program in this field may be reduced to two proposals, as set forth in an "Analysis of Causes of Labor-Management Conflict in the Auto and Aircraft Industries" prepared by four ranking officers of the union.

(1) Discharge cases should be first subject to negotiation before final action is taken. The experience of the union, as cited in this statement, has clearly demonstrated that the most frequent cause of strike explosions is the arbitrary discharge of workers without previous warnings or discussion. When such disputes affect union officers or committeemen, the life of the union itself appears menaced in the mind of the average worker. . . .

(2) For those managements responsible for provoking stoppages, penalties equivalent to those suffered by equally guilty workers should be applied. The obvious equity of this principle would go far toward restoring worker confidence.[2]

Thus far managements of the automobile industry have resisted all efforts of the union to incorporate these provisions in contract or practice. They insist upon retaining the power to initiate disciplinary actions, allowing the union to contest their propriety through the grievance procedure. It need scarcely be remarked that the present situation is far from stable. The ultimate solution is far from clear.

[2] The union statement, dated July 6, 1944, appears in *Investigation of The National Defense Program,* part 28, with the above quotation appearing on page 13686.

Wages. While the impact of the union on management's freedom to determine wage rates is generally recognized, the complexity of the problem and the numerous ways in which authority has been shared are sometimes overlooked. In this section we can do no more than suggest the avenues opened by the union in sharing such authority with management.

Methods of payment in the industry include straight salary (primarily for clerical or office employes); hourly rates; and piece rates, which may be for an individual or for a group, and are almost always accompanied by guaranteed hourly rates. Production jobs are grouped into categories of similar skills, required efforts, and job conditions which are known as job classifications. Each job classification is given its wage rate, which may take the form of a "band" within which a worker is placed on the basis of his experience, seniority, and ability. In the case of piece rates, the amount per piece is determined on the basis of time-studies of the operation involved. The process of establishing job rates, whether hourly or piece, permits considerable discretion, especially since thousands of such rates must be determined. The union has consistently asked for greater participation in the exercise of this discretion. The problem is a difficult one, since the setting of an individual rate—among thousands of such rates—does not involve nor permit collective bargaining in the sense of negotiating *general* conditions. On the other hand, the factors to be considered in determining an individual rate are not referable to a clear set of standards permitting a judicial decision of what that rate should be—a condition essential to their being handled by a grievance procedure culminating in arbitration. As a result, the problem is met by a process which may be described as "fractional bargaining" or "specialized bargaining,"[3] in which union representatives at several administrative levels and locations negotiate for rates applicable to categories of workers who represent only fractions of the total bargaining unit. At the same time union and management officials must bear in mind the over-all relationship of the many individual rates, so that some wage *system* evolves.

The condition stated in one important contract is rather generally applicable: "The establishment of wage scales for each operation is necessarily a matter for local negotiation and agreement between the Plant Management and the Shop Committee, on the basis of the local circumstances affecting each operation, giving consideration to the relevant factors of productivity, continuity of employment, the general level of wages in the community, and the wages paid by competitors." Any *general* wage increases won by the union in national negotiations are applied to the classification rates so established.

The false impression should not be created, however, that the union always participates with management in the *initial* determination of classification and piece rates, or in the redetermination of such rates at times when methods of production, equipment used, or other factors change. Such is sometimes the case. Under existing agreements, however, management generally retains the authority to set rates initially and it generally exercises this authority. Subsequent to such unilateral determination of the rate, the union may challenge it through the grievance procedure, or through other established bargaining procedures. It is usually at this point that "negotiation and agreement" take place, but throughout the duration of such negotiation the original rate as set by management remains in effect. In the words of one contract, "When negotiations are completed, such classification and rate shall become a part of the local wage agreement, and the negotiated rate, if higher than the temporary [management] rate shall be applied retroactively to the date the production employes started on the job, except as otherwise mutually agreed."

[3] Paul H. Norgren has used the latter term in *The Swedish Collective Bargaining System* (1941), p. 216.

The joint negotiation of rates sometimes involves a restudy of the job, with the union observing or participating. Contracts may specify the conditions under which such a job study must be made, as for example that the operation must have run for at least 24 hours or five working shifts, whichever is shorter; the employe observed must have knowledge that his operation is being studied; the study must take into consideration all details of the complete operation; the method of manufacture and the quantity and quality of production must have previously been satisfactorily established.

No permanent machinery for the resolution of deadlocks between union and management in the negotiation of rates is customarily provided. If the dispute is settled by arbitration, the resort to arbitration must be a matter of agreement at the time. The major contracts specifically provide that the determination of rates is not referable to the impartial chairman or umpire. His sole point of entry in wage controversies consists of deciding, when requested, whether a particular operation may properly be placed in an existing classification. Thus he may rule that "employees classified under Classification #510, Drill Press, who are performing the operations on radial drills covered by this grievance are improperly classified." In some cases he may likewise rule that "operators . . . who are classified under Classification No. 1025, Milling Machine-Production, and are operating Cincinnati tracer controlled Hydromatic Milling Machines, be reclassified under Classification No. 1157, Profile and Mill, and that they receive such retroactive pay to which they would have been entitled had they been so classified at the time they began their operations on these machines . . ." The impartial chairman rendering the above decisions construed his power, in another case, in the following way:

> Under the contract the Appeal Board [on which the impartial chairman has the deciding voice] has the authority, on proper petition, to decide in which of any existing classifications a particular operation should be placed. It does not have the authority to create new classifications or to determine that a wage or rate of pay provided for an established classification is improper, or that a particular operation in a classification should carry a wage or rate of pay different from that provided for the classification.

Because the thousands of wage rates in the automobile industry are individually determined, even though attention is paid to the relationship between rates, cases invariably arise where workers on one job believe they are being underpaid relative to workers on another job. These "wage inequities" require further negotiation. They may be handled by procedures permanently available, or by temporary commissions appointed for that purpose.

The determination of classification and piece rates by no means settles the problem of wages. In addition, numerous special cases must be provided for. Mention of only a few of these will be made, to indicate the extent of union participation in this area of management:

> Piece-work allowances will be given in addition to piece-work earnings to compensate for production interferences or abnormal conditions not contemplated in the time-study, but no allowances will be given for delays of less than 15 minutes.

> Piece-work average earnings [estimated over a prescribed period of time] will be paid to an employe temporarily assigned to a job other than his own, or when he is forced to produce in the face of handicaps that require constant attention to matters not normally involved in his operation, or when because of a breakdown or material shortage he runs less than his full complement of machines.

> When a worker is required to re-work parts that are spoiled: if spoilage is due to his own faulty workmanship he is paid only his occupational day rate; if due to incorrect

specifications, faulty gauges, faulty instructions or faulty stock, or if due to some-one else's work, he is paid his average piece-rate earnings for the time involved.

A contract may also contain a number of clauses specifying the wage rate to be paid to employes who are transferred to a higher-paid classification (the rate may differ depending upon whether he has had previous experience on the new job); to employes who are transferred from a higher-paid classification to a lower-paid classification; to employes who are transferred from a higher-paid classification to a lower-paid classification and then to an intermediate classification; to an employe who formerly worked in one plant of the company and who is employed as a new man in another plant. There may also be clauses relating to wage rates for an employe assigned to a group operating on a group piece-rate basis—the payment depending upon whether he is an experienced employe, a transfer from another department but inexperienced on the new job, or a new inexperienced employe. A minimum hiring rate for new employes is generally also specified.

Even these detailed provisions do not exhaust the union's role in the field of wages. Certain general provisions loom very important. Among these are the provisions established in many contracts that wage rates for women shall be set in accordance with the principle of equal pay for comparable quantity and quality of work on comparable operations; that a "differential" (for example, of five or ten per cent of earnings) be paid to those required to work on the second or third shift; that time-and-a-half be paid for work under certain circumstances, and double time on other occasions; that employes reporting to work and not previously informed that work was not available shall be given "call-in time," generally equal to pay for two or three hours, depending on the contract.

While part of the union program consists in making more general throughout the industry certain of these concessions which may have been secured in only particular instances at the present time, the union also has on its agenda wage action which looks to further gains. Among the advances which it seeks are the following:

1. Complete elimination of piece work. The wage incentive should not be used to extract extra energies from workers over and above a fair day's work. Moreover, under an incentive or piece-work system, somehow the pay check never adds up to what the worker has anticipated.

2. Corporation-wide wage agreements, with rates for classifications the same in all plants of the company regardless of geographical location. Along with this, union participation in the initial setting of rates.

3. At a later date, uniformity of wage rates throughout the industry. Business competition must not proceed on the basis of wage inequalities, but "must be founded upon the relative efficiency of management techniques, productive skills, technological improvements and the resulting superiority of the product."[4]

4. The guaranteed annual wage.

Hours. Although the Fair Labor Standards Act has removed many of the questions concerning hours of work from the bargaining table, the union still exercises an important voice in the discretionary area still remaining—which includes, of course, any provision obtained through negotiation for a shorter work week than that specified in the Act. (Thus as part of its long-range program the union has announced the goal of a 30-hour week.)

In most contracts the union and management have joined in establishing some definition of the work week. This may range from the more binding clause specifying

[4] From Walter P. Reuther, *Our Fear of Abundance*, p. 6, reprinted by the UAW-CIO from the *New York Times Magazine*, September 16, 1945.

that "Regular manufacturing operations shall be confined to five (5) consecutive eight-hour days, Monday to Friday inclusive, except for continuous operations" to a provision which simply states that "The employe's working week shall be a calendar week beginning on Monday at the regular starting time of the shift to which he is assigned." No contract with a major company limits the amount of time which an employe may spend on the job, providing instead for penalty payments of time-and-a-half or double time for work exceeding eight hours in one day or 40 hours in one week, the amount of the penalty payment depending upon the circumstances under which the additional time is worked.

In the case of continuous or seven-day operations, the company may schedule days off for the employe other than those regularly scheduled for the work force as a whole. The employe may thus be required to work Saturday or Sunday, taking other days off in the middle of the week in their stead. Since Saturday or Sunday work must be compensated at overtime rates except on continuous operations, the union seeks to restrict the number of operations designated as continuous. Questions of this nature may be threshed out in the grievance procedure and may be finally passed upon by the umpire, if necessary. Thus in one case the umpire ruled:

It must be concluded, therefore, that since there appears to be no regular need for seven days of work by any one of the shifts involved in the East Boat Dock operations, Sunday must be regarded as the employee's day of rest, and the Company is not entitled to a schedule setting a day of rest other than Sunday. If the employees are called to work on Sunday, they may not without their consent be given a day off during the week in order to avoid premium pay for the seventh day.

The established shift hours have been fixed largely by custom, but at least one major contract provides that "any change in the established shift hours or lunch period shall be first discussed with the Shop Committee as far in advance as possible of any such change."

Equalization of hours is a principle which has become widely established in one form or another. One application of this principle has already been noted in the provision for the part-timing of seniority employes down to 32 hours before a reduction in force is undertaken. Extra work in periods of part-time operation may likewise be equalized among employes engaged in similar work. In addition, all the important agreements have some form of the following provision found in one of them:

When, in the judgment of Management, overtime is required for a given Department, the regular employees assigned to the Department will work such overtime periods. All reasonable means will be employed to equalize overtime among shifts. When, in the judgment of Management, overtime is necessary for employees on a given classification within a Department, the employees regularly performing the operations involved shall work such overtime periods. Where such overtime is of a continuing nature, Management, insofar as is practicable, will rotate such overtime among qualified employees within the Department.

A further question in this area of management is involved in the definition of what constitutes hours of work for purposes of pay. As previously remarked under wages, the principle has been established that employes reporting for duty without prior notification that no work is available are entitled to "call-in time" of two or three hours, depending on the agreement, which are to be considered as hours worked for purposes of pay. It is also generally established that chief stewards or shop committeemen engaged in handling grievances are to be paid for time so spent, as hours worked. Rest periods of ten to fifteen minutes are compensated for. Time lost in effecting repairs, or in checking tools out and in at the beginning and end of the shift are considered at time worked. More troublesome has been the question of "wash-up time" on jobs especially dirty. An allowance of five to ten minutes has become the practice in some shops, though unofficially and sometimes against the wishes of higher management.

Employe Advancement Policies. The union has won the right to participate in the determination of vacation policy in all the major companies. Provisions vary considerably, but the union's interest commonly extends to questions of the duration of vacations, eligibility standards, payment, and timing. The major contracts make no provisions for payment for legal holidays not worked. In event work is required, however, a penalty payment of double time is specified. A company spokesman voices his belief that the time is not far off when holidays will be paid nonworking days. "It's been granted in the East and it's been granted on the West Coast. We feel it closing in on us. One of these days we'll have paid holidays."

None of the principal contracts in the industry makes any provision for jointly determined or administered retirement benefit plans. The question of retirement benefits was brought to the fore in 1946 when one of the Big Three companies dismissed certain employes because they had passed the age of 65. While the union secured the temporary rescinding of this action, it recognizes the need for substituting young men for superannuated employes. To meet this need it is proposing, as a contract term, the provision of "adequate retirement pensions." It intends, as well, to secure the "establishment of social security plans, financed by employers and providing life insurance, sickness and accident benefits, supplementary unemployment insurance."[5]

Promotions. Automobile contracts commonly specify that management is free to promote employes to higher-paid jobs on the basis of merit and ability, but where these two factors are equal the employe with the greatest seniority shall be given preference. The union is empowered to protest decisions, on the ground of unfair discrimination, through the grievance procedure. This type of provision would seem to satisfy management's desire for discretionary authority in selecting workers for advancement. As a matter of fact, however, some management officials assert that the clause does not operate as intended. In the words of one industrial relations director: "The union is constantly pressing for more consideration for seniority. The infrequency of union grievances on this score is misleading. Actually, operating management gives in to union pressure many times, because of the difficulty of proving greater ability and in order to avoid a fight with the union. I'm convinced that in many of our promotions seniority gets more consideration than either merit or ability—the clause in the contract notwithstanding."

Even without such unofficial pressure to recognize the seniority principle, management is far from free to promote as it wills. Its judgment as to whether a man is abler or possesses more merit than another may be called into question through the grievance procedure and taken to the umpire for final disposition. Significant in this respect is one decision in which the umpire stated:

Some members of Management or supervision seem to think that it is sufficient for them to form and assert strongly the belief that one employee is superior to another. That is clearly not enough. They must be able to support this belief with specific, concrete reasons. [The contract] expressly declares that disputes as to merit and ability are subject to the grievance procedure. The several agencies of the grievance procedure, including the Umpire, are thereby given a positive task to perform. The provision is not an empty formalism; and the agencies of the grievance procedure,

[5] Walter P. Reuther, *A Program for UAW-CIO Members*, p. 7.

including the Umpire, are not expected merely to rubber stamp the assertions of one side or the other, or to make decisions merely on the basis of the strength or positiveness of the assertions. To perform their tasks they must be given adequate basis for judgment. A supervisor's testimony that he honestly believes one employee to be superior to another with respect to the promotion is certainly a factor to be considered. It is not, however, either conclusive or sufficient. The supervisor must be prepared to state the basis of his belief and to support it, not by repeated assertion, but by specific and understandable evidence—evidence which relates to capacity for the job in question, not merely to the employee's general character. I am speaking, of course, only of promotions to jobs within the jurisdiction of the Union.

Union officials make no secret of their desire to obtain greater recognition for seniority in advancements. They have listened to management's argument that straight seniority lessens incentive. "The younger workers don't have any incentive to work harder because they know that advancement will go to the older men. And the older men don't have any incentive because they know that promotions will come to them anyway." To some degree union men have recognized the validity of this criticism. At the same time, they will reply that there is no other satisfactory method of eliminating favoritism from promotions or of preventing discrimination because of union activity.

The union has officially shown no interest in the promotion of employes out of the bargaining unit, though occasionally wildcat strikes have broken out in protest over the appointment as foreman of a man personally objectionable to the workers.

Health and Safety. The typical contract provision in this area specifies that "The Company shall continue to make reasonable provisions for the safety and health of its employees during the hours of their employment. The Company shall provide protective devices and other equipment necessary to protect the employees from injury and sickness." Recommendations or complaints under a provision such as this are funneled through the grievance procedure. In some companies the union is also accorded equal representation on a safety and sanitation committee.

It is probably true that the union is dissatisfied with its share of authority in this sphere, and occasional concerted group protests over safety or health conditions have been staged. Under a clause such as that cited, says one union official, "the company feels it has sole authority to set up all provisions for health and safety, including medical examinations, choice of doctors, determination of when and where ventilation will be installed, and so on. The union wants a voice in those matters. We raise grievances, but the company takes its time in complying with any agreement they make. We try to be responsible and live up to the contract in protesting conditions, but sometimes the company puts us in a position where we can't order the men in to work under conditions where we wouldn't work ourselves. In a paint department, where materials were being baked in ovens, the members said to us, 'O.K., if you tell us to go back in that oven, at 117 degrees, with no ventilation and no drinking fountains, we'll go back. But we don't think you'll tell us to.' How do you think we feel?"

PROCUREMENT OF MATERIALS AND PARTS

The union has shown little interest in this category. Insistence on working with union-made parts has seldom arisen as an issue since the union has effectively organized such a large portion of the industry. An occasional contract may contain a provision like the following: "The Company shall continue to use its best efforts to keep the production of work parts, tools, dies, fixtures, and maintenance in the Plant, insofar as practical and efficient to do so. When necessary to deviate from this practice the Union shall be informed of the reason before work is sent out."

PRODUCTION

In this category the union has concerned itself only with those areas of management here discussed.

Job Content. In general it may be said that the basic job content (though not the specific operations of a job) is set forth in the job classifications on which wage rates are based, and in the determination of which the union frequently participates. Despite this procedure the question continues to arise as to whether an employe may properly be required to perform certain operations as part of his job.[6] This question is one in which the international union has not been involved, except insofar as its representatives are called into some stage of the grievance procedure. The issue is primarily raised in one of two ways: either as a direct grievance, in which additional pay is sought for the performance of operations not considered a part of the job; or as a secondary grievance involving a protest over disciplinary action taken against an employe or group of employes refusing to perform what management construes as part of their job.

The former type of dispute generally arises as a request for reclassification, a matter previously discussed in the section under wages. Disputes of the second type may be illustrated by an arbitration case in which it was related that a group of five men, employed as checkers of a given classification, told the foreman through their spokesman "that they would not check shipping releases; that they would not put up, count out or check materials for shipment; that they would not show material handlers what material to be put up or counted out; and that they would not show material handlers what material to load on the trailers." When the men continued to refuse to perform these operations, as not properly part of their jobs, the leader was discharged. The discharge was protested through the grievance procedure. Disciplinary action was ruled justified, but the penalty reduced.

In other cases a union official, such as chief steward, may instruct the men that certain operations are not properly part of their jobs and countermand, either explicitly or impliedly, a foreman's orders requiring those operations. Thus in one grievance a chief steward was penalized for allegedly advising two employes not to change cutters on their machines, since that was not part of their responsibility. In the words of the foreman, as reported, "I then turned to [the chief steward] and told him that he wasn't the boss and had no right to tell any employee what to do. He said he didn't exactly tell them what to do—he remarked to them that 'if he was running the machine he wouldn't do it'—this he repeated to me at this time. I then told him to go back to work. He said 'that ain't bargaining.' " A penalty of three days suspension was then imposed, protested, but upheld by the impartial chairman.

Management in the industry expresses concern that the plaguing problems of jurisdictional lines which have developed *between* the older craft unions may loom just as important *within* the newer industrial unions. The problem is essentially a different one, however. It is rooted in wage consciousness rather than job consciousness. With the multiplicity of job classifications, each with its own rate, workers are eager to call attention to some operation they are performing which may provide grounds for reclassifica-

---

[6] One company has attempted to clarify the situation by having the following clause inserted in its contract: "In order that there will be no misinterpretation of what is considered an employee's regular job the following distinction is made. It consists of all parts regularly assigned to the employee's machine or group of machines, bench, or assembly station, *or work group.* In addition, it is the prerogative of Management to route new parts, with or without piece-work prices, over such machines as the dictates of proper load distribution require. All new parts, originating from new or changed engineering specifications, routed to the employee's station, therefore, are to be considered part of his regular assignment."

tion to a higher rate. The grievance procedure is one way of calling attention; refusal to perform the singled-out operation unless paid a higher rate is another.

In one other way has the union displayed an interest in job content. It has sought to limit supervisory employes from performing production functions, with the obvious intent of preserving such work for its own members. It has secured this objective through contract clauses limiting the job content of management representatives, as in the typical provision: "Supervisory employes shall not be permitted to perform work on any hourly-rated job except in the following types of situations: (1) in emergencies, when regular employes are not immediately available; (2) in the instruction or training of employes; and (3) in the performance of necessary work when production difficulties are encountered on a job."

Methods of Operation. At times minor union officials, or rank-and-file members, have attempted to share in the determination of methods of production—as for example by an insistence on working with a multiple instead of a single drill press, or an objection to a foreman's instructing welders as to what flame should be used in their torch. Again it may fairly be said that the union has officially shown no express desire to share authority in this field, except insofar as it has upheld, in the grievance procedure, members or representatives who have contested managerial authority.

Rates of Operation. Contracts commonly provide that rates of operation, or production standards, "shall be established on the basis of fairness and equity consistent with the quality of workmanship, efficiency of operations, and the reasonable working capacities of normal operators." Management remains responsible for the initial determination of standards, or for changes as a result of new production techniques, but any complaint by the union or its members must be entertained. Upon such complaint, the union is entitled to complete information as to how the standard was set. If dissatisfied with this explanation, the union may appeal through the grievance procedure, with the umpire or impartial chairman empowered to deliver a final ruling. The latter's power, however, is limited to a decision as to whether the production rates established are justified in accordance with the "fairness and equity" clause of the contract; he has no authority to determine what the rate shall be.

The time-study method is widely used as the basis for management's determination of operating rates. Union objections are generally directed to inadequacies of a particular time-study. Thus it may argue, as it has, that "sufficient time was not taken to make a proper and complete time study," or that "the proper consideration has not been given to the time requirements of beginning the operation, of selecting, fitting, loading and unloading the arbors, and of performing miscellaneous operations such as roll and checking the run-out." Decisions as to whether the union's criticisms are well-founded are often extremely difficult to make, requiring a technical knowledge not often possessed by the arbitrator. Recognizing this limitation, one impartial chairman, upon the presentation of such a grievance, secured the consent of both parties to have an independent time-study made by an engineering firm on whose judgment, experience, and honesty both would rely. Although the decision in this case went against the union, it is interesting to note that the union regards this procedure as establishing a precedent, despite the impartial chairman's clear statement that it was not to be so understood.

The methods of establishing speeds of operation outlined in the contracts and developed by the umpires have failed to resolve all disputes. Indeed, it may be said quite accurately that the question of operating rates is one of the thorniest issues separating the union and company managements today. Union officials make no secret of the fact that the union has lowered production rates, but express surprise that this should evoke criticism. "One of the purposes for which we organized our union was to slow down the assembly lines to a pace that was in keeping with the way a human being ought to work."[7] In the words of one top union official: "A fair day's work is a hard thing to measure, sometimes. I mean, I don't want any of our people standing around, I want them to work steady, but I don't want them to be like race horses, either."[8]

Managements on the other hand deny that standards are set so high as to overtax the worker. Quite the contrary, there is widespread if not universal belief in their ranks that the union has now arbitrarily lowered production rates to the point where workers must consciously hold back or kill time so as not to exceed them. This, they say, is true regardless of whether pay is on an hourly basis or by the piece. The statement by an official of one company that "employes limit their daily production, reach a certain maximum and then loaf the rest of the day" is affirmed in other quarters.

To charges such as this the union has two answers. One is a proposal that the union be given a voice in the initial determination or redetermination of standards, rather than a protest through the grievance procedure. The workers will live up to standards jointly agreed upon, it claims. This proposal was raised at least as early as 1936 and was one of the issues in the protracted Chrysler strike of 1939. Management's answer given in those days is the answer still given today: "When shop stewards handle the throttle of production you have surrendered the plant." The other union proposal is the guaranteed annual wage, which, it says, will eliminate the worker's fear that he is hastening his own unemployment when he exerts himself on the job.

Standards of Quality. Like methods of operation, this is an area in which the union has shown no official interest. Any challenge to managerial authority has come in isolated instances, as in the case of an assistant steward disciplined for refusal to obey orders and for encouraging a slowdown. In his defense brief he stated on his own behalf that "this case is predicated upon the fact that [the assistant steward] had, on numerous occasions during his employment with the company, been in arguments with supervision to pass bad workmanship, and [the assistant steward] will introduce evidence showing that this is not the type of inspection that the standards of aircraft and the machine standards call for during the war period."

One of the major companies has claimed that occasionally a union committeeman will lower rates of operation by telling the workers not to produce so much and to pay more attention to quality, that the union cannot afford a reputation for poor workmanship even if this means less production. A top union official says that if such situations are accurately represented by the company the men involved are violating the contract, as standards of quality remain within the company's purview and not that of the union.

DISTRIBUTION

The union has not sought in any significant way to secure a voice in this category. The only area in which it has displayed any concern is in the encouragement of a market to receive the desired output. Officials have expressed interest in increasing output and sales in what are now "off seasons" by decreasing quantities produced and sold during present peak seasons; flexible pricing has been suggested as one means of accomplishing this objective. It may safely be said, however, that no important foothold has been obtained by the union in matters of distribution, nor has any union program in this field received careful definition or emphasis.

[7] Statement of Walter Reuther, UAW president, in *Investigation of the National Defense Program*, part 28, p. 13179.
[8] Statement of R. J. Thomas, then UAW president, now first vice president, in *Investigation of Concentration of Economic Power*, Hearings before the Temporary National Economic Committee, U.S. Congress (1940), part 30, p. 16377.

COORDINATE ACTIVITIES

Line of Products. No sustained concern with this area has been shown by the union. During the reconversion period Walter Reuther, later UAW president, made proposals for the utilization of unneeded automobile plants in the manufacture of prefabricated housing and lightweight railroad rolling stock. His proposals received no serious consideration by management, however, and were not pressed as demands.

Company Organization. Most management officials regard the unionization of foremen as a direct threat to organizational structure of the company. As yet the UAW has explicitly disavowed any interest in enrolling foremen as members. This statement of intent has not been accepted at full value by management, however. "Conditions may change," says one official, "the area is a dynamic one. The UAW may someday find itself in the position of having to organize foremen to prevent some other national organization from coming in and organizing them." Certain union representatives admit they have not closed the door to this possibility. If foremen, who rule on grievances in the first step of the procedure, are themselves represented by the union bringing the grievance, the present grievance procedure will break down and probably will have to be discarded, company officials believe. This result, if it comes, will necessarily have a profound effect upon the status and position of the foreman in the company organization. What the outcome may be management will not now even predict.

Some management representatives believe that the union has affected company organization, again with respect to the foreman, in still another way. Thus one says: "The union circumvents the foreman by appealing decisions over his head. This robs him of any real authority he may have. He can't make his decisions stick any more. The upshot is that in some companies the shop steward has more authority than the foreman." In support of this statement he referred to the Detroit hearings before the special senate committee investigating the national defense program.[9] The official quoted above viewed the consequence as a breakdown of company organization. It may as logically be viewed as an attempt to modify the organizational structure in such a way that the distribution of authority follows new lines.

Nor is it difficult to find evidence of the troubled state of company organization in its lower frames. Grievances have been appealed to impartial chairmen in which the employes and union committeemen have admitted to intimidating supervisory officials. "The men thus admit that X [a job foreman] was at least intimidated into leaving the building by the threats of the workers and that the committeemen did accompany him down the aisles, down the stairs, to the street floor, and to the outside door." In other cases, union officials in the shop have overruled the orders of supervisors. "X admits that he directed the employes to work as they had worked in the past, that is, not to use the new forms."

In one further significant way has the company's organizational structure been modified. The importance of the function of the office of impartial chairman or umpire has been apparent in the previous discussion. This function consists primarily in ruling whether there has been executive compliance with administrative or directive agreements, or administrative compliance with joint directive decisions. In the establishment of an agency independent of both management and union, yet integrated into the company's structure, a significant change in corporate organization has been accomplished. The umpire becomes an official of the company as certainly as is the corporate president. This development has been a direct result of the growth of collective bargaining.

[9] Part 28; testimony of Packard officials beginning at page 13284 is especially pertinent.

Prices of Products. The UAW's interest in prices has become generally known as a result of the General Motors 1945–1946 negotiations and strike, in which price policy played an important part. The demand for a wage increase without an accompanying increase in the price of General Motors products was based on the argument that "Wage policy for the nation requires that reconversion wage adjustment be absorbed (except in isolated cases) out of industry's existing price levels." [10] The threat of inflation was emphasized as requiring such a policy in the public interest. The so-called National Citizens Committee which the union assembled to weigh its case reported:

> From the record it is clear that the Union in its refusal to accept a wage increase that involves price increase has lifted the whole matter of collective bargaining to a new high level by insisting that the advancement of Labor's interest shall not be made at the expense of the public. The union has shown a sense of social responsibility that indicates its growing maturity and is certainly to be commended.[11]

When the union failed to win the agreement of General Motors not to increase product prices, and price increases were granted to the automobile manufacturers on the ground of increased wage costs, the union sought to contest the price allowances in the federal courts.

While the price issue was raised in other major automobile negotiations than those with General Motors, reports of management officials were to the effect that the heart of the union bargainers was not it. In the words of one official: "When the company started talking price, the union men waved it aside, indicating they felt that was up to management. Some of us asked specifically if they would raise no objections to price increases by the company. They replied, 'Well, the union policy is that you're not supposed to do it.' But they showed no real concern and never made it an issue."

A desire to influence the price of the products which they make is largely limited to those who follow the leadership of the incumbent president and grows out of a conception of broad economic objectives. It is thus not confined to price policy in a period of inflation. "We have said that wages and prices and ability to pay must have a relationship if we are to achieve a full production, full employment, full consumption economy."[12]

Mr. Reuther has also shown an active interest in the use of pricing policy to eliminate or soften seasonal fluctuation in production. He has advocated a sliding price plan under which cars would sell at the highest price during the peak period and at the lowest price during the low production period. "We have already suggested to individual manufacturers that they establish a sliding scale of prices in an effort to level off the peaks and valleys of their sales curve. . . ."[13] This proposal has, however, met with the opposition of the other three top union officials, who fear that it "must inevitably lead to correlated proposals to reduce wages as prices are cut."[14]

Collective Bargaining. The union of course shares authority with management in the determination of the bargaining procedures to be employed. Little effort has been made to formalize the procedure of renegotiating the contracts except to provide for notification of a desire to reopen the contract within a specified period prior to its expiration,

[10] *Purchasing Power for Prosperity,* UAW-CIO (1945), p. 9.

[11] *Report of National Citizens Committee,* UAW, p. 10.

[12] Statement before the General Motors Fact-Finding Board appointed by President Truman, *New York Times,* December 29, 1945.

[13] Walter P. Reuther, *The Challenge of Peace,* UAW, p. 16, reprinted from *International Postwar Problems,* April, 1945.

[14] *New York Times,* April 19, 1946.

frequently 60 days, and for a reply by the other party within a specified time, for example, ten days. The grievance procedure is spelled out in detail, however. No point will be served by examining that procedure except, perhaps, to take notice that impartial chairmen or umpires are provided for in all of the Big Three companies, and are empowered to rule on virtually all disputes arising under the contract.

Union Penetration of Managerial Areas: Steel

The United States Steel Corporation and those major independent producers customarily grouped as "little steel" provide the focus of our attention in this industry. Although a number of unions engage in collective bargaining with these businesses, as indeed with virtually all major corporations, we shall confine our attention to the major union involved, the United Steelworkers of America.

The principal contracts in the steel industry contain management clauses of the same type that is found in the automobile industry. A typical clause is the following:

The management of the works and the direction of the working forces, including the right to hire, suspend, or discharge for proper cause, or transfer, and the right to relieve employees from duty because of lack of work or for other legitimate reasons, is vested exclusively in the Company, provided that this will not be used for purposes of discrimination against any member of the Union.

As previously pointed out, clauses of this nature are valid only for the duration of the contract and are subject to the limitations otherwise provided for in the contract. It is interesting to note that while the above clause, taken from the 1946 Carnegie-Illinois agreement, is identical with that appearing in much earlier agreements, the content has ceased to be the same. For "the management of the works and the direction of the working forces" have been subjected to increasing limitations due to other provisions obtained by the union in collective bargaining, as well as through contract interpretations arising from grievance proceedings. Such management clauses are in effect a statement that management reserves complete authority in all areas where it has not agreed to share authority with the union.

FINANCE

The union now has no voice in this category. It has, however, shown interest. Officials have stated that when collective bargaining becomes established on an industry-wide basis, a goal toward which the union is working, it will be concerned with the share of the business income which is distributed to the owners. The president of the union, Philip Murray, has officially suggested that the business policy be adopted of setting aside earmarked reserves for the purpose of compensating workers displaced by technological developments.

PERSONNEL

Type of Personnel. Apprenticeship programs to promote the professional competency of new employes and employes seeking advancement to higher-rated positions have been established jointly by the union and management in some companies. The union has defined matters of interest to it in such programs as "selection, a progressive schedule of wages, job training, periodic examinations, ratios [of apprentices to journeymen], classroom instruction and adjustment of complaints," and a system of administration and supervision.[1]

Size of Force. The Steelworkers have interested themselves in the size of the work force in several ways.

They have in a number of instances made specific requests, via the grievance procedure, for the addition of a worker to a crew which they considered undermanned. A typical case requests the addition of a "spell-hand" (relief man) to relieve and assist cranemen in specified mill pits during the winter months. The arguments advanced are that the cranemen must otherwise undertake work which they should not be required to perform in addition to their normal work, that the lack of an additional helper makes for inefficient operations, that there have been changes in health and sanitary conditions justifying the additional help.[2]

The union has shared authority in determining the over-all size of the work force by securing an agreement, in some companies, to a sharing of work down to three days before a reduction in force is undertaken. The size of the force is thus maintained while the number of manhours is reduced.

The Steelworkers have been deeply interested in the question of technological unemployment, a condition which has affected large numbers of their people in past years. While agreements have been reached in specific instances under which displaced workers have been carried on the payroll until they could be absorbed elsewhere in the plant, the union has not yet obtained general acceptance of its proposed policy that "Those workers for whom there are no openings when they are finally displaced should be employed in some capacity until regular jobs open up for them. The wages paid to those workers until they are placed on regular jobs should be charged to the original cost of the technological improvement."[3]

Hiring. The contracts generally specify that new employes will be regarded as probationary for the first 260 hours of actual work. In rehiring after layoffs, employes return to work on the basis of ability to perform the required work and physical fitness, and where these are equal the length of continuous service is the governing factor. A few contracts specify in addition that if all three of these factors are relatively equal, local management and the union grievance committee may agree "that the factor of family status, namely, the number, age and physical condition of dependents of such Employees, shall be given consideration."

Layoffs. The provisions governing layoffs are the same as those governing rehiring: The following factors as listed below shall be considered; however, only where both factors "a" and "b" are relatively equal shall continuous service be the determining factor:

---

[1] *Industrial Training*, a Steelworker Union Handbook (undated), p. 6.

[2] In one instance where such a request was granted and the company later sought to eliminate the added job as unnecessary, an arbitration board ruled that the company could not tender its general managerial rights as proper authority for elimination of a job which had been instituted in settlement of a grievance. The grievance settlement was said to take on the nature of a supplemental agreement between the two parties. "This is not to say that a job so established must be continued forever. In case there should be proper reason in the opinion of either Party it is possible to seek an adjustment. Such an adjustment might conceivably, under the Contract, be accomplished through a new Agreement between the parties, a new Grievance, or by the job being discontinued with the right of the Union to bring a Grievance claiming that the alleged reasons for discontinuance were improper. In this last case it would then be the responsibility of the Management to show specifically that the reasons are proper."

[3] *Investigation of Concentration of Economic Power*, part 30, p. 16507. *Technological Unemployment*, Steelworkers Union Handbook (undated), pp. 38 and 39, contains amplification of this proposal.

a. Ability to perform the work;
b. Physical fitness;
c. Continuous service.

This clause would suggest that the factor of continuous service, or to use the more common term—seniority—on which the union would prefer to place greatest stress, had been pretty well buried. Actually, arbitration decisions in grievance cases have often made seniority the deciding factor. This has come about due to an insistence by the union, sustained by arbitration boards, that ability and physical fitness must have some objective measurement if they are to be given weight. It is worth citing from a case turning on this issue.

The contention of the Company in the present grievance is that Management retained certain employees with less continuous service because these employees had more than relatively equal ability to perform the work. At the arbitration hearing this Board sought to make a determination of the relative abilities of the aggrieved employees by comparing the three employees . . . with the greatest continuous service who were let go with the five employees with the least continuous service who were retained. The judgment that the latter five employees had greater ability than the other three was found to be solely the opinion of the immediate supervisor. This opinion was not based on any objective data such as records of production or amount of incentive earnings. Instead, it rested solely on a belief that the work being performed by the five employees was more arduous than the work of the three older men and also upon an alleged greater versatility of the five employees.

This Board finds that the harder work allegedly being performed by the five employees with the least continuous service does not demonstrate in any way a greater ability on the part of these employees. Each of the eight employees being compared was working on a special type of equipment. Each is acknowledged to have been doing satisfactory work. Because the work required by certain of the machines may have been more arduous than that required by others clearly does not establish the possession of a greater ability on the part of those employees performing the work. It is admitted that the three employees with the greater continuous service could have learned to perform the work of the other five employees quickly—probably more quickly than the five employees could have learned to do the work of the three employees. Since the seniority setup is based on departmental seniority and not on job seniority, mere occupancy of the job does not establish a prior claim to that job. The contention of the Company, consequently, is narrowed down to the judgment of the supervisor that the five employees had a greater ability to perform the work because of an alleged greater versatility. Inquiry discloses that the supervisor thought of greater versatility in terms of a "greater readiness to do the work." The Company has submitted nothing to give support even to this narrow contention in the case of the five employees with the lesser continuous service who were retained. It is evident that this was merely a subjective opinion of the supervisor.

On the basis of this reasoning, the board ordered a payment of back wages for the period of layoff to the aggrieved workers.

The provision for part-timing of seniority employes before a general layoff, appearing in some contracts, has already been mentioned.

The union is now seeking a voice in certain more controversial matters relating to layoffs, one old and one new. Of long standing is its claim that technological advancements should not be made the basis for dismissals, but that workers so displaced should be reabsorbed in the course of the company's regular labor turnover. More recently in one of the "little steel" companies it has challenged management's authority to retire men at age 65. It wishes to make retirement a selective matter, allowing each case to be heard through the grievance procedure where the worker prefers to continue at his job. The company, on the other hand, maintains that such selective retirement is unworkable and that insistence on it transcends the union's functions.

Allocation. In general, management's right to allocate and transfer workers, as set forth in the general management clause, has not been subject to any important limitations. Grievance cases have arisen on this issue, however, in which workers have contested the authority of the foreman to assign them to some work in addition to their normal job, or require them to perform another job rather than remain idle because of temporary mechanical breakdown or material shortage. Management customarily maintains that it has complete authority in this field. In the words of the assistant industrial relations director at one of the large plants: "Our legal staff has even gone so far as to say that management can require a production worker to clean spittoons if it wishes. This is pushing the right too far, however. Sometimes a right stretched too far ceases to be a right, and we don't intend to take chances on losing this one by a stupid use of it." Other union grievances have protested the removal of a worker from one shift to another, but have failed to receive support from the arbitration boards.

Discipline. The major contracts commonly provide for a formal procedure to be followed by management *prior* to disciplinary action which may result in suspension or discharge. The union may observe but does not participate in this procedure to which management has contractually agreed. In all cases where it is believed that an employe's conduct may justify suspension or discharge, the employe is first suspended or provisionally discharged. This initial suspension lasts for no more than five days, during which time the employe may, if he wishes, request a hearing and a statement of his alleged offense before his department head, the general superintendent, or the plant manager, with or without the presence of his union committeeman, as he chooses. After this hearing or in the event a hearing is not requested, management may then conclude whether the suspension should be converted into a discharge, or whether the suspension should be revoked. In the latter case the employe receives payment for time lost while suspended. If the suspension is upheld, extended, or converted into a discharge, the employe is then at liberty to protest such disciplinary action through the usual grievance procedure. At this time the union enters the picture as a participant to present the employe's point of view.

The union has taken the position that management, in the person of the foreman, "must be able to give valid and almost statistical proof of cause before he fires a man," and recognizes that "to the traditional foreman" such a requirement "seems like an insufferable invasion of his rights, if not a death blow to his executive standing. And many of the higher executives still misunderstand and resist this compulsion of satisfactory collective dealings."[4]

The Steelworkers are able effectively to insist on such a rigid policy with respect to discharges because arbitration boards are empowered to pass on "just cause" for discipline. This means that it is the impartial chairman of the arbitration board *and not management* who must ultimately be convinced that disciplinary penalties are merited. The same objective evidence that we saw was required to demonstrate greater ability in cases of layoff must be offered to support any discipline imposed.

Illustrative of this requirement of evidence to support penalties for infraction of working rules is a case where a millwright in a blast furnace maintenance department was given a six-day suspension for allegedly refusing to repair the springs of a "larry car." The board, on hearing, found that the foreman's instructions to the employe were not

[4] *Production Problems,* Steelworkers Union Handbook (undated), p. 23.

clear and therefore could not be used to sustain the charge. "Since it has not been reasonably established that the aggrieved employee was insubordinate nor that he used profane or abusive language toward the foreman, this Board allows the grievance request." (The request was for the removal of the charge from the employe's record and the payment of wages lost for the period of suspension.)

In a somewhat similar case, involving the discharge of five employes for alleged leadership in an illegal work stoppage, the terminal grievance decision stated in part: "The Umpire feels that justice as well as sound labor relations calls for a degree of proof that is correlative with the high degree of the severity of the charge and penalty imposed. The burden of proof must, of course, be placed upon the Company, proof that the complainants are, beyond a reasonable doubt, guilty of violating [the contract]." Finding the evidence insufficient, the umpire rescinded the managerial discipline.

Determination of "just cause" involves not only establishing whether evidence exists to support the charge, however. It likewise involves judgment of whether the circumstances adduced justify the disciplinary action taken. Thus in a case where an employe had been a participant in an altercation with another worker but was found not to have provoked the argument which led to a blow struck by the second worker, the board found that a suspension penalty was unwarranted, although a reprimand was in order.

The union's sharing of managerial authority in matters of discipline has raised at least two important problems in the steel industry. One involves the question of whether the union should exercise greater discrimination in determining if an employe has a legitimate grievance. The other is set forth in the assertion encountered in some quarters of management that the union seeks to use its power over disciplinary actions to contest managerial authority generally.

In two grievance cases coming to arbitration the union took the position that men fired for illegal striking should not have been so disciplined because the company had not established that they were the ringleaders in the unauthorized action. In another case the union argued against the discharge of a group of men, ringleaders of an unauthorized walkout, on the ground that all who were involved had not similarly been penalized and that the discharge was therefore discriminatory. The shifting position of the union in these instances raises the question whether the union seeks simply to obtain justice in the application of discipline to the workers, or whether it is out to shield them from *any* discipline imposed by management. It should be made instantly clear that no judgment is implied in this question. The fact is that the union's responsibility in such cases has not adequately been established. It is not yet generally agreed whether the union is obligated to exercise its discretion in the grievances it presents, or whether it has an obligation to act as attorney for any worker-client who may seek its services. This question is discussed in Chapter 12. It is mentioned here only to indicate that such uncertainty in this area has led to misunderstandings between union and management which have only heightened the latter's feeling that its authority is being sharply challenged.

The second problem, involved in the charge by some management people that the union has challenged managerial authority generally by challenging its disciplinary power, is akin to that encountered in the automobile industry. It involves the use or threat of wildcat strike in the event of disciplinary action which the workers find objectionable. If the union contests management's authority to discipline in such a fashion, say these critics, management has lost the power to run its plants. At the same time it is fair to observe that general managerial criticism of this nature is not found in the steel industry as it is in automobiles. In one of the largest steel plants in the world, the industrial relations director and his assistant agreed that while it was true that fear of direct worker action or of challenge via the grievance procedure has restrained some foremen from properly enforcing the contract and from disciplining offending workers, this was not a serious problem.

One further question respecting discipline has been raised in this industry but has not as yet become widespread in its impact. In one important instance where a company promulgated an Employe's Manual setting forth rules of conduct for the employes with penalties attaching to their infraction, the union charged that the company owed to it the obligation of bargaining with respect to those rules prior to their publication. The company refused to bargain, but agreed to submit the question to arbitration, which was done. At the same time the union brought charges of an unfair labor practice before the National Labor Relations Board. While the Board refused to uphold the charge on the ground that the union had sought redress by other means, it expressly noted that insofar as management's exercise of its right to frame rules of conduct touched its day-to-day relationship with its employes the union had a right to be consulted.[5] With this construction of the Wagner Act the employes come into possession not only of a right to question disciplinary action—a right established under their collective-bargaining agreement—but an equally important right to participate in the determination of the rules under which they may be penalized before those rules may be promulgated.

Wages. The types of wage payments in effect in the steel industry include salary, and hourly, tonnage, incentive, or piece-work rates. The major contracts provide that rates in effect as of the date of the agreement shall remain in effect for its duration, except where changes are permitted by the rate-adjustment provisions of the agreement itself. The union has construed this provision as preventing the company from changing any existing method of payment. "This means that no incentive plan may be added to an hourly rated job or any existing form of incentive changed or any tonnage or piece-work rate changed to an hourly rate or to an hourly plus tonnage or incentive."[6] In at least one grievance proceeding it has secured the company's acquiescence in this interpretation, and employes who had been transferred from hourly rate to salary by the company were put back on hourly rate in settlement of the grievance raised by the union.

Because the contracts recognize that "changing conditions and circumstances may from time to time require the installation of new wage rates, adjustment of existing wage rates or modification of wage rate plans," provision has been made for a "rate establishment and adjustment" procedure.

When a new job is to be established, as a result of new manufacturing processes, new products, new departments, or new occupations, management retains the right to develop an appropriate hourly, tonnage, incentive, or piece-work rate. The proposed rate is explained to the union grievance committee, whose agreement is sought either on the establishment of that rate or on its installation for a trial period. With or without such agreement management is thereupon free to install the rate, but if it is installed without agreement it is subject to challenge through the grievance procedure at any time within 90 days.

---

[5] *Matter of Timken Roller Bearing Company,* NLRB Case No. 8–C–1815 of August, 1946. Although neither "big steel" nor "little steel" was involved in this case, the company, a steel fabricator, is one of that group of large corporations with which our study is generally concerned.

[6] *Guide for Interpretation of 1945 Agreement,* Steelworkers Union Handbook (1945), p. 7.

When changes are made in equipment, method of processing, material processed, or quality or production standards which would result in a substantial change in job duties, or where over a period of time a number of minor changes of this nature add up to a substantial change from the original job specifications, management may make appropriate adjustments of the former rate. Such adjusted rates are explained to the union representatives and their agreement is sought. To this end negotiations may be held, following the grievance procedure. If it develops in the course of such negotiations that additional study of the job is needed, the company will undertake the study, seeking the union's cooperation in conducting it. If no agreement between the parties is forthcoming despite these efforts, management has the choice either of instituting the rate it has developed, or of setting a temporary rate for a trial period. In the former case, the employe may contest the rate via the grievance procedure at any time within 90 days. If management elects the alternative of a trial period, the employe is guaranteed a minimum of his straight time average hourly earnings over the three months preceding the change in job content. After the expiration of the trial period, the employe may challenge the rate through the grievance machinery at any time within 30 days.

In the case of rate establishment for new jobs and rate adjustment on changed jobs, any increase in rate obtained in the grievance procedure is made retroactive in the manner agreed upon in the contract.

In contesting a rate set by management under its powers defined in the rate establishment and adjustment clause, the union may bring to bear one or both of two principal arguments. It may charge that a rate lowered through a rate adjustment was illegally changed because there had been no substantial change in job duties or requirements; or it may charge that the rate set was improper because it was not in line with other wage rates in the plant. Illustrative cases may be cited. In one the union presented both arguments to contest management's action in lowering a tonnage rate for checkers. Management had acted on the ground that interplant shipments were being made *without* weighing and checking and that the number of such shipments had substantially increased, altering the job content. The arbitration board found that management had acted within the scope of its authority, but that the new rate was out of line with other rates in the plant.

In another case, management adjusted a wage rate following the installation of new patenting furnaces. The union contended there had been no substantial change in job duties and that the adjusted rates were out of line. The arbitration board gave extensive consideration to the grievance. On the first point the Board found that the changes in job requirements were "substantial" and, "accordingly, give contractual justification to the installation of new rates." With respect to the second point, it said: "The incentive rates on the new furnaces are a product of (a) anticipated earnings and (b) production standards. The anticipated earnings represent the amount of incentive earnings which would be earned by the worker working at normal incentive pace. The production standards represent the amount of production expected in working at normal incentive pace. Both the anticipated earnings and the production standards which combine to determine the rates are protested by the Union." It thus became necessary to examine both of these elements. Standards, the board held, had been based on adequate time studies. They were thus found to be proper. As regards anticipated earnings, however, the board ruled that the incentive activity required to meet the new production standards had increased by a measurable percentage. Although this had been recognized by management, the board contested the arithmetical computations by which the percentage increase had been figured. Substituting its own method of calculation the board arrived at a different figure. It thereupon ordered an increase in the anticipated earnings rate from $0.98 to $1.005 per hour.

Even from this abbreviated discussion it becomes clear that independent managerial authority in the determination of occupational wage rates is confined to cases where new jobs are established or where the content of existing jobs is changed. And even in this limited area it retains no final authority. Such managerial decisions must be defended and justified before a board of arbitration in the selection of which the union participates, and which constitutes the ultimate authority in this field.

It is unnecessary to do more than mention certain general contract provisions relating to wages similar to those already discussed in the automobile industry. These include penalty payments for overtime; the payment of "allowed time" when workers report to their jobs without prior notification that no work is available, or begin work which lasts for less than four hours; the allowance of shift differentials and joint agreement on rules as to how such differentials shall be applied when overtime or incentive work is involved; and the requirement that women must receive the same pay as men for performing the same quality and type of work. All these matters have become subject to joint determination.

In two other areas the union has made important gains through the assistance of the War Labor Board. These are provisions for minimum daily wage guarantees and the elimination of so-called wage rate inequities.

The minimum daily wage guarantee simply provides that those employes who have an established occupational hourly rate are guaranteed that they will receive not less than that rate times the number of hours worked during the day. For those employes who have no occupational hourly rate, the guarantee consists of the common labor rate times the number of hours worked on any one day. Such a minimum daily guarantee is of advantage to those employes who are working on an incentive, tonnage, or piecework rate and whose earnings for the day either do not average the occupational hourly rate which in some cases may have been established for their job, or, in the absence of an occupational hourly rate, do not average the common labor rate.

The elimination of wage-rate inequities has developed into a program of wide ramifications. This program had its inception in a petition by the union to the War Labor Board for the approval of a principle stated as "equal pay for similar work throughout the industry." While denying the union's request as so stated, the Board directed that intraplant wage discrepancies should be eliminated, and the number of job classifications should be reduced. It set forth four principles to guide union and management in the negotiations which were ordered to accomplish this:

1. Describe simply and concisely the content of each job.
2. Place the jobs in their proper relationship.
3. Reduce the job classifications to the smallest practical number by grouping those jobs having substantially equivalent content.
4. Establish wage rates for the job classifications, taking into consideration the wage-rate relationships in comparable plants in the industry. Reduction of out-of-line rates should not affect the wages of present incumbents of the job, however.

This directive was incorporated into the major contracts in the industry, and the program has been underway since the early part of 1945. The working out of the program has taken place primarily in the Carnegie-Illinois Steel Corporation, to this date. The magnitude and significance of this task should not be underestimated. They can only be suggested here.

At the start, the joint committee selected approximately 142 jobs, several from each department, which were found most frequently throughout the plants of the company. This was done in the belief that this number of jobs, when properly classified, would serve as guideposts or bench marks to which practically all other jobs could be compared and placed in their proper relationship.

As the program has proceeded, the methods of its succeeding phases have been reduced to written agreements between the corporation and the union. The first agreement covered the procedures regarding review of classifications for production and maintenance jobs. Essentially, it consisted of a joint decision that twelve factors were to be considered in determining the relative worth of jobs. These were listed as preemployment training, employment training and skill, mental skill, manual skill, responsibility for materials, responsibility for tools and equipment, responsibility for operation, responsibility for safety of others, mental effort, physical effort, surroundings, and hazards. For each of these twelve basic factors a score sheet was developed, which established as many levels or categories of that factor as were considered to exist. Thus three categories or levels of preemployment training were concretely defined, nine levels of employment training and experience, six levels of mental skill, and so on. Each category or level is related to one or more of the bench-mark jobs. The lowest category of the factor is considered as base, and all higher levels are given a relative numerical classification.

Every job is subjected to this classification procedure, and scored on the basis of the twelve factors. The score of all factors is then totaled and rounded off to become the job class, on the basis of which jobs may be ranked in relative importance. All jobs of the same job class are to be given the same wage rate.

The second agreement between union and management arising from the wage-inequities program covered the description and classification of repair and maintenance men. The full content of this agreement, like the others of this program, cannot be suggested here. One of its major provisions, however, consisted in joint agreement that for certain defined journeyman jobs, known as "trade or craft jobs," job content should be supplemented with a measurement of the varying qualifications and abilities of the individual employes for purposes of eliminating wage inequities and establishing standard rates. It was thus agreed that for each job class for a trade or craft, developed according to the procedure outlined in the first agreement, three hourly wage rates would be established: (1) a "standard rate" equal to the plant standard hourly wage-scale rate for the respective job class of a job; (2) an "intermediate rate" at a level two job classes below the standard rate; and (3) a "starting rate" at a level four job classes below the standard rate. Precise guides for the advancement of a worker from the starting rate through the intermediate rate to the standard rate were laid down.

The significance of this agreement can be properly appreciated only when the policy which it establishes is compared with the practice of the past. Whereas only three wage rates will now be provided for the job of a machinist, in one plant the joint commission was reported to have found some 38 different rates in effect. Where previously there had been quotas set for the number of men in a given wage-job category, such quotas will now be eliminated so that a man's wage will be determined by the defined content of his job and an objective measurement of his ability. In the words of one union representative, "Under this program a worker won't have to wait for a dead man's shoes."

The third agreement in the program established the principles upon which plant standard hourly wage scales are to be set when the task of classification has been accomplished. Comparison between the standard hourly wage rate, as so set, of a nonincentive job and the existing hourly wage rate of that job will disclose the extent of a wage-rate inequity, if any exists. In the case of an incentive job the comparison will be between the standard hourly wage rate plus "equitable incentive compensation" and the actual average hourly earnings. Insofar as is possible within the monetary limits to which the union and management have jointly agreed, such wage inequities as are found will be wiped out. If this cannot be accomplished at one time, because of the sums involved, it has been agreed that all future rate changes must be in the direction of eliminating the inequity. The inequity may result in the lowering as well as the raising of present rates. Wage rates of present job incumbents will not be reduced, however, and "the normal turnover of employees shall be utilized in the elimination of out-of-line wage rates." The standard hourly wage rates culminating from this extensive program will be incorporated in the basic collective-bargaining agreement between company and union.

This brief summary does little justice to the magnitude of the task described. It is perhaps sufficient to indicate the extent to which the union is sharing managerial authority in establishing a complete and comprehensive wage schedule.

The union is not completely satisfied with its role in the determination of wages. It is driving for advances on two fronts. A resolution adopted by the executive board of the international union at its July, 1945 meeting affirms the union's intent to establish uniform job classifications and uniform wage rates for these classifications throughout the basic steel industry; this is the request which was denied by the War Labor Board. It is also in the forefront of those unions which are pressing for the establishment of a guaranteed annual wage.

Hours. Agreements in the steel industry customarily provide that the normal work schedule consists of five consecutive working days followed by two days of rest, except at times when shifts are changing. Departures from this normal schedule may be made by management after prior conference with the union, but union agreement to such departures is not a prerequisite to management's exercise of its right. There are, however, certain limitations upon this authority. (1) Departures from normal operations must be necessary in the interest of efficient operations. There is little question but that management, if called upon by the union via the grievance procedure, would have to offer proof of the existence of this condition. (2) Most managements have agreed that effort on their part should result in no less than 85 per cent of the work force operating on normal schedules. If called upon by the union grievance committee, management must make an accounting of its performance in this respect. However, in figuring the 85 per cent, all departures from normal which have been mutually agreed upon are included as normal.

While determination of starting times rests with the company, and the company may change schedules from time to time to suit varying conditions of business, it may make no indiscriminate changes and all changes must be made known to the union as far in advance as possible. But what are indiscriminate changes? The union has offered the following examples. An employe is scheduled on the day turn of 8 to 4, Monday through Friday. During the week management determines that for an emergency it wishes to have the employe report on Saturday, which would be the employe's sixth day in the payroll week. Management therefore tells the employe not to report on one of his scheduled days during the week, even though work is available, in order to avoid paying him overtime for Saturday. Or an employe is told not to report on a scheduled day during the week in order to have him come out on the seventh day, thereby avoiding the payment of double time. These cases, say the union, would represent indiscriminate changes. Its position has been upheld by at least one arbitration board which passed upon a case embodying some of the circumstances cited by the union as example. The board held that since workers had been rescheduled solely to avoid the payment of overtime, they were to be compensated for the turns they had lost as a result of this action of management.

Questions as to what constitute hours of work have mainly concerned call-in time and allowed time. The former provides for payment for two hours if workers are not previously instructed that work is not available, while the latter guarantees at least four hours pay once a worker begins his shift. These provisions do not apply in the event of breakdown, strikes, or "acts of God."

As previously mentioned, certain contracts make provision for reducing the number of hours in the work week to spread employment in time of curtailment of output.

Employe Advancement Policies. The union participates with management in determining the duration and eligibility requirements for vacations, and the amount of vacation pay. No provision is customarily made for payment for holidays not worked. Where work is required employes are paid overtime rates. The union has made little headway in the area generally designated as "social security." It does, however, have a full program including:

1. The establishment and joint administration of adequate retirement plans.

2. Provision for dismissal pay. In cases where plants or portions of plants are closed down, this should mean severance payments of four weeks' wages to those with more than three years of continuous service, and eight weeks' wages to those with more than three years of continuous service. In cases of technological unemployment, displaced workers who for various reasons cannot be reabsorbed in other jobs should be paid dismissal wages of ten per cent of their earnings for a ten-year period, and not less than $500 to those with less than ten years' service.

3. Sick leave of seven days per year, with pay, for employes of one to three years' service, and 14 days for those with more than three years' service.

4. Group insurance plans, jointly established and administered, to provide for death, accidents, hospitalization, and medical care.

Demands relating to portions of this program have already been raised by the union in bargaining conferences. One "little steel" company has flatly refused to bargain on these matters, claiming they are subject solely to managerial determination. The issue will no doubt loom importantly in the near future.

Promotions. Most of the major contracts explicitly recognize that promotional opportunity "should increase in proportion to length of continuous service."

In recognition, however, of the responsibility of the Management for the efficient operation of the works, it is understood and agreed that in all cases of promotion . . . [within the bargaining unit] . . . the following factors as listed below shall be considered; however, only where factors "a" and "b" are relatively equal shall length of continuous service be the determining factor:

a. Ability to perform the work;

b. Physical fitness;

c. Continuous service.

The determination of the unit within which these factors shall be applied in the event of promotion is subject to local agreement. Thus in one important works, a local agreement spells out in detail that job seniority units are to be established in specified instances (such as Front Side of Furnaces Nos. 1, 2, 3, 4, E, 5, 6, 7, 8, 9, and 10, in the Blast Furnace Division, with each numbered group constituting a single combined seniority unit, Ladle House and Pig Machine, Sintering and Dehydration Plants, etc.); department seniority units are to be established in other instances (such as Production Planning Department, Time and Payroll Bureau of the Accounting Department, the Chemical Laboratory, etc.); and division seniority units in still other instances (such as the 12" and 16" Alloy Bar Mill of the Rolling Mill Division, the #1 Billet Dock of the Rolling Mill Division, etc.).

"Continuous service" may likewise be locally defined. Thus in computing service for promotions within a departmental seniority unit, the parties may agree that only the following service may be considered: (a) continuous service with the corporation prior to March 16, 1937; (b) continuous service from March 16, 1937, to October 1, 1945, in one of the thirteen plant divisions of which the departmental seniority unit is a part; and (c) continuous service in the departmental seniority unit itself since October 1, 1945.

Despite the wording of the promotion clause, which appears to place primary emphasis on ability and physical fitness, in actual operation seniority frequently becomes the controlling consideration. The union has been able to secure this desired objective through the insistence that management must be able to demonstrate, by objective standards, that a junior employe is actually more qualified than one with greater seniority before it may promote him. Arbitration boards have inclined to support this view in grievance cases coming before them. Thus in one important case, the board, referring to the contract provisions, said:

The first paragraph sets forth a guiding principle in recognizing that "promotional opportunity and job security . . . should increase in proportion to length of continuous service." Adherence to this principle in the event of a promotion means that the qualified candidate with the longest continuous service has a superior claim to the job. Ordinarily, the factor of continuous service will be sufficient to determine which employee is entitled to the promotion. However, the remaining portion of the quoted provision grants the Company the right to promote an employee with less continuous service if his ability to perform the work is more than relatively equal to that of another candidate.

The use of this right must be exercised with care, particularly in view of the guiding principle mentioned above. First, the difference in the respective abilities of the candidates for a promotion must be more than "relatively equal" in order to waive the use of continuous service as a governing factor. A minor difference in ability is insufficient. The difference must be great enough to mean an appreciably superior performance. Second, the difference in ability is confined by the agreement to the performance of the work required by the particular job. Obviously, ability which is not evidenced in superior performance on the job in question cannot be used in making a decision on a promotion. Third, the difference in ability to perform the work must be demonstrable. A mere opinion that the given difference in ability exists is not sufficient. As a party to the Agreement, the Union has the right to require reasonable proof in the case of a claim that one candidate for a promotion has an ability to perform the work more than relatively equal to that of another candidate. If the Union is not convinced by the Company's effort to substantiate the claim, it has the right under the Agreement to seek a determination by this Board. Such a determination requires demonstrable evidence on behalf of the claim. The seniority provision clearly implies that the alleged difference in ability must be reasonably demonstrated.

With these cautions in mind, this Board finds that the Company has not made a sufficient showing on behalf of its contention that X, as compared with the aggrieved employee [Y], had more than relatively equal ability to perform the work of Serviceman "C." That he was more able generally seems to be probable. However, the evidence submitted to this Board does not demonstrate reasonably that he was able to perform the distinctive work of Serviceman "C" appreciably superior to Y. The part played by X in devising an improvement in the Gato valves is the only objective item of evidence introduced on his behalf. It does not constitute any substantial showing of a superior ability to perform the work of Serviceman Class "C." In the instance of Y, the only objective evidence submitted is the record of an instance of insubordination. The incidents surrounding the alleged insubordination are too inconclusive to accept the matter as showing a recognizable inferior ability to perform the work of Serviceman "C." The remaining material submitted on behalf of a greater ability of X consists of the judgment of supervision that he was more cooperative, willing to work and resourceful. It has not been shown that whatever difference existed between the employees in the degree of possession of these traits would mean an appreciable difference in ability to perform the distinctive work required by the position of Serviceman "C."

On the basis of these considerations, the Board reversed the company's choice of employe for advancement, and ordered the promotion of the senior worker retroactive to the date of the filing of the grievance.

To provide the necessary objective indication of greater ability the company has introduced "merit ratings" by supervisors as evidence. The union has at times contended that since merit ratings are only expressions of opinion it would refuse to recognize them as demonstrating superior ability. Nevertheless, the same board which rendered the above decision has advised that such ratings will be accepted as evidence providing they have been maintained over a period of years rather than made up at the time of promotion.

The promotional system has raised one other important question. The above method of determining who shall be promoted is applicable only to employes in the bargaining unit. Since foremen are excluded from the bargaining unit of production employes in the steel industry, the company retains the right to promote whom it will to foreman positions. The union has taken the position that in times of production cutback, foremen should not be allowed to exercise seniority to recover a production or maintenance job. There have been wildcat strikes in support of this position. Union representatives have at times said that they would consent to such "bumping," returning the demoted foreman to his former production job, if they had a voice in who was promoted; but when the company exercises that right unilaterally, the company—and the promoted worker—must take his own chances. The result has been that on occasions a company has had difficulty in getting an able worker to accept a foreman's job, because he feels he is being "promoted into insecurity." The effect of a recent arbitration award denying the union's position remains to be seen.

Health and Safety. Clauses under this heading commonly provide that the company "shall continue to make reasonable provisions for the safety and health of its employes," that it shall provide protective devices, wearing apparel, and other equipment necessary to protect employes from injury, and that it shall install necessary heating and ventilating systems. Union claims that the company has failed to live up to this agreement may of course be presented through the grievance procedure, and a number of such claims have in fact been made. They have taken the form of requests for a spell-hand to provide heat relief for "push-off operators," summer relief in the coke-ovens department when the temperature reaches 85 degrees instead of the customary 90, or erection of working platforms in the open-hearth department by qualified carpenters rather than by the bricklayers themselves, to guarantee against defective scaffolding. The important fact from our viewpoint in this study is not whether the union's position is upheld by the arbitration board—and it often is not—but that management's alleged errors of omission or commission are judged on the basis of an objective determination whether the conditions charged either exist or warrant remedy. Thus before rendering decision the board may examine the record to ascertain whether the push-off operators are subject to health or safety hazards, or to discover how many instances of heat prostration have occurred among coke-oven employes when the temperature ranged between 85 and 90 degrees, or to determine the number of injuries sustained by bricklayers due to unsafe working platforms.

PROCUREMENT OF MATERIALS AND PARTS

The only area of this category in which the union has shown much interest has been in the company's relations with outside contractors. In some negotiations the union has expressed a desire to limit the freedom of the company to establish such relations, arguing that it opens possibilities of depriving members of jobs. Thus far management has successfully resisted this view, however.

PRODUCTION

In this category the Steelworkers have shown no real interest in any except those areas here discussed.

Types of Machinery. The official union policy has been not to oppose technological improvements in the industry but to provide for their orderly introduction. "This means that technological improvements should be installed at such times and under such conditions as not to displace workers, bankrupt communities, close up complete mills, and otherwise disrupt the social fabric of industrial districts."[7] To the extent the union is able to secure the acceptance of this policy it does not determine whether new or improved types of machinery will be introduced into the mill, but it may participate in the timing of their introduction.

Job Content. Questions as to whether an employe may properly be required to perform certain operations as part of his job arise in the grievance procedure. The nature of such cases can best be illustrated by excerpts from one coming to arbitration:

The aggrieved employees are Traveling Tablemen operating moving tables in the Roller sequence. During a roll change, the Tablemen assist other members of the Rolling Crew. One of the tasks involved in the roll change is the removal and the placement of shoe bolts on the roll stands. In the spring of 1945, Management instructed that these shoe bolts be tightened with wrenches and sledge hammers, a task which had been discontinued for several years but which had been performed previously by Roll Helpers. The Union contends that the assignment of this task has increased excessively the work of the Table Operators and asks that the Roll Helpers be restored to the crew since the work belongs to them. . . .

The evidence, even though fragmentary, indicates that Traveling Tablemen tightened the shoe bolts with sledges and hammers some years ago when the practice was being regularly followed. Further, it is apparent that during the period of so-called laxness in tightening the shoe bolts, this task of tightening them with wrenches and sledges was done occasionally by Traveling Tablemen. . . . On the basis of such evidence, it is not reasonable to assume that the task of tightening the shoe bolts was an entirely new duty for the Traveling Tablemen, beginning in May, 1945.

This Board finds that the Company has not violated any provisions of the Agreement in requiring the Traveling Tablemen to fasten the shoe bolts with wrenches and sledge hammers.

In general, however, the union or its members contest not so much changes in job content as wage adjustments which are made or which it believes should or should not

[7] *Investigation of Concentration of Economic Power*, part 30, p. 16507.

be made as a result of the changed job content. The wage-inequities program discussed earlier involves the description of all jobs, it is true, but it is understood that such descriptions are solely for purposes of classification. They may not, therefore, be used to freeze the requirements of any particular job. When this program has been completed, management will remain free to alter the content of any described position, subject to two conditions: (1) the changed job content may require that the job be placed in another classification, carrying a different rate; (2) the changed job content may require the adjustment of an incentive or piece rate to permit earnings equal to the standard hourly rate plus "equitable incentive compensation."

Methods of Operation. Occasional instances have arisen when union members have sought to contest a company's method of production. Disputes have thus arisen at particular plants as to whether a scarfing operation might be eliminated or whether ingots from the pits should be rolled top first instead of bottom first. Such isolated examples, however, provide no basis for a finding that the union has sought generally to share managerial authority in this area.

Rates of Operation. While complaints that employes are not giving full effort or full time to their jobs are met with in the steel industry as in other basic industries, they are far from being as prevalent. Moreover, the steel industry is distinguished in that, under the leadership of the Carnegie-Illinois Steel Corporation, a serious attempt is being made to meet the problem in a manner intended to bring cooperation rather than conflict from the union.

In discussing the impact of collective bargaining on managerial authority in the steel industry, it becomes apparent that a major effect has been the elimination of personal opinion as the basis for management decisions in certain areas of concern to the union; more correctly, the effect has been to require that only when opinions are supported and substantiated by the facts may they be accepted as a valid exercise of managerial authority. In layoffs and promotions, management may depart from the seniority rule only when it demonstrates that a man has greater ability. The wage-inequities program is premised on an objective measurement of the factors which enter into job classification so that wages may be determined by system. Standard hours of work must be observed unless it can be shown that departures from normal are necessary to efficient operations. Provisions for safety and health will be tested by objective standards. Discipline will be upheld only when supported by evidence. It is now proposed that this same test of objectivity be applied to the setting of rates of operation.

The program, which is starting from simple beginnings and stems out of the wage-inequities agreements, involves a refinement of current time-study practices. The first agreement of that series enunciated the principle that:

Classification will be made on the basis of performance of a "Fair Day's Work," defined as follows: "A fair day's work is that amount of work that can be produced by a qualified employee when working at a normal pace and effectively utilizing his time where work is not restricted by process limitations."

Example: A normal pace is equivalent to a man walking, without load, on smooth level ground at a rate of three (3) miles per hour.

The third agreement in the wage-inequities series added the corollary:

The term "equitable incentive compensation" shall be understood to mean extra compensation over and above the rate of a fair day's pay for the job in proportion to the actual performance required over and above the performance rate of a fair day's work on the job.

Starting from the initial union–management agreement that a fair pace is represented by a three-mile-an-hour gait without handicaps, it is proposed that additional examples of fair pace, illustrative of steel operations, be adopted as further bench marks.

It is felt that the adoption of a number of examples as standard for a fair day's work pace will make easier the task of establishing clearly the normal pace for all other operations, as well as to demonstrate to all concerned both in management and the working force the objectiveness and fairness of the program as a whole and of the individual standards established.[8]

Whether the program meets with success will probably depend as much upon the degree of support accorded by the union as upon the nature of the program itself. While the initial surveys are being undertaken by management, final results will be subject to negotiation.

DISTRIBUTION

The union has shown no interest in this category except in a most general way. It is planning in terms of an iron and steel industry which annually will *produce and market* some 80 to 85 million tons of products. It believes the economy can and must support such a program and utilize such an output. Its long-range plans are based on this belief. As yet, however, it has shown no desire to share authority in this field.

COORDINATE ACTIVITIES

In this category the union has shown an interest only in those areas here discussed.

Company Organization. The unionization of foremen has posed the same problems in the steel industry that were referred to under automobiles. The Steelworkers, like the Automobile Workers, have as yet disclaimed any intent of including foremen within their organization. Despite this policy important questions are raised involving their relationship with foremen's unions. The same considerations which were previously discussed are applicable here, and there is no necessity of repeating them.

Occasionally there has been shown a more direct interest in the organizational structure of the company, where the security of employes has been involved. In one important works a stoppage occurred in protest over a managerial decision to decentralize maintenance work, permanently transferring approximately 30 per cent of the maintenance workers to production units. The union's position was that it would oppose such a move unless guarantees could be worked out covering seniority rights, utilization of skills, earnings, and subsequent transfers. The case came to arbitration, with the board ruling that the grievance had no standing since it alleged no violation of the contract.

Selection of Key Personnel. Only random interest has been shown in this area, seldom by official expression and then only by local units. One company official relates how a local union officer advised a newly appointed superintendent that he might as well go back to the open hearth as "you won't last here sixty days." An international union representative advises that in a smaller plant one of the superintendents was fired as the result of a union demand. Such instances, however, are scattered and rare.

Prices. The Steelworkers have been concerned with the industry's price policies but as yet have made no effort to share authority in this field. A price-cutting program in

---

[8] From remarks by H. L. Dawson, Chief Industrial Engineer, Carnegie-Illinois Steel Corporation, before the Industrial Relations Committee of the American Iron and Steel Institute, Pittsburgh, June 19, 1946 (mimeo). The corporation proposes that the bench-mark standards be developed through motion pictures of workers on the job.

the Spring of 1938 brought protests from the union's international president, who saw in the move a threat to wages.[9] The Steelworkers did not, however, join the Automobile Workers in seeking to affect the prices of their products in the postwar reconversion period. Top union officials have stated that as industry-wide bargaining comes, the organized workers must participate in the determination of pricing policy.[10]

Collective Bargaining. Bargaining procedures employed are a joint product. No procedural details need be discussed, except to mention that the acceptance of permanent arbitration boards to interpret and enforce the contracts is on the increase. The inauguration of this arrangement in the United States Steel Corporation in 1945 may be expected to hasten its spread throughout the industry.

A discussion of the Steelworkers' interest in managerial problems would not be complete without mention of the union–management cooperation programs which this union has sponsored. Its active support of such programs, beginning in the early years of its experience, led to the establishment of an engineering department within the union whose primary function is the promotion and development of systems of cooperation. The underlying premise is that the union should assist in "making industry able to meet the demands of labor for higher wages, shorter hours, security of the job and better conditions."[11]

The program starts with the appointment of a joint research committee, which is empowered to examine into all phases of the company's operations.

. . . The general objective is, of course, to plan months and sometimes years ahead. These plans cover what the mill is going to produce, what raw materials and machinery will have to be purchased, what funds will have to be borrowed, and what labor staff will be required to process and ship the product. These predictions are not only made for the entire period planned, but also scheduled so that the materials, the funds, and the workers will be on hand for uninterrupted production.

These forecasts should be based upon study as to where sales effort may be most effective. Where such studies are made, and are used in selling effort, forecasts based on them will have a substantial accuracy. For the sales staff is thus organized to turn predictions into actual sales.

Forecasts based upon sales research and management of the kind described should be used as a basis for calculations of the tonnage of raw material needed, and for the other parts of master planning.[12]

Basic to this cooperative undertaking is an agreement that economies effected shall not react against the interests of the workers. Normal labor turnover is to be the medium through which workers whose jobs have been made unnecessary are to be reabsorbed or removed. Moreover, the benefits of economies and increased business are to be shared with the workers since they have been jointly responsible for them.

Ever since the Steelworkers became interested in union–management cooperation of this nature, they have repeatedly emphasized that "no cooperative program should be undertaken without full understanding and agreement on both sides."[13] Cooperation is not a bargaining demand, it is an offer of help from the union which management is free to reject without running a risk of recrimination. To this date, therefore, the program has not been based on any planned drive to penetrate additional management areas not encompassed in the collective-bargaining agreement, though management's

[9] An account of the circumstances is given in *How Collective Bargaining Works*, p. 529.
[10] Golden and Ruttenberg, *The Dynamics of Industrial Democracy*, p. 315.
[11] *Production Problems*, Steelworkers Union Handbook, p. 2.
[12] *Production Problems*, Steelworkers Union Handbook, p. 8–9.
[13] *Production Problems*, Steelworkers Union Handbook, p. 5.

fear that this is an inevitable result of the program has limited its spread. It has thus primarily been confined to small companies in the industry, and even then chiefly to companies which were "sick" or ailing.

There is some reason to question, however, whether the initial union attitude that union–management cooperation must only be a voluntary affair will be retained indefinitely. There is some reason to believe that actual demands for such a program may ultimately be sponsored by the union in collective-bargaining negotiations. The Steelworkers are already supporting two proposals which look in this direction. Their leadership has been in the forefront of those advocating industry councils on which labor would be represented and which would be empowered to act in all areas of business operation. This is simply union-management cooperation formalized. Likewise, the Steelworkers have been leading in the fight for a guaranteed annual wage. They realize that such a guarantee has meaning only if applied to a guaranteed number of workers. If business conditions seem to require the dismissal of a number of employes, or the reduction of wages, union representatives make no secret of the fact that they will want to know whether such action is necessary. This means an examination of managerial decisions in all the major categories—finance, personnel, procurement, production, sales, and what have here been called coordinate activities. Experience gained in the administration of union–management cooperation plans may be used in formulating proposals designed to avoid the necessity of wage cuts or reductions in force. Union–management cooperation may thus be brought home to "big steel" and "little steel" in the form of definite demands.

Whether these events will materialize is speculative. What is more certain is that some of the union's leaders are thinking in these terms, that they no longer regard themselves as a force merely reacting to managerial decisions in certain areas of business operation but as a force which itself can influence the whole range of industrial economic activity.

Union Penetration of Managerial Areas: Meat Packing

The "Big Four" meat packinghouses have been organized primarily by three unions, the United Packinghouse Workers of America, the Amalgamated Meat Cutters and Butcher Workmen of North America, and the National Brotherhood of Packinghouse Workers. Of these three unions the first has secured the greatest following among the employes of the large corporations and our attention will be largely focused upon its relations with the management of the industry. For the most part its agreements are corporation-wide, supplemented by local agreements negotiated at the plants.

General management clauses of the type found in other industries are likewise found in the meat-packing contracts, vesting in management the "right to hire, suspend or discharge for proper cause, or transfer, and the right to relieve employees from duty because of lack of work, or for other legitimate reasons." While it is explicitly recognized that this right is subject to the limitations of the contract, it is a safe generalization that meat-packing managements feel that the unions have transcended these bounds and are seeking further enlargement of their authority. In the words of one company representative, "In what areas haven't they tried to intervene?"

FINANCE

The United Packinghouse Workers has not sought to bargain directly on any of the areas of this category. It has sufficiently interested itself in company policy with respect to matters of finance, however, that some managements are already adopting a defensive attitude with respect to their sole propriety in making decisions of this nature. One general superintendent thus asserts, "They think they are concerned with the use of surplus and the size of surplus. They have argued that surplus should be used to increase wages. And they'd like to dispose of our net earnings for us, interesting themselves not only in wages and surplus but also in the dividends to stockholders." In the area of accounting procedures, the UPWA has been critical of the companies' cost-accounting techniques, which it regards as permitting the concealment of the amount of profit properly attributable to meat as distinguished from by-product operations.

The union's interest in these areas has been due to their impact on the wage-paying ability of the companies. It has touched on decisions in this category not in an attempt to bargain with respect to them directly, but in bargaining on the wage issue.

PERSONNEL

Type of Personnel. The union has secured agreement that choice of personnel will not be governed by consideration of race, sex, color, creed, or nationality. The large numbers of Negro and Mexican workers in the industry have made this issue an important one. While the very number of such workers constitutes evidence that the

307

companies have not pursued discriminatory policies in adding employes to the payroll, the union's actions in this field have been directed primarily to assuring nondiscrimination in their assignment to specific tasks. Despite company denials, the union persists in maintaining that Negroes and Mexicans have been barred from certain types of jobs. It cites by way of example "the case of the company which, although it had Negro watchmen, had never employed any of them in its offices or stock rooms. The matter was presented to the management through the local union, with the outcome that the company finally saw the wisdom of removing the ban against employing Negroes in this position."[1] At the same time the union recognizes that a large part of its efforts in this direction must be centered on an educational program within the union. It has not denied that some existing discriminatory practices result from worker attitudes as well as those of management.

Size of Force. The only manner in which the union has evidenced any interest in this area has been in occasional protests that an operation is undermanned.

Hiring. The most common provision with respect to hiring practices lays down the rule that before new employes may be hired, the seniority list for the department involved must have been exhausted, and employes in other departments desiring to transfer to the job opening must have been given the opportunity. It is sometimes agreed that when hiring new help, the company shall give preference to former employes whose services were satisfactory. In rehiring following layoffs, seniority governs.

Layoffs. The principle that layoffs shall be on the basis of departmental seniority has become rather firmly established in this industry. The administration of this directive has at times resulted in disagreement. Even such a question as what constitutes the department within which seniority shall apply has had to be taken to arbitration for settlement.

Another difficulty in applying the seniority principle has concerned the question of whether a senior employe may "bump" the man next below him, at time of reduction in force, or whether an employe so displaced from his regular job shall be given the job of the man with least seniority in the department, obviating the disturbance of employes in the intermediate classifications. An arbitrator in one company has ruled that the parties have committed themselves to the process of "bumping" at times of layoff. Thus a bone trimmer who had been earning 88 cents an hour was ordered to be put on the job of separating viscera at 83 cents an hour, displacing the incumbent on the job who had lesser seniority, instead of being assigned to the job of saving chitterlings at 72½ cents an hour, as the company had done.

The union has sought, thus far unsuccessfully, to establish the principle that the company may not retire a person for age unless the worker himself so desires or unless he is unable to fill his job.

Allocation. Only a handful of rules governing the assignment of a worker to a job have been mutually agreed to. The nature of these, as well as the enlargements upon them sought by the union, indicates that the union's interest has been as much in job satisfaction as in job security in this area.

Illustrative of the provisions which seek to preserve job security in the event of transfers are the following: An employe transferred to another department at his own request retains for 90 days his seniority in his original department, to which he may return within that period if he so decides. An employe transferred to another department at the direction of the company has the right, in the event of layoffs in the new

---

[1] Statement submitted to the Subcommittee for a Permanent Fair Employment Practice Commission of the United States Senate Committee on Education and Labor, United Packinghouse Workers of America (mimeographed, undated), p. 6.

department or the elimination of that department, of returning to his original department.

In the early part of 1944 the union raised the issue of job satisfaction:

There is nothing in the present agreement, however, which assures employees an opportunity for a job in another department; under these circumstances an employee who may desire to get into the maintenance department because he has some skills as a mechanic may request such a transfer; whether or not the transfer is granted, however, even in the event an opening should occur, would be entirely subject to the judgment of the employer. It is that situation that the Union desires to correct. . . .[2]

The remedy suggested by the union was granted in negotiations by two of the major packers, and ultimately included at the direction of the War Labor Board in the two remaining cases. The contract clause embodies a "waiting list" system assuring the following arrangement:

Under the Union's suggested plan, John Jones would advise the person who keeps the [waiting] list that he desires to be transferred into Department X; when an opening occurred, if John Jones had more seniority than anyone else on this waiting list who had also designated Department X, he would be transferred into that Department and the same rule with reference to his ability to do the job as applied for promotions in his regular Department would apply in this case as well.[3]

In some of the largest corporations, the union has also obtained agreement that no employe may be permanently transferred without his consent in writing. It has attempted, as yet without widespread success, to establish the additional principle that temporary assignments should be made on the basis of seniority, with the less desirable work going to employes with the least seniority. Thus, as related in one grievance proceeding, a worker "in the smoked meats department was put to work on dog food temporarily, although there were men with lesser seniority in his department whom he and the Union believed should have been given this other work to do while he was left in the department." The arbitrator denied the Union's position, however, holding that under the present contract management remained free to make temporary assignments without regard to seniority.

Discipline. The belief that management's disciplinary authority has been undermined by the union is prevalent in this industry, as in those previously discussed. Such a feeling stems from two sources: (1) the work stoppages of organized groups in protest of discipline imposed; and (2) a rescinding of disciplinary penalties as a result of union appeals via the grievance procedure. The first has been discussed in connection with the automobile and steel industries and needs no further elaboration here.

Arbitration, as the terminal step in most of the grievance procedures, has resulted in the laying down of certain principles governing the imposition of discipline. These principles are at present in an ill-defined state. They are by no means as clearly developed as in the automobile industry, for example. The interesting fact is that insofar as it is possible to discern the growth of a body of custom or practice, there is reason to believe that it is headed in the direction of an enunciation of the same types of principles as are to be found in the automobile and other industries.

1. There must be a clear statement of rules and an equal enforcement of them.

[2] Brief submitted by the United Packinghouse Workers of America, CIO, to the Panel of the National War Labor Board (Cases No. 111-5760-D, 111-6000-D), UPWA (undated) p. 205.

[3] Brief submitted by the United Packinghouse Workers of America, CIO, to the Panel of the National War Labor Board (Cases No. 111-5760-D, 111-6000-D) p. 205.

"These rules, however, appear to be none too precise. . . . In addition, the evidence was quite convincing that at least a significant number of employees were unfamiliar with the published edition of these rules. . . . Since X appears to have followed what was at the time, if not customary, at least condoned procedure, and since the Company must assume some joint responsibility for the general relaxation in the adherence to the rules, it was unnecessary to single X out, without warning, for disciplinary action, when other employees had evidently been engaging in the same mal-practice."

2. There must be adequate evidence to support the charges.

"We have here a case where there is some circumstantial evidence of apparent intent to do wrong, but neither conclusive proof of such intent, nor the act itself. The Arbitrator was impressed by the testimony which indicated that the behavior of the men might be related to an attempted theft, but he was also struck by the testimony that the men could have been in that location for reasons unconnected with attempted theft. . . . Having not been proven guilty, the men must be presumed innocent. Having committed no crime, no punishment is in order."

3. The employe has a right to know the offense with which he is charged.

"The Company declares that it decided on the length of suspension in the case of each employee on the basis of its judgment of his responsibility for the disturbance and on the basis of his past conduct record. It may be that the judgment of the Company was sound and valid in the instance of each employee. However, the Company has not made known the considerations which led it to apply differential penalties to the employees. This arbitrator does not have any information on any of the employees . . . which permits him to determine whether a given differential penalty was given for proper cause. He merely wishes to point out that any of the employees and the Union as his official agent have the right to know why a different penalty was given to him and the right to secure redress in the event of unfair discrimination."

4. The employe has a right to know the penalty to be imposed.

"This is a misuse of the penalty of indefinite suspension. It should be recognized that an indefinite suspension is in the nature of a temporary and indeterminate action pending the ability to fix a definite penalty. Its justification is to allow for an investigation and for the formation of a decision as to what should appropriately be a determinate penalty. Its use beyond this point is without warrant. The affected employee is entitled to know his status. To keep him in a state of uncertainty, so that he does not know what to expect and is unable to make plans, cannot be reconciled with the ethics of employer-employee relations."

5. The penalty must accord with the offense.

"This Arbitrator can see the desirability of imposing on X some form of disciplinary action sufficiently grave to drive home the seriousness of having used a knife; he cannot see the justification of giving her the same penalty that was given to Y when her guilt was infinitely less than his."

On occasions the union has itself sought to participate in the meting out of discipline for offenses. It has brought pressure against a company to secure the discharge of an employe alleged to have engaged in agitation directed against Negro employes. It has at times imposed fines or taken other disciplinary action against its own members who have participated in unauthorized stoppages.

Wages. Agreements as to the setting of wage rates in the meat-packing industry are much less specific than in the industries previously discussed. As a general proposition the company is obligated to notify the union in advance, where possible, of any proposed new rates or changed rates, and in any event, within three days after such a rate is introduced. The advance notification is designed to permit the union to offer suggestions, but it may also challenge the rate by the grievance procedure after it has been set. The clauses, familiar in other industries, barring the company from changing rates except where there has been a change in the job are not generally to be found, though the union has at times placed reliance, to achieve the same result, on a general clause barring changes in "working conditions now in effect" unless as a result of collective bargaining.

The union has expressed dissatisfaction with this method of establishing rates, and has sought the right to participate with management in the determination of all rates.

Provision, therefore, should be written into the agreement to the effect that whenever an hourly rated job is to be changed to a piece-work job or whenever there are to be changes in present piece-work rates, such changes must be arrived at through negotiations with the Union or under the grievance machinery, and if an emergency arises requiring immediate adjustment, a situation which at the present time is not within our contemplation, the contract should provide that the change finally agreed upon should be retroactive to the date that the change was initiated. In order to avoid abuse, however, it should be made clear that no rate can be changed except in the face of a real emergency.[4]

The problem of combination and multiple or split rates has been a peculiarly thorny one in the meat-packing industry. A combination job is one where an employe works on two or more differently rated jobs at the same time. A multiple or split job is one where an employe is assigned to two or more jobs between which he alternates. The union has sought payment, for all time worked, of the highest rate involved in the combination job. While it has secured this result in certain isolated cases, more generally it is agreed that the worker shall be paid an "equitable rate of pay for all hours worked on such jobs." The union has been more successful in the field of multiple or split jobs, obtaining agreement that when a worker is assigned to a job with a higher authorized rate than his regular rate, or when he is assigned to a job with a lower rate than his regular rate, he is to be paid the higher of the two rates. This provision has not ended the difficulty, however, as the question has been raised as to what constitutes a man's "regular rate" when he is working on several jobs, each carrying a different rate. One answer given in arbitration has been that a worker's regular rate is the rate which he is paid on the operation consuming the major portion of his working time.

Questions of classification arise in this industry, as in those already analyzed. They take the form of a union contention that Jones, now classified under electrical maintenance and performing the work of a trouble shooter, at the rate of $1.05½ an hour, is actually doing the job that properly falls under the classification of wireman, at a rate of $1.12 an hour. Matters of this sort may be processed through the grievance procedure and be settled by arbitration, as the terminal step.

In this industry, too, are to be found general provisions such as those previously encountered: a differential in favor of night workers, equal pay for women performing equal work, penalty payments for overtime, and "call-in" time.

The principle of a minimum daily guarantee for piece workers, quite similar to that found in the steel industry, has been established here as well. As a result, piece-work earnings are calculated on a daily basis, and a worker is guaranteed an amount

---

[4] Brief Submitted by the United Packinghouse Workers of America, CIO, to the Panel of the National War Labor Board (Cases No. 111-5760-D, 111-6000-D, 111-5763-D), p. 123.

no less than the basic hourly rate of his job times the number of hours worked in the day. In one arbitration award the corollary has been laid down that the daily calculation of earnings is applicable to overtime as well as straight time.

A more important wage guarantee is to be found in the provision that each employe is entitled to at least 36 hours' pay in each week of employment, subject to the provisos that he must be present each day for the full time worked by the gang of which he is a part, and that his gang is not one customarily hired by the day, such as snow-shovelers. This 36-hour guarantee takes effect after an employe is called to work on the second work day of each week. Thus employes who are laid off at the end of the first working day of the week do not benefit by its provisions. An arbitration award has elaborated this guarantee system by holding that overtime hours must be considered as straight-time hours for the purpose of determining whether an employe has received the 36 hours of work to which he is entitled. On the other hand, an employe who refuses to work when work is available, regardless of whether overtime is involved, has his guaranteed number of hours reduced by the hours of work which he refused.

Guarantee time, as this system has come to be known, was in effect prior to the designation of the UPWA as a collective-bargaining agent, though the number of hours originally guaranteed was fewer than at present. The system is now a matter of contract, however, and the union has pressed to raise the guarantee from 36 to 40 hours.

New directions in which the union is attempting to push forward in this area of management include a guaranteed annual wage, under which the company would assure to each employe 52 weeks of 40 hours each year, within his department, with the company retaining an unlimited right to lay off employes, but only after 52 weeks' notice; and elimination of geographical wage differentials.

Hours. In this traditional area of collective bargaining the scope of managerial authority has been progressively lessened, and the union is not yet satisfied with the results. Companies have generally agreed to make every effort to limit the working day to eight hours and the working week to 40 hours, with the understanding that this agreement does not actually restrict the amount of time an employe can be required to work. The latter proviso constitutes the nub of the hours problem—"that no employe will be required to work unreasonable hours."

The operations of the meat-packing industry are such that occasions arise necessitating overtime work. Meat may come in in exceptional quantity, for example, and there will be no "surplus" butchers to put on the job. The packers have contended that due to the uneven flow of livestock they have little control over scheduling of the handling, slaughtering, and dressing operations. They point out that working the employes longer than normal hours in fact penalizes the company, since it involves penalty pay, so that they can scarcely be charged with scheduling overtime simply through wilfully ignoring the employes' welfare.

The Packinghouse Workers have refused to accept these arguments, however, claiming that methods of controlling the flow of livestock to permit shorter workdays and work weeks are available. It is their intent to prod the managements into making use of them. They seek to do this by defining more precisely, by number of hours in the day or week, what constitutes "unreasonable hours." They are also pressing for a five-day week, by requiring premium pay for the sixth consecutive day of work in any week.

We recognize unreservedly that the imposition of penalty payment for the sixth day worked would have the tendency to make such work costly to the Companies and thereby they would use their ingenuity to plan their operations in such a way so as to avoid it to the extent that it is possible to do so, and we submit that it is the intention of the Union to establish a 5-day week for this industry.[5]

As a challenge to the companies' present unilateral determination of the number of hours which shall be worked in any day, organized groups of workers have replied with a unilateral determination of their own—by simply walking off the job. The union has not hesitated to admit such unofficial action by its members as failure to return to work after lunch on Saturday, or refusal to work longer than eight hours when not informed how long management planned to keep them on the job that day, or quitting at the end of ten hours. "We do not believe that such refusal to work can be properly considered a stoppage, since perpetual motion cannot be expected of the human machine . . ."[6]

The Packinghouse Workers have also sought to protect Sunday as a day of rest. To the agreement that on operations requiring Sunday work another day of rest may be designated they have attached the rider that work may not be considered regular Sunday work until a gang has worked four consecutive Sundays. As a further precaution against indiscriminate scheduling of Sunday work they have secured agreement that when worked but not regularly scheduled it shall not be considered ground for laying off a worker on a customary workday, as a means for "making up" for the penalty Sunday rates.

Other provisions affect the scheduling of hours of work. Employes required to work more than five hours without a meal period must be paid time-and-a-half for hours worked in excess of five until a meal period is granted, except under certain circumstances. And employes required to work more than five hours after the first meal period are to be allowed 20 minutes of paid time for a second meal, which is furnished free by the company. Relief periods and spellout time may not be changed except by agreement. As far as practicable, there must be an equal distribution of hours of work within each department.

As in other industries, there have been some difficulties in defining what constitutes hours of work. In meat packing, hours of work for which payment must be made include "call-in" time, when workers report for duty without previous notification that no work is available; rest periods; meal times under certain conditions, as mentioned above; time spent in preparing tools and equipment; time spent in changing clothes, up to a prescribed maximum; time involved in returning from distant assignments; and time occupied in receiving instructions at the commencement of the working day.

Employe Advancement Policies. The union has joined in contractual provisions governing the length of vacations, service requirements, and vacation compensation. Penalty rates must be paid when specific holidays are worked, but as yet the union has not secured the payment for holidays not worked, which it seeks.

Any benefits for sickness, accidents, or retirement remain under the control of management, with the exception of one major corporation, which has incorporated a sickness and accident plan in its contract with the union. Under this plan, employes with one year of continuous service are eligible for half wages for a period

[5] Brief submitted by the United Packinghouse Workers of America, CIO, to the Panel of the National War Labor Board (Cases No. 111-5544-D, 111-5760-D, 111-6000-D, 111-5763-D, 111-5914-D), p. 183.
[6] Brief submitted by the United Packinghouse Workers of America, CIO, to the Panel of the National War Labor Board (Case No. 111-5760-D), p. 217.

dependent upon their length of service. A waiting period of one week is specified for employes of less than ten years' employment with the company. The goal of the union in this area is the establishment of a fund to provide employes and their dependents with medical, surgical, and hospital care, and to offer disability payments to employes permanently disabled and survivor payments to families of workers whose death results from sickness or injury. The union is also interested in establishing the principle of severance pay, at the suggested rate of one week's pay for each 26 weeks of service with the company.

Promotions. By joint agreement, promotions within the bargaining unit are based on departmental seniority. When a departmental seniority list has been exhausted, vacancies are filled from the waiting list of applicants from other departments, on the basis of plant seniority. The senior employe must be able to perform the job or learn the job "within a reasonable time" in order to benefit from this arrangement.

Several questions have arisen with respect to the operation of this promotional system and have received answers in arbitration. Under one ruling, an extended period of time cannot be required of a man to demonstrate his capacity to hold the better job. "In the arbitrator's view, a period of thirty days is ample for a determination of the ability to perform the duties of a newly assigned job. A total of some five to six months on permanent assignment to a job can hardly be interpreted as necessary to establish ability to perform."

In a second important ruling, an arbitrator held that where management selected a man with lesser seniority because the senior employe did not have the requisite ability, the burden of proof in any grievance brought on behalf of the senior worker rested with the union rather than with the company. "Here the Union had the burden of convincing the Arbitrator that the Company was wrong in refusing to recognize either present ability to perform or ability to learn performance within a reasonable time." No other cases turning on this issue are available in the meat-packing industry, but it is worth noting that this decision reverses the rule being hammered out in arbitral awards in the automobile and steel industries.

Lastly, several decisions have held that an employe who refuses a promotion to which he is entitled by virtue of his seniority, must be offered the job again should a vacancy develop for the second time. "People do change their minds, as everybody knows; and the fact remains that X still had the appropriate seniority."

Safety and Health. Control over this area still rests almost exclusively with management. Some contracts obligate the company to maintain standards conducive to the health and safety of its employes, but no attempt has been made by the union to spell out what constitutes such standards. An agreement between one of the large packers and the National Brotherhood of Packinghouse Workers does, however, detail sixteen items of safety equipment which the company agrees to furnish.

The UPWA has been acutely conscious of matters of safety and health, and has at times irritated managements by insisting that the industry's record in these particulars is not a good one. It has maintained that only by joint attack upon these problems is it possible to obtain the desired remedial results. Nevertheless, it has not sponsored a program as concrete in this field as, for example, its proposals on social security.

PROCUREMENT

While the union has shown an interest in the characteristics of the flow of livestock, it has not attempted to exercise any control in this category.

PRODUCTION

The union's influence in matters of production has been felt almost exclusively in issues affecting the rate of operation. The nature of its impact in this area is by no means uniform, however. In certain contracts it has secured management's agreement that there shall be no change in production standards unless it is found that an error has been committed in setting them or unless the operation has been changed so that the amount of work required to perform the job is changed. In one major corporation it has received the guarantee that when standards are changed, the new standards must permit the same opportunity for premium earnings as existed under the previous standards, except where there were initial errors in the production requirements. Violation of these agreements may, of course, be tested in the grievance procedure.

In other large packing companies the union has not even attained the right to protest production standards through grievance proceedings. One result has been friction between union and management based on alleged slowdowns and stoppages, which the workers claim in fact represent nothing more than an inability to keep up with the standards set for them. In some cases controversies of this nature succeed in injecting into the grievance procedure questions of standards which could not be appealed in their own right. This may occur when management disciplines employes for failure to meet production requirements, and the union appeals the disciplinary action by presenting grievances. In disposing of the question of discipline, the arbitrator sometimes inescapably must pass upon the production standard—though only over the company's objection. Thus in one case the arbitrator ruled that discipline imposed upon five employes for failing to keep up with production standards should be revoked and the men compensated for their wage losses. While taking pains to point out that he was not involving himself in an argument with management as to whether the standards set were fair, nevertheless in the circumstances of this case "the record and the testimony indicate to him that these men were passing hogs because they could not reasonably handle them."

The Packinghouse Workers are not satisfied with such a backdoor entrance to questions of the rates of operations, however. They have signified their desire to obtain the right to negotiate directly with management on the establishment of job standards.

DISTRIBUTION

The union has shown an interest in regularizing the level of output by eliminating seasonality. The packers have rejected such projects, by and large, with the argument that "you can't change a sow's habits." The union leadership is not content with this reply, however, wondering if a sow's habits cannot be changed with regulated breeding, as has been done to some extent in the case of poultry. As yet they have made no issue of the matter.

COORDINATE ACTIVITIES

Company Organization. Both the United Packinghouse Workers and the Amalgamated Meat Cutters and Butcher Workmen have enrolled foremen in their unions, though in separate bargaining units, thus injecting the same questions respecting company organization as were found in the industries previously discussed. In still another way has the foreman become the focus of controversy. The union, has, in arbitration, successfully maintained that an employe who moves into a supervisory position loses his seniority rights, since these are specifically reserved for members of the bargaining unit. It has therefore been held that when a foreman is returned to the bargaining unit, either as a result of demotion or layoffs, he has no seniority in the department in which he is placed, but must enter at the bottom of the seniority list. As in the case of the Steelworkers, such "promotions into insecurity" pose a serious problem for management in finding men to fill their foremen's ranks. This problem again raises the question of the place and status of the foreman in the organizational structure of the company.

Research and Development. Mention has already been made of the union's interest in this area. While making no bargaining issue of these matters, the union has gone on record as strongly favoring "extensive research and experimentation which will bring about a greater per capita consumption of meat."[7] It sees potentialities for lower production costs and expanded markets both at home and abroad in the development of dehydration, further experimentation in the preparation of cuts, improvement of livestock feed crops, and research in animal breeding and feeding. As yet, however, the Packinghouse Workers have not indicated in what ways, if any, they intend to participate in such programs.

Collective Bargaining. While the union shares with management decisions as to methods of negotiation, there has been no formalization of the process of contract bargaining. With respect to the grievance procedure, argument centers chiefly around the place of arbitration as the terminal step. Under War Labor Board decisions arbitration of issues arising under the contract became a widespread practice. The companies have, on the whole, shown little enthusiasm for this procedure and some have sought to eliminate it. The union has opposed and will continue to oppose any such effort. Because of this differential regard for grievance arbitration the system has not been fully integrated into the company structure. Its future is uncertain.

[7] *Meat During Post-War—Will There Be Enough?,* a Post-War Plan for Meat Packing, UPWA (undated), pp. 13–14.

Union Penetration of Managerial Areas: Public Utilities

We shall here be concerned with a composite of several industries, which for present purposes we shall simply designate as "public utilities." Specifically, the companies involved are those providing light, heat and power, telephone, telegraph, and radio-telegraphic service. The unions involved are the International Brotherhood of Electrical Workers (IBEW), the Utility Workers' Union of America (UWUA), the National Federation of Telephone Workers (NFTW), the Commercial Telegraphers Union (CTU), and the American Communications Association (ACA). While this composite treatment does not permit the same degree of generalization possible in the industries previously discussed, there is enough similarity respecting relations with the unions and economic considerations of the businesses to warrant this treatment. At the same time, we shall be able to examine the degree of union penetration in a larger segment of the economy than if attention were confined to a single industry of the public-utilities field.

Clauses specifying the general powers of management which are not disturbed except as set forth in the collective agreements are almost invariably to be found. While the wording differs among agreements, the general purport is the same as has been found in those industries already analyzed. As we have already discovered, the significance of such clauses is better understood by examining the limitations on managerial freedom imposed in the contract or in practice than by any affirmative statement of unilateral authority. In what ways have the unions in this field secured or asserted the right to share in managerial decisions?

FINANCE

No union of those mentioned above has sought the right to bargain directly on matters affecting corporate financial arrangements. Varying degrees of interest in this category have been shown, however. The IBEW has not hesitated to bring the financial policies of the company into its collective-bargaining presentation, but this has been solely for purposes of demonstrating ability to grant wage increases. More directly, on one occasion the ACA asked the president of a large corporation "to go to Jesse Jones, Head of the Federal Loan Administration and the RFC, for the purpose of getting more money from that source to meet our wage demand. [He] did so and returned from Washington with the news that the RFC would not make any additional loan for this purpose."[1] The NFTW has maintained that in the telephone industry "too much money is taken out of the business in the form of dividends. There is absolutely no economic justification for maintaining the $9.00 dividend on A.T.&T.

---

[1] American Communications Association, *Report from the International Executive Board to the Sixth National Convention* (1942), p. 13.

stock. It should be much lower."[2] While such actions and comments evidence a deep interest in corporate financial decisions, they do not indicate any present intent of making them issues of the bargaining table.

PERSONNEL

Type of Personnel. In some cases the union has obtained agreement that there shall be no discrimination against women in the policies of the company. In the light and power field it has sometimes made the composition of work crews, by types of skill, a contractual matter. In telegraphy, where professional competence is not only important but measurable, there has been joint agreement as to the qualifications which must be possessed by new employes. These have at times been spelled out in considerable detail; for example: "At transmitting stations and at receiving stations where U.H.F. [ultra high frequency] equipment is used, operators shall hold at least a valid Second Class Radiotelegraph Operator's license with at least three (3) years experience on said license except that an employee of the Company may be promoted if qualified and if he possesses a valid 2nd Class Radiotelegraph license." Or, again, in another company: "Applicants for employment as Radio, Automatic and Teletype Operators will be required to demonstrate during a test, under school conditions, using message texts comprising plain-language, figures and five-letter code, possession of the following operating qualifications." These qualifications are stated in detail for various grades of operators in terms of minimum speeds for perforating, transcribing ink-recorder signals, aural reception, and hand sending.

Size of Force. The unions have played an active part in this area of management, concerning themselves with the size of the work force required to perform specified operations, as well as with the over-all size of the staff. In the light and power industry it has sometimes secured agreement on how many men must be employed in a work gang, or that the existing size of the maintenance and construction force shall be maintained. The ACA has petitioned the Federal Communications Commission to make mandatory the employment of two technicians per radio watch. In one company there has been agreement as to the regular complement of employes in the various listed senior classifications, such as six senior operator technicians for the New York office, three senior automatic printer operators, two senior telephone operators, and so on.

Total force requirements have likewise been affected in several ways. In some companies there have been agreements on part-timing of employes prior to layoffs, thus preserving the size of the force while reducing the manhours of employment. More importantly, the ever-present danger in the telephone and telegraph fields of mass layoffs due to technological advancements has been met in some degree by joint policies protecting the employes. These may take the form of an agreement that all employes of given seniority shall be protected in their jobs regardless of technical improvements, or that no more than a specified number of employes as of a given date may be furloughed as a result of mechanization, or that no "regular employe" will be dismissed during the lifetime of the agreement as a result of changing technologies. The NFTW is now faced with the prospect of a reduced need for telephone operators as a result of the imminent advent of long-distance subscriber dialing, and is seeking to work out with the companies how this technological development may be met with the least cost of jobs in the industry. There have sometimes been agreements limiting the number of part-time employes who may be hired. Reversing the

---

[2] *The Telephone Worker*, December, 1945, p. 7.

problem, the ACA during the war concerned itself for a time with the need for recruiting additional workers to assist in manning telegraphic services.

Hiring. In some companies there has been agreement that before new employes may be hired preference will be shown to regular employes desiring the opening, or to employes who are on furlough from another department due to reduction in its work load. Thus in the latter case one agreement specifies that no new employes shall be hired in any classification at any office within two years from the start of involuntary furloughs through force reduction unless laid-off employes who are eligible and qualified have declined employment. At least one important agreement provides that no new employes will be hired during the six-month period prior to mechanization changes in the classification or offices affected, to allow for the absorption of employes already on the rolls who otherwise would be displaced. In some cases employment preference is given to union members even though not formerly employes of the company. Rarely, there is provision for a closed shop, under which the union supplies employes on request of the company.

Rehiring subsequent to reductions in force generally follows the inverse order of layoffs.

Layoffs. In determining the order of layoffs, the seniority factor is most commonly applied. It is probably generally correct to say that even where companies have resisted strict application of the seniority principle, they have at the same time accepted it as a principle, seeking only to reserve discretion in its application. One union representative has thus said that "in practice the companies are willing to observe seniority—it is simply a matter of their not wishing to be tied down by a contractual requirement."

Methods of applying seniority vary in detail. Some provide for nothing more than observance of length of service in making layoffs within the seniority unit. Others provide more elaborate systems of effecting reductions in force. All demonstrate the impact of the union. Several examples may be cited.

In one electric utility, selection of employes for layoff is based solely on length of continuous service with the corporate system. In the event of force reductions in a department which functions as a department in more than one company of the system, the number of employes laid off in each company must be proportionate to the number of employes in the department in each company. In event of a surplus of employes in any department, employes who have transferred to that department within the previous year must be retransferred or laid off before other employes are affected. Alternative arrangements may be adopted by agreement of the company and the union.

In the traffic department of a telegraph company, the force is listed in the order of seniority and the list divided into three equal parts, designated as the senior, middle, and junior groups. In event dismissals become necessary, the senior and middle groups are retained full time, while a work-sharing arrangement is introduced in the junior group, down to six hours a day. Any layoffs required by the work load affect first the employes in the lower half of the junior group, in inverse order of seniority. When this half-group has been exhausted, the seniority list is redivided into senior, middle, and junior groups, and the process repeated.

In one telephone company, the following procedure has been jointly established:

(a) Temporary and occasional employees shall be laid off first.

(b) Next in order, employees with less than two years of net credited service shall be laid off, in the order of service (shortest to longest).

(c) After making the layoffs outlined in (b) next above, should additional force adjustments be required, the Company may give consideration to the transfer of employees to other exchanges in the District or Division having employees with shorter terms of service.

(d) After making the adjustments required by (a) and (b) above and permitted by (c) above, if further force adjustments are deemed necessary, the Company agrees to bargain with the Union at the General Level for all departments on the following matters:

1. Whether part-timing should be substituted for further layoffs.
2. Whether a combination of part-timing and layoffs should be instituted.
3. Whether the extent and composition of the departmental work groups should be changed.

(e) If after the bargaining provided for in (d) next above has taken place, it should be decided that further force adjustments shall be accomplished by layoffs, such layoffs shall be made in accordance with the following provisions:

1. Layoffs shall be in the inverse order of seniority (shortest to longest) among employees performing essentially the same type of work in the particular department of the Company or subdivision thereof in which it is applied.
2. When an employee is notified by the Company that he is to be laid off, that employee shall have the right to select another job, in his department, which is essentially of the same type of work he is then performing, provided the selected job is not in another state and provided further the employee currently filling the selected job has the least seniority of all the employees in his state performing essentially the same type of work.[3]

The required notice to employes, in the event of layoff, varies among companies, ranging up to 15 days.

Allocation. Agreements as to the assignment or transfer of employes may be classed as prohibitive (those foreclosing management from taking certain kinds of action) or prescriptive (those establishing the nature of the action which management must take under given circumstances). In addition, there are some clauses which rest discretion with the employe.

In the class of prohibitive agreements are found provisions that no employe may be transferred without his consent; or that employes with company seniority exceeding five years may not be transferred against their wishes from one locality to another; or that employes of one major department of the company shall not be assigned to jobs in another major department except in an emergency or when arranged with the local shop committee; or that temporary assignments of employes carrying them out of their locality may not exceed three months.

In the prescriptive agreements, which determine how transfers may be effected,

---

[3] Compilation of "typical contract clauses" has become a popular pastime indulged in by research agencies—private, governmental, business, and union. The mass of provisions governing a particular area of management which is thus thrown at the reader to some extent dulls his appreciation of their significance. He is led into a comparison of one clause with another, with the result that the basic significance of any one of the clauses is sometimes lost. It is hoped that contract clauses such as that just cited will be here read for the purpose for which they are reproduced—as an indication of the degree to which the union has shared in making managerial decisions. Seniority has become somewhat of a "stale" subject to all of us, but if the above contract provision is re-read not with an eye to the type of seniority involved, but with a thought of how this provision affects the discretion of corporate management, the old words become surcharged with new meaning and one is left with a sense of being a witness to if not a participant in a profound evolutionary change in our business system.

seniority is the most commonly accepted factor, though its action may be modified in some cases by provisions reserving certain limited discretion to management. It is probably an accurate representation of the unions' position to say that the general rule which they seek to apply is that where employes desire to make a change to a given opening, the employe with greatest seniority shall be chosen; but where employes prefer not to change, the employe with the least seniority is to be selected. Other prescriptive agreements in this area of management provide that the assignment of shifts or tours of duty shall be based on seniority, and that in the event of mechanization or technological advancements, employes whose jobs are made obsolete will be retained for new positions.

As mentioned, some agreements respecting assignment of workers rest discretion with the employes under stated circumstances. Thus when a class of work is transferred from one department to another or from one city to another, employes may be given the option of transferring with the work or of being assigned to other work for which they are qualified within the same department or city. Again, in the event of changes in operating methods, employes may be given a choice of retraining to meet the demands of the new methods or of transferring to a different assignment.

Discipline. Almost universally established is the right of the employe or the union to protest disciplinary action by means of the grievance procedure, which commonly provides for arbitration as the terminal step. In some instances, if grounds for discipline are established, the penalty imposed by management may not be modified by an arbiter. In other cases such modification may be permitted. Provisions respecting discharges of employes for cause are sometimes more strictly drawn. Thus the company may agree not to dismiss any regular employe without first warning him in writing, except for certain specified offenses when prompt action is deemed essential. Occasionally the union may secure agreement that any notation in the employe's record of improper performance of duties must first be reviewed by him, or that his employment record is available for his inspection upon request.

From time to time an arbitration decision may state some principle of disciplinary action. Such occasional decisions have not, however, built up a body of precedent or doctrine in any of the industries of the public-utilities field in the same manner in which the arbitral awards of the automobile, steel, and meat-packing industries have done.

Wages. A common type of wage agreement among public utilities specifies a rate band for given occupational classifications, within which the individual rates of employes are placed. In addition there are frequently systems governing the wage progression within the band, sometimes stated with considerable elaboration.

Thus in one power and light company there is provision for progressive wage increases within a progression band and for merit increases within a merit band. The progression plan operates automatically. For merit increases, the company is obligated to advise the union five days in advance of proposed increases for the selected employes. The selection of an employe or the failure to select an employe for merit increase is subject to union protest through the grievance procedure.

In one telephone company it has been agreed that the basic weekly wage rate for each employe shall be determined on the basis of four considerations: his title classification, his location (for this purpose three zones of company operation have been defined), his ability, and his length of service in the title classification.

In order that wage rates may be equitably determined, tables of wage rates attached have been established, which give, for each title classification in each wage zone, the intervals at which employees are considered for wage rate increases and the new rate which will be established if the increase is granted. The maximum rate for each title classification and wage zone is also shown. Wage rate increases shown on the table of wage rates up to and including the increase which establishes the rate shown for the forty-ninth (49th) month shall be granted automatically. Wage rates shown beyond this point represent the wage progress which will be made by employees who meet the requirements of their jobs in the normal time intervals. Wage increases as shown on this guide beyond the rate shown for the 49th month may be deferred or withheld from employees who, in the judgment of Management, do not meet the requirements of their jobs in the normal periods of time. When an increase is withheld the employee's supervisor shall notify the employee of such action, and at the same time inform the employee of the reasons therefor in writing. If the employee is dissatisfied with such action, he or the Union may deal with it as a grievance.

In one wire company, job classifications have been given minimum rates, job rates, and maximum rates. Employes meeting the requirements of the job are given automatic wage increases to the job rate, and merit increases in the discretion of management above the job rate, but failure of the company to grant an increase in either event is subject to protest through the grievance procedure, culminating in arbitration.

Certain provisions are to be found in most agreements, such as payment of overtime rates under specified conditions, night differentials, "call-in" time, and expense allowances. The latter, providing for travel, board, and lodging, have been of considerable importance in the public-utility field because of the use of repair and maintenance crews which operate away from their home office. Other provisions perhaps less commonly found call for the payment at a higher rate of an employe assigned to temporary work in a higher classification than his regular job, differentials to a worker assigned temporarily to supervisory duties, advantageous treatment for the employe transferred to an office having higher or lower wage schedules than that from which he moves, and adjustment of the wages of similarly qualified workers in a given classification when a new employe is hired at a rate above the minimum for that classification.

In some few cases, guaranteed work weeks or guaranteed annual wages have been negotiated.

Hours. In all cases the normal hours of work per week are set by joint agreement. In some companies the normal week, generally ranging from 35 to 40 hours, applies to all employes. In other companies the number of hours varies with the classification of employes. Thus in one corporation an employe may have a normal week of 35, 39, 40, or $45\frac{1}{3}$ hours, depending upon the classification within which he falls.

Supplementing agreement as to the number of hours per week are provisions governing the scheduling of those hours. It may be understood that employes will be scheduled on consecutive workdays "where practicable," or, more binding, that the work week may not be split. Again, it may be agreed that the hours of work shall be spread over five days, except in the case of certain types of workers whose hours may be scheduled over a period of six days. In some instances union and management have agreed that, service requirements permitting, a minimum time interval of 12 hours must elapse between the end of one tour and the beginning of the next. Necessary Sunday work may be assigned on a rotational basis within a given classification. Split tricks may not be assigned to regular employes. All of these provisions are not to be found within a single company, but they are not uncommon and few collective agreements in the public-utilities field are without one or more of them.

In a number of companies the employe must be informed, in advance, of his schedule for the coming week if changes of hours or rotation of shifts are practiced. An alteration of the schedule may then be permitted only under certain circumstances, such as, in one agreement, the company's obligation to meet service requirements of a substantial duration (for which advance notice of at least 72 hours is required), or to provide relief on account of sickness or other unexpected absence of employes (requiring advance notice of 24 hours), or to provide relief on account of vacations (necessitating advance notice of 72 hours). As a guarantee against short-notice changes in schedules, the union has at times secured agreement to a condition of the type that "when an employee is required to work a tour other than the one shown on his weekly work schedule and he has not been notified by Friday of the preceding week of such change of assignment, he shall be paid for those hours worked before or after his regularly scheduled tour at one and one-half times his regular rate."

Overtime provisions have been important in this field. The union effort to obtain a greater degree of control over the assignment of extra hours of work has met with resistance due to management's insistence that in a public utility the requirement of continuous service must take precedence. The results of union efforts are nevertheless to be found in many important agreements. One specifies that no employe will be required to work more than 12 hours in any workday unless the employe so desires. Another limits the amount of overtime which may be required by management to four hours on any tour of duty. In a number of companies it is agreed that overtime is to be distributed equitably among all the employes available on a rotational basis. It has sometimes been understood that where employes desire overtime it shall be granted to those with the greatest seniority, but where overtime is not desired, it is to be given to those of least seniority. At least one important union, the Federation of Telephone Workers, is seeking agreement that no overtime may be required but may be worked only by voluntary consent of the employes. As yet, however, this principle is not to be found anywhere in the telephone industry.

The question of what constitutes hours of work, for purposes of pay, has received numerous answers. Included in working time are relief periods, travel time, "call-in" time, time "on call," and time during which a foreman requires line-gang employes to wait for assignment to hotel or lodging accommodations.

Employe Advancement Policies. Liberal vacation plans were often to be found in public utilities prior to the advent of collective bargaining. They have now been incorporated into collective agreements and thus come under the joint jurisdiction of union and management. In general it may be said that employes not required to work on a holiday which falls within their normal schedule nevertheless receive their full pay for that day. It is likewise commonly agreed that work on the specified holidays, varying from five to eleven in number, shall be limited to what is necessary to provide continuous service. When employes are required to work, they receive penalty rates of pay.

As in the case of vacations and holidays, numerous companies in the public-utilities field provided for sickness benefits, pensions, and other forms of employe benefits without any compulsion of collective bargaining. With the arrival of unions and their establishment of formal relations with management, such benefit systems have to a degree become embodied in collective agreements, thereby becoming contractual rights of the employes rather than company gratuities. Thus in some companies it is contractually agreed that the existing system of sickness allowances shall be continued for the life of the contract. In others, the benefits are now spelled out in the agreement. Severance allowances are similarly treated. Where provided for, they usually envisage payments to employes whose services are being terminated for other reason than discipline, with the size of the payment dependent upon length of service.

As yet the unions have made less progress in subjecting pension systems to joint management, although in some instances they have secured agreement that an existing pension plan may not be modified without the consent of the union, or less frequently have obtained minority representation on the pension committee. The importance with which a union views this latter right may be judged from the following extract from an official union report:

. . . Before union representation on the committee was provided for, the P & B [Pension and Benefit] Committee, then composed of only company representatives, held perfunctory meetings and decided upon cases involving sick benefits, death benefits and pensions on a purely technical basis taken from their interpretation of the existing plan.

Following the addition of a union representative to the committee, a decided change occurred in the disposition of cases submitted to the committee. The Union was successful in winning benefits for members who had been denied benefits when their claims were sent through the regular channels of the P & B Committee Secretary who took it upon himself to turn down their claims made on the basis that, in his opinion, there was no compensation due under the plan.[4]

The unions are not satisfied with the present systems of benefits. They seek liberalization of the sickness and severance allowances. They want greater representation on pensions committees. With respect to the latter, the attitude of the Federation of Telephone Workers is probably typical. It denies that pensions must be viewed as company gratuities. It claims that in the case of the telephone companies the pension plan has been in effect for so long that management would be unable to withdraw it now even if it wished. It has become, in fact, an employe right, for full protection of which the federation asks for the power to name a representative to the pension committee and to subject all committee decisions to the grievance procedure. It has stated that unilateral managerial action to modify the pension system, even where such modifications constitute improvements and liberalizations of the plan, "is considered as being on the borderline, at least, of an unfair labor practice."[5]

Promotions. The question of the weight to be accorded the seniority factor in selecting employes for promotion has been an important and a contested one in the public-utilities field. It is probably accurate to say that unions in the telegraphic and radio-telegraphic industry have been more successful in emphasizing seniority than have unions in gas, light, and power companies, and that the latter have been more successful than unions in the telephone industry.

One arrangement in the telegraphic field provides that vacancies within the bargaining unit must be posted by management for a specified period, during which time interested employes may bid for the job. The names of all applicants are submitted to the union, which has the right of making suggestions and recommendations to the company. Management is thereupon privileged to make its selection, but subject to

---

[4] American Communications Association, *Report to the Seventh National Convention* (1944), p. 21.

[5] *The Telephone Worker*, December, 1945, p. 7.

the important requirement that seniority shall govern if an employe has the minimum qualifications for the job. Protests of violation of this rule may be presented in the grievance procedure. Such protests have in fact been made, with one union seeking to establish the further principle that determination of what constitute minimum qualifications must be submitted to impartial judgment. Thus in one instance where a senior employe had been refused promotion to a position of manager-operator of a transmitting station on the ground that he was not technically qualified, the union secured company assent to an impartial examination of the man's qualifications, by an engineer selected by the president of a state university. Although the examiner ruled that the protesting employe was not qualified for the position he sought, the union was satisfied at having settled the issue by such independent appraisal of his ability.

In the case of promotions to positions outside the bargaining unit, the union is sometimes authorized to submit recommendations and make representations on behalf of an employe, but final decision is reserved exclusively to management.

In gas, light, and power companies, it is sometimes provided that seniority controls only where two or more employes are equally competent, or where a number of factors such as ability, physical fitness, and regularity of attendance are equal. In a few companies union membership confers a preferential status in advancements, under the agreement. At least one union has expressed an interest, in negotiations, in the promotion of its members out of jobs in the bargaining unit into supervisory positions, but has brought no pressure to convert its interest into influence.

In the telephone industry there is almost a complete absence of any provisions effectively controlling promotions. The most that has been gained by the union is recognition of seniority as a factor, though managerial opposition has prevented the attachment of any specific weight to be accorded it. Nevertheless, the union has at times brought grievances charging insufficient consideration of seniority in the selection of employes for promotion.

Miscellaneous provisions have been agreed upon in one or more of these three branches of the public-utilities field. Thus in some instances the company may agree not to promote a duly certified union representative, if such promotion affects his status as a union representative, without obtaining prior consent of the union. In one major corporation it has been agreed that in considering employes for promotion, minor errors and infractions appearing in his record which occurred six months or more prior to the time of review of his record shall be disregarded, except that if an infraction has been repeated over a period of time it shall be considered. In some companies there is provision for special training of employes to make them eligible for advancement. At times it may be agreed that an employe temporarily assigned to a job which represents a promotion shall be confirmed in that job after he has held it a specified length of time.

Health and Safety. In addition to general provisions obligating the company to "continue to make reasonable provisions for the safety and health of its employees," there are at times more specific agreements as to practice and policy in this area. These vary from company to company. Examples may be cited. "In job assignments and in assignments to do specific pieces of work only such employees shall be used as have the necessary judgment, skill and ability to safely perform the work to be done." "Work by field forces in stormy weather, excepting emergency work for which protective apparel will be provided, shall not be required in the vicinity of outside live wires or live wire service equipment . . ." ". . . where local conditions are such that the public transportation system is inadequate or unsafe for a female released from duty at midnight or later and before 6:00 A.M., the Company agrees to reimburse the employee for the cost of the necessary taxi fare to her home within the limits of the city . . ."

PROCUREMENT

Most of the unions mentioned in this section have been concerned with the question of the contracting out of certain types of work by the company. Their interest has been in preserving jobs for their own members. One result has been a limitation upon management's authority to contract out work under given circumstances. Thus it may be agreed that a company will use its own employes on specified types of work, generally of a maintenance or construction nature, employing outside contractors only when none of their own employes is available. As a variant, management may agree to terminate contracts with independent contractors before laying off its own employes for lack of work. Some companies have consented not to let out a contract for given types of work without prior information to the union, concurrently agreeing that wherever practicable such work will be given to their own employes.

This effort by the company's employes to obtain job security at the expense of an outside group of workers has sometimes led to jurisdictional disputes in which the company finds itself caught in the middle. In several instances management may have agreed to a provision such as one of those recited above, only to find that an attempt to use its own employes on a class of work customarily regarded as belonging within the jurisdiction of an established craft provokes a strike of the craft workers employed by contractors on other company operations. On such occasions the management has sometimes proclaimed its indifference to which group of employes actually performs the operations, insisting that the problem be settled between the contending unions. Nevertheless, it may be pointed out, without implying judgment, that the situation has in some measure been the result of the union's penetration of the managerial role of determining the company's relation with its subcontractors and suppliers.

One other way in which certain of the unions have exercised influence in this area has been through securing management's agreement that it will employ only contractors who have negotiated agreements with the same union or with unions belonging to the same parent federation of which it is a member.

PRODUCTION

Machinery and Equipment. The comments of one union leader are generally applicable to all the unions here under discussion. "We will not only not fight technological improvements but we will encourage and promote them, if our program is accepted by the companies. That program simply demands that in any technological advance there must be a three-way split of advantages: something for the workers, desirably not only job and wage protection but also additional benefit; something for the public, in the form of improved service and possibly lower rates; and something to the company, in the form of increased profits or lower operating costs. This last we don't have to worry about since it is the only one of the three benefits that is now assured. If and when this program is wholeheartedly accepted, then the union will be very much interested in affirmatively promoting the technological improvement of the industry."

Meanwhile, the unions have not sought any voice in determining the types of machinery and equipment to be placed in use. Resistance to technical change such as characterized unions of earlier years has been largely replaced, in the case of all the unions in this field, by a policy of protecting their members from the adverse effects of the change. Actual promotion of mechanical improvements appears to remain as only a future possibility.

Job Content. The system of job classification noted in connection with industries discussed earlier has been spreading with some rapidity in the public-utilities companies. Under this system each employe is assigned a company classification, which embraces a collection of related job duties which he is capable of performing and which reflect his normal work. The union's primary interest in such classifications lies in the wage rates attached to them. It has for this reason sought classifications precisely or narrowly enough defined so that employes doing work which calls for greater skill than that normally required by their classification will be paid appropriately, either by being shifted into the higher classification or by being paid its rate for the time during which they are performing its duties.

To achieve this end some unions have felt the necessity of bargaining with respect to the classification descriptions. They have obtained partial concession in a number of important companies by the agreement that official job titles or the essential duties thereof will not be changed or abolished without mutual consent. If negotiations to establish the content of the classification result in disagreement, the grievance procedure, terminating in arbitration, may in some instances be invoked. In other important companies, however, these concessions have not been obtained. Management fears that the establishment of rigid classifications, subject to negotiation, means the encouragement of job jurisdictions preventing effective utilization of the employes' time. This situation has arisen at one electric utility, for example, where due to certain improved practices the time of boilermakers is no longer fully occupied by their former duties. The company has sought to make full use of their time by assigning them to such odd jobs as keeping equipment clean, but has encountered the strong objection of both the workers and the union, who maintain that tasks of this nature fall outside their normal skilled work and should be assigned to others. This company has so far refused to recognize that the union may negotiate on the content of the job, retaining the view that it is within management's authority to assign workers to such tasks as it may choose, including the dilution of their normal work classification with duties extraneous to it.

In the telephone industry, where management still rejects the union point of view, the Federation of Telephone Workers is pressing for a model contract clause specifying that "the Company shall not create new job classifications or add to or subtract from the job duties of existing classifications without bargaining and agreeing upon with the Union for a wage rate and working conditions for the new or changed job classification."

In a number of instances the unions have also sought to limit the job content of supervisory management, by insisting, with some degree of success, that foremen, chief operators, or other first-line supervisors may not perform nonsupervisory work except under certain specified conditions.

Methods of Operation. For the most part, union interest in this area has been spasmodic. There has been insistence that the "hardware" on poles carrying wires—insulators, conductors, and the like—must be installed in the air rather than on the ground. In one case the union secured the abandonment of a company practice requiring the employes to keep a record of the number of telegraph messages sent per hour and the number of wires or channels worked. The employes forced this abandonment not by refusing to enter the record, but by entering the arbitrary number of 20. Protestations by the company were met by "job action" or threat of strike, sometimes actually carried out. As noted in a subsequent arbitration proceeding, "the Company retreated in the face of these threats." When the company attempted to reinstate the practice, the union objected and forced the matter to arbitration, where it was ruled that "a matter such as this which has historically been an issue between the management and its employees comes within the category of a matter pertaining to a condition of employment." As such, it was removed from the sphere of unilateral action by the company, and reintroduction of the practice could be undertaken only after negotiation with the union.

Examples such as the above are not, however, typical. Such occasional union intervention in methods of operation betrays no sustained interest or official drive to secure a voice in this area. It constitutes at the present time a relatively infrequent irritant to management.

Rates of Operation. Because of the nature of the services rendered by the public-utilities corporations, there has been less incentive for unions to seek the right to bargain directly on working speeds or work quotas. The union's share in the area of disciplinary authority has given it a power to protect employes who might be discriminatorily penalized for failure to meet standards deemed excessive. In some companies it has also secured inclusion of a policy clause in its contract specifying something to the effect that the company will not use "improper supervisory methods" to stimulate employes to work at speeds "beyond their individual ability to perform within proper accuracy standards." Claims that such a clause has been violated may be processed through the grievance procedure.

DISTRIBUTION

The unions have shown little interest in this category. Indication that they will not hesitate to intervene, however, if management's decisions threaten the status or security of their members is offered in the union protest over the continuation of "skip-a-month" billing practices, after the end of World War II. This practice had resulted in the elimination of a number of jobs during the war, which the union sought to have restored at its termination.

COORDINATE ACTIVITIES

Company Organization. One of the unions under discussion, the IBEW, has for some time accepted foremen as members and in some cases has consolidated them with production and maintenance employes in the same bargaining unit. In early 1946 by its own count it had agreements covering foremen with at least 126 power and light companies, and had not relaxed its campaign to secure further enrollments. Of more recent organization, the UWUA likewise seeks membership among supervisory employes. The problems relating to company organization engendered by the unionization of foremen have been previously discussed and require no repetition.

A clear example of union participation in this area is offered by the concern of the ACA with the proposed merger between the Western Union and Postal Telegraph companies. Failing in their efforts to halt the consolidation, its officials and legal representatives worked tirelessly to secure modifications of the proposed merger legislation designed to protect the rights and benefits of Postal employes. Its influence was evident in the postponement of legislative action, in the terms of the merger act as finally passed, and in the delayed closing of a number of Postal branch offices.

Prices. The industries we are now discussing must be distinguished from those previously analyzed by the absence of competitive pricing. The prices or rates for the services of all the companies we are interested in at the moment are set by public commissions or agencies, and are subject to change only upon their approval. It is thus the case that any union influence over price policy in the public-utilities field must be exercised upon governmental commissions rather than upon corporate management itself. Such influence is scarcely "bargaining" in any traditional meaning of the word, but it may take the form of reacting to management's proposals to the commission for reasons which in other industries would be expressed at the bargaining table. Thus an affiliate of the Utility Workers Union opposed management-proposed rate reductions on the argument that they were premised on continuation of bimonthly billing, a practice which had eliminated a number of jobs. The ACA in 1946 opposed increased rates for Western Union by brief and personal pleading before the Federal Communications Commission, holding that before such increases were granted a thorough study was needed of the industry, including its labor policy, mechanization program, operating practices, and management policies. In exchange for a wage increase, the CTU agreed to cooperate with management officials in seeking rate increases. The NFTW has stated as its policy: "There may be isolated cases where rate increases will be necessary to make possible the payment of better wages. These cases should be few, though, and they will be largely confined to the independent branch of the industry. Where they are found, the unions should see that they are raised, not to help the companies, but to see that rates are adequate to maintain decent wage levels. But there must be no general upward revision in telephone rates. Such a step would be as harmful to unions as it would be to the companies. Both would suffer from the loss of public good will."[6]

Perhaps significantly, union leaders have occasionally expressed the personal opinion that the unions should be represented on the rate-making commission itself.

Collective Bargaining. Procedures for the negotiating of contracts remain in an informal state, for the most part. With respect to the settlement of grievances arising under the contract, arbitration as a final step is almost universally accepted. Except for a few departures from the rule, however, the arbiter is appointed at the time the issue is raised or, while designated in advance, is engaged on an ad hoc basis. A permanent, readily available court of last resort is still not a widely established institution in public utilities.

[6] *The Telephone Worker*, December, 1945, p. 7.

INDEX